Kenya: A Study in Physical and Human Geography

D1393932

Francis F. Ojany
Senior Lecturer in Geography
University of Nairobi

Reuben B. Ogendo
Associate Professor of Geography
University of Nairobi

Longman

Longman Kenya Ltd
PO Box 45925
Shell and BP House (2nd floor)
Harambee Avenue
Nairobi

Longman Tanzania Ltd
PO Box 3164
Dar es Salaam

Longman Uganda Ltd
PO Box 3409
Kampala

Longman Group Ltd
London and Harlow

First published 1973

ISBN 0 582 64550 6

Printed by Kenya Litho Ltd., P.O. Box 40775, Changamwe Road, Nairobi.

Contents

Preface

One of the main problems facing mankind in the developing countries of the world today is the urgent need for accelerated economic development. In Africa, this problem is not only pressing and challenging, but exciting because of the changes that have taken place. Before independence, development was directed and determined by the colonial administrator. Following the attainment of independence, the pace, guidance, motivation and policy making passed into the hands of the leaders of the independent African states. This change has made Africa the focus of world interest, so that accelerated advancement and positive achievements are easily noticeable. In our view, the materials we have gone through in this work show positive and significant achievements in Kenya since 1963. The rest of the world is also keenly watching to see what type of leadership Africa will give the world. Will Africa evolve a middle-of-the-way system between capitalism and socialism? We would like to believe that the African way and method has valuable aspects that should enrich both capitalism and socialism.

We believe that economic development and modernisation in Africa can only follow from a detailed knowledge of the continent's environment circumstances. Development demands the fullest knowledge of the physical nature of the continent; both its possibilities and limitations must be fully appreciated beforehand. Only with the aid of such knowledge can new developments be constructively evaluated.

No work on the geography of Kenya as detailed as the present volume, had been published. It was to fill this gap that we felt encouraged by virtue of our profession to undertake its preparation. We intended it primarily for use in the Upper Secondary School forms and for the geography students who study the regional geography of Africa at University level. We think that it presents a fairly detailed treatment of the geography of Kenya.

Beyond the corridors of Geography Departments, we aimed at providing a work that should meet the requirements of many entrepreneurs, field officers, government administrators and local economic planners. Furthermore, we hope that the various Kenya examples that are examined herein will be useful to other scholars and to all those interested in a proper understanding of Kenya. It is also our hope that other countries may find in th book something worth trying out, for example the wel known Kenya 'Harambee' spirit.

We have not ignored the general reader. A number o the topics discussed should form vital reading for man non-professional geographers. The tourist wishing t know something about Kenya—its history, nation heritage, its people and development—should find muc of interest.

Without the help of many people and organisation we could not have produced the book. We have benefite by reference to many published and unpublished work especially those of the various Kenya Governmer Departments and parastatal bodies, including the re search departments of the East African Community. W have drawn much useful information from the work o other geographers, economists, agriculturists and demo graphers. We have also drawn heavily from our ow researches in the various aspects of Kenya's geograph In this respect we hope that our varied interests ha been of value.

We wish to thank the Kenya Information Departmer for allowing us to use a number of photographs fror their excellent collection. We have endeavoured t acknowledge our sources in footnote form and in th references given at the end of each chapter. We also ow a great debt of gratitude to many of our colleagues wh willingly gave us the benefit of their rich experience. I particular we wish to thank Professor S. H. Ominde an Dr R. S. Odingo, whose own geographical contribution we found extremely helpful. We are also grateful Professor Ominde for considerable assistance wit mapping materials in the department and for advic The University of Nairobi has been extremely helpfu especially in its declared policy of actively encouragin individual research and the publication of the results.

Although we have mentioned many who have helpe us with information, we also wish to point out that th opinions expressed in the book and any errors o omissions are our responsibility.

The chapter and other arrangements adopted for th book are straightforward. In a brief introduction w have included a historical note on the making of th modern Kenya. Part 1 examines those aspects which might be termed physical, while Part 2 examines those aspects which might be called human and economic. Part 3 gives a brief conclusion and closes with 'future outlook'.

We have shared the writing freely although each of us has contributed more in areas of personal interest. We hope that the product will stimulate more research in the many pressing aspects of the African environment.

If any one theme has been highlighted, it is the need to extend research work into the low potential areas of Kenya.

F. F. OJANY
R. B. OGENDO

NAIROBI
FEBRUARY 1973

Acknowledgements

The publishers are grateful to the following for permission to use their photographs or diagrams:
Kenya Statistical Abstract; Ardea Photographics (6A, 6C, 6E); Camera Press Ltd (3A); Barnabys Picture Library (6B); S. K. Runcorn 'Continental Drift' (Academic Press, 1962) (2.9); *Principles of Physical Geology* by A. Holmes, Nelson 1966 (2.13); *An Economic Geography of East Africa* by A. M. O'Connor, G. Bell and Sons, 1966 (9.2)

List of illustrations

Maps and line drawings

Photographs

To our parents

Part 1

Chapter 1
Location and Historical Background

The Location of Kenya in Africa

This chapter has two main aims: the first is to examine the geographical location of Kenya within the African continent and the second is to give the historical background of the creation of the Republic. These two aspects should be explained from the outset, if Kenya's geography is to be understood properly.

Location

The Republic of Kenya is located on the eastern part of the vast continent of Africa and forms an important part of East Africa. Apart from sharing boundaries with its East African Community neighbours such as the Republic of Uganda to the west, and the United Republic of Tanzania to the south, it is also bordered by the following countries (see Fig 1.1):
1 Ethiopia in the north
2 the Republic of Sudan in the north-west
3 the Republic of Somalia in the east.

Kenya is bordered in the south-east by the Indian Ocean, which is an important outlet and means of sea contact. This contact is focused on Mombasa, Kenya's main gateway to and from the sea. Both Uganda and nothern Tanzania are also served by Mombasa.

Kenya is located approximately between latitudes 4°21′N and 4°28′S; and between longitudes 34° and 42°E. It is almost bisected both by the Equator and by longitude 38°E. As indicated on the accompanying map, (Fig. 1.1), the three East African republics of Kenya, Tanzania and Uganda are full members of the recently formed East African Community which was established in the form of the East African High Commission during the colonial era. It was later known as the East African Common Services Organisation (EACSO) as independence came to the relevant East African countries. The Community is an important economic union which, it is hoped, will ultimately also be a political confederation.

Outside the East African Community are the five inner neighbours comprising the states of Ethiopia, Somalia, Ruanda, Burundi and Zambia. These are potential members of the Community, which nearly all of these countries have applied to join. It is likely that they will be accepted as full or associate members.

The other neighbouring countries such as Zaire (formerly Congo Kinshasa), the Republic of the Sudan, Malawi, Madagascar and, perhaps later, Mozambique, might become members of a greatly expanded Community, perhaps better called 'Eastern Africa Economic Community'.

Size

With an area of 224 960 sq miles (582 646·4 km²), Kenya is about 2·5 times the size of Uganda and 2·4 times as large as the United Kingdom. Kenya could, however, be packed into Tanzania about 1½ times. Water occupies about 2·3% (5 171 sq miles: 13 392·9 km²) of the area of the country, thus leaving 219 789 sq miles (569 253·5 km²) of dry land, of which about two-thirds is either semi-desert or desert. Thus between only 54 947·3 and 73 189·7 sq miles (or 142 313·5 to 189 561·3 km²) of Kenya can be used profitably by its 11 million people. The greater part of the suitable area is in the wetter south-western part of the country, but there is also a narrow strip along the Indian Ocean in the south-east which is habitable to a variable extent.

Administrative and Industrial Units

Kenya falls into provincial and district units for both administrative and industrial purposes. The administrative units indicated in Fig. 1.2 are those for 1968 whilst the industrial units (Fig. 1.3) are demarcated by the 1961 administrative units, owing to their relatively longer period of use for census purposes.

There are seven large administrative provincial units and one provincial district unit. The largest province is the Rift Valley, 67 131 sq miles (173 869·3 km²). The other provinces in order of size are: Eastern (60 628 sq miles or 157 026·5 km²); North-Eastern (48 997 sq miles or 126 902·2 km²); Coast (33 385 sq miles or 86 467·2 km²); Nyanza (6 414 sq miles or 16 612·3 km²); Central (5 087 sq miles or 13 175·3 km²); Western (3 054 sq miles or 7 909·9 km²), and Nairobi extra-provincial district (264 sq miles or 683·8 km²).

1

In this study the units referred to most often, especially in the industrial and other economic studies, are the district industrial units as distinct from the current administrative districts.

The latitudinal location of Kenya and its varied surface configuration combine to create a physical environment with a range of characteristics varying from equatorial proper to temperate. However, since the greater part of Kenya is unsuitable for agricultural activities, those aspects of our study which are associated

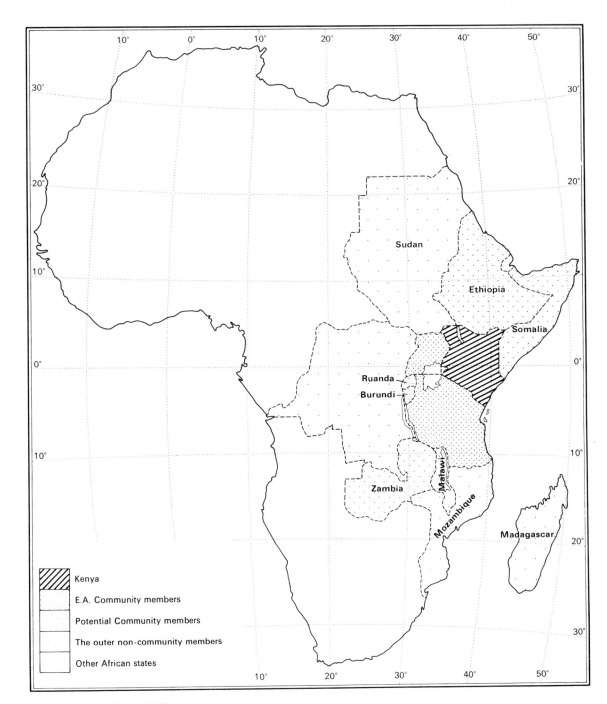

Fig. 1.1 Location of Kenya in Africa

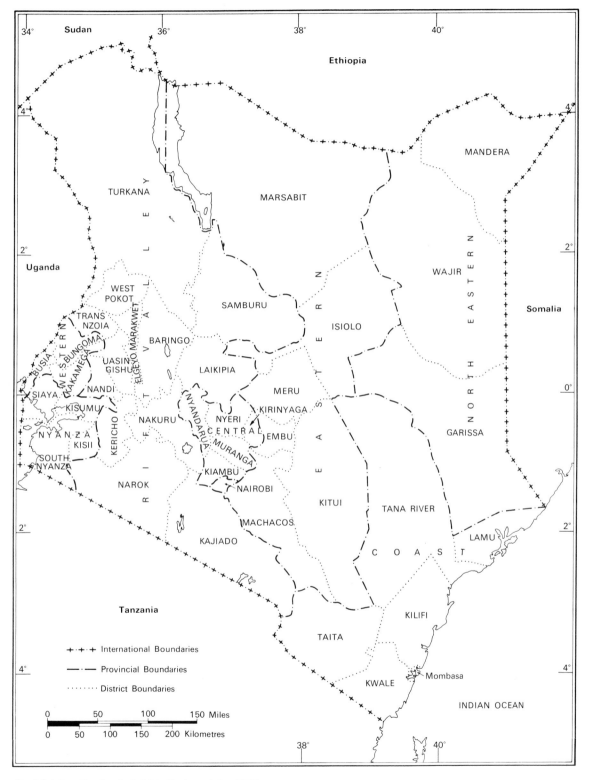

Fig. 1.2 International and administrative boundaries, 1968

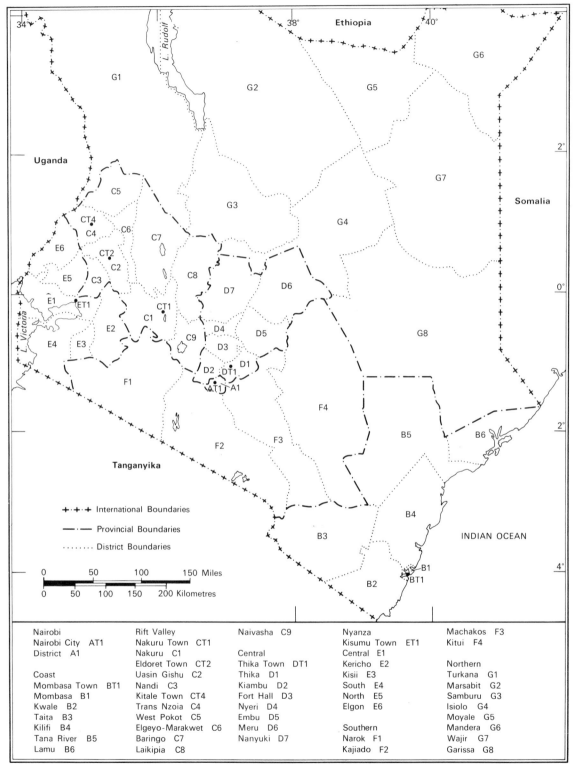

Nairobi	Rift Valley	Naivasha C9	Nyanza	Machakos F3
Nairobi City AT1	Nakuru Town CT1		Kisumu Town ET1	Kitui F4
District A1	Nakuru C1	Central	Central E1	
	Eldoret Town CT2	Thika Town DT1	Kericho E2	Northern
Coast	Uasin Gishu C2	Thika D1	Kisii E3	Turkana G1
Mombasa Town BT1	Nandi C3	Kiambu D2	South E4	Marsabit G2
Mombasa B1	Kitale Town CT4	Fort Hall D3	North E5	Samburu G3
Kwale B2	Trans Nzoia C4	Nyeri D4	Elgon E6	Isiolo G4
Taita B3	West Pokot C5	Embu D5		Moyale G5
Kilifi B4	Elgeyo-Marakwet C6	Meru D6	Southern	Mandera G6
Tana River B5	Baringo C7	Nanyuki D7	Narok F1	Wajir G7
Lamu B6	Laikipia C8		Kajiado F2	Garissa G8

Fig. 1.3 International and administrative boundaries, 1961

with economic activities based on natural or imported organic resources are confined mainly to the more habitable south-western and coastal belts of Kenya.

The Making of Modern Kenya

African countries will surely go down in history as the countries where historical events exercised the greatest influence on geography, and Kenya provides one of the best examples where this is the case. It is not possible to find a logical geographical rationale to Kenya's human geography, without first gaining an insight into the historical events which culminated in the creation of the country.

The story of the making of modern Kenya must surely start with the East African coast which, from the evidence available (thanks partly to the early Greek and Arab geographers), has been in contact with Europe, North Africa, Arabia and Asia, for nearly two thousand years. This is a long period and for a detailed account of it the reader is referred to two excellent accounts recently written by Neville Chittick (1968) and F. J. Berg (1968).

To the Greek and the Roman world, the East African coast was known as *Azania*. To the Arabs, much of what was to become the Kenya and Somalia coasts was the *Land of the Zenj*, that is, the land of the black people. The Zenj Empire was founded about AD 998 and the present Sanye and Boni tribes are probably its only known descendants. Rhapta, probably near the Rufiji delta, was the best-known town.

There were three crucial events which were to have permanent consequences on our geography. The first was the appearance of the Portuguese in the area following Vasco da Gama's call at Mombasa and Malindi in 1498. Then came permanent organised Arab rule along the coast, and lastly, came the systematic scramble for Africa by the European colonising powers. Those who came to our area were the British, the Germans and the Italians.

Vasco da Gama found a number of thriving trading sites along the East African coast founded by Arabs from Oman. Portuguese interest in the area followed but their attempts to subdue the Arabs met with a firm rebuff when they were defeated first in 1698, and then finally in 1728. The Arabs took over the town of Mombasa including the famous Fort Jesus, which the Portuguese had built, but were challenged by the Mazrui Arabs who were already well-established in the Takaungu, Mombasa and Lamu areas under the leadership of Ali bin Osman. A stalemate was only avoided after the 1830s when Sayyid Said, the supreme ruler of Muscat, decided to transfer his administrative centre to Zanzibar in 1832. By 1837 he had subdued the ruling Mazrui family. After this the coastal areas saw a period of considerable prosperity.

Despite considerable activities along the narrow coastal belt, the Arabs did little to establish their authority inland. They were traders and were content to confine their attentions to ensuring that their caravan routes into the interior in search of ivory and slaves were reasonably safe. In any case, they did not wish to embark on a major test of strength with the interior tribes such as the Masai people, who had considerable military ability.

British interest in what eventually became Kenya also began at this time. In December 1823 the survey ship HMS *Barracouta*, under Captain Vidal, called at Mombasa. The already defeated Mazrui Arabs found in Captain Vidal a possible ally against the Imam of Oman. However, despite verbal assurances, Vidal did not succeed in persuading his home government to acquire an interest in the area. British interest was only pioneered by private enterprise. In 1884 Sir William Mackinnon acquired a trading concession from Sultan Barghash of Zanzibar and then founded the British East Africa Company to trade with the interior of East Africa, particularly with Uganda where an established system of African government was already in existence. Pioneer missionaries including Rebmann, Krapf and Hannington also appeared, not only to spread their mission, but also to help eradicate the slave trade. It was at this time that European nations began the rush for colonial possessions in Africa. A Royal Charter was granted to the British East Africa Company in 1888 and the company changed its name to the Imperial British East Africa Company. As already noted the Company had its main interest in Uganda, so that the vast stretch of country from the coast to Uganda was of little immediate interest.

The East African Protectorate

The Company had the estimated inadequate budget of about £250 000 with which to provide a safe corridor for its caravans to Uganda as well as floating its operations there. There was thus added pressure for a British government takeover of this intermediate territory. This was done on 1 July 1895 when the British Government declared as a protectorate the land between Mombasa and the eastern edge of the Gregory Rift Valley. This protectorate was known as *The East African Protectorate* (Fig. 1.4). At first it was ruled by the British diplomat based in Zanzibar, but in 1904 Sir Donald Stewart was appointed its Commissioner and Commander-in-chief with his base in Mombasa.

The Mazrui Arabs who had not expected to be ruled by the British rebelled against the new rule and were only subdued after a bitter struggle lasting nine months and not until the British had brought soldiers from India.

The transport system to Uganda had all along been unsatisfactory. In 1895 it was decided that the British efforts in Uganda could only pay if a railway line was built from Mombasa. This decision was to have permanent and important repercussions. The construction of the railway which finally reached Kisumu in 1901 had necessitated the importation of Asian labourers

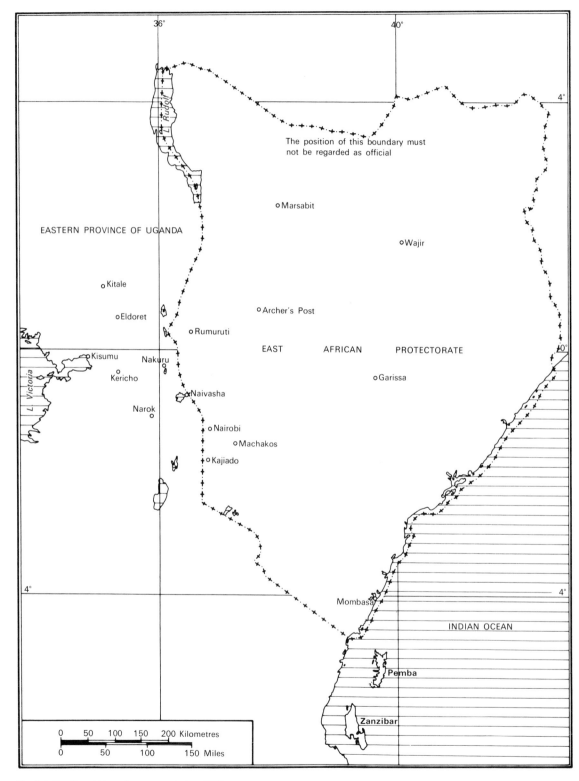

Fig. 1.4 The East African Protectorate before 1902

from India. Traders and other adventurers appeared and set up trading posts along the railway line and began to explore other hitherto unknown parts of the Protectorate.

These developments soon became more than could be competently organised by a consular institution. The next Commissioner was Sir Charles Eliot and he did not hide his strong feelings that the Protectorate be recognised as a colony, and that European farmers be introduced into the cooler highlands to enable the railway to pay for itself. He also demanded that the African population be subject to taxation.

The Demarcation of the Boundaries

The actual extent of the East African Protectorate was very vague especially to the south and north. When substance was given to the Protectorate, it was divided for administrative purposes into three provinces (Fig. 1.5) viz: Seyidie, Tanaland and Ukambani. Each of these was further subdivided into a number of districts each named after its main settlement. No attempt was made to make the boundaries of these provinces or districts conform in any way to the ethnic composition of the indigenous population, let alone find a rational base.

In 1907 the headquarters of the Protectorate were moved from Mombasa to Nairobi, which since July 1889 had been the headquarters of the Uganda Railway. At the turn of the century, the European settlers had forced the Government to preserve the 'White Highlands' for their exclusive use while the African inhabitants were allowed only to live in native reserves and were subject to alienation by the Europeans at will. This meant that the indigenous African population were for all practical purposes tenants in their own land at the pleasure of the British Government. In 1915 settler agitation forced the British Government to extend their own lease of the White Highlands to 999 years instead of 99 years. At the same time, the Indians were also agitating for themselves, some of their prominent leaders even demanding that the Protectorate be annexed as a part of the Indian Empire. The other extreme demand was of course that the Europeans should create a 'white man's country' out of the Protectorate.

Another major internal boundary change came on 5 March 1902 when the British Foreign Office decided to transfer the eastern province of Uganda, the area between Naivasha and Kisumu, to the East African Protectorate. It has been said by many authors that this was done to add more land to the White Highlands and also, since it was a populous area, to provide cheap labour for the European farmers. Following this addition, the provinces were also reorganised. The new area was divided into Nyanza and Naivasha Provinces. The new pattern is shown in Fig. 1.5. Altogether six provinces were created and these were maintained until after the First World War.

During the intervening years individual and occasional explorations into the dry north were also undertaken. As the result of these, Marsabit, Garba Tula and Archer's Post were formally established in 1901 and this northern area became officially known as the Northern Frontier District in 1910.

Soon after the 1914–18 War, an influx of European settlers began to arrive in the country. Many of these were ex-servicemen who knew little about farming. These people were partly responsible for the hectic political manipulations which followed. They regarded the country as a white man's country in which the interests of the indigenous African population were to be secondary. Major internal provincial boundary changes were therefore to be expected. In 1926 the Turkana *Extension from Uganda* (see Fig. 1.8) was transferred to Kenya. Expansion into the north-east into Jubaland was also continued and the administrative boundaries of the Protectorate as at 1918 are shown in Fig. 1.6. There were by this time eight provinces. The main changes included the creation of Jubaland Province and the extension of Kenia Province (as Kenya Province) by the inclusion of Meru and Embu Districts. There was also considerable revision of the district boundaries in Nyanza.

Declaration of Colony Status

In 1920 the Protectorate was declared a Crown Colony and renamed Kenya. The narrow (10 miles or 6·25 km wide) coastal strip which had been leased from the Sultan was, however, still recognised as a Protectorate. This pleased the white farmers, who had by this time added another 4 560 acres to the White Highlands. In 1926, the Government made a small concession to the African population by agreeing to delimit and define the African reserves. Twenty-three such native reserves were gazetted and it was also understood that these could not be alienated to the Europeans without the consent of the African District Council concerned, and not until the Colonial Secretary had also agreed. This assurance was invalidated as soon as valuable minerals were detected in the Reserves. In 1930, the *Native Lands Trust Ordinance* was hurriedly passed to give the Government power to exclude from the native areas any lands found to be mineraliferous.

However, because of the conflict over the ownership of Kenya between the three races–Europeans, Asians and Africans–a new administrative pattern was proclaimed by the British Government in 1924 (known as Proclamation No. 54). The main European farming areas were virtually given small regional district governments by being carved out of the native districts and being made Extra-Provincial Districts. Ten such Extra-Provincial districts were declared–Trans Nzoia, Uasin Gishu, Kisumu–Londiani, Nakuru, Naivasha, Turkana, Laikipia, North Nyeri, Nairobi and Mombasa. The other main change was the rationalising of the Coast Province and the changing of the former Kenya Province to Kikuyu Province, after it had been decided to preserve

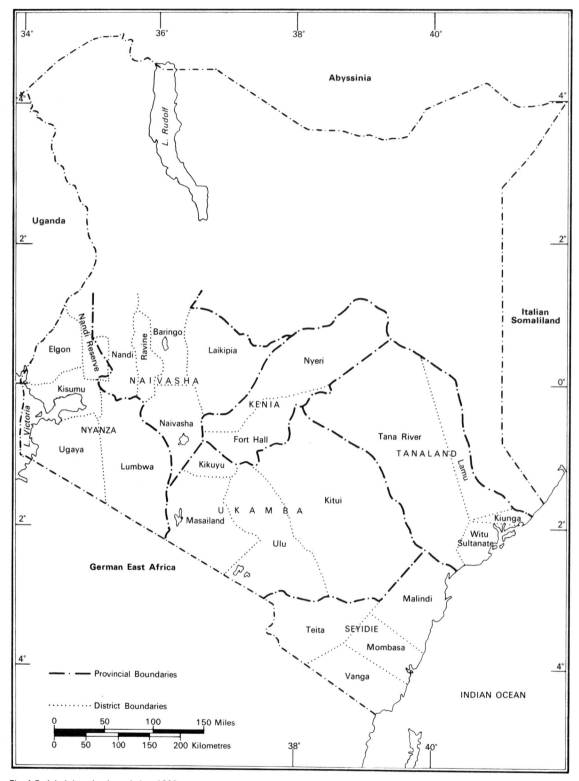

Fig. 1.5 Administrative boundaries, 1909

8

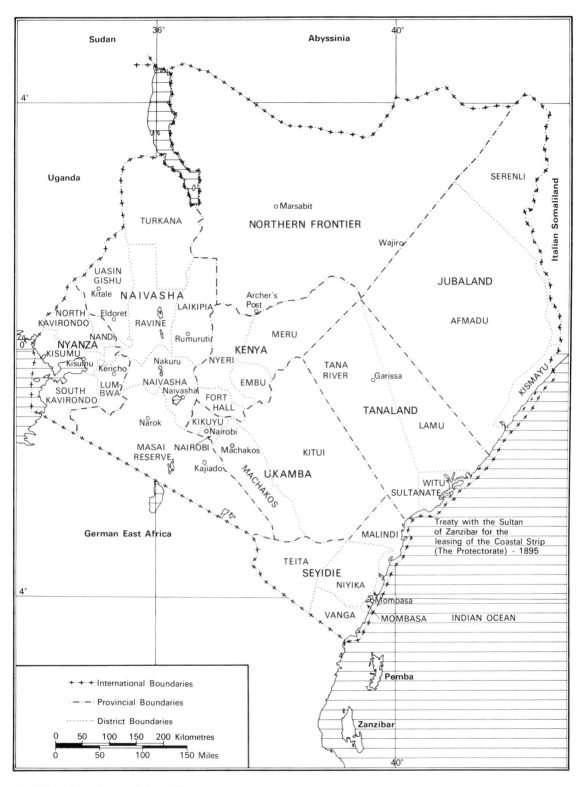

Fig. 1.6 Administrative boundaries, 1918

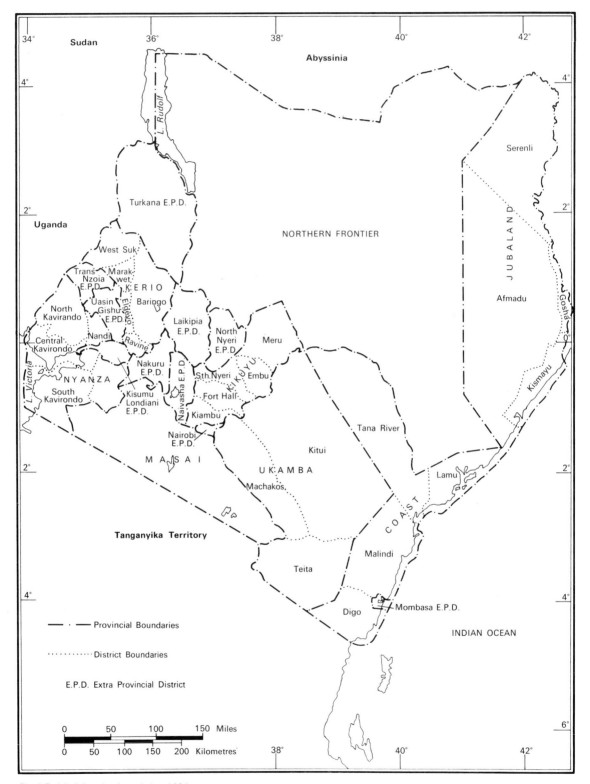

Fig. 1.7 Administrative boundaries, 1924

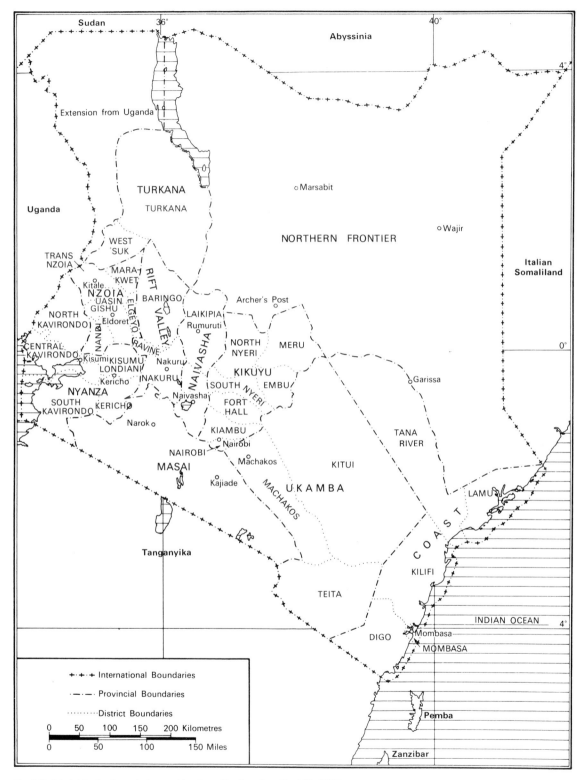

Fig. 1.8 Administrative boundaries resulting from Proclamation No. 158, 1929

the name Kenya for the new country. These details are shown in Fig. 1.7.

Even after the above changes had been implemented, Kenya was still subject to rapid political change, and the internal struggle between the three races soon precipitated new boundary changes. These were announced in the form of Proclamation No. 158 of 1929. The most significant change was certainly the surrender of Jubaland Province to Italian Somaliland. The changes had been agreed in the Treaty of London (15 July 1924) between Italy and Britain and demarcated on the ground in 1927. It was finally ratified by the two governments in 1933. Other important internal changes affected Kerio Province and some of the former Extra-Provincial Districts in the vicinity. Out of these were created three new provinces – Nzoia, Rift Valley and Naivasha Provinces (Fig. 1.8). These changes in fact gave the green light for local government in Kenya to be conducted on racial and tribal lines. Nevertheless they did not satisfy the people.

In April 1932, the British Secretary of State for the Colonies set up another commission under Sir Morris Carter to consider the needs of the indigenous inhabitants with regard to land, and also to define more exactly the 'White Highlands'. As the result of his report a new provincial map (Fig. 1.9) was drawn. The White Highlands were defined as totalling some 16 700 sq miles (43 253 km²). The Reserves were to be known as *Native Lands* and in them business was to be run on tribal lines. Nzoia, Naivasha and the Rift Valley Provinces were joined into one large Rift Valley Province, as were Kikuyu and Ukamba Province which became Central Province. Masailand became an Extra-Provincial District.

The above alterations lasted only until 1959 because of the increasing tempo of the political struggle among the three races. A State of Emergency was declared in 1952 and land ownership became the most sensitive issue in Kenya. The British efforts to withhold independence from the Africans precipitated the 1961 administrative boundaries (Fig. 1.10). The Akamba were separated from the Kikuyu and put together with the Masai. The three tribes who were thought to have been most involved in the Emergency were put together in Central Province.

As independence appeared inevitable, the Africans began to lose political unity and probably through the old technique of divide and rule, tribalism in Kenya reached its pre-independence peak. The people of the present Western Province had come together in 1948 and founded a common togetherness under the name *Abaluhya* (people of 'Oluhya').[1] Similarly, all the tribes in and around the Rift Valley who use the general word *Kalei* ('I say'), when calling one another, came together in the early 1950s as the *Kalenjin* people. At the coast too, nine small tribes joined and became the

Miji Kenda[2] group. As a result when the final conference met to discuss the granting of independence on 12 December 1963, an unworkable and cumbersome regional system (Fig. 1.11) had to be inherited by the new Prime Minister. This new provincial set-up emphasised tribal differences and although the post-independence African government has time and again changed and altered it, the great distances which separate a group in some provinces and the difficulties of closer administrative liaison make the whole system difficult to operate.

Since Independence the main changes have involved the creation of the North Eastern Province in 1965 out of the larger Coast Province of 1962. The present provincial and district boundaries are shown in Fig. 1.12.

International Boundaries

We have traced the internal boundaries without specific note of the evolution of the international boundaries apart from the boundary with Somalia. The straight line which this boundary takes is typical of the European 'paper boundaries' in Africa. Little consideration was paid to points that mattered. We must also note that the demarcators had little information to go by.

The demarcation of the boundary with Ethiopia was first discussed in 1947 and a Boundary Commission was set up. The present boundary was then mapped on the ground in 1955 with minor amendments being agreed in 1963. These amendments were then actually mapped in 1964. There followed protracted discussions at ministerial level, and on 13 June 1970 the two Heads of State finally ratified the discussions by signing the treaty in a colourful ceremony at Mombasa.

In 1926, Turkana was transferred from Uganda to Kenya. The grazing areas to the north were agreed and marked on the ground in 1938. This latter boundary was generally known as 'the Red Line'. More recently (1968), it has been adjusted to give the 'Ilemi Triangle' to Kenya (Fig. 1.13).

With regard to the boundary with Uganda, the section from Lake Victoria to Mount Elgon has been adequately demarcated and is fully mapped. Further north, from Suam River to the Turkana Escarpment is also mapped but no details of official demarcation have been published or gazetted. The Karasuk area which lies to the east of this undemarcated section was up to 1969 administered for Kenya by the Uganda Government. In late 1969 the Government of Kenya took over the administration of the area and renamed it Karapokot. In the 1969 census taken by Uganda, this Karasuk area had a population of 13 796 people. The final northern stretch of the Turkana Escarpment was demarcated and mapped in 1959–60, but at the time of writing it does not seem that this has been formally recognised in any later document. On the whole, the Uganda-Kenya boundary is a

---

[1] Originally the people of different homes would get together around a fireplace (Oluhya) in the evenings for discussion. *Abaluhya* was the acceptable word for all the 'Oluhya' groups coming to find a common identity. Linguistically *Abaluhya* means people of one tribe.

[2] These were the Chonyi, Digo, Duruma, Giriama, Jibana, Kambe, Rabai and Ribe.

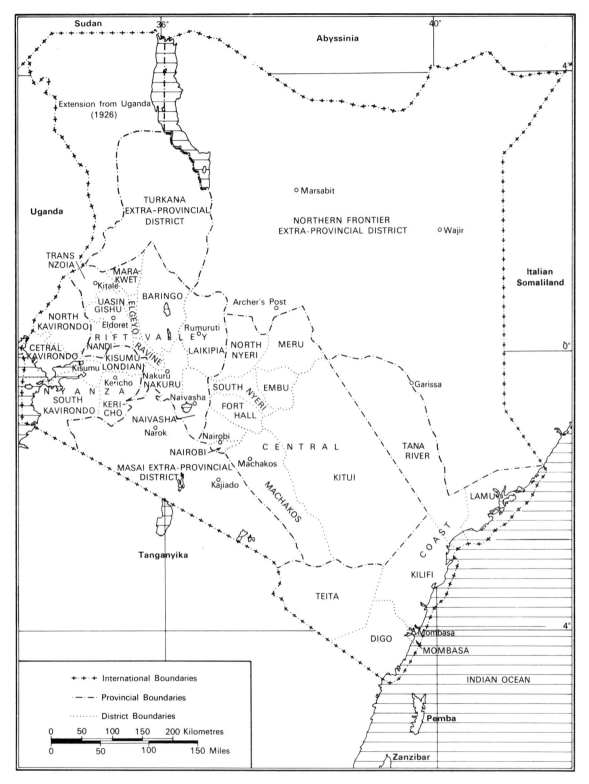

Fig. 1.9 Administrative boundaries resulting from the Carter Commission, 1933

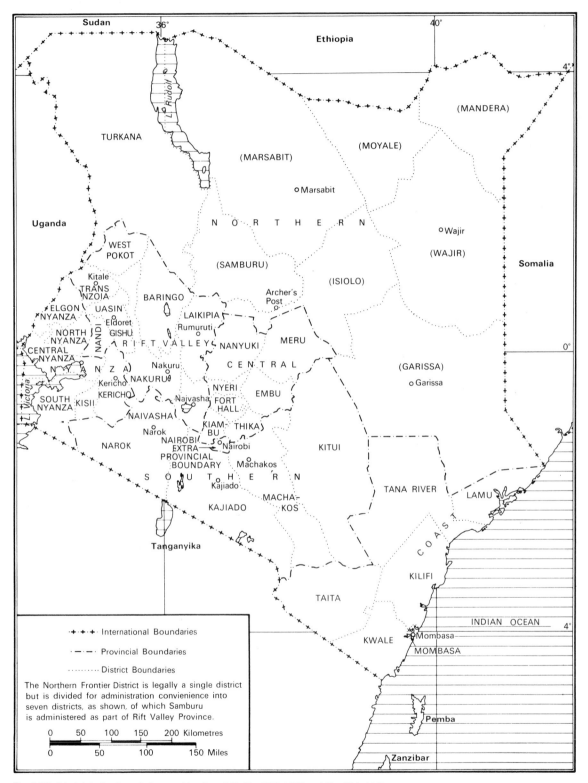

Fig. 1.10 Administrative boundaries resulting from L.N. No. 207, 1959 and No. 386, 1961

14

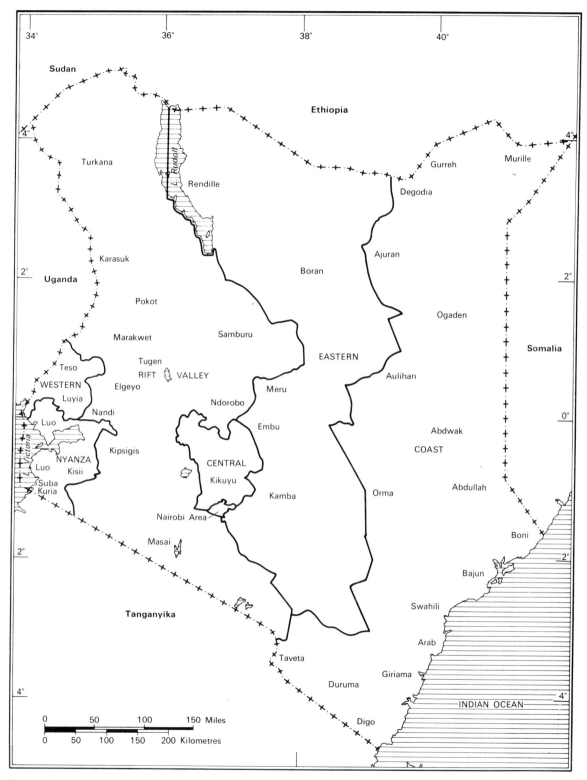

Fig. 1.11 Regional boundaries resulting from the Regional Boundaries Commission, 1962

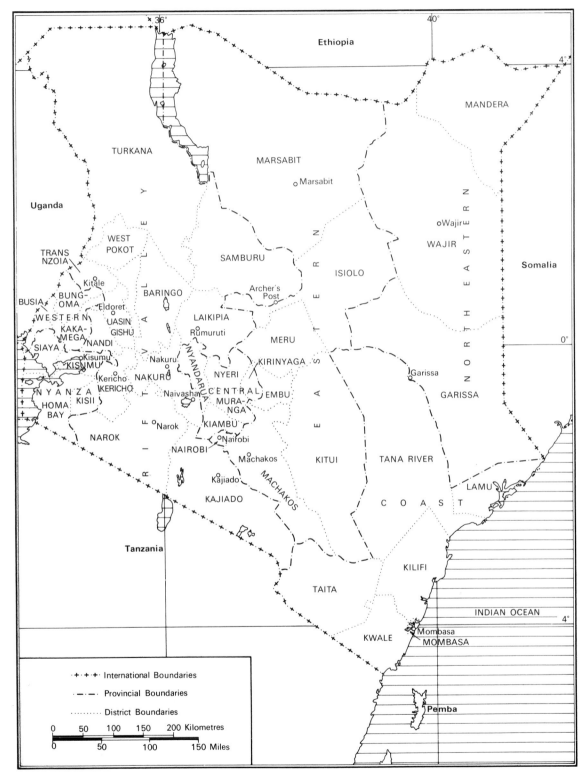

Fig. 1.12 Present provincial boundaries as proclaimed at Independence, December 1963

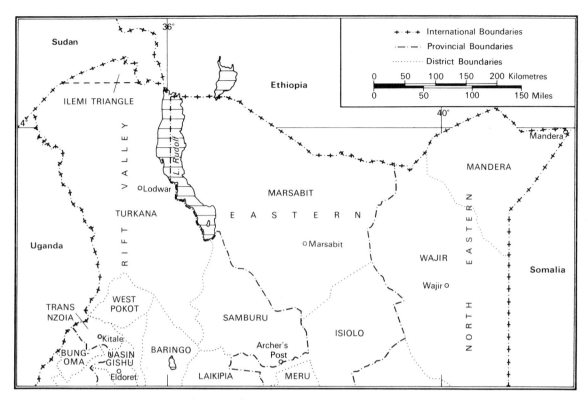

Fig. 1.13 Present international boundary of Northern Kenya

peaceful boundary. It cuts through tribal areas so that in most places the same tribe lives astride it in both states. We have already noted the case of the Karapokot people. The Iteso, the Basamia, Banyala, Bahayo and Bagwe sub-tribes live on both sides just as the Babukusu whose kinsmen in Uganda are the Bagisu. The Banyala, Bahayo and Bagwe who live in Uganda are more usually known as the Basamia.

The present relatively straight boundary with Tanzania was fixed by a Boundary Commission which reported in 1907 following the Anglo-German agreements of 1886, 1890 and 1893. The section from the Indian Ocean to Lake Jipe was re-demarcated in 1956–57 and was fully mapped during the period. This boundary has both the Masai and the Luo people on either side but since the two states are in close cooperation and understanding, this situation causes no difficulties. The Kuria and the Digo tribes are also divided by the boundary.

Territorial waters at present are confined to three nautical miles although these may be extended to twelve nautical miles offshore. Such legislation would be welcome as it would safeguard against a lot of possible inconvenience.

References

CHITTICK, N. 'The coast before the arrival of the Portuguese' in *Zamani: A Survey of East African History*, EAPH/Longman, 1968.

BERG, J. F. 'The coast from the Portuguese Invasion' in *Zamani: A Survey of East African History*, EAPH/Longman, 1968.

Kenya Report of the Regional Boundaries Commission HMSO, 1962.

OJANY, F. F. 'The geography of East Africa' in *Zamani: A Survey of East African History*, EAPH/Longman, 1968.

Chapter 2
Geology

Geography and Geology

It was William Morris Davis (1850–1934) who first recognised that 'All the varied forms of the lands are dependent upon–or, as the mathematician would say, are functions of–three variable quantities, which may be called structure, process and time.' The truth of this dictum has been widely acclaimed by the students of both geomorphology and geology, particularly the former. In the above statement is implied another fundamental fact: that the face of the earth is always undergoing change. The form of the earth's surface at any given time is its *physiography*. The successive changes of surface relief and climate during Geological Time is *palaeogeography*. The study of palaeogeography, as of structural geology, is more naturally the field of the geologist.

From the above introductory comments, it will be seen that there is a close relationship between physical relief and geology and although this fact is known to students of geography, we do not believe that all geographers do more than make passing references to the richness which sound geological knowledge can add to their subject. We believe that without proper understanding of the underlying rocks, knowledge of landforms and of human geography tends to be superficial. *Process* is also important because rock weathering and the rate of soil erosion are largely dependent on the climate which in turn produces distinctive landforms. Similarly most lithological soils are due to the effect of climate, slopes and denudation. That these interrelationships can only be adequately appreciated after careful observation of the processes at work together with the underlying geology cannot be disputed.

A few examples from our own area may serve to illustrate our point. The pre-Cambrian rocks, when subjected to weathering and erosion, commonly produce unique residual hills known as *inselbergs*. These may be finger-like (also known as sugar-loaf), domed or castellated into tors, depending on the nature of the

Fig. 2A General view of the granitic and tor landscape in Seme Location, near Kisumu. Note the finger tor on the skyline on the right

Fig. 2B Close-up view of the tors, Seme Location. The influence of vegetation and man, through his cultivation, in aiding rock disintegration can be appreciated from this picture

joints in the rock. Beautiful examples of these residuals can be seen in Maragoli and Seme locations of west Kenya and in the semi-arid parts of eastern Kenya. Similarly, the quartzites in the Kisii Series produce the smooth rounded ridges so typical of parts of Kisii District where these rocks occur.

Tectonic disturbances, including volcanicity, have different impacts on the landscape. The radial drainage patterns which develop on lava cones are markedly different from the rectangular drainage patterns that tend to develop on lava plateaus. Equally distinct are the parallel drainage patterns which result on the lava dipslopes and which characterise the Kikuyu dipslope. One further illustration might also be cited. We believe that to understand the origins of the well-developed marine platforms which occur around Mombasa Island and the entire Kenya coast, the corresponding raised beaches, degraded cliff-lines and coastal creeks, a sound knowledge of the eustatic movements which occurred during the last Quaternary period is necessary.

Thus an understanding of the past geographies of the land is vital for an intelligent interpretation and appreciation of the topography of any country. These facts in effect illustrate the close relationship between geography (especially geomorphology) and geology. Wills (1950),

one of Britain's most outstanding geologists, expressed this close link in these words: 'I prefer to think of Geology as the geography of the past, and Geography as the geology of the present. . . . The successive geographies of the region are sketched in an attempt to trace the gradual evolution of the present physical make-up of the country.'

Kenya's topography has been very strongly influenced by its geological history. Hence to understand its relief, including the form of its rivers, the student must be fairly well informed on its geology. Because of this fact, we shall examine the main groups of rocks that occur in Kenya and the structural geology of the country in slightly more detail.

Fig. 2.1 shows the distribution of the main rocks that occur at the surface in Kenya. Their stratigraphical divisions and the respective major earth movements during each period, we have summarised in Table 2.1. Thus, unlike in many African countries where the surface rocks are predominantly pre-Cambrian in age, in Kenya Cainozoic volcanic rocks and Quaternary sediments cover large areas. Volcanic rocks alone cover nearly 29·8 % of the total land area of the whole country. Similarly, unlike other African countries, in Kenya the younger rocks are much more important economically.

Table 2.1 *Economic uses of Kenya rocks*

Systems	Representative Rocks	Tectonic Events	Main Economic Uses (after Pulfrey (1960))
Recent	Soils, alluvials, sands. Hot springs—trona and other evaporites. Volcanic ashes	Rise to present sea level. Minor volcanicity and grid faulting.	Trona, salt, sands, brickearths, meerschaum, guano
Pleistocene	Moraines on highest peaks. Coral reefs and sandstones at coast. Interior sediments, alkaline and pyroclastic lavas	Grid faulting, major volcanic eruptions in rift south of Nakuru, Nyambeni and Marsabit areas. 3rd major faulting of Rift Valley and Kano Rift, alkaline dykes intruded	Limestones, cement, diatomite, gypsum, bentonitic clays, kaolin
Tertiary	Coastal sediments. Large quantities of volcanic rocks of the highlands. Interior Miocene Beds	1st and 2nd major faulting of Rift Valley. Warpings, major regional uplift in central Kenya alkaline and carbonatite intrusions	Limestones, building stones, carbon dioxide, ballast, lead, batytes
Cretaceous	Danissa Beds, Maheran Sandstones, Freretown limestones and siltstones	Stability. Probable commencement of carbonatite intrusions	
Jurassic	Limestones and shale in coastal areas. Daua Limestone Series and Mandera Series	Slight uparching and tilting: Faulting in N.E. Kenya	Limestones and shales, shales, gypsum
Triassic Permian Carboniferous (Karroo)	Duruma Sandstones, Mansa Guda Formation	Gentle tilting, warping and tilting of mesozoic rocks. Erosion	Ballast
Bukoban	Kisii Series—Acid and basic volcanics, quartzites and other sediments	Gentle warping faulting. Dolerites and pegmatites intruded	Soapstone, cassiterite
'Basement' (The Mozambique Belt)	Quartzites, crystalline limestones schists, gneisses including Kusae, Kasigau Series, Turoka and other formations	3rd period of N.E. trend folds in north Kenya. Early recumbent folds. Major period of orogenesis. Granites, granodiorites, pyroxenites, eclogites etc. intruded	Asbestos, kyanite marble, limestones, vermiculite, garnet
Kavirondian	Arenaceous and argillaceous sediments. Conglomerates, hornblende andesites etc.	Metamorphism with isoclinal folding with N.E. and S.E. trending axes. Granites, syenites and dolerites intruded	Gold, silver
Nyanzian	Sandstones, conglomerates, quartzites, phyllites, limestones, pelites volcanics and ironstones	Slight metamorphism of Ablum and Embu Series. Granites, epidiorites. Gabbros	Gold, copper, zinc, chromite, cobalt, silver, corundum and other minor minerals

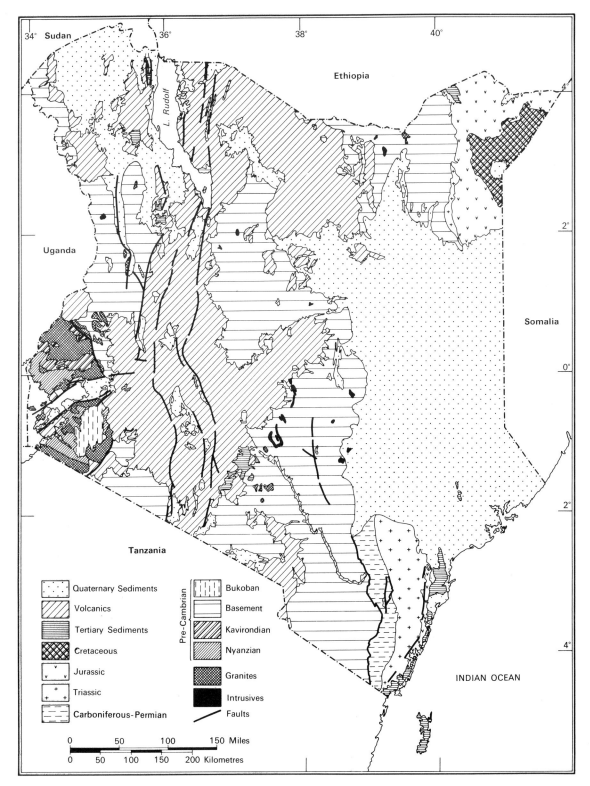

Fig. 2.1 The geology of Kenya

<table>
<tr><td>Quaternary Sediments</td><td rowspan="5">Pre-Cambrian</td><td>Bukoban</td></tr>
<tr><td>Volcanics</td><td>Basement</td></tr>
<tr><td>Tertiary Sediments</td><td>Kavirondian</td></tr>
<tr><td>Cretaceous</td><td>Nyanzian</td></tr>
<tr><td>Jurassic</td><td>Granites</td></tr>
<tr><td>Triassic</td><td></td><td>Intrusives</td></tr>
<tr><td>Carboniferous-Permian</td><td></td><td>Faults</td></tr>
</table>

0   50   100   150 Miles

0   50   100   150   200 Kilometres

History of the Geological Mapping of Kenya

The details of Kenya's geology are not fully known because the geological investigations and mapping of the country have not been completed. What has been accomplished as well as what is still to be done is illustrated in Fig. 2.2. A department for geological surveys was formally established in Kenya in 1932 and its first geological report, that of the Loldaike-Ndare Area, was published in 1933. Since its foundation, the department has had a slow but steady growth in which financial worries have not always been absent. In 1952, it was manned by sixteen qualified geologists largely due to the financial grant from the British Colonial Development and Welfare Vote. At the beginning of 1968, the department had an establishment for eight geologists besides the services of four other geologists largely as a result of technical assistance from the Canadian Government (who sent in three geologists) and the British Government (who paid the other geologist). Despite these difficulties, the Mines and Geological Department is well-established and has the best earth science reference library in the country.

Having established the historical record, we can now turn our attention to the examination of first the rocks and then structural geology.

1. Rock Types

Pre-Cambrian

Relatively little detailed research has been done on these rocks. Their advanced age, their complicated deformations and contortions and their highly altered nature due to both thermal (heat) and metasomatic (chemical) metamorphism have meant that to study these rocks is an extremely difficult task.

Prior to 1951, it had been assumed that the Basement System rocks were the oldest rocks in Kenya because their appearance showed a more advanced degree of metamorphism than either the Nyanzian or the Kavirondian systems. In 1951, however, Professor Arthur Holmes suggested that the Nyanzian and the Kavirondian rocks might in fact be older. This was soon proved to be the case in Tanzania but in Kenya conclusive evidence was not forthcoming until 1965. In that year, Sanders, using isotopic age determinations using potassium-argon (K:Ar) and rubidium-strontium (Rb:Sr) techniques, as well as the structural and metamorphic evidence, showed that some of the Nyanzian rocks formed the foreland against which the sediments which were later to form what are now known in East Africa as the Basement System rocks (the Mozambique Geosyncline) were deposited. The Nyanzian System rocks are thus the oldest rocks in Kenya. They are commonly dated as lower pre-Cambrian. The Basement System are middle or even upper pre-Cambrian. The reason why the Nyanzian System rocks do not show such a high degree of alteration in hand specimen is that they were mainly altered by thermal metamorphism and the full impact of this process cannot be fully appreciated through physical observations.

Nyanzian and Kavirondian Systems

These two systems are treated together because they occur in close juxtaposition and because they have a number of other similarities. They occur in western Kenya on either side of the Nyanza (Winam) Gulf.

The Nyanzian System covers much of Siaya District and wide areas of South Nyanza District. The Kavirondian System is best developed as a horseshoe-shaped belt about 10 miles (16 km) wide from Busia town through Butere, with Kakamega town marking its northern boundary.

Nyanzian System These rocks consist of great thicknesses of various types of ancient volcanic materials in which basalts, tuffs, trachytes, andesites, rhyolites and greywacke are very common. The volcanics were interbedded with a number of coarse-grained sediments such as conglomerates, quartzites and banded ironstones. The whole system was later intensely altered during archaean times by heat rising from greater depths (thermal metamorphism) and during these processes mineral belts were interjected in association with other intrusions.

Kavirondian System Indications are that these rocks are younger than, and may in fact be sedimentary derivatives of, the Nyanzian System. Lithologically, they consist of alternating bands of sandstones, grits and mudstones with water-lain conglomerates. Besides its widespread occurrence in west Kenya, two small isolated outcrops, one near Embu township (hence the name *Embu Series*) and the other near El Roba in Kenya's northern border (known as *Ablum Series*) are regarded as belonging to this system. Like the Nyanzian and the Kavirondian Systems, both the Embu and the Ablum Series are characterised by the occurrence of banded ironstones and dolerites and their fold trends also appear to be similar to those of the main systems.

Basement System

These rocks cover wide areas in the country. The original sediments (mainly sandstones, grits, shales and limestones) were probably laid down in one vast geosyncline (called the *Mozambique Geosyncline*) or in a series of geosynclines which extended over much of eastern Africa on what Sanders (1965) has called 'a deeply sheared granite-migmatite complex'. What have been known as the Basement System rocks form a mantle rock which, as Sanders has also shown, constitutes 'supercrustal Folded Metasediments'. The term *Basement System* is now clearly inappropriate and a misnomer. Contemporary geological opinion now prefers to call the system the *Mozambique Belt* which in Kenya is subdivisible into the *Kamba Group, Turoka Group, Loita Group* and *Turbo*

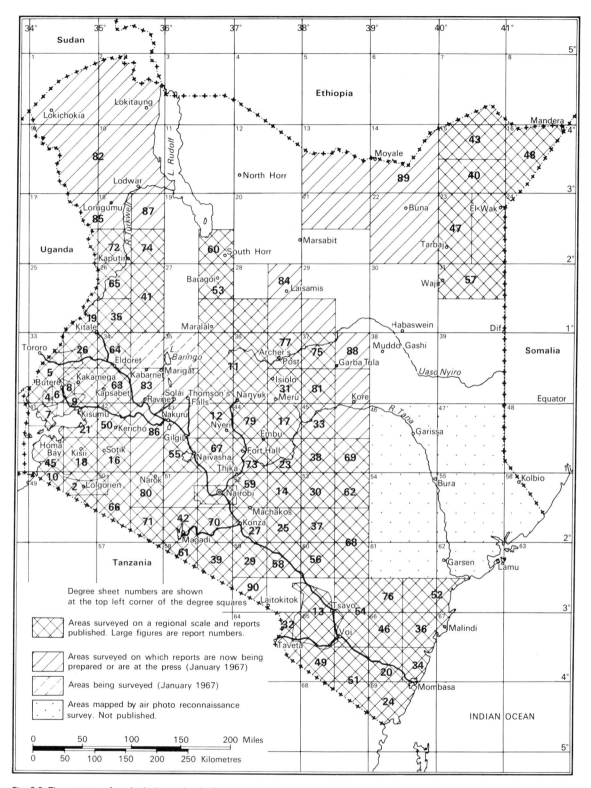

Fig. 2.2 The progress of geological mapping in Kenya

Fig. 2C Ngwane River, Machakos, during the dry season. Note the distinct bedding and dipping of the gneissic rocks of the Basement System

Group, depending on the locality of occurrence.

The Mozambique Belt sediments were intensely metamorphosed to give a variety of rocks including gneisses, schists, marble, quartzites and other more complicated types. The metamorphism appears to have occurred in two phases during Cambrian times. Each phase was accompanied by injection of granites (granitisation) and migmatites (migmatisation).

Kisii Series

These lie unconformably on the older rocks. They are the Kenya members of the *Bukoba System* rocks which are much more extensively developed in Tanzania. They are estimated to be approximately 670 million years old and are confined to the area around Kisii in western Kenya where they form a thick 2 500 feet (761 m) capping that forms the impressive Kisii Highlands which rise to 6 700 feet (2 030 m) above sea level in places.

Stratigraphically the rocks show three divisions with the lower and the upper group being composed mainly of lavas. The middle group is lithologically different in that it is dominated by ferruginous siltstones and quartzites which in Manga Ridge form prominent scarps and free faces.

In other localities, the lower lavas (mainly basalts) have been altered metasomatically into non-magnesium soapstones. The soapstones have been worked for a number of years by the local people to make carvings which sell as 'Kisii carvings'.

Intrusives in the pre-Cambrian Rocks

Intrusives into the pre-Cambrian rocks cannot be said to have been extensive. However, where they occurred, they had important geographical repercussions in that their injection was in places accompanied by the introduction of mineral belts. Also the intrusives, being more resistant to erosion, now form erosional remnants which add diversity to the present relief.

These ancient intrusives are mainly granitic and were especially typical in western Kenya where they now rise above the general ground level to form tors, smooth exfoliation ridges, bare-rock surfaces and other inselbergs including whalebacks. In other parts of the country, they are scattered. Examples occur in Ukambani, the northern parts of Uasin Gishu and near Moyale in northern Kenya. The apparent absence of these intrusives in central Kenya may be partly because they have been buried by later volcanic rocks. The imposing Doinyo Sapuk (Kilima Mbogo), which rises to 7 041 feet (2 146 m) above sea level and juts by some 2 000 feet (600 m) above the surrounding plains, is a metadolerite which may well be a portion of a larger dyke intrusion. Besides granitic and doleritic intrusives other more complicated rocks such as migmatites are also known to be present. Most of these intrusives are probably all of archaean age and may have been contemporaneous with the archaean metamorphism. This would also support the view that some of the 'intrusives' were merely metamorphic rocks that were altered by metasomatism.

Jurassic Rocks

These outcrop in two localities in Kenya. The more extensive outcrop is in the north-east where the *Daua Limestone Series* cover more than 6 500 sq miles (16 800 km²) in the two districts of Mandera and Wajir. In this area, the rocks form thick series of beds which suggests deposition in a neritic environment. In the coastal area

Table 2.2 *Succession of Palaeozoic-Mesozoic sediments in Kenya*

System	Stage	North-east Kenya		Coastal Kenya	
Cretaceous	Neocomian	Marehan Sandstones Marehan Danissa Beds Series		Freretown Limestone	
—	—	—	—	—	—
Jurassic	Tithonian	Mandera Series Dakacha Limestones Hereri Shales			
	Kimmeridgian	Seir Limestones Muddo Erri Limestone Rahman Shales	Daua Limestone Series	Rabai Shales	
	Oxfordian				
	Callorian	Rukesa Shales		Miritini shales	
	Bathonian	Murri Limestones		Kibiongoni Beds	
	Bajocian			Kambe Limestone	
	Lias?	Didimtu Beds		— — — — — —	
Trias		Mansa Guda Formation		Mazeras Sandstones/ Shimba Grits	Duruma Sandstones
				Mariakani Sandstones	
	— — — — — — — — —			Maji ya Chumvi Beds	
Permian- Carboniferous?				Taru Grits	
Pre-Cambrian		Metamorphosed Sediments of the 'Basement System'			

N.B. — — — — — — — Dashed lines denote unconformities.

near Mombasa, the *Kambe Limestones* are about 1 500 feet (460 m) thick and lie discordantly on the Mazeras Sandstones. On their western margin, these rocks are faulted against the Triassic rocks.

It looks clear that the deposition of these beds followed a Jurassic Sea invasion in which tropical conditions prevailed and in which coral polyps certainly thrived. A shallow epicontinental sea with intermittent changes in its level would create such an environment. As Table 2.2 shows, the deposits are an alternation between limestones, sandstones and shales. The palaeogeography of eastern Africa at the time is sketched in Fig. 2.3. The rocks (Kambe Limestones, the Kibiongoni and the Upper Jurassic Shales) also serve to illustrate the importance of lithology of a rock in influencing relief. The Kambe limestone forms the 'Foot Plateau' of Caswel (1956), while the soft shales form the low ground into which the Port Reitz and Port Tudor waters have extended and the rivers also pick the shales to extend their headstreams inland more easily.

Cretaceous Rocks

Except for the Freretown Limestone of Mombasa, cretaceous sediments are confined to north-eastern Kenya in the area around El Wak and Finno where the

Fig. 2D Massive Kambe limestone rocks in Kilifi District, Coast Province. They form prominent residual hills in the area

25

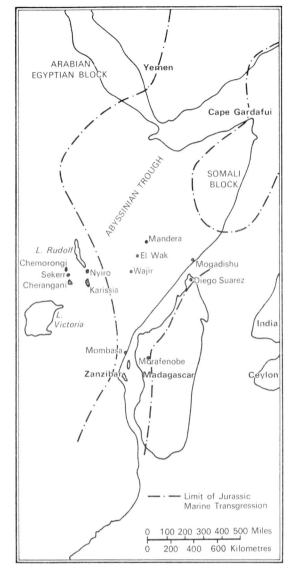

Fig. 2.3 The palaeogeography of Eastern Africa during the Jurassic

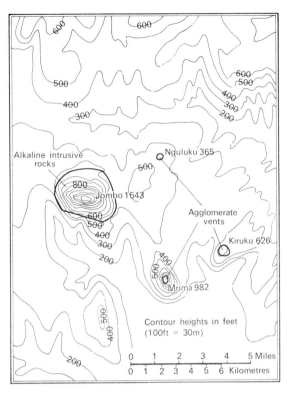

Fig. 2.4 Influence of Jombo intrusives on relief

Wien anticlinorium, the Jabich and the Godobi ridges (see Figs. 2.5 and 2.6).

Intrusives into the Mesozoic Rocks
These include the rocks that compose Jombo, Mrima and Kiruku hills. Evidence shows that the intrusives are post-Jurassic in age and it has also been thought that they may be of the same age as the tertiary carbonatites of west Kenya. Fig. 2.4 shows the influence of these intrusives on the present landscape.

The Cainozoic Period

Under this period we include both the Tertiary and the Quaternary. The period was marked by significant changes in the palaeogeography of the area. Much of the present Kenya remained above sea level and protracted subaerial erosion took place. Secondly, the period witnessed widespread tectonic disturbances and extensive volcanic eruptions. The tectonic activities included continental uplifts, faulting, warpings and archings. Continental sediments were also deposited in at least three small areas in the country. The full succession of the Cainozoic sediments is summarised in Table 2.3.

Maheran Series outcrop. The Series are made of two important beds–the Danissa Beds and the Maheran Sandstones and Quartzites. The Danissa Beds could have been deposited in a deltaic condition as a result of a marine invasion from the north-east. The Maheran Sandstones on the other hand contain siltstones and also exhibit ripple marks. They could thus have been deposited in a shallow sea with a shifting shoreline as has been suggested by Baker and Saggerson (1958).

Again the above lithological differences show well on the present relief. The quartzites and the flaggy sandstones form ridges and residual hills such as the Bur

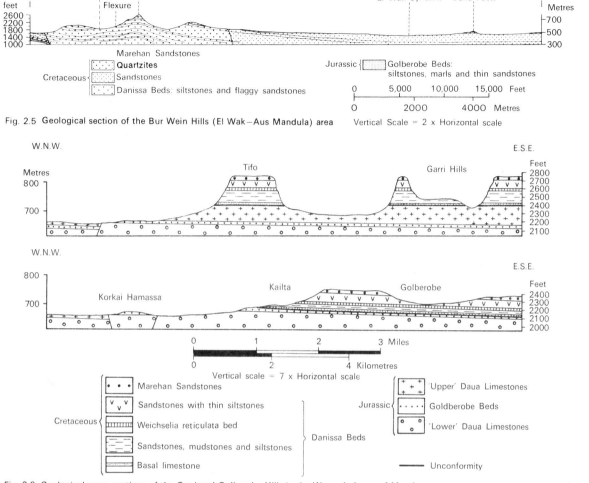

Fig. 2.5 Geological section of the Bur Wein Hills (El Wak—Aus Mandula) area

Vertical Scale = 2 x Horizontal scale

Fig. 2.6 Geological cross-sections of the Garri and Golberobe Hills in the Wergudud area of Mandera

Table 2.3 *Cainozoic succession in Kenya*

Period	Interior and west Kenya	North-east Kenya	Coastal Kenya
Recent	Soils including laterites. Alluvium, spring deposits and evaporites in interior lakes e.g. Magadi trona	River soils including Kankar limestones, laterites and surface sands	Alluvium and beach sands
Upper Pleistocene	Loams, sheet limestone, mudstones, siltstones, tuffs, pumice lavas, fluviatile sediments	Red and brown clays having nodules	Windblown sands, Raised alluvial deposits
Middle Pleistocene	Lake beds in floor of Rift, Kanjeran Beds. Rawe Fish Beds	Thin laminated limestones, sandstones, conglomerates and ironstones. El Wak Beds	Kilindini sands, Mombasa Crag, coral reefs
Lower Pleistocene	Miriu Gravel. Lower Rawe Beds. Kanam Beds	Gypsum, limestones, sandstones and clays. Wajir Beds	Magarini sands?

Volcanics

Tertiary and Quaternary volcanics outcrop over nearly 67 250 sq miles (166 870 km²) in Kenya. In composition they are characteristically alkaline. The main rock types include phonolites, nephelinites, trachytes, basalts, basonites and tuffs.

Volcanicity has a constructional effect on the pre-existing topography and the impact of the Cainozoic volcanic activities in Kenya must be seen in this way. They buried a large part of the country and in the process considerably altered the drainage patterns and channels. The pre-volcanic land surface was likely to be one of low relief during the mid-Tertiary period (Fig. 2.7).

Lava outpours thus built some of the present great highlands in Kenya while repeated uplifts raised some of the then residual plateau remnants to their present great heights. Around Nakuru, the thickness of the lava is about 6 000 feet (1 830 m). In Nairobi, a borehole near the main railway station struck the 'Basement Rock' at a depth of 3 900 feet (1 190 m). In the main composite cones of Mounts Kenya and Elgon, the present thicknesses of the volcanic material are 12 760 (3 900 m) and 10 180 feet (3 085 m) respectively. Such major changes must have considerably affected the climate and the whole palaeogeography of our region.

The sequence of the volcanic eruptions has not been fully worked out but it is clear that the Kapiti phonolite was one of the earliest lava outflows in the country. Isotopic age of the Athi River phonolites has given an

Fig. 2E Njorowa Gorge (Hell's Gate), Naivasha, showing the columnar structure formed by comendite volcanoes. Fischer's Tower, one of three in the area, stands as though guarding the gate.

age of 13·4 million years and some of the youngest pumice rocks from Njorowa Gorge are about 29 000 years old. It seems that from that date, eruptions continued intermittently into the Quaternary. Table 2.4 summarises the chronology as far as it is known.

Table 2.4 *Chronology of volcanic eruptions in Kenya*

Period	Volcanic Events
Recent	Teleki and Andrew cones in N. Kenya, geothermal activities—hot springs. Upper Menengai volcanics. Basalts in Rift Valley, Simbi Crater. Olivine basalts of Chulu Hills
Upper Pleistocene	Eruption of the main cones in Rift Valley floor—Longonot, Suswa. Early eruptions in Chulu Hills. Eruption of tuffs, pumice showers, Kijabe basalts and Eburu volcanics and comendites. Parasitic vents of Mt. Kenya
Middle Pleistocene	Extensive eruption of pyroclastics in Naivasha area. Aberdare tuffs and trachytes. 2nd major eruption of Mt. Kenya
Lower Pleistocene	Homa basalts. 1st major eruption of Mt. Kenya. Olivine basanites, basalts and trachytes in Limuru, Kijabe and Simba areas. Initial activities in Homa area
Pliocene	Main eruption of Lower Menengai volcanic series. Nephelinites, trachytes, pyroclastics, phonolites and tuffs in Rift Valley and Naivasha. Londiani agglomerates, Kedowa, Mau, Kinangop and Bahati tuffs. Beginnings of Sattima series—Laikipia and Aberdare eruptions. Main eruption of Mt. Elgon
Middle Miocene	Londiani and Rumuruti phonolites, Simbara Series. Gwasi and Samburu volcanics. Extensive fissure eruptions—Kapiti, Yatta and Kericho phonolites

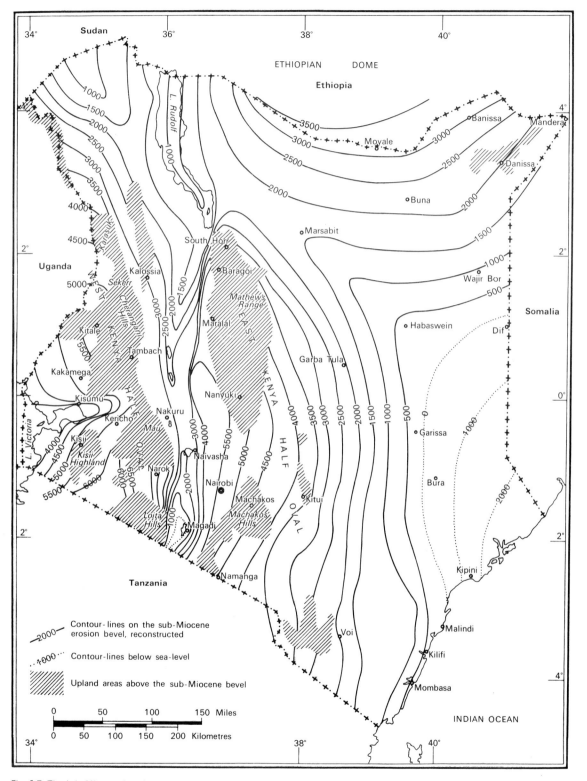

Fig. 2.7 The sub-Miocene bevel

In Kenya, both Fissure (or Linear) and Central (or Vent) type volcanic eruptions occurred. The plateau-building types were probably the more widespread. Thus Kenya's great lava plateaus include Kapiti plains, Kericho, Laikipia and the Uasin Gishu. In each of the above cases, the eruptions appear to have flowed from a fissure situated somewhere close to the present main rift valley zone. Central type cones are of course exemplified by the dominating and imposing Mounts Kenya and Elgon and partly by the Aberdare and Mau Ranges, as well as other smaller examples.

In magnitude, the Kapiti, the Simbara and the Kericho lava eruptions were the most extensive and indeed the most spectacular episodes that must be attributed to geologic disturbances of the first magnitude.

Each one of the above eruptions covered many hundreds of square miles and each involved hundreds of cubic miles of magmatic material. Writing on the Kericho phonolites, Binge (1962) states: 'If an average thickness over this area of only one-tenth of a mile (161 m) is assumed, though a maximum depth exceeding one thousand feet (305 m) has been observed . . . it can be estimated that the volume of the lavas exceeds one hundred cubic miles (417 km^3). This estimate is low as no allowance has been made for the additional thousand sq miles (2 590 km^2) covered by the Mau Forest Reserve beneath which the phonolite flow will almost certainly extend up to the edge of the Great Rift Valley.' The widespread occurrence of pyroclastic materials indicates that some of the eruptions were of the *nuées ardentes* class. Similarly the widespread occurrence of tuffs indicates that lava ash showers were also characteristic.

Lacroix (1908) classified volcanic eruptions into Hawaiian, Strombolian, Vulcanian and Pelean types. To these four classes, other authors have added Plinian, and the Icelandic types. When dealing with extinct or dormant volcanoes, it is not always easy to classify the eruption in question. However, using the rock materials as evidence as well as the topographic form of the remnant lava materials, we can say that Mount Kenya is an example of a Vesuvian type eruption. The Mau and the Aberdare Ranges are only partly in this class because of their 'fissure roots'. The plateau lavas are Icelandic examples. We must nonetheless conclude that most of Lacroix's classes were represented in our region.

Origin of the Yatta Plateau The outline of the Yatta phonolite (Fig. 2.8) presents one of the most perplexing volcanic outcrops known anywhere. The problem is how to account for a continuous outcrop of lava some 180 miles (290 km) in length, and averaging only between 2–3 miles (3–5 km) in width and only about 20–50 feet (6–15 m) in thickness. Its outer edge has certainly been considerably eroded by gully-head erosion and scarp retreat along the point of contact with the underlying basement rock.

Two main theories have been advanced to explain its emplacement. Gregory (1921) thought that the lava flowed down a pre-existing river valley. Schoeman (1948),

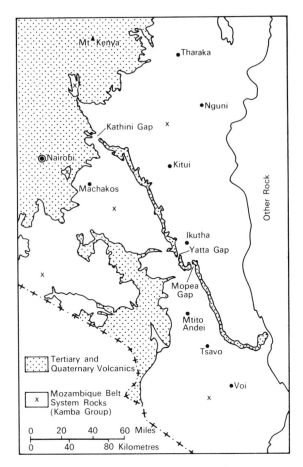

Fig. 2.8 The extent and shape of the Yatta phonolite

Walsh (1963), Saggerson (1963), and Temperley (1955) have since supported this school of thought. The second theory was first advanced by Dodson (1953). It explains the feature as due to eruption along a fissure zone. Sanders (1963) found grounds to support this latter view. Either explanation accepts that in its present form the lava is an erosional remnant. It is probably true to say that any theory that invokes river valley flow must first be sure that such a valley existed in the first place. In this sense the examination by one of us (Ojany 1971) of the early drainage pattern in Kenya is important here. The pre-volcanic drainage pattern seems to have been simple west-east streams, without any channels along the line of the present Yatta Plateau. It is therefore probably true that those who explain it as fault guided have more evidence in their support.

Quaternary Period

i *Pleistocene* We have shown that volcanic activities continued into this period (i.e. into the last million years). The bulk of the Mount Kenya and the Nyambeni eruptions occurred during this time. The Marsabit lava plateau, the Chulu Range and many of the rocks now

Table 2.5 *Quaternary sediments in north-east Kenya*

Recent	River soils and windblown sands	
Upper Pleistocene	Red and brown clays with calcareous nodules	
Middle Pleistocene	Thin laminate limestones Ferruginous sandstones and conglomerates Gypsite and gypsum } Wajir Beds Impure limestones	Partly contemporaneous with El Wak Beds
Lower Pleistocene?	Sandstones Clays and sands } Wajir Beds	

exposed on the floor of the Rift Valley are all due to Pleistocene eruptions.

This period also saw the deposition of extensive terrestrial sediments. In some of these sediments have been found datable fossils – both mammalian and artifacts.

The main area is in western Kenya with Kanam and Fort Ternan where fossils of Upper Miocene age include that of the family *Hominidae* (named *Kenya pithecus wickeri* by Leakey). Table 2.5 gives the more important sediments.

In some localities, the sediments are more than 500 feet (150 m) thick and their varying lithologies indicate climatic oscillations. The thin laminated impure limestone beds suggest the occurrence of widespread shallow lakes which were common in most localities during the Kamasian pluvial. The gysiferous deposits would then suggest an interpluvial that followed.

Along the Kenya coast, the Pleistocene pluvials and interpluvials were marked by fluctuations in the level of the sea. We might note here that the evidence which correlates the East African pluvial phases with the temperate glacial phases, and the interpluvial phases with the interglacial phases, has not been proven beyond doubt but most students of the tropical Pleistocene period accept this correlation as meeting the facts known to date. The tropical sea level dropped during glacial periods and rose during the interglacials. This is because during glaciations much water was locked up in temperate and higher latitudes and tropical and other mountains as snow. During the interglacial this snow melted and so raised the sea level. In the tropics the glacial period also meant cooler and wetter (more rainfall) conditions. This meant that the lake levels of inland lakes rose (at the sea coasts, the opposite took place).

During the Kamasian pluvial, the sea level dropped by some 200 feet (61 m) below its present level (this was the time of the greatest glaciation in temperate lands). A marine platform was cut at this low level and coral polyps grew and thrived from this platform. This coral rock increased its thickness during the subsequent inter-

pluvial. As the sea level fluctuated, so barrier reefs were formed with the enclosed zones now being filled with coastal lagoonal sands. The chronology of these events along the coast is summarised in Table 2.6.

During the same period, the floor of the Rift Valley was filled by much larger lakes than the present smaller ones. Diatomaceous beds near Naivasha and the evaporite deposits and, in particular, trona from Lake Magadi show these conditions.

ii *Holocene* Rocks of this age include thick lacustrine and fluviatile deposits that now occupy the sites of the former lakes. They are particularly important in the Rift Valley floor following widespread dessication after the Pleistocene.

Although there are no important active volcanoes in Kenya, it is quite clear that volcanic activity is not entirely extinct. While we may regard our region as one of extinct and dormant volcanoes, the region cannot be said to be wholly free from possible activities. Count Teliki volcano, to the south of Lake Rudolf, last erupted in 1895. The numerous minor parasitic cones in and around the Chulu Range, Simbi Crater near Kendu Bay, and other sites in the Rift Valley, including the Menengai Caldera, and in the Lake Rudolf area, are all known to have shown activities during the last two hundred years.

The present-day activities are, however, exclusively geothermal. They include steam and gas fumeroles, as in the Menengai Caldera, Longonot and Eburu area, hot springs, as at Maji ya Moto, and blow-holes. The shores of Lake Hannington are studded with fumaroles, hot springs and geysers. McCall (1967) has made an admirably comprehensive study of these features. One of the carbonatite springs near Eldoret has been used as a spa in the last few years. Volcanologists usually interpret such geothermal activities as diagnostic of the last stages of volcanic activities.

Other Pleistocene features in Kenya include glacial moraines in the higher parts of Mounts Kenya and Elgon and in the Aberdares. Most of these were deposited during the last glaciation when the snowline was lower

Table 2.6 *A correlated sequence of events along the Kenya coast*

Geological time-scale	Terminology of climactic stages	Sea level changes (Kenya)	Major palaeogeographical events at the coast (partly after Caswel, 1956)	Kenya artifact cultures	General Pleistocene terminology	Alpine glacial sequence of Europe	Sea level changes (Europe)
Holocene	Post-pluv-ial { Nakuran, Makali-an }	Rise and aggradition to the present sea level	Deposition of windblown sands. Deposition and silting in Ports Tudor and Reitz, and drowning and silting of creeks	Wilton, Gumblian, Elmentaitan	Post-glacial period	Post-glacial	Flandrian transgression
Upper Pleistocene	Gamblian pluvial			Magosian, Stillbay, Capsian	Last glacial period	Würm glaciation	Generally low
	Third interpluvial	15 feet (4·6 m) OD 30 feet (9·1 m) OD	15 feet (4·6 m) raised beach, caves and platform 30 feet (9·1 m) marine platform 100 feet (30·5 m) knickpoint	Fouresmith	Last interglacial period	Last interglacial	25 feet (7·6 m) OD 60 feet (18·3 m) OD
Middle Pleistocene	Kanjeran pluvial	C−150 feet (45·7 m)	Cutting of deep channels	Pseudo-Stillbay, Acheulian	Penultimate glacial period	Riss glaciation	Very low
	Second interpluvial	C−100 feet (30·5 m)	Coral reefs grow 200 feet (61 m) knickpoint 120 feet (36·6 m) terrace	Acheulian	Penultimate interglacial period	Great interglacial	170 feet (51·8 m)
Lower Pleistocene	Kamasian pluvial	C−200 feet (61 m)	Cutting of marine platform upon which the coral grew	Chellean	Ante-penultimate glacial period	Mindel glaciation	Very low
	First interpluvial	C−200 feet (61 m)	250 feet (76·2 m) knickpoint		Ante-penultimate interglacial period	First interglacial	200 feet (61 m)
	Kageran pluvial				Early glacial period	Gunz glaciation	Lower
Pliocene		C−300 feet (91·4 m)	Deposition of Midadoni beds, Deposition of Magarini sands in a semi arid condition				C−300 feet (91·4 m)

than its present level. Baker (1968) found what he termed 'great' and 'very marked' moraines which he dated as Gamblian I wet phase and 'oldest' moraines which he dated as of Kanjeran pluvial in the Mount Kenya area. The other recent deposits are soils including alluvial soils and sands in eastern Kenya.

Intrusives into the Tertiary Rocks

These are not widespread apart from alkaline plutonic intrusives which may be connected with volcanicity and rift faulting. The main ones form part of the carbonatite complex of western Kenya. These include Rangwe, Homa Hill and others in the Koru area. There is evidence to show that these centres are connected structurally with the Elgon and Moroto centres of Uganda. On the other hand the Mrima and Jombo centres, near the Taita hills, appear to be isolated examples.

2. Tectonic Activities

Our knowledge of the tectonic events in Kenya since the deposition of the Nyanzian sediments is incomplete. The pre-Cambrian mountain-building movements which affected the Nyanzian, and later the Kavirondian sediments can be conceived from the 'upturned remains' of the above rocks. The Basement rocks were also later subjected to another major orogenesis.

Apart from the above events, our area experienced no other tectonic disturbances apart from restricted thermal and heat-flow activities which affected the Kisii Series probably during and soon after their deposition. This long period of relative stability was dominated by

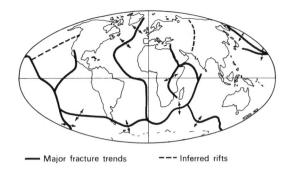

—— Major fracture trends   – – – Inferred rifts

Fig. 2.9 Tectonic features of the globe

extensive erosion which continued uninterrupted until towards the close of the Jurassic period. By this time, the entire region had been reduced to a vast surface of low relief. Then from the early Cretaceous, a series of earth movements interspersed with short phases of stability and erosion followed. The movements included uplifts, upwarps, downwarps, tilting and faulting, including rift valley formation. It was also during these tectonic disturbances that volcanic activities took place.

Rift Valleys

Kenya is the country where the Great African Rift System is best seen and there are some magnificent viewpoints for this. This tectonic features is now known to be part of the world-wide system of almost continuous rift valleys which girdle the entire earth (Fig. 2.9). The

Fig. 2F View of the Rift Valley from near Longonot looking east to the Kikuyu Escarpment, which rises to 8 500 feet (2 600 m). Mount Margaret (6 365 feet) (1 940 m), one of the cones in the Rift Valley, is clearly seen

Fig. 2G The Nyando fault-line scarp, in the Kano Plains near Kisumu. Note the prominent granitic tor that juts above the skyline of the upthrown side, and the straightness of the base of the escarpment. The plain formed by the downthrow is under sugar cane cultivation (the Kibos-Chemelil sugar estates), as seen in the foreground

system thus constitutes one of the main first order features of the earth's surface. Its true origin, why it occurred, and when it occurred, present great challenges to geology.

The East African portion of this feature is unique in that in this area is the greatest expanse of a rift valley occurring on the land surface and thus directly accessible for on the spot study. It is therefore not surprising that the term *rift valley* was first used by Gregory (1896) for the 'Great Rift Valley of East Africa'. Gregory was also the first scholar to recognise it as a tectonic feature due to faulting. He defined the term to mean a long strip of country let down between normal faults or a parallel series of step faults. Later Willis (1928) used the alternative term *ramp valley* but this use has not been continued.

The Form of the Rift System
The Great African Rift Valley continues through the territorial grounds of many nations. Together with the Palestinian portion, the closely related parts of the system stretch over a distance of more than 3 500 miles (5 600 km). It has an average width of between 20–35 miles (32–56 km) but in Kenya the various sectional widths differ a great deal. Across the Kano Plains its width is 25 miles (40 km). In the Magadi section it is 35 miles (56 km), in the Baringo area it is 60 miles (97 km). Further north in the Lake Rudolf area, it is at its widest, being 105 miles (169 km) at the southern end of the lake and a little over 200 miles (322 km) at the northern end of the lake. The lowest parts of the rift floor are at the extreme ends; the level of Lake Magadi is 1 900 feet (584 m) and that of Lake Rudolf 1 230 feet (375 m).

To understand the Rift Structure an investigation should not confine itself to the political boundaries.

In fact over much of its length, the Rift Valley in Kenya is made up of complicated and in places *en échelon* faults which do not form a single rift valley but rather a rift system. Fig. 2.10 shows this. In many places the faults are asymmetrical and the amounts of displacement differ. Fig. 2.11, explains the terms commonly employed when referring to tectonic displacements. The Kenya system forms a gentle S-curved furrow that runs from north to south through the centre of the country (along the crest of the Kenya Dome). The only notable exception to the above is the Kano Rift of west Kenya which is bounded by two normal faults and has thus determined the west-east trend of the Nyanza (Winam) Gulf. Within the main rift are many minor north-south trending faults (known locally as *Grid* or *Sykes faults*, so named after L. J. Sykes who first studied them in 1939). The average throw of these Grid faults varies from about 10–50 feet (3–15 m). They are the most recent movements in our area and are

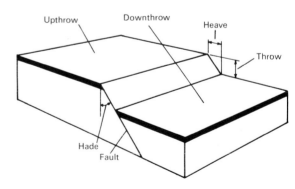

Fig. 2.11 The terminology of faulted topography

34

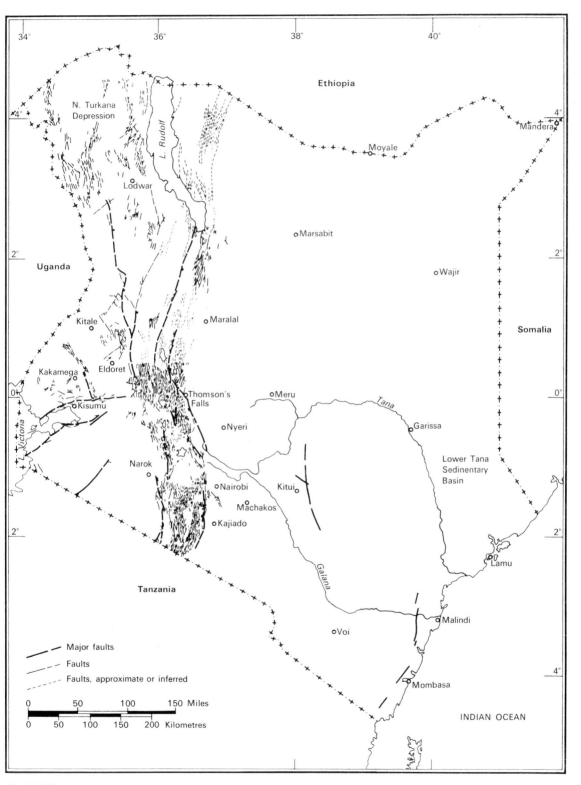

Fig. 2.10 The rift system

35

mostly Holocene features. The amounts of displacement involved in the main fault lines are tremendous. In the Central Highlands it is between 6 000 and 10 000 feet (1 830–3 050 m). The Nyando fault in the Kano Plains has a throw of 2 000 feet (610 m) while the Kendu fault to the south has an average throw of 1 200 feet (3 660 m).

The Origin of Rift Valleys

The tectonic displacements of the earth's crust which form rift valleys have not been fully explained. What we now know is the result of work not only on the East African section but also on the Red Sea and Ethiopian sections and the Rhine Rift Valley. Thus although in East Africa the tensional theory is commonly attributed to Gregory, it should be remembered that he had the idea from other workers such as De Lapparent (1887), Uhlig (1912) and Suess (1891). Gregory, thus following the then familar 'fallen keystone' concept, advanced the view that the Kenya section of the Rift Valley was the result of tensional forces on the uparched axial portion of the earth. Since then men like Cloos (1955) have demonstrated using models that distension can cause faulting in this manner. Recently the work of Freund (1965) has also tended to support this view.

In Uganda, Wayland (1921) invoked the compressional theory and Willis (1928) gave him support following the latter's work in the Red Sea area. Other workers have invoked vertical movements (Dixey 1956, Troup 1949), while others have invoked magmatic pressure, isostatic collapse and so on. More recently crustal separation in the manner of continental drift has also been advanced (for example by Girdler in 1969). King (1962) explains the origin of the Central African Rift Valley System simply as being the results of the powerful uplifts and warpings to which the interior of the African continent has been subjected since the Pliocene time. The rift valleys thus formed at the axes of the crest which cracked open due to tensional forces along the uplifted arch.

It is apparent from the above summary that the rift valleys have been formed as a result of a combination of a number of forces and it is not anough to explain them simply as due to tensional or compressional forces acting by themselves. Current opinion tends to favour tensional forces together with some amount of large scale uplifts (that is anticlinal arching), gravitational and isostatic collapse and some degree of crustal separation (in the manner of continental drifting). Isostatic adjustment is necessary to ensure that the borders rise and slope away from the tips of the depressions (Holmes 1965).

The Kenya Rift System seems to have been produced in the manner outlined above. The sequence in each locality certainly differed in its details. McCall (1967) has shown that in the Lake Hannington area (Fig. 2.12) at least eight main phases of activities occurred before the present form was produced.

Wayland favoured compressional forces partly because of the negative gravity anomalies (Fig. 2.13) which

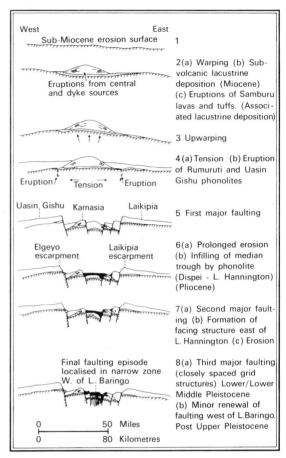

Fig. 2.12 Diagrammatic representation of the successive stages in the formation of the Rift Valley in the Lake Hannington sector

Bullard (1936) had shown to exist in the rift valley floors. Such readings suggest that the floors contain light material. It is not really necessary to invoke compression to account for the negative gravity readings.

The other point to be explained when discussing rift valley formation is the driving mechanism or the source of the energy to cause motion. The swell uplift has been accepted. We should also note the separation of the Arabian block from the eastern Kenya and Somali block. This area tells more vividly the closeness to continental drifting that would seem to be going on so that the force must be similar (though much weaker) to that responsible for the continental drift as a whole.

The Age of the Kenya Rift System

The tectonic disturbances which produced the East African Rift System did not take place at the same time. Even in the Kenya section alone, the movements have continued over the last 20 million years. Tectonic activities that account for the 'Basin and Swell Structure'

36

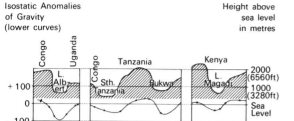

Isostatic Anomalies
of Gravity
(lower curves)

Height above
sea level
in metres

Fig. 2.13 Profiles across four African rift valleys with the corresponding gravity anomalies, determined by E. C. Bullard and plotted by A. Holmes. A marked deficiency of mass is revealed beneath each of the rifts

in Africa go back to the carboniferous times and the movements appear to have continued intermittently to this day. The rift system in Zambia, Malawi and parts of Tanzania appears to be slightly older than the main Kenya fault lines. That the Malawi troughs are filled with sediments of Karroo age has tended to lead to the view that these fault lines are older, but this interpretation is not accepted by all geologists.

In Kenya, the present major fault lines certainly seem to be younger if one judges by the freshness of their scarps. The earliest probably appeared in late Miocene, and another phase of major faulting is known to have occurred in Pliocene and Quaternary times. The Grid faults are the youngest, and many of them belong to the last 5 000 years.

Considerable rejuvenations along old fault lines appear to have been characteristic in the rifting processes.

References

DAVIS, W. M. (1909) *Geographical Essays*, Dover Publications, 1954.

WILLS, L. J. *The Palaeogeography of the Midlands*, University of Liverpool Press, 1950.

HOLMES, A. 'The sequence of the pre-Cambrian orogenic belts in South and Central Africa', *Intern. Geol. Congr. 18th session*, 1951, pp. 154–269.

SANDERS, L. D. 'Geology of the contact between the Nyanza Shield and the Mozambique Belt in Western Kenya', *Bull. No. 7, Geol. Surv. Kenya*, 1965.

PULFREY, W. 'Shape of the sub-Miocene erosion bevel in Kenya', *Bull. No. 3, Geol. Surv. Kenya*, 1960.

CASWEL, P. V. 'Geology of the Kilifi-Mazeras area', *Report No. 34, Geol. Surv. Kenya*, 1956.

CASWEL, P. V. 'Geology of the Mombasa-Kwale area', *Report No. 24, Geol. Surv. Kenya*, 1953.

SAGGERSON, E. P., and MILLER, J. M. 'Geology of the Takabba-Wergudad area', *Report No. 40, Geol. Surv. Kenya*, 1957.

BAKER, B. H., and SAGGERSON, E. P. 'Geology of the El Wak-Aus Mandula area', *Report No. 44, Geol. Surv. Kenya*, 1958.

JOUBERT, P. 'Geology of the Wajir-Wajir Bor area', *Report No. 57, Geol. Surv. Kenya*, 1963.

BINGE, F. W. 'Geology of the Kericho area', *Report No. 50, Geol. Surv. Kenya*, 1962.

LACROIX, A. 'La montagne Pelée après ses éruptions', *Ac. Sci. Paris*, 1908, pp. 74–93.

GREGORY, J. W. *The Rift Valley and the Geology of East Africa*, Seeley Service, London, 1921.

SCHOEMAN, J. J. 'Geological reconnaissance of the area west of Kitui Township', *Report No. 14, Geol. Surv. Kenya*, 1948.

WALSH, J. 'Geology of the Ikutha area', *Report No. 65, Geol. Surv. Kenya*, 1963.

SAGGERSON, E. P. 'Geology of the Simba-Kibwezi area', *Report No. 58, Geol. Surv. Kenya*, 1963.

TEMPERLEY, B. N. 'Geology and groundwater conditions in the Kibwezi-Chulu area', *Technical Report No. 2, Ministry of Works, Hydraulic Branch*, 1955.

DODSON, R. G. 'Geology of southeast Machakos area', *Report No. 25, Geol. Surv. Kenya*, 1953.

SANDERS, L. D. 'Geology of the Voi-South Yatta area', *Report No. 79, Geol. Surv. Kenya*, 1963.

BAKER, B. H. 'Geology of Mount Kenya area', *Report No. 79, Geol. Surv. Kenya*, 1968.

RANCORN, S. K. (Ed) *Continental Drift*, Academic Press, New York, 1962.

SYKES, L. J. 'Notes on the geology of the country surrounding Nairobi', *Geol. Surv. Kenya*, 1939.

BAKER, B. H. 'The Rift System in Kenya', *East African Rift System, Upper Mantle Committee, UNESCO Seminar, Nairobi*, 1965.

WAYLAND, E. J. 'Rift valleys and Lake Victoria', *15th C.R. Intern. Geol. Congr. Sect. 6, Vol. 2*, 1929, pp. 323–353.

KING, L. C. *Morphology of the Earth*, Oliver and Boyd, 1962, pp. 293–295.

BULLARD, E. C. 'Gravity measurements in East Africa', *Phil. Trans. Royal Soc. London, Vol. 235A*, 1936, pp. 445–531.

HOLMES, A. *Principles of Physical Geology*, 2nd edn, Nelson, 1965, pp. 1044–1108.

MCCALL, G. J. H. 'Geology of the Nakuru-Thomson's Falls-Lake Hannington area', *Report No. 78, Geol. Surv. Kenya*, 1967.

GIRDLER, R. W. 'Drifting and rifting of Africa', *Nature, Vol. 217*, 1968, pp. 1102–1106.

CLOOS, E. 'Experimental analysis of fracture patterns', *Bull. Geol. Soc. America, Vol. 66*, 1955, pp. 241–256.

DRAKE, C. L. and GIRDLER, R. W. 'A geophysical study of the Red Sea', *Geophys. Journal, Roy. Astron. Soc. Vol. 8*, 1964, pp. 473–495.

Chapter 3
Relief and Drainage

The relief of Kenya can be described as being both simple and extremely diversified, and the statements would not be contradictory. A glance at the relief map (Fig. 3.1) may give the impression that the country's topography is fairly simple. But such a survey will nonetheless reveal the two most distinct physical regions into which the country most naturally falls, *viz, lowland Kenya*, which includes all the land below 3 000 feet (915 m), and *upland Kenya* (Fig. 3.2). This distinction is important and indeed fundamental as the landscape ecology (that is, the combined physical and human landscape) in the two regions contrasts sharply. Generally, lowland Kenya is largely a negative environment which presents exciting development challenges. Upland Kenya on the other hand must be viewed as the backbone of the Republic.

However, a detailed scrunity of the landscape will again show that Kenya possesses one of the most complicated and diversified physical environments that can be found in any country. Every landform and landscape type – equatorial, tropical, savannah, aeolian, glacial, volcanic, tectonic, etc. – is present in Kenya. Such an environment must afford considerable, if not unlimited, scope for the study of geomorphology. It is the product of both endogenetic and exogenetic agencies and our aim in this chapter is to trace and explain this evolution.

Kenya's structural geology is dominated by a gentle dome-shaped asymmetrical shield (Fig. 3.3). This is true irrespective of the direction of the line of the section one chooses. The land rises very gently westwards from the east until about 3 000 feet (915 m) above sea level. Above this height, the climb to the west becomes much steeper and a more obvious obstacle to transportation routes as the true upland environment is reached. Mount Kenya (17 058 feet or 5 200 m), an imposing composite volcano situated right in the heart of the country, is Africa's second highest peak.

Although the various features of the country have different origins, generally the entire terrain is dominated by a succession of extensive well-preserved plateaus at different heights above sea level. The height of these plateaus and their apparent similarity in form, can be used as a rational basis for dividing the whole country into the physiographic units as shown in Fig. 3.4. Our map does not show the maximum number of divisions.

Fig. 3A General view of Mt Kenya from Naro Moru, with Point Batian clearly visible

Fig. 3B Close up view of Mt Kenya

38

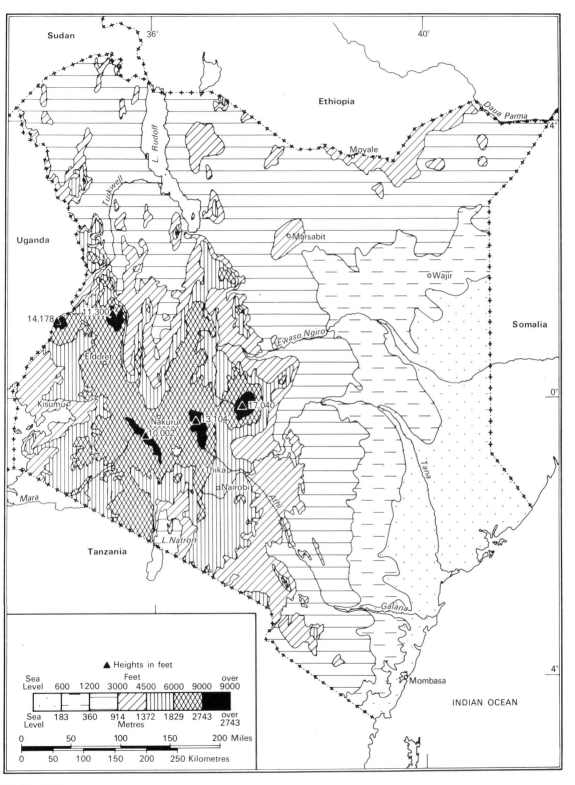

Fig. 3.1 Relief

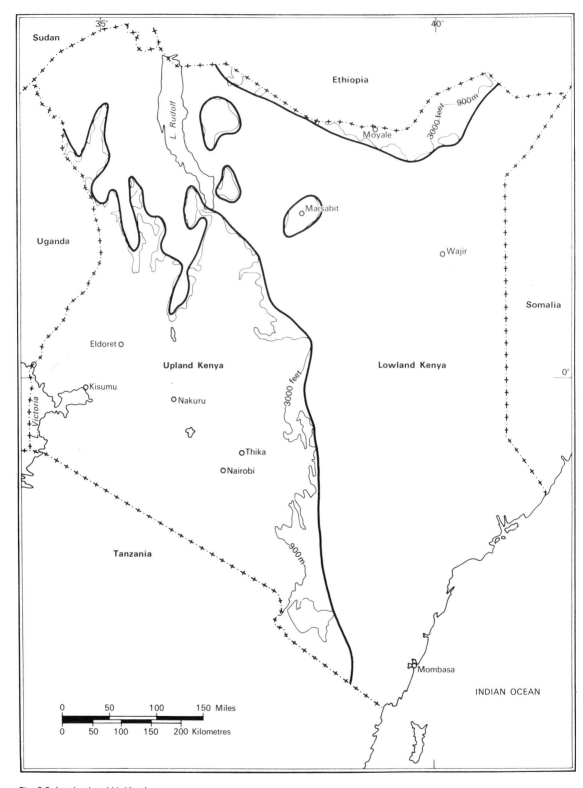

Fig. 3.2 Lowland and highland

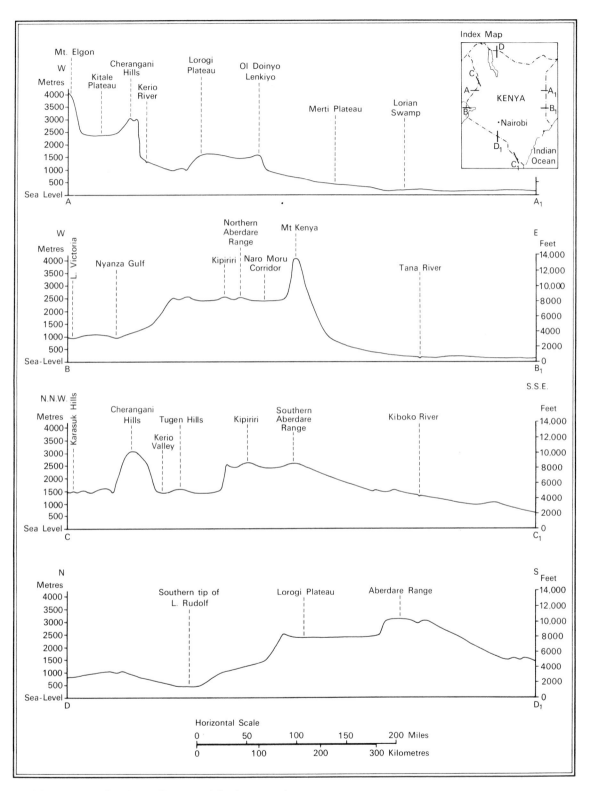

Fig. 3.3 Selected relief sections to illustrate variation in topography

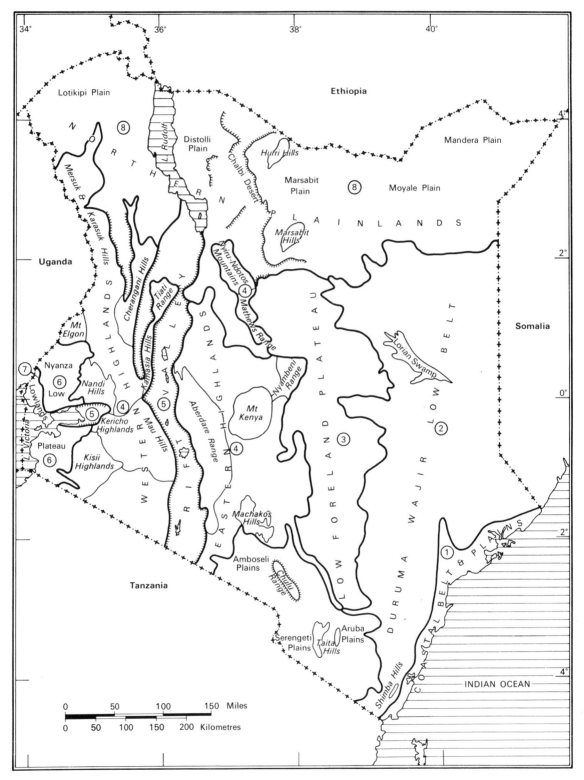

Fig. 3.4 Physiographic regions (simplified)

For a more detailed study, the reader should study Ojany's 1966 paper. The rest of the details of the relief can then be usefully studied under each region.

The Coastal Belt and Plains

A properly developed coastal plain has not been attained along the Kenya coast. This is because the present sea level is a young feature. The area, as we have noted, has been subjected to periodic eustatic changes almost since the Carboniferous period. Consequently, only an ill-defined coastal plain can be traced below 500 feet (152 m) and even then a true plain is very narrow. It has an average width of 2–5 miles (3–5 km) and is only found below the 200-foot (61 m) contour. Near the mouth of the Tana River it widens out to about 10 miles (16 km). Between 200 and 500 feet (61 and 152 m), an ill-defined low plateau (locally known as the *Foot Plateau*) is found covering mainly the Jurassic rocks belt.

Quaternary sea level changes, already noted, left well developed geomorphological features along the coast. The greatest fall in sea level appears to have taken place during the Kamasian Pluvial. It enabled the coastal rivers to cut deep channels, which reached their maximum extent into the then sea level. During the Holocene, when the sea level rose, the old river courses were drowned to form the present coastal creeks. Mombasa Island was formed following the drowning of two closely spaced rivers – Mwachi (Reitz Creek) and Kombeni (Tudor Creek). The soft, easily erodable Jurassic shales behind the coral rock into which Port Tudor and Port Reitz now spread out also helped bring about complete isolation of the island. Mtwapa Creek also spreads out inland where these soft rocks occur.

But the sea level in rising has not attained the very high levels that it reached during the third interpluvial. Thus abandoned cliff-lines (now degraded, in places), stacks, raised platforms, and raised beaches are well displayed in appropriate areas along the coast. A near-perfect abandoned cliff-line forms the steep slope above which the Oceanic Hotel is built, while the Mama Ngina Drive below it is an excellent example of the 30 foot (9 m) raised platform. Another well-preserved abandoned cliff-line can be seen a few yards before the Shelly Beach Hotel. The raised platforms are best seen on either side of the entrance to the Kilindini Harbour. Raised beaches are well seen as one descends towards most of the hotels and cottages along the coast. Most of the cottages are in fact built on them.

The Duruma-Wajir Low Belt

This is an extensive region that has an obvious uniformity in that it is dry, monotonously flat and very uninspiring. It is separated from the coastal belt by a rather ill-preserved series of hills which other authors have termed the *Coastal Ranges*. These ranges are clearly part of this region which rises very gently from 500 feet (152 m) to about 1 000 feet (304 m). Much of this region shows a well-developed planation surface of Upper Pliocene age. In its southern portion, a number of residual hills including Shimba (1 453 feet or 443 m), Jibana (1 028 feet or 314 m), Lali (1 394 feet or 426 m) and Kulalu (1 453 feet or 443 m) jut above the main surface and also appear to show an accordance of summit. This does suggest that these residuals, although partly the product of the porous nature of the Duruma Sandstones, also record a higher and therefore older erosion surface.

The Lorian Swamp is an important feature in the area. During exceptionally wet seasons, it can hold a considerable volume of water from the Ewaso Ngiro River and it then functions as an important local stream, flowing into Somalia.

With irrigation, it is possible that this region may support considerable cattle ranching and some cotton, kenaf, sugar cane and groundnut cultivation, especially along the Tana Valley. The large quantities of Quaternary sand deposits in the area are partly due to the numerous west-east seasonal streams that disappear in the region but also to extensive weathering of the gneissic rocks. In the extreme north near Wajir, the features begin to be wind-formed.

The Low Foreland Plateau

This region lies between 1 000 and 3 000 feet (304 and 915 m) above sea level. Much of it is flat, and desolate and dry. Except for the volcanic plains of Amboseli, the region forms one extensive erosion surface of late Tertiary age, from which numerous small inselbergs rise abruptly. The inselbergs are in different stages of destruction with the Taita Hills, which rise to 7 248 feet (2 208 m), as the most important single group on this otherwise monotonous plain. It is evident that from such a large mass of residuals (Taita Hills group) a number of smaller inselbergs will in due course separate out by selective erosion.

The formation of inselbergs has been debated considerably. From their writings, it is clear that all the Kenya students of landform genesis are agreed that the inselbergs are formed by lateral planation. This is the process by which the extensive deep-seated weathered mantle at the foot of the hill is removed. Two types of these inselbergs are present: those marginal to the main hillmasses, known as *marginal type*, and those which now appear to occur freely over the landscape, known as *ubiquitous type* inselbergs. It is clear that these residuals are still being formed at the present time and those already formed are undergoing further destruction.

The terminology applied to these residual hills has been rather confused. It is clear that the actual shape and form of each inselberg has been influenced by the nature of the bedrock. Resistant rocks of great age are more suited to inselberg development. Thus, plutonic rocks, if well-jointed with both vertical and horizontal joint

Fig. 3C Maikuu hill, one of the inselbergs in the Wami Hills, Machakos District. It can be seen about 40 miles (64 km) from Nairobi to the right of the Mombasa road

planes, will weather more easily along these lines of weakness to give *castellated tors*. If there are no horizontal joint planes, then the rocks weather to give *finger type* or *sugar-loaf type inselbergs*. If, however, the joint planes are well apart and vertical, then *domed inselbergs* result. Gneissic rocks on the other hand form *slabby type* inselbergs in conformity with their original sedimentary nature. Commonly only the bare rock shows above the general plain and hence the term *bare-rock inselbergs*. The important point to note here is that all these different forms are merely various types of inselbergs. Figs. 3.5 and 3.6 illustrate some of these.

The area between the Serengeti Plains and the Amboseli Plains is dominated by the imposing Chulu Range, which rises to 7 134 feet (2 173 m) above sea level. Beyond this range but to the south of the Emali-Simba railway line area, small youthful volcanic cones jut above the plain. These cones should not be mistaken for inselbergs.

1. Kit Mikai, in Seme Location, (Kisumu District). an example of castellated tors.

2. Ihonga Mrui in Iresi area (Kakamega District). Finger type or sugar loaf form.

Fig. 3.5 Inselbergs and tors

44

Fig. 3D Ol Doinyo Nyegi, which rises over 1 000 feet (300 m) above the Rift Valley floor, near Magadi. It is formed by sheets of porphyritic obsidian and the rims are faulted. A smaller ash cone can also be seen. The bulk of the mountain is filled with plateau trachytes

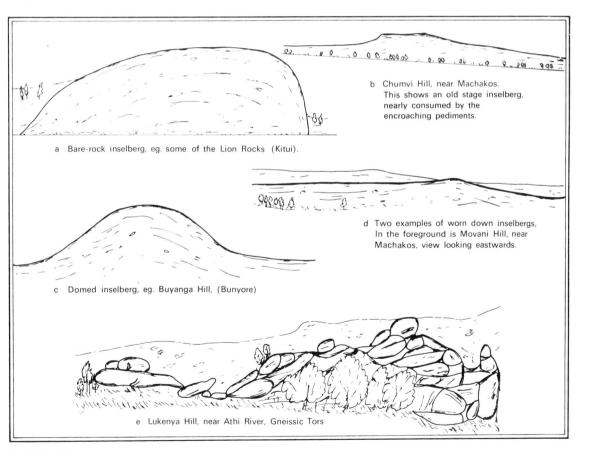

a Bare-rock inselberg, eg. some of the Lion Rocks (Kitui).

b Chumvi Hill, near Machakos. This shows an old stage inselberg, nearly consumed by the encroaching pediments.

c Domed inselberg, eg. Buyanga Hill, (Bunyore)

d Two examples of worn down inselbergs, In the foreground is Movani Hill, near Machakos, view looking eastwards.

e Lukenya Hill, near Athi River, Gneissic Tors

Fig. 3.6 Inselbergs and tors

The Kenya Highlands

The Kenya Highlands are famous particularly for their role in the historical development of the nation. As defined in this work, these highlands possess tremendous physical diversity although the unity of the region is evident by virtue of its great height. No single contour can be used to delimit the lower part of the region, for other factors must also be considered. Breaks of slope and the general appearance of the terrain are other important details of the landform to be borne in mind.

The Great African Rift Valley bisects the region into the western and the eastern highlands. Two sharply contrasting landscapes occur: there are the *old upland massifs* which are erosional remnants of old planation surfaces of pre-Miocene to late-Jurassic age on the one hand, and the relatively younger *Tertiary–recent volcanic highlands and plateaus*, with which we must now include those areas which have been called the *intermediate lava plateaus* (Ojany 1966), on the other.

The Western Highlands

This sub-region is well-defined to the north by the sharp ravine-like gullies cut into it by the northward flowing fault-guided streams, and to the west by the 5 000 foot (1 520 m) contour along which an important change of slope seems to be continuous. The sub-region is dominated by a number of important topographic units as shown in Fig. 3.4. The Cherangani Hills rise to 11 300 feet (3 444 m) to form the highest non-volcanic point in Kenya. To the west of the Cherangani are situated the Mersuk and Karasuk Hills and the Kitale-Kapenguria Plateaus. The Kisii Highlands provide an example of a maturely dissected scenery on which is preserved some excellent remnants of the Gondwana Summit Plain (see King 1965).

The rest of the sub-region is largely a result of constructional activities of Tertiary volcanicity. Again a number of individual plateaus dominate the scene. The imposing Mau Hills, Mount Elgon, the Kamasia Hills

Table 3.1 *Outline of the highest mountain ranges and hills*

Mountain/ Range	Average height		Length		Width		Peaks	Height	
	feet	m	miles	km	miles	km		feet	m
Mt Kenya			75	121	75	121	Batian	17 058	5 199
							Nelion	17 022	5 188
							Lenana	16 355	4 985
Mt Elgon							Wagagai	14 178	4 321
							Sudek	14 140	4 310
							Koitobos	13 830	4 215
Aberdare Range	11 000	3 353	40	64	15	24	Lesatima	13 104	3 994
							Kinangop	12 816	3 906
Cherangani Hills	9 000	2 743	30	48	25	40	Chemnirot	11 500	3 505
							Sondang	10 520	3 206
							Kaisungol	10 370	3 161
Sekerr Range	8 000	2 438	7	11	3	5	Seger	10 910	3 325
Mau Range	9 000	2 743	50	80	25	40	Melili	10 165	3 098
Nyiru								9 203	2 805
Longonot								9 111	2 777
Subugo								8 803	2 683
Ndoto Mountains	7 000	2 136	30	48	20	32	Bokhol	8 313	2 534
Nyambeni Range	6 000	1 829	12	19	6	10	Itiani	8 245	2 513
Ol Doinyo Orok								8 376	2 553
Ngong Hills	8 000	2 438	7	11	2	3	Ol Lemoya	8 074	2 461
Kasithit Hills	6 000	1 829	20	32	10	16	Losiolo	8 104	2 470
Mt Suswa								7 732	2 357
Kulal								7 520	2 292
Mathews Range	6 000	1 829	30	48	10	16	Langiyo	7 792	2 375
							Warges	8 820	2 688
Chulu Range	6 000	1 829	30	48	10	16	Ridge	7 134	2 175
Taita Hills	5 000	1 524	30	48	10	16	Vuria	7 248	2 209
Doinyo Sapuk								7 041	2 146
Karasuk Hills							Kachangalau	9 145	2 787
Gwasi Hills								7 454	2 272
Mt Loldian								9 874	3 010
Timboroa								9 496	2 894

Fig. 3E Koma Rock, a *kipuka*. This is one of the many former marginal inselbergs near Nairobi which were engulfed by lava flows during the eruption of the Kapiti phonolites. It rises above the lava field like an island above the sea

and Tiati Range are obvious examples. The youthful stage of the cycle of erosion can best be illustrated by the present form of the plateaus and especially of Kericho Plateau. The compactness of the land has not had time to be altered very much despite the high rate of erosion.

The Eastern Highlands

Like its western counterpart, this sub-region is very distinct above the Low Foreland Plateau. As the eastern boundary of this unit goes down to about 3 000 feet (915 m), the sub-region is consequently even more diversified. It has within it relics of the old upland massifs; Tertiary to recent volcanic highlands and plateaus, intermediate lava plains as well as non-volcanic plateaus. The most important remnants of the *old upland massif* here are the Machakos Hills and the

Northern Mountain Ranges which include the Nyiru-Ndotos and Mathews Ranges. These old land surfaces are much dissected and in Machakos a mature topography has been attained in the Mbooni-Kilungu upland environment. The lower parts of these hills record lower erosion surfaces including the sub-Miocene at 4 000–5 000 feet (1 216–1 520 m) and a late Tertiary surface below 4 000 feet (1 216 m).

From the point of view of general height of the land, the volcanic landscapes dominate the sub-region. The two masses which command the whole area are of course Mount Kenya and the Aberdare Ranges, which rise to 13 104 feet (3 992 m). The juxtaposed position of the Aberdares Range and the Mau Hills on the opposing shoulders of the Rift Valley, while possibly co-incidental, is too neat to be an unrelated arrangement, and it appears to be an area whose geomorphological history has not been fully worked out. To the north-east of Mt

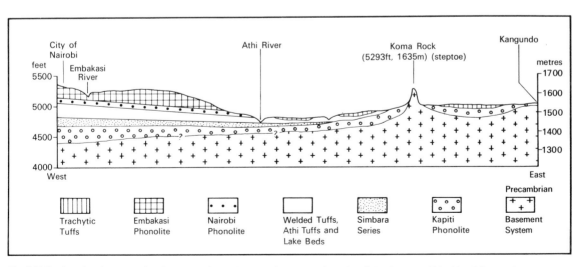

Fig. 3.7 Section showing pre-volcanic topography and islands (steptoes) above lava fields between Nairobi and Kangundo

Kenya is situated the Nyambeni Range which rises to 8 245 feet (2 513 m) at the Itiani Peak. This range dominates the Meru country. The rest of the country which lies to the north and north-west is dominated by the Laikipia Intermediate Plateau.

The landscape to the south of Mt Kenya and the Aberdare Range is dominated by the Kiambu and the Ngong dipslopes on the west and by a series of stepped lava plateaus which form interior plains east of Nairobi. Of these inland plains, the Embakasi, the Thika and the Kapiti Plains are the best known. The Embakasi Plain is still in its initial stage of erosion, while the Kapiti Plain has now been eroded to the late youth stage. Above the Thika and Kapiti plains, old residual inselbergs that were not quite covered by the lava flows jut above the plains to form excellent examples of *steptoes*, *kipukas* or *dagalas*, as these features have been called by other workers (Fig. 3.7) (see Cotton 1952). Koma Rock and Kongoni Hill are perfect examples of this. On parts of the Thika and Athi Plains disused termite hills associated with Kirichwa Valley tuffs now form fascinating mound topography whose origin has caused considerable debate (see Ojany 1968). The narrow plateau formed by the Yatta Phonolite forms one of the most unusual relief features of its kind known. Its surface is practically intact although it is undergoing active scarp retreat along its edges by headward gully erosion.

The Kenya Rift Valley

We have already noted that fracturing and differential movements of the earth's crust have both been important episodes in the geologic events in Kenya. The main valley (see Figs. 2.9 and 3.4) runs meridianally through the Kenya Highlands and continues into Tanzania. In the Distolli Plain, the faults are not so impressive due to later volcanic eruptions and sand dunes. In other places displacements of the order of 4 000–6 000 feet (1 216–1 824 m) are typical.

As the faults occurred in a series of parallel faults, the sides of the main valley are typically stepped, although lower down into the valley bottom these benches or platforms mark the former lake levels. Also in the floor of the valley are a number of younger volcanic plugs and cones. The more important cones are, from north to south, Silali (5 008 feet or 2 355 m), Menengai (7 475 feet or 2 279 m), Longonot (9 111 feet or 2 776 m), Suswa (7 732 feet or 2 355 m) and Shombole (5 132 feet or 1 564 m). The tops of these cones have been either partly or wholly blown off to form craters while that of Menengai is large enough to be classed as a caldera.

Little is left of the original Pleistocene lake but smaller lakes still dot the whole length of the rift floor. Unlike the main Rift Valley, the Kano Plains Rift Valley is smaller and has an almost perfectly flat floor.

Fig. 3F Aerial view of the upper rim of the Longonot crater in the Rift Valley. Note the well-rimmed parasitic cone, the erosion rills and the sharp edge of the crater rim

The Nyanza Low Plateau

This is a low plateau with a gentle but obvious slope towards Lake Victoria which shows that structurally it is part of the down-warped Lake Victoria Basin. But over much of its length it is dominated by an extensive erosion surface at an altitude which ranges from 4 000–5 000 feet (1 216–1 520 m). Above this plain, especially to the east of Maseno, is the higher, much dissected, granitic tor and bare-rock inselberg landscape of the Maragoli Hills. This higher landscape suggests a higher surface at 6 000 feet (1 824 m), but much of it has now been destroyed. Here the local influence of bedrock shows vividly.

A series of three parallel stepped faults occurs below Maseno towards the lake and their effect is well marked on the landscape. In south Nyanza too, Lambwe Valley was caused by faulting.

Along the southern slope in particular, volcanic cones such as Gwasi Hills (7 454 feet or 2 271 m), Gembe Hills, Ruri Hills, and Homa Hill, stand out and dominate the skyline.

The Nyanza Lowlands

This is a relatively minor region. It is a low lying swampy tract of country very much prone to flooding, and embraces the Yala-Nzoia Lowlands between Port Victoria, Ukwala, Boro and Yimbo.

The Northern Plainlands

This is the most extensive of the regions and covers the whole of Northern Kenya. It is also the least known of the regions due to its remoteness. It is an area dominated by extensive low lying interior plains that range in height between 1 200 and 3 000 feet (366 and 912 m) and in this respect it might be said to form the natural continuation of the Low Foreland Plateau. It is also an area of considerable aridity. The plains have had different origins. From west to east, the Lotikipi Plains are made up of Quaternary sediments, the Distolli Plains are of lava and dune plains, the Marsabit area is a lava plateau, the Moyale area has been carved by erosion out of basement rocks, and the Mandera Plain is of Mesozoic sediments.

The only features that interrupt the general monotony and aridity of these plains are a number of prominent volcanic cones – such as Marsabit (4 687 feet or 1 428 m), the Kulalu (7 520 feet or 2 292 m) and the Hurri Hills (4 854 feet or 1 479 m), the Lokwanamoru, Lorionet, Mogila and Loriu Ranges, and Songot Mountains. Many of these cones are composite, and around Marsabit are found a number of smaller craters (the Gofs) and other cones. In most places, the edges of the lava plateaus form prominent scarps which add diversity to the landscape. The dunes and the extensive sand plains are formed by the mantle from these volcanics. To the east of Distolli Plain, there is a true desert environment in the Chalbi area and here in particular aeolian processes are dominant.

The Drainage Pattern

Fig. 3.8 shows the present pattern: although the stream density might appear high, perennial streams are much fewer. Water shortage is therefore one of the main features of the environment. Table 3.2 gives a summary of the basic information about these rivers.

The present drainage network is fairly simple because the main rivers radiate either from the central dome formed by the Kenya Highlands or from the southern foothills of the Ethiopian Highlands. Minor tributaries will, of course, reflect local details but even these are still merely consequent on the original slope of the land. Thus the conical volcanic mountains are drained by simple radial streams such as on the slopes of Mounts Kenya and Elgon and in the Rift Valley cones. Similarly, the dipslopes of the Aberdare Range, including Kiambu and the Meru Range, are drained by simple parallel consequent streams. Also in the Rift Valley many of the rivers are fault-guided and are endoreic. In the highland areas, most of the rivers still exhibit youthful characteristics with waterfalls and river capture. Again, the rivers that drain into Lake Victoria are essentially parallel streams on the slope formed by the edge of the downwarp to the centre of this lake. Note also the many parallel tributaries of the Lower Tana. Some of these patterns are illustrated in Fig. 3.9.

Factors Responsible for the Present Pattern

The forces which have been responsible for the present pattern are now well understood. They are earth movements which included regional tectonic uplifts, downwarping and faulting. These events in turn precipitated volcanic eruptions of an unparalleled scale in Africa. These eruptions, as we have noted, buried at least 30 per cent of the previous topography and endogenic forces generated by pressure from the uprising molten magma were enough to cause the 'rise to the rift' which many workers have rightly noted. It is reasonable to conclude that it is these forces which caused the *Kenya Dome* or the *Kenya Half Oval* of Willis. Apart from the above movements, intermittent and uneven regional uplifts have also affected the coastal zone since the late-Carboniferous period. The present pattern is thus the result of modifications by the above events.

An important geomorphological problem is the form of the early pattern before the events alluded to above occurred. Much of the early Tertiary drainage must have been adjusted to that topography (Fig. 2.7). Pulfrey has suggested the existence of a *topographic low* along the present main Rift Valley and other workers including Gevaerts have since confirmed this. If this is accepted, then it would seem to imply some form of drainage lines towards the centre of this *topographic low* very much

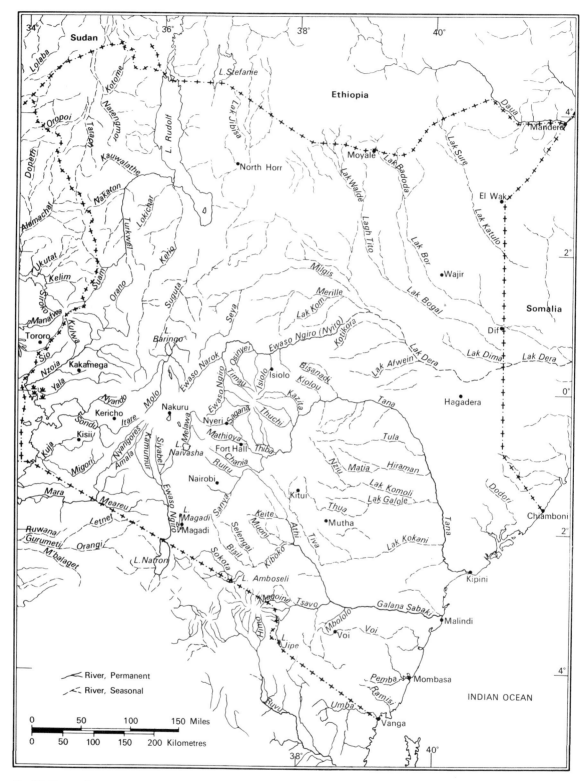

Fig. 3.8 Present drainage pattern

50

Table 3.2 *Main Kenya rivers*

Rivers	Length		Basin Area		Remarks
	miles	km	sq miles	km²	
Tana	440	708	24 000	62 160	Last 200 miles (322 km) to sea navigable by launch
Athi-Galana-Sabaki	340	547	17 000	44 029	Last 100 miles (161 km) to sea navigable by canoe
Mara	180	290	3 000	7 770	Half of this river is in Tanzania
Nzoia	160	258	5 000	12 950	—
Suam-Turkwel	220	354	8 000	20 720	90 miles (145 km) perennial
Ewaso Ngiro (North)	330	531	22 000	56 980	180 miles (290 km) perennial
Ewaso Ngiro (South)	85	137	2 000	5 180	60 miles (97 km) perennial
Kerio	220	354	2 500	6 475	70 miles (113 km) perennial
Yala	110	177	1 000	2 590	—
Sondu/Miriu-Kipsonoi	68	109	2 000	5 180	Called Sondu/Miriu by the Luo, Kipsonoi by Kipsigis
Kuja	55	89	2 000	5 180	—
Melawa	67	108	300	778	—
Voi	130	209	2 100	5 439	50 miles (80 km) perennial

as at the present time in the rift area.

Both Fuchs and Cooke showed that a low watershed probably existed somewhere to the south of the present Lake Rudolf area. Rivers to the north of that watershed drained to join the Kangen River in the Sudan. Riverine fish evidence appears to confirm this interpretation and to judge by the present nature of the middle part of the Turkwel River, it seems that this river formed the headwaters of the pre-Miocene river which Ojany (1971) has called the *Proto-Turkwel.*

The situation to the south of the above watershed has also been examined by a number of scholars including Joubert, Dixey (1946) and Cooke. They show that this lower part of the watershed formed part of the Ruvu (Pangani River). This view is plausible since the Ruvu Valley below Arusha-Chini in Tanzania looks fairly old. The resistant rocks which form the North Pare and the Lelatema Hills are much worn down. These facts would lend support to the view that this part of the rift system is fairly old–probably pre-Miocene. Also in the Kajiado-Namanga area, the present underfit Bissil (or Kajiado) River has a very wide valley carved out of very resistant rocks. This fact can be seen along the road to Namanga. It is clear that the present valley could not have been cut by the little water that now flows through it during the wet season. The valley must have carried more water formerly, and as it can be traced to join the Namanga River the present Kajiado River probably formed the headwaters of the proto-Ruvu River during the early Tertiary period. Another tributary probably ran along the present site of Lake Natron (Fig. 3.10).

The pattern in other parts of the country at the time can also be sketched out. The pattern in western Kenya is now fairly well known. The main changes were associated with the formation of Lake Victoria. The downwarping of the depression in which water ultimately collected to form the lake did not begin until the Miocene period and continued into the Pleistocene. The downwarping is the more recent manifestation of the Basin and Swell movements of Africa. The present rivers in western Kenya formed the headwaters of the main Uganda rivers (Fig. 3.10), and these early rivers have been called the *proto-Kagera, proto-Katonga* and *proto-Kafu.* Temple is an important author in connection with this topic (1971, etc.).

The situation in eastern Kenya is less known but it is here that one of us has carried out field work over a number of years. The problem hinges on the shape of the sub-Miocene level (see Pulfrey, Saggerson and Baker). The maps suggest the need for west-east consequents along the dipslope of the East Kenya Half Oval. It should also be noted that this is the part of Kenya which has suffered least from tectonic disturbances and volcanicity. Field work in the critical area of the Machakos Hills showed clearly that the Keite River is the oldest in the area, and that to the east of the present Yatta Phonolite the Thua River is another misfit stream that now appears beheaded. Keite thus appears as the original headwater to the eastward-flowing Thua. This is not a new idea: it had been suggested by Champion and also later by Gregory (1921). Geological considerations clearly suggest that this was an area dominated by a few west-east master streams that were superimposed on the eastern Half Oval.

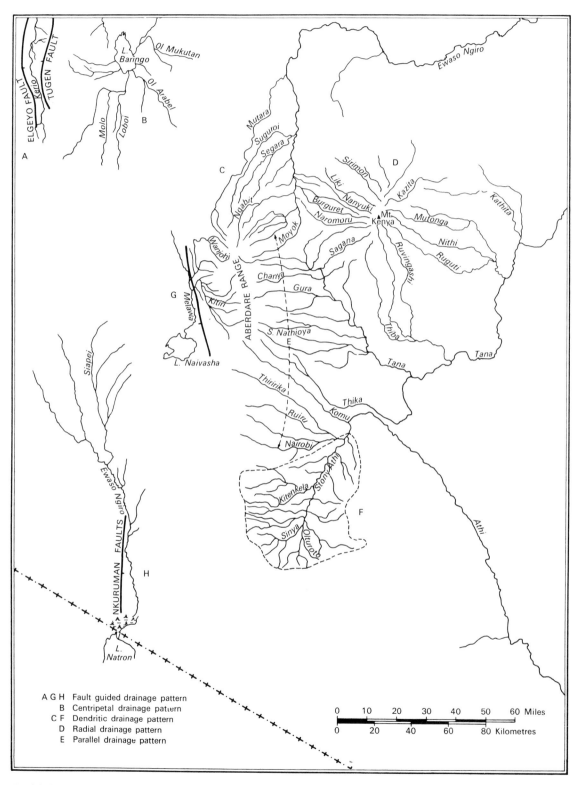

Fig. 3.9 Some examples of drainage patterns in central Kenya

A G H Fault guided drainage pattern
B Centripetal drainage pattern
C F Dendritic drainage pattern
D Radial drainage pattern
E Parallel drainage pattern

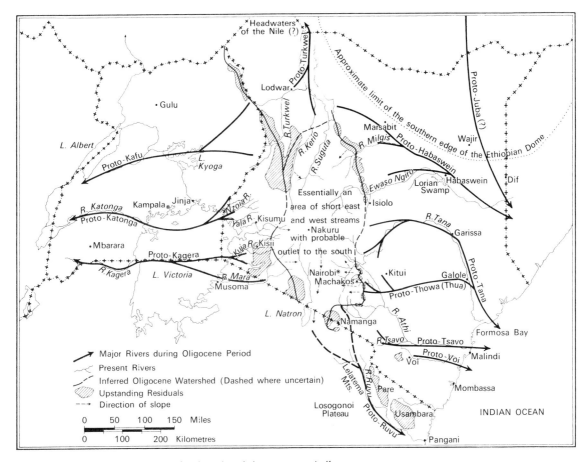

Fig. 3.10 A suggested reconstruction of early tertiary drainage patterns in Kenya

In north-eastern Kenya, two factors can help us in the reconstruction. We assume a radial pattern from the Ethiopian Dome. In this we are in agreement with Pulfrey's 'Primitive Juba River', which in accordance with our terminology is called *proto-Juba*. The other factor is more debatable although we see it as proven by the present knowledge of the area. The Habaswein Depression has been shown to be the product of erosion. It is therefore a feature of considerable age, probably pre-Miocene. This is reasonable in view of the tremendous amount of sedimentation that has gone on here. The sediments appear to have been laid down from the adjoining higher ground by river deposition. This might have been the proto-Habaswein River which had as its tributaries parts of the present Milgis and north Ewaso Ngiro Rivers; the proto-Habaswein must also have had other tributaries from the Ethiopian Dome.

The early Tertiary drainage pattern as depicted in Fig. 3.10 differs in some fundamentals from that suggested by Pulfrey (Fig. 3.11), but the authors are of the opinion that new facts which were not available to Pulfrey warrant the changes. It is difficult to see how Pulfrey's primitive *Athi River* could have climbed the two half ovals which Pulfrey's sub-Miocene bevel shows.

Kenya Lakes

There are various types of basins or depressions in which water has collected to form lakes. The origins of the hollows are associated with the main processes which have been responsible for the present topography, and so any genetic classification of lakes really involves classifying the origin of the basins which hold the water. There are four main categories: tectonic, volcanic, glacial, and coastal or floodplain. The tectonic lakes can further be sub-divided into two sub-classes: lakes due to downwarping, of which Lake Victoria is the classic example, and the rift valley lakes, i.e. those which now occupy the lowest parts of the floor of the Rift Valley. Of the latter sub-class, Lake Rudolf (2 473 sq miles or 6 405 km²) is the largest; others are Logibi, Baringo,

Fig. 3G Tiva River, on the Machakos-Kitui road, during the dry season. Note the inselberg on the left.

Fig. 3H Aerial view of Lake Elmenteita. Note the former lake levels on the left

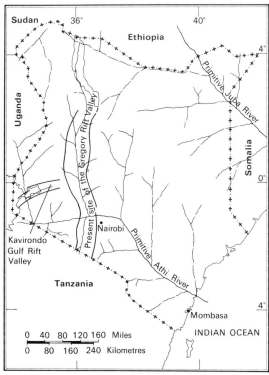

Fig. 3.11 Possible early Tertiary drainage pattern in Kenya

Hannington, Nakuru, Elmenteita, Naivasha, Magadi, Kwenia and Amboseli. Kwenia, Amboseli and sometimes Nakuru dry up during the dry periods. We know that these rift valley lakes are merely the remnants of what was a much more extensive lake or series of lakes that occupied the floor of the Rift Valley during the last pluvial period. The present remnants are therefore generally small and very shallow, with the exception of Lake Victoria which has a surface area of 26 418 sq miles (67 493 km²) and is the largest lake in Africa.

The volcanic lakes are also of very small dimensions. Examples of lava damming such as produced Lake Kivu are not present in Kenya. Instead, our examples are confined to small crater lakes, and while many are seasonal, others like Simbi near Kendu Bay and Lake Paradise in Marsabit are permanent.

The glacial lakes occupy the glacial corries of Mt Kenya and so are really tarns. The main ones are: Michaelson, Hohnel, Enchanted and Carr's Lakes. Others such as Lake Alice and Lake Ellis were caused by damming by glacial moraines.

The coastal lakes include those which occupy marshy ground both along the coast and near the Yala Swamp near Lake Victoria. Lakes Gambi, Mukunguya, Bilisa and Shakababo are in the lower Tana River near Garsen. Shakababo is really an ox-bow lake. Lake Kanyaboli in the Yala Swamp is fed by the River Yala, as is Lake Namboyo. In the same vicinity are found at least three small ox-bow lakes along the River Nzoia.

Table 3.3 *Kenya lakes*

Lake	Area		Length		Width		Average depth		Height over MSL	
	sq miles	km²	miles	km	miles	km	feet	m	feet	m
Victoria*	26 418	67 493	175	282	140	225	150	46	3 720	1 134
Rudolf	2 473	6 405	154	247	20	32	—	—	1 230	372
Baringo	50	129	11	18	4·5	6·8	17	5	3 200	975
Magadi	40	104	16	26	2·5	4	—	—	1 900	579
Naivasha	44–74	114–191	10	16	5	8	11	3	6 150	1 875
Amboseli (seasonal)	0–44	0–114	0–13	0–21	0–6	0–10	0–2	0–0·6	3 900	1 188
Jipe	15	39	7·5	11·8	2	3	—	—	2 300	701
Hannington	13	34	12	19	1·25	2	—	—	3 200	975
Nakuru (seasonal)	2–12	5–31	1–5	2–8	1–2·5	1·6–2	2	0·6	5 765	1 757
Elmenteita	7	18	4·5	6·8	1·5	2·4	—	—	5 850	1 783
On Mt Kenya										
Hohnel	0·03	0·08	0·25	0·4	0·12	0·2	—	—	13 760	4 194
Michaelson	0·05	0·13	0·25	0·4	0·19	0·3	—	—	13 010	3 965

[1] Only a small portion is in Kenya.
Source: *Atlas of Kenya*, 1959

References

OJANY, F. F. 'The physique of Kenya: A contribution in landscape analysis', *Annals Assoc. American Geographers, Vol. 56*, 1966, pp. 183–196.

CASWELL, P. V. 'Geology of the Mombasa-Kwale area', *Report Geol. Surv. Kenya, No. 24*, 1953.

GREGORY, J. W. *The Great Rift Valley*, John Murray, 1896.

SAGGERSON, E. P. 'Geology of the south Kitui area', *Report Geol. Surv. Kenya, No. 37*, 1957.

SAGGERSON, E. P. and BAKER, B. H. 'Post Jurassic erosion-surfaces in eastern Kenya and their deformation in relation to rift structure', *Quart. Jnl. Geol. Soc. Lond, Vol. 121*, 1965, pp. 51–72.

SANDERS, L. D. 'Geology of Kitui area', *Report Geol. Surv. Kenya, No. 30*, 1954.

BUDEL, J. 'Die doppelten Einebnungslfachen in den feuchten Troppen', *Zeitschrift für Geomorphologie, Vol. 1*, 1957, pp. 201–228.

KING, L. C. *Morphology of the Earth*, Oliver and Boyd, 1965.

COTTON, C. A. *Volcanoes as Landscape Forms*, Whitcombe and Tombs, 1952.

OJANY, F. F. 'The mound topography of the Thika and Athi Plains of Kenya: A problem of origins', *Erdkunde, Archiv für wissenschaft Geographie, Band XXII*, 1968, pp. 269–275.

WAYLAND, E. J., COMBE, A. D., and SIMMONS. *Summary of progress of the Geological Survey of Uganda for the Years 1919–29.*

WALSH, J. 'Geology of Ikutha area', *Report Geol. Surv. Kenya, No. 56*, 1963.

WILLIS, B. 'East African plateaux and rift valleys', *Studies in Comparative Seismology*, Carnegie Inst. Pubn. 1936.

DIXEY, F. 'Erosion and techtonics in the East Africa rift system', *Quart. Jnl. Geol. Soc. London, Vol. 102*, 1946, pp. 339–388.

DIXEY, F. 'Some observations on the physiographical development of central and southern Africa', *Trans. Geol. Soc. South Africa, Vol. 41*, 1938, pp. 113–170.

COOKE, H. B. S. 'Observations relating to Quaternary environments in east and southern Africa', *Trans. Geol. Soc. South Africa, Vol. 60*, 1958, pp. 1–73.

PULFREY, W. 'Shape of the sub-Miocene erosion bevel in Kenya', *Bull. Geol. Surv. Kenya, No. 3*, 1960.

GEVAERTS, E. A. L. 'Report on the geology and ground-water conditions in the Nairobi and surrounding areas', *Technical Paper, Public Works Dept., Hydraulic Branch, Kenya* (unpublished) *No. 3*, 1957.

FUCHS, V. E. 'The geological history of the Lake Rudolf Basin, Kenya Colony', *Phil. Trans. Roy. Soc. Series B, Vol. 229*, 1939, pp. 219–274.

JOUBERT, B. 'Geology of Namanga-Bissel area', *Report Geol. Surv. Kenya, No. 39*, 1957.

HOLMES, A. *Principles of Physical Geology*, 2nd edn., Nelson, 1965.

CHAMPION, A. M. 'The Thowa Rivers', *Jnl. E.A. and Uganda Nat. Hist. Soc. Vol. 3*, 1912, pp. 13–20.

OJANY, F. F. *Drainage development in Kenya: Studies in East African Geography and Development*, ed. S. H. Ominde, Heinemann, 1971.

Chapter 4
Climate

In Kenya, as in other East African countries, the systematic collection of all weather data is done by the East African Meteorological Department. This is one of the major scientific organisations of the East African Community and was first established in 1929, although the measuring of rainfall had been started in Mombasa back in 1891. By 1960 there were more than 170 stations all over Kenya with records of over 30 years' duration to enable a good analysis of the climate of the country to be made. Since agriculture, including pastoralism, plays a dominant part in the Kenyan economy a thorough understanding of climatic characteristics and variations is of the utmost importance.

The main factors which control the climate of any place are latitude, altitude, character of prevailing winds, the distance from the sea or from any sizeable water-body, and topography. Topography is especially important when the area under study has diversity of relief which can form barriers to the prevailing winds. Vegetal cover is also important, but normally it is a result of the other factors already noted.

The pressure belts are also important. These shift with the apparent movement of the overhead sun and cause seasons. The greatest insolation, usually directly below the overhead sun, creates the lowest pressure. The low pressure belt is known variously as the *heat trough*, the *equatorial trough* or the *intertropical convergence zone* (ITCZ). It is usually the point for convergence of winds and the creation of air masses. An air mass is a large body of air which may cover hundreds of square miles, and which has a definite source region and a marked uniformity of temperature and humidity throughout its entire length, width and depth. As such a body of air moves, it will be known by its source region, and as it moves across a tract of country, it transports and introduces its own particular climatic characteristics throughout the country over which it passes. In this way it influences the weather of the places. The convergence of air masses as noted above normally results in the upward movement of air over the area of low pressure, which in turn causes cooling, condensation and precipitation. Air masses (also known as airstreams) are therefore important mainly as carriers of moisture.

The Air Masses in Kenya

Kenya is dominated particularly by three distinct air masses. During the months from November to March, very dry winds from the Sahara Desert dominate the western part of the country. This dusty air mass is called the *harmattan* (or *Egyptian air*). In the eastern parts of the country, the equivalent airstream has an Arabian source, and is thus known as the *Arabian* (or *Indian*) *north-east trade winds*. This north-easterly variety is of course the north-east monsoon which has crossed a stretch of the northern part of the Indian Ocean. It is thus a maritime airstream and brings some rains to the coastal lands during this period.

By about the month of April, the wind system has reversed and many of the central, southern and eastern parts of the country begin to feel the influence of the south-east trade winds from the Indian Ocean. On crossing the Equator this airstream becomes the *south-east monsoon* and as these winds have crossed a vast body of water (i.e. the southern Indian Ocean) they are the source of the main rains in Kenya. This air mass persists more or less with the same vigour and consistency until about August.

From about the month of July, at the time when the south-west trade winds are still quite strong, high winds associated with them penetrate through Equatorial Africa as the *Congo airstream*. This air is extremely unstable and convectional storms easily and freely develop in it. Its influence is felt mostly in the western parts of Kenya. The climatic swing that we have traced above, gives Kenya her climatic seasons (Figs. 4.1 and 4.2). Monthly variations in the rainfall received in the different parts of the country form an important factor in the water shortage problem in the country. This month to month variation is even more meaningful if read against the prevailing wind situation for each month because in this way the source of the rainfall can be seen (see Figs. 4.3 to 4.8). The eight stations from which the readings have been taken are Lodwar, Mandera, Kisumu, Nanyuki, Garissa, Nairobi, Voi and Mombasa (Findlater, 1968).

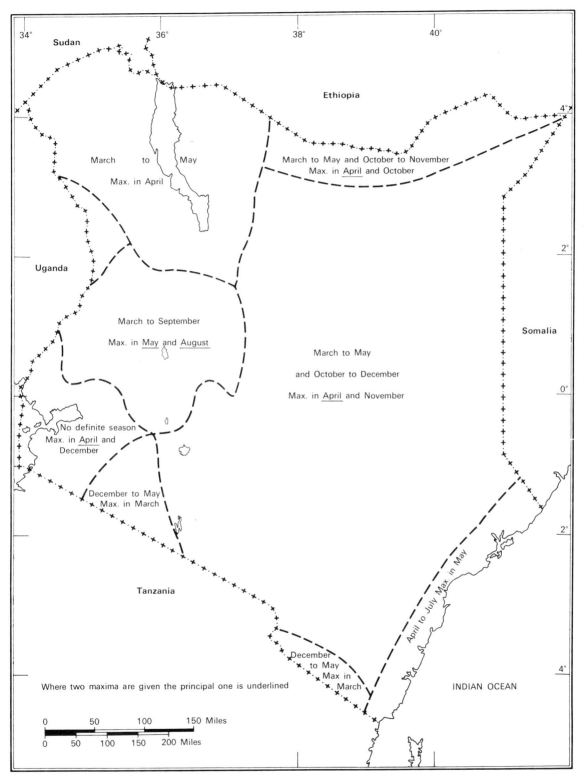

Fig. 4.1 The rainy seasons

34° 36° 38° 40°

Sudan

Ethiopia

March to May
Max. in April

March to May and October to November
Max. in April and October

4°

Uganda

2°

March to September
Max. in May and August

Somalia

March to May
and October to December
Max. in April and November

0°

No definite season
Max. in April and
December

December to May
Max. in March

2°

Tanzania

April to July Max. in May

Where two maxima are given the principal one is underlined

December
to May
Max in
March

4°

INDIAN OCEAN

0   50   100   150 Miles

0   50   100   150   200 Miles

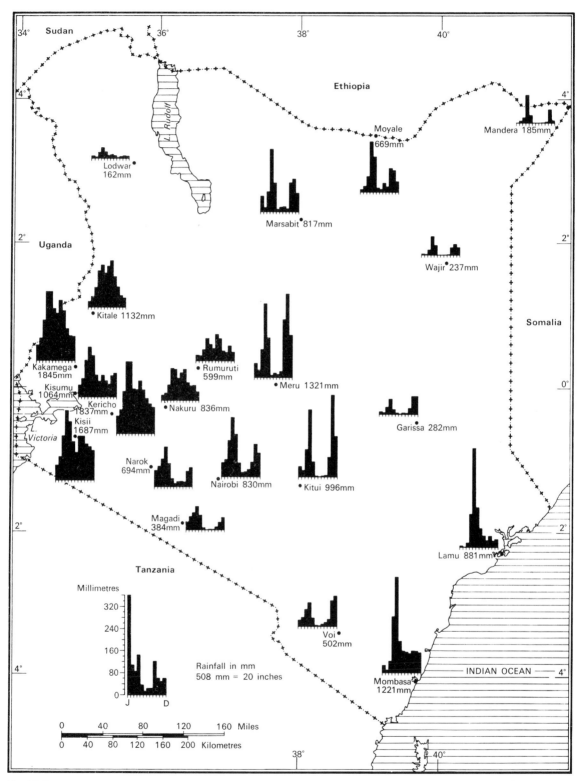

Fig. 4.2 Located columnal diagrams of rainfall

Summary of Month by Month Rainfall Variations

January The north-east monsoon is becoming very powerful and bifurcates to give an easterly wind through the low corridor between the Ethiopian Highlands and the Central Highlands of Kenya, and a northerly wind which dominates the extensive flat plains east of 38° E. This bifurcation results in dry, generally clear air, and consequently this is normally one of the driest months in Kenya.

February Conditions are still very similar to January and this is the other main dry month.

March Important changes are beginning to emerge. Although the north-east monsoon is still present, a belt of convergence is beginning to develop as the winds (especially those of lower levels) begin to acquire a southerly origin. As a result of these changes, rainfall brought by the southerly winds is a welcome feature. These winds mark the beginnings of the main wet season known as the *long rains*.

April The south-easterly winds are now well established. April is thus the wettest month in Kenya with rain fairly general and widespread over the whole country. At low levels the winds are clearly the south monsoon.

May During this month the south monsoon is becoming firmly established especially over the flat land to the east of 38° E. These southerly winds are particularly dominant in the coastal areas of the country and as a result these areas receive their maximum rainfall during this month. Many coastal stations record over twenty rainy days. To the north of the equator, the winds are divergent with the flow through the northern corridor being fairly strong at this time.

June The south monsoon is now dominant especially in the flat area east of 38° E. But in parts of northern Kenya the winds are still mainly from the east. Taken altogether, the rainfall totals over the whole country begin to show a marked drop.

July As would be expected, this is near the time of maximum development of the north monsoon. On crossing the equator, these winds curve to become part of the south-east monsoon. Again, this is a dry month. We should note here that the rains of western Kenya come partly from the unstable Congo airstream and partly from convection thunderstorms associated with breezes introduced by the pressure of Lake Victoria and augmented by the Congo airstream.

August The south monsoon is still present so that the situation is similar to July.

September In the highland zone, light wind, mainly from the east appear. Above 10 000 feet (3 048 m), the north-easterlies are beginning to re-establish themselves at the expense of the south monsoons. Again, this is a dry month.

October The south monsoon has almost disappeared and is replaced by the strengthening north-easterlies, especially above 10 000 feet (3 048 m). Some convergence takes place between these two winds which brings about

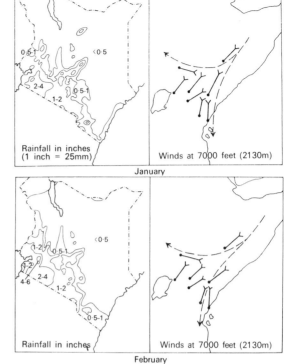

Fig. 4.3 Climatic conditions (January/February)

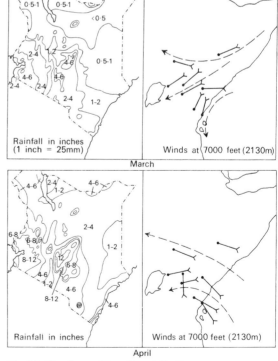

Fig. 4.4 Climatic conditions (March/April)

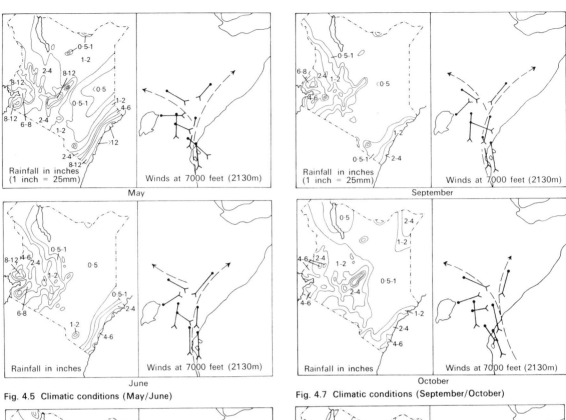

Rainfall in inches
(1 inch = 25mm)

Winds at 7000 feet (2130m)

May

Rainfall in inches

Winds at 7000 feet (2130m)

June

Fig. 4.5 Climatic conditions (May/June)

Rainfall in inches
(1 inch = 25mm)

Winds at 7000 feet (2130m)

September

Rainfall in inches

Winds at 7000 feet (2130m)

October

Fig. 4.7 Climatic conditions (September/October)

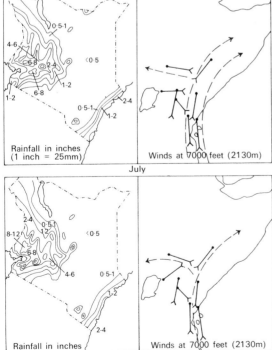

Rainfall in inches
(1 inch = 25mm)

Winds at 7000 feet (2130m)

July

Rainfall in inches

Winds at 7000 feet (2130m)

August

Fig. 4.6 Climatic conditions (July/August)

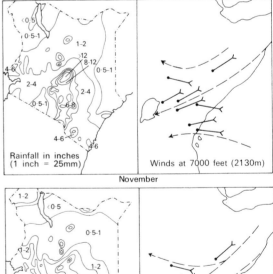

Rainfall in inches
(1 inch = 25mm)

Winds at 7000 feet (2130m)

November

Rainfall in inches

Winds at 7000 feet (2130m)

December

Fig. 4.8 Climatic conditions (November/December)

60

Table 4.1 *Distribution of rainfall in Kenya*

Rainfall		Area		Percentage of total area	Accumulated percentage
inches	mm	sq miles	km²		
0–9	0–253	60 800	157 470	27·0	27·0
10–19	254–507	80 700	209 011	35·9	62·9
20–29	508–761	40 800	105 692	18·1	81·0
30–39	762–1 015	18 800	48 692	8·4	89·4
40–49	1 016–1 269	.11 000	28 490	4·9	94·3
50–59	1 270–1 523	7 500	19 425	3·3	97·6
60–69	1 524–1 777	3 700	9 583	1·6	99·2
70–79	1 778–2 031	1 500	3 885	0·7	99·9
80 +	2 032 +	200	518	0·1	100·0

Source: D. R. L. Prabhakar.

Table 4.2 *Summary of annual rainfall over selected stations*

Station	Maximum		Mean		Minimum		Average number of rainy days
	inches	mm	inches	mm	inches	mm	
Nairobi	62	1 570	35	879	17	437	120
Mombasa	74	1 887	47	1 204	28	709	145
Nakuru	60	1 515	34	871	21	541	137
Eldoret	72	1 826	38	973	18	462	134
Nyeri	52	1 321	36	922	18	460	100
Wajir	20	513	10	249	3	74	29
Kisumu	74	1 884	50	1 278	37	942	139
Magadi	24	621	16	398	6	153	67
Voi	47	1 201	21	538	7	184	72
Lodwar	20	498	6	165	1	19	23

some precipitation. These winds mark the beginnings of the *short rains*.

November The north-east monsoon is now dominant at 7 000 feet (2 134 m) while traces of the southern monsoon are also evident at lower levels. Convergence is now more widespread and this month normally records the peak of the short rains especially in the eastern highlands.

December There is still a general strengthening of the north-easterly or easterly flow of winds which is the sign for the southward spread of dry and clear weather. The short rains have disappeared or are quickly tailing off.

From the above survey certain important conclusions can be reached. The most important clearly is that large parts of the country have drought lasting more than six months. We also note that a very small fraction of the country gets over two inches (50 mm) of rainfall in every month of the year.

The Mean Annual Rainfall

Fig. 4.9 shows the mean annual rainfall for the country. Again, the compelling conclusion which strikes one is the general inadequacy of the amounts received by large parts of the country. Shortage of water is one of the most basic problems of development in Kenya. Two other characteristics of this rainfall are also important but are not apparent from the maps. These are the great variability in the annual total and the considerable uncertainty in the time of year when the rains can be expected (see Fig. 4.10). Planned agriculture therefore is made very difficult.

The reason for these large rainfall variations is partly the tremendous topographical contrasts, including the great altitudinal range, and partly the distribution and presence of large water bodies such as Lake Victoria and the Indian Ocean. Lake Victoria plays an important part in the local climate. During the day it acts as a cold reservoir and air moves from it to replace warm rising air in the adjoining land areas. This initiates the cooling lake breeze. During the night, the reverse takes place. Along the eastern and south-eastern shores, however, it appears that the prevalent easterly winds meet the land breezes and the two bring about subsidence of air and so a small amount of rainfall. This is the reverse of the convergence of the western shores. Prominent topographic features stand out as islands or pockets of high oro-

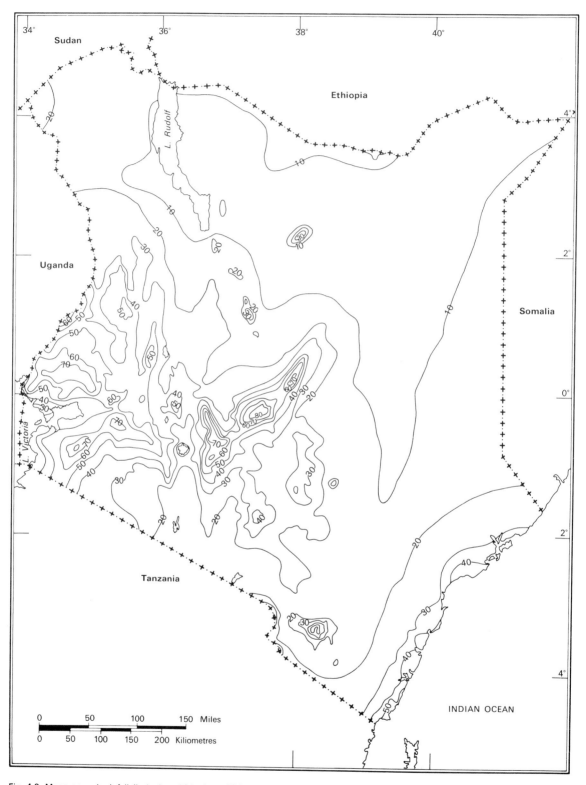

Fig. 4.9 Mean annual rainfall (in inches: 10 inches =254 mm)

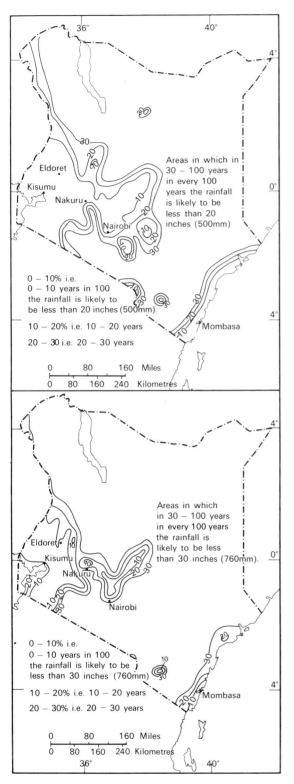

Fig. 4.10 Rainfall probabilities

graphic rains as the mean annual map clearly shows. On the other hand, the lowland of the Rift Valley zone, especially between the Aberdare Range and the Mau Hills, is a dry corridor.

A more serious drought, however, characterises the low corridor of northern and north-eastern Kenya which is in fact part of the dry region that covers north-eastern Africa and Arabia. This dry belt forms one of the greatest climatic anomalies in Africa. How can this semi-desert and desert condition be explained? It is the largest tropical dry region of the world. As is revealed by our monthly rainfall figures, this dry region gets its limited rains mainly during the transitional seasons of April to June and September to November. Flohn (1966) has advanced the view that the unusual lack of summer precipitation in the area must be explained by a combination of all possible divergence effects, four of which he lists as follows: directional divergence caused by overheating of the Ethiopian Highlands; speed divergence produced by northward increase of the pressure gradient; frictional divergence in coastal parallel winds; deflection of the wind-driven ocean surface currents and cold upwelling along the coast. It appears therefore that any rains in the dry parts of eastern Kenya are brought about by the seasonal movement of the convergence between the trade winds. These usually take the form of violent storms which occur mainly during the afternoons or evenings. Destructive squalls, coupled with thick rising sands, are also very common in these parts and especially around Lake Rudolf. The drought in this area is thus due to a semi-permanent divergence, which is due, at least in part, to constant funnelling of air around the two highlands of central Kenya and Ethiopia.

Droughts and Floods in Kenya

Droughts and floods are common features of the Kenyan climate. Both these extremes are due to important major rainfall anomalies and, of course, cause great difficulty for an essentially agricultural people like the Kenyans, who have also to farm large marginal areas. Little research has been done on these vital aspects of our rainfall. Both climatological records and oral knowledge show that major droughts, with serious results to both man and game, have occurred in the following years: 1928, 1933–4, 1939, 1942–4, 1952–5, 1960–1, and 1965. Major floods in certain low-lying parts of the Nyanza Gulf, and the Lower Tana Basin in particular, occurred in 1937, 1947, 1951, 1957–8 and 1961. These anomalies in rainfall have caused widespread famine as drought brings about crop failure while excessive rain causes flooding of the fields during the crucial growing period. A further hazard appears to be that serious droughts in Kenya have commonly been coupled with an invasion of locusts.

In Kikuyuland the 1928 drought resulted in the serious 'famine of Thika'. Among the Kalenjin, especially in the marginal Tugen areas, the 1933–4 drought brought the

Fig. 4A Kau village on the Tana River, north-west of Kipini. The village had to be evacuated during the 1961–62 floods

Fig. 4B A flooded and isolated village in Bunyala Location in Western Province on the shores of Lake Victoria. The Samia Hills can be seen in the background

famine known as *kimouito*, so called because people ate hides and skins. The 1942–4 drought resulted in the *kiplelgowo* famine, again so called because so many animals died as a result, and the countryside was littered with white bones. Amongst the Kipsigis, the *Kiplelgowo* is known as the *rubet ab sigirok* (the famine of the donkeys), because people ate donkey meat. The 1952–3 drought brought the *rubet ab biasi* (the potato famine) because there was nothing to eat but potatoes. The 1965 famine was nicknamed *bandek ab Amerika* (the American yellow maize famine) because American yellow maize was sold throughout Kenya at that time.

In Luoland also these droughts brought starvation. Some of the most disastrous were *ke[1] choka, ke nyangore, ke otuoma, ke nyangweso*, and *ke otonglo. Ke choka* is also so known by the Abaluhya people. *Ke nyangweso* and *ke otuoma* may have been the same famine following the 1933–4 drought. *Ke nyangweso* was also associated with a major locust invasion. *Ke otonglo* followed the 1942–4 drought and was so-called because for the first time the smallest measure for grain/flour cost 10 cents.

The above sequence appears to suggest some physical phenomenon not clear as yet, which influences atmospheric conditions to affect rainfall amounts.

Hailstorms in Kenya

Hail is an ice-pellet, normally associated with cumulonimbus clouds. In tropical areas, a hailstorm commonly follows a day of intense heating of the earth's surface which produces convectional overturning and rapid ascent of air currents. Hailstorms are an important form of precipitation in western Kenya. These areas are not only densely peopled, but also under intensive cultivation (both for subsistence and well-developed large-scale farming). Hailstorms are also a particular characteristic of the Lake Victoria zone where the main East African thunder belt also occurs (Fig. 4.11).

The hailstones in East Africa are much larger – they have been known to be an inch (25 mm) in diameter – than those of temperate regions. They therefore cause a lot of damage to crops and their control is thus an urgent matter for research. Sansom (1961) has reported that a single storm in a tea estate in Kericho in September 1958 caused damage estimated at £10 000 and also that, over a five-year period, in western Kenya loss of coffee due to hail amounted to over £100 000!

Not enough is known on the causes or control of hail. The optimum height for hail however appears to range between about 5 000 and 9 000 feet (1 500–2 750 m). Sansom, who has done more work on this, has shown that hail is a rainy season phenomenon which can be expected in the afternoon especially at the beginning and end of the season. It may be that the well-defined breezes from the lake contribute to their development by aiding local wind conveyance in the area (Fig. 4.12).

[1] The Luo word for famine is *kech*.

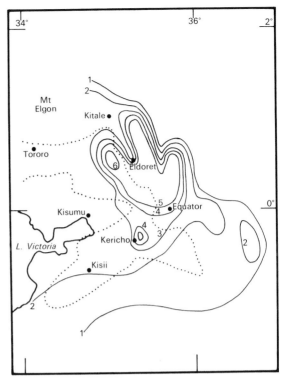

Fig. 4.11 The hail belt of Western Kenya. Solid lines denote average annual frequency of hailstorms. The dotted line encloses areas with over 50 inches (1 270 mm) average annual rainfall

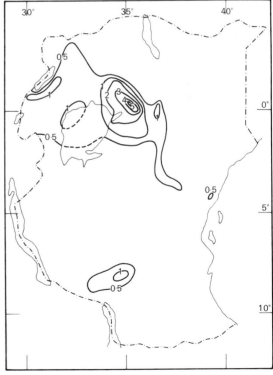

Fig. 4.12 Average annual frequency of hail in East Africa

65

Temperature

Height and aspect are the two factors which exert the greatest influence on temperature in Kenya. But below 500 feet (152 m) above sea level and around Lake Victoria the influence of land and sea breezes is more important. The highland areas in Kenya are the regions with low temperatures while the low-lying parts stand out as areas with higher temperatures (Fig. 4.13).

As would be expected in a country like Kenya, there is a large range in both the minimum and maximum temperatures from below freezing point in the snow-capped Mt Kenya to over 40°C in some parts of the north and north-east. From existing records, Ettrick Estate, near Eldama Ravine, has recorded the lowest absolute temperature of minus 3·3°C while Chagaik Estate in Kericho has recorded minus 2·2°C. An absolute maximum of 41·8°C has been recorded by Magadi Soda Co Ltd at Magadi on the Rift Valley floor. Two other stations, Mandera DC's office and Taveta Homer Bros have each recorded 40°C.

The low-lying northern plainlands are the hottest areas generally and here maximum temperatures commonly exceed 35°C, with March as the hottest month. Night temperatures in these areas are generally above 20°C. Nyanza and Western Province both show great variations from hot, stuffy, low-lying plains to cool pleasant temperatures in the hills surrounding Kakamega, Kericho and Kisii. Here we should, of course, note the cooling influence of the lake breeze. The hottest months are from October to March.

The Rift Valley, including the adjoining highlands, shows a large diurnal range of over 20°C. The hottest parts are the low-lying Rift Valley floor with Magadi frequently recording over 40°C. The central areas of Kenya, including Nairobi area, generally enjoy pleasant temperatures with a daily range of about 15°C. Nairobi Railway Station, for example, has recorded an absolute maximum of 32·7°C and an absolute minimum of 3·9°C.

The coastal belt is an area of fairly high temperatures with a very small diurnal range of 7–9°C. The region is thus particularly sticky, especially as the humidity is also very high throughout the year (all months have RH of over 70%). The coolest months here are July and August, when afternoon temperatures may average 28°C and nights 20°C.

Atmospheric Pressure, Relative Humidity, Sunshine and Cloud Amounts

Atmospheric pressure is affected by altitude and readings are commonly taken at the main synoptic hours since these hours would give a fair approximation to the maximum and minimum of the mean daily pressure wave. There is an expected rise of about 3 millibars between the two readings.

Relative humidity too is highest about dawn (6 am) and lowest about 3 pm. This again is to be expected as the

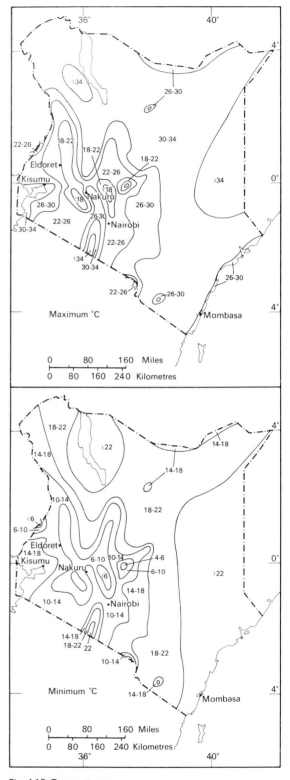

Fig. 4.13 Temperatures

Table 4.3 *Summary of temperatures over selected stations °C*

Station	Height in metres	Absolute maximum	Mean maximum	Mean minimum	Absolute minimum
Lodwar	506	39·8	34·9	23·7	17·2
Wajir	244	39·4	33·6	22·1	15·0
Garissa	128	46·1	34·3	22·5	13·9
Lamu	30	35·0	29·2	24·1	17·2
Mombasa	16	35·6	30·1	23·4	18·9
Voi	560	37·3	30·5	19·4	11·5
Nairobi (Met. HQ)	1 798	29·7	23·6	11·6	2·5
Nanyuki	1 946	30·3	23·7	8·5	0·7
Magadi	613	41·8	35·0	23·2	16·8
Narok	1 890	32·1	24·5	8·5	0·3
Nakuru	1 836	33·8	26·4	10·0	3·3
Equator	2 762	24·9	18·3	8·0	3·5
Kitale	1 896	31·8	25·4	11·2	4·2
Kericho	1 890	32·2	24·0	11·1	0·1
Kisumu	1 146	36·9	29·4	17·1	11·0

Table 4.4 *Annual summary of other climatic elements from selected stations*

Station	Atmospheric pressure (mb)	Relative humidity %		Cloud amount		Average sunshine (hrs)
	3 pm	6 am	3 pm	9 am	3 pm	
Lodwar	—	62	30	3·9	4·2	3 582
Mandera	983·7	73	43	4·4	4·3	—
Wajir	—	—	48	5·1	4·2	—
Garissa	—	—	45	6·1	5·0	—
Lamu	—	86	75	4·5	3·3	3 242
Malindi	—	—	72	4·5	3·7	—
Mombasa Airport	1 005·2	93	66	5·5	4·6	2 987
Voi	—	87	45	5·5	6·1	—
Nairobi (Met. HQ)	820·3	95	52	6·4	5·7	2 503
Nanyuki	806·9	89	51	4·9	6·6	2 172
Magadi	940·9	—	35	4·4	4·4	—
Nakuru Airport	810·7	94	47	4·8	6·4	2 584
Kisumu	884·2	85	47	5·1	5·5	2 842

insolation increases, while the rather high range between the two readings (see Table 4.4) is due to high temperature changes. Similar changes can be expected with cloud amounts (measured in eighths). The rainy seasons appear to show an increase in maximum cloud amounts.

Sunshine is measured in hours per day and monthly totals can easily be compiled. On the whole the longest hours of sunshine are in the drier areas.

Climatic Regions

Having examined the various climatic elements and the factors which go to produce these, we are now in a position to attempt a division of the country into the prevalent climatic types. In this exercise we must note though that very little detailed information is available for the northern parts of the country. Although climatic change from area to area is gradual, there are obvious differences, for example, between the climate along the Kenya coast and that in the highlands or around Lake Rudolf. These differences should be noted.

According to Miller's classification, Kenya has a *hot climate*: the narrow coastal belt is classed as *equatorial (A₁) type*, and the rest of the interior as *tropical continental (A₃) type*. These two subgroups correspond to Finch and Trewartha's *tropical rainforest* and *tropical savanna* climates.

In most cases the above generalisations are acceptable. However, because of the great variation of height in

Kenya, the localised influence of Lake Victoria, and the relatively low rainfall totals in our region, the climate over Kenya shows considerable modifications from the textbook examples of hot climates. As a result, seven climatic types can be recognised in Kenya. Six of these are variations of the hot climate but the other, we suggest, is a variation of a *hot desert* climate (Fig. 4.14).

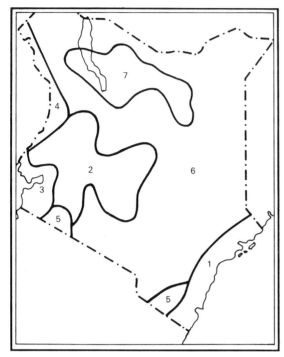

Fig. 4.14 Climatic regions

1. Modified Equatorial Climate of the Coast

As in other equatorial climates, this region has no dry season, but has a well-developed double maximum in May and October. Also, it has high average temperatures and humidity throughout the year. But the Kenya coast differs from the equatorial climate which is well known for its high annual rainfall (of convectional origin) totals, in that it receives much lower totals.

2. Modified Tropical Climate of the Kenya Highlands

This modification is caused by the high and varied relief. The resulting climate is therefore much cooler than a tropical continental climate and may be described as a *highland sub-tropical* climate. The amount of rainfall received at different places here depends very much on the position of the station in relation to the rain-bearing winds. Thus Meru, on the north-eastern slopes of Mt Kenya, receives 52 inches (1 320 mm) a year while Nyeri,

on the south-western slopes, only receives 29 inches (737 mm) a year.

This region enjoys the best climate in Kenya. Day temperatures are cool, pleasant and fresh while nights may be chilly.

3. Modified Equatorial Climate of the Lake Victoria Basin

Here also modifications result from relief and the influence of this body of water. Although there is no really dry month, rainfall totals in the region show considerable variations and are, in any case, much lower than in a typical equatorial climate.

The enclosed basin form of Lake Victoria tends to increase temperatures although the lake itself exerts a cooling influence, and they are still lower than in an equatorial climate.

4. Modified Equatorial Climate of the North-western Border

This appears best in the Karasuk areas and is really a continuation of the climate of eastern and northern Uganda. High relief introduces a welcome lowering of temperature in parts of the area.

5. Tropical Climate of the Narok and Southern Taita/Kwale Areas

Again, this is part of the tropical climate which dominates the central mainland of Tanzania. The high relief of such hills as Loita exerts a cooling influence so that taken altogether the climate here is more tolerable than the semi-desert climate of eastern Kenya.

6. Tropical Continental/Semi-desert Climate of Eastern Kenya

This vast region receives less than 20 inches (500 mm) per annum. The mean temperature is 22–27°C with the very wide range of about 11°C. The skies are generally clear and great variations in the mean annual rainfall can be expected.

7. Desert Climate of Central Northern Kenya

A considerable stretch of northern Kenya receives less than 10 inches (250 mm) of rainfall and climatologically may be regarded as desert. We have already shown that this aridity is a continuation of that of Arabia. Wajir and Lodwar belong here. Between 1931 and 1960, Wajir had a mean annual total of 9 inches (237 mm) while Lodwar had an average of 6 inches (162 mm) over the same period. Their respective mean annual temperatures between 1936 and 1962 were 29·3°C and 27·9°C. The great annual variations typical of this climate may be illustrated by the fact that Lodwar Meteorological Station in 1933 received 0·7 inches (18 mm) and in 1936

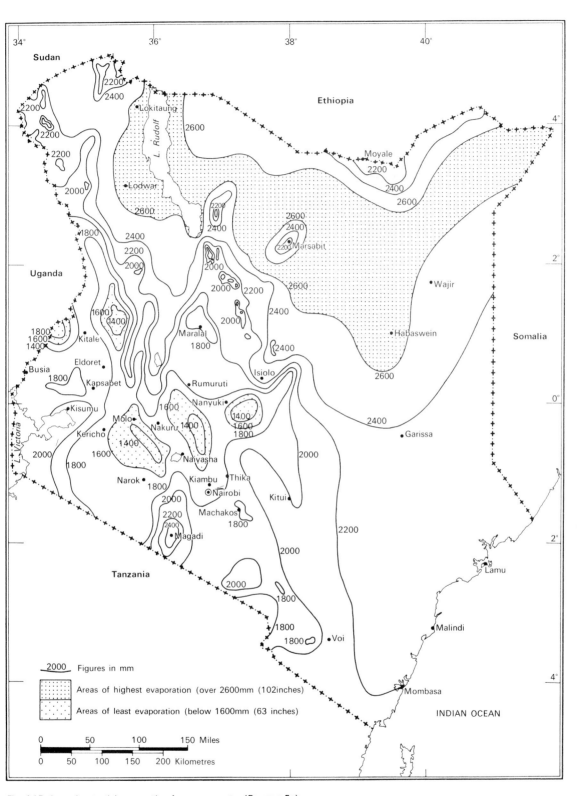

Fig. 4.15 Annual potential evaporation from open water (Penman Eo)

the same station recorded 15 inches (369 mm). The figures for Wajir (DC's Office) range from 20 inches (514 mm) in 1951 to 3 inches (74 mm) in 1949.

As has already been noted, the winds are characterised by widespread subsidence or divergence, so no clouds will form. The skies are therefore cloudless and visibility is only hindered by sandstorms, which are a common occurrence.

Water Balance

The study of water balance became important during the 1950s following the work of Thornthwaite in 1944. The term *water balance* means the balance between the total amount of precipitation received by a particular place and its loss through evaporation. Of the total water precipitated on any piece of ground, some is lost by evaporation and some is absorbed by the roots of plants before being transpired through the leaves. These two ways of disposing of some of the precipitation are collectively known as evapotranspiration (i.e. evaporation plus transpiration). The rest of the precipitation then becomes known as *surplus water* and it is this amount that infiltrates into the soil or reaches the rivers and seas as run off.

The rate of evapotranspiration at any place will of course depend on a number of climatic factors, the main ones being temperature, insolation, wind velocity, length of day and humidity. When all these factors attain a state in which maximum evapotranspiration can take place, this maximum is known as *potential evapotranspiration*. Potential evapotranspiration differs from *actual* evapotranspiration in that the latter is influenced not only by the prevailing climate but also by the amount of vegetation cover as well as the moisture present.

When actual evapotranspiration is less than the potential evapotranspiration, then the place is said to have a *moisture deficit*. On the other hand, when water is in excess of the water requirements, then a state of *moisture surplus* will be attained. Some of the surplus moisture will then be used to re-establish the moisture reservoir of the soil before the remainder drains off.

Garnier (1960) has shown that the elements of water balance of any place are related as follows:

$$P = PE + (S - D)$$

(where P· = precipitation, PE = potential evapotranspiration, S = water surplus, D = water deficit).

The above equation however has not taken into consideration the soil storage capacity.

The method for computing the water balance has been given by Thornthwaite and Mather (1957) who also show that before it can be done it is necessary to know:
a mean monthly or daily air temperature;
b mean monthly or daily precipitation;
c necessary conversion and calculating tables;
d information on the water holding capacity of the depth of soil for which the balance is to be computed.

No detailed work has been done on Kenya's water balance although Woodhead (1968) has carried out studies of potential evaporation in Kenya (Fig. 4.15). The Department of Meteorology at the University of Nairobi in 1970 put a post-graduate student on a project to calculate the mean annual potential evaporation in Kenya as Obasi (1969) had done for Nigeria. The latter's work showed that, although more laborious, Penman's (1948) method is more accurate than Thornthwaite's (1944).

Water Resources in Kenya

The conservation, study and management of Kenya's water resources are carried out under a Department of Water Development which was formerly under the Ministry of Natural Resources but has recently been organised under the Ministry of Agriculture.

The Department has divided the whole country into the five drainage areas shown in Table 4.5.

One of the many functions of the Water Development Department includes the collection of hydrological data giving the records of many river gauging stations. In 1967 the hydrometric stations which were operating in the whole country were as shown in Table 4.6.

A lot of data has already been collected by the department and more emphasis must now be directed to its analysis.

Rate of Evaporation

Although not enough work has been done in this field, evaporation from open water surfaces in Kenya is high, being nearly half of the total rainfall in some places. The Water Department estimates that below 1 000 feet (300 m) it is more than 100 inches (2 540 mm), and that

Table 4.5 *Drainage areas*

Drainage area	Area (approximated)		% of total area of Kenya
	sq miles	km²	
1 Lake Victoria	18 900	49 000	8·4
2 Rift Valley	49 000	127 000	21·8
3 Athi River	27 000	70 000	12·0
4 Tana River	51 000	132 000	22·7
5 Ewaso Ngiro	79 200	205 000	35·1

Table 4.6 *Hydrometric stations*

Type	Drainage area					Total
	1	2	3	4	5	
River gauging stations	101	57	66	95	42	361
Water level recorders	11	2	6	15	8	42
Standard rain gauges	224	150	220	161	73	828
Autographic rain gauges	16	8	12	14	4	54
Storage rain gauges	—	—	1	21	20	42
Evaporation pans	22	13	22	15	9	81
Full hydrometeorological stations	4	2	6	6	2	20

Source: O. S. Cege, 1968.

Table 4.7 *Mean annual rainfall and mean annual evaporation for selected stations*

Station	Latitude	Longitude	Altitude		Mean annual rainfall		Mean annual evaporation (EO)	
			feet	m	inches	mm	inches	mm
Lodwar	3° 07'N	35° 37'E	1 662	506	6·6	167·2	106·8	2 714
Garissa	0° 29'S	39° 38'E	420	128	11·7	302·1	93·4	2 374
Katumani	1° 35'S	37° 14'E	5 250	1 600	32·1	816·2	70·4	1 790
Koru	0° 07'S	35° 16'E	5 313	1 620	72·7	1 845·1	75·6	1 919
Magadi	0° 53'S	36° 17'E	2 010	613	16·1	409·1	101·8	2 585
Lamu	0° 16'S	40° 54'E	99	30	35·5	902·5	91·1	2 327
Mombasa Airport	4° 02'S	39° 37'E	180	55	41·5	1 053·7	86·7	2 205
Kisumu (Met.)	0° 06'S	34° 45'E	1 254	382	50·8	1 288·6	83·1	2 018

Source: Water Development Department. 1968.

Table 4.8 *Total surface water resources of Kenya*

Drainage area	River	Mean annual run-off	
		cubic yards (millions)	m³ (millions)
Lake Victoria	Nzoia	2 511	1 920
	Yala	1 263	966
	Nyando	654	500
	Sondu	1 616	1 236
	Kuja-Migori	1 138	870
	Others	2 354	1 800
	Sub-total	9 536	7 292
Rift Valley	Melawa	242	185
	Gilgil	36	28
	Molo	51	39
	Perkerra	165	126
	Others	565	432
	Sub-total	1 059	810
Athi River	Athi	980	749
	Tsavo	180	138
	Njoro-Lumi Springs	383	293
	Others	150	115
	Sub-total	1 713	1 295
Tana River	Tana-Garissa ·	6 148	4 700
Ewaso Ngiro	Ewaso Ngiro		
	Archers Post	967	739
KENYA		19 423	14 836

Source: Director of Water Development Department. 1968.

above 10 000 feet (3 000 m) it is about 50 inches (1 270 mm). The work of Woodhead (1968) also gives useful information on the rate of evaporation from a number of localities in Kenya. He also gives the accuracy factor which he considered the data available to him at the time. In Table 4.7, we give a selection of stations with their mean annual rainfall and mean annual evaporation (EO).

Surface Water

Kenya is not rich in surface water resources. The only really important surface water area is the Lake Victoria Basin. The Tana River area is also important, but the value of this is slightly reduced by the very high evaporation rate. The Water Development Department gave this information based on available records on Kenya's total surface water resources.

Ground Water

Kenya's surface water deficiency is nearly made good by the considerable amount of ground water available. Much of this ground water has not been developed save in the area around Nairobi where some conservation measures have been undertaken.

In Kenya the water table is slightly deeper than in other parts of Africa (it is reached at an average depth of 260 feet (80 m) below the surface). Nonetheless, Kenya's rural water supply depends on developing this ground water. This fact was realised fairly early in the history of Kenya's development when the first borehole was drilled in 1927, and by the end of 1967 there were 3 627 boreholes in this country. This is discussed further in Chapter 12.

References

Atlas of Kenya, Surv. Kenya, 1970 edn.

FINDLATER, J. 'The month to month variation of mean winds at low level over eastern Africa', *East African Met. Dept. Technical Memorandum, No. 12*, 1968.

FLOHN, H. 'On the causes of aridity of north eastern Africa', trans. H. T. Morth, *East African Met. Dept.*, 1966.

SANSOM, H. W. 'The occurrence of hailstorms in British East Africa', *Estratto da Nubila, Anno IV, No. 2*, 1961, pp. 34–51.

EAST AFRICAN METEOROLOGICAL DEPT. *Climatological statistics for East Africa and Seychelles, Part 1*, 1964. (N.B. Various other publications of this department have also been consulted in writing this chapter.)

MILLER, A. A. *Climatology* (Revised edn.), Methuen, 1953.

THORNTHWAITE, C. W. 'An approach toward a rational classification of climate', *Geog. Review, Vol. 38, No. 1*, 1948, pp. 55–94. See also original article in *Trans A.G.U. Vol. 26, Part V*, 1944, pp. 683–693.

GARNIER, B. J. 'Maps of the water balance in West Africa', *Bulletin de l'I.F.A.N., T.XXII, Series A, No. 3*, 1960, pp. 709–722.

THORNTHWAITE, C. W. and MATHER, J. R. 'Instructions and tables for computing potential evapotranspiration and the water balance', *Drexel Institute of Technology Publications in Climatology, Vol. X, No. 3*, 1957, pp. 181–311.

WOODHEAD, T. 'Studies of potential evaporation in Kenya', *Dept. Water Development/E.A.A.F.R.O.*, Nairobi, 1968.

OBASI, G. O. P. 'Mean annual potential evapotranspiration in Nigeria', *Dept. of Meteorology, University of Nairobi*, 1969 (unpublished).

PENMAN, H. L. 'Natural evaporation from open water, bare soil and grass', *Roc. Roy. Soc. London, Series A., Vol. 193*, 1948, pp. 120–145.

CEGE, O. S. 'Kenya's water resources and their development', *Hydrometeorological Survey of the Catchments of Lake Victoria, Kyoga and Albert*, 1968, pp. 46–52.

PRABHAKAR, D. R. L. 'Kenya's water resources: A general assessment of current research programme and future needs', *Water Department, Nairobi*, 1968 (unpublished manuscript).

Chapter 5
Plant Geography

Our aim in this and the next two chapters is to examine more directly plants and animals (including man) as they live in their homes (or habitats), and especially the effects upon them of man and his activities. The influence of man particularly on the vegetation cover of the earth is of such great significance in practically all the habitable regions that there is today little true natural vegetation still left.

For those who are more interested in biology, especially botany, and especially readers who intend to study biogeography, it is perhaps useful to comment briefly on the botanical nomenclature (naming system) used in this and the other chapters of the book.

In order to deal effectively with and name systematically the almost limitless variety of plants on the earth, the plants are sorted into groups. The plant groupings are organised so as to create a hierarchical system of classification. It is generally accepted by most biologists that the groupings (or *taxa*, singular *taxon*) consist of: *divisions* (or *phyla*), *classes*, *orders*, *families*, *genera* (singular *genus*) and *species*.

The originator of the nomenclature was the great Swedish botanist Linnaeus. He used the binomial system by which only two names were given, at any time, to each plant species, so that the same two names were never again given to any other plant species. Linnaeus introduced (in Latin) *generic* and *specific* names. For example, all the species of the well-known rose (flower) plant belong to the genus *Rosa*; hence every rose plant species has the first or *generic* name *Rosa*. Then the various rose species are given *specific* (or distinctive) names, e.g. *Rosa setigera*; the specific name *setigera* is either as descriptive as possible or has some evolutionary historical connotation, or a combination of both qualities.

Note the endings of the names denoting the *order* and *family* of the rose group of plants. The rose belongs to the order Ros*ales* and to the family Ros*aceae*. This system of endings is common in the botanical nomenclature. Note also that the first letter of the *generic* name is always a capital letter, whilst the first letter of the second part of the *specific* name is left small, e.g. *Pennisetum clandestinum* (Kikuyu grass). As ideas amongst botanists regarding a universally acceptable classification of the plant kingdom are changing rapidly none is attached to this chapter.

Like human society, a complex plant community is made up of classes or groups, each group having its characteristic structure. Thus the various plant species in the more complex plant communities fall into ecological groups or classes. Although in each plant community the species may vary both in height and life-form, members of the same ecological groups are similar in both their life-form and their relation to the environment. An ecological group, therefore, is an aggregate of species making similar demands on a similar habitat.

Where a plant community consists of woody plants, herbs, and others, a number of layers or strata (such as the tall tree layer, shorter or smaller tree or shrub layer, herb layer, and many other lower layers) are usually formed. Apart from these layers consisting of the self-supporting plants, there are also other plants such as climbers, parasites, mosses and lichens.

Each of the plant communities found in Kenya has special features which differentiate them.[1] Whether they be trees or grasses, the characteristic plant species of the various communities constitute what are normally called the dominant species. Two or more plant communities may be alike in that their respective dominant species are trees or grasses, but they may differ in terms of the specific dominant tree or grass species involved in their composition. When two or more plant communities have trees (or grasses) as their dominant species, then they are said to have the same life-form. The latter plays an important role in fashioning the general structure of the relevant plant community. Generally speaking, plant communities are specific entities complete with their characteristic plant species, compositions and typical structure. The vegetation mosaic of the earth is, in essence, made up of the various units of plant communities. Differences ob-

---

[1] e.g. various types of forest or woodland such as *Brachystegia-Afzelia*, *Manilkara-Dalberga/Hyparrhenia*, *Combretum schumannii-Cassipourea*, *Combretum-Hyparrhenia*, *Acacia-Themeda* and many others. These communities differ from one another in that their characteristic tree species are respectively *Brachystegia*, *Afzelia*, *Manilkara*, *Dalberga*, *Combretum*, *Cassipourea* and *Acacia*.

served between plant communities are often due to variations in such environmental conditions as:

a climatic factors, including seasonal changes, microclimates, local and regional climates, light intensity, air temperature and humidity, rainfall and winds;

b physiographic factors, which are influenced by the nature of the geological strata and geodynamic processes;

c edaphic factors dependent on the soil and its physical and chemical characteristics, soil water and air contents and the allied elements;

d biotic factors, associated with the activities of living organisms such as plants, animals and especially man.

Although the various habitat factors enumerated above are classified separately, they often act and react upon one another. In general, however, the climatic factors have a dominant influence over all the other habitat (or environmental) factors.

In ecology, there are three levels of integration, that is, three principal types of ecological systems, namely the individual, the population and the *ecosystem*. Individuals and populations rarely exist alone in nature. They are usually found in *association* with other plants and animals. This complex community of living things consists of spatially ordered systematic organisations which use energy and raw materials in their united function. It is this community of plants and animals, together with the environment which controls it, that is termed the *ecosystem*.

In our study of the various types of ecosystems, it is important to observe that man and his activities (be they constructive or destructive) form the focal point of our interest. Thus, in this chapter as well as in all the others — and especially the next two — our aim is to investigate the association which exists between the various vegetation belts (the results of the mosaic formed by the many plant communities) and the numerous animal species existing in Kenya, particularly man. Such an approach would perhaps serve as the best foundation for the effective study of Kenya's ecological regions. Many of the economically applicable ecological relations are examined in the chapter on ecological regions, where it is amply indicated that a good knowledge of these regions is the key to a better understanding of Kenyan agriculture, the basis of the country's economy.

Although moisture and temperature are generally responsible for the existence of the variety of the plant communities in Kenya, the more significant of the two climatic factors is moisture. Apart from the higher moisture and lower temperatures which characterise the highlands, mists are an important factor both in the highlands and in the coastal zone, where they exert considerable influence on the relevant vegetation belts. However, a vegetation study which lays too much emphasis on rainfall alone can be misleading. Throughout Kenya, especially in the semi-desert and desert vegetation region, evaporation is a factor of major importance. Temperature also seems to be the deciding factor between certain of the major vegetation units

under similar total rainfall, as is notably the case between the *Combretum-Hyparrhenia* scattered-tree grassland and the highland grassland vegetation units (Fig. 5.1). In a tropical country such as Kenya, an attempt to assess the relative significance of moisture and temperature must go together with the appreciation of the fact that, unlike the temperate zones, it is always low moisture and high evaporation rate, and not normally low temperature, which are more likely to limit the growth of plants.

The Climatic Vegetation Types

Both altitude and aspect of the land, to a large extent, induce the climatic differences which appear so marked in Kenya. Broadly speaking, Kenya consists of an enormous area of plains which supports semi-desert vegetation. Although there are a number of outliers of the highland region scattered in various parts of it, the semi-desert region of Kenya stretches to the north-east and east. Comparatively moist vegetation types cover the south-western quarter of Kenya. This part of Kenya consists mainly of the highland mass, including the Lake Victoria Basin to the west. The coastal belt is covered by a relatively moist tropical zone.

The classification of Kenya's vegetation was pioneered by Shantz in 1923. While this early study is greatly appreciated because it provides a valuable perspective into this complex problem, recent researches in this field have rendered Shantz's work outmoded. Thus, Shantz's 'savannah' is here referred to as 'scattered-tree grassland' — a phrase which speaks for itself. For some of the plant communities, sub-titles which indicate the dominants are used.

The main Kenya vegetation units (Fig. 5.1), which are examined in some detail below, are shown in Table 5.1.[1]

1. Forest and Mountain Communities

a *Highland forest (and highland grassland)* Considerably limited in its extent, this vegetation covers certain parts of the Kenya Highlands, where it is found on isolated masses of the highlands at altitudes varying from 6 500 feet (1 976 m) to 9 000 feet (2 736 m). Although the rainfall may vary from 35 inches (889 mm) at the drier transitional fringe to 90 inches (2 286 mm) on some of the wetter eastern slopes, this vegetation normally receives an annual rainfall averaging between 40 inches (1 016 mm) and 50 inches (1 270 mm). Moreover, it is often reinforced by mountain mists, so that the distribution of the community is determined by both comparatively low temperatures and high moisture. Big areas in this region are covered with open undulating grassland with relatively small forest areas patchily distributed, but becoming more prominent on the wetter eastern slopes.

[1] D. C. Edwards, 'The ecological regions of Kenya', Emp. Jnl. of Exptal. Agric., Vol. 24, No. 94, 1956.

Table 5.1 *Vegetation units in Kenya*

Major plant communities	Minor plant communities

1 Forest and mountain communities	a i Highland forest community
	  ii Highland grassland community
	b Mountain summit communities
	c i Coastal forest and ⎱ communities
	  ii Coastal grassland ⎰

2 Grassland communities	a Low tree-high grass *(Combretum-Hyparrhenia)* or scattered-tree grassland community b Grouped-tree grassland community c i Scattered-tree grassland and open grassland *(Acacia-Themeda)* community ii Scattered-tree grassland and open grassland (types other than *Acacia-Themeda*) community
3 Semi-desert and desert communities	a Desert dry-bush with tree (grass-bush) community b Desert scrub community c Desert scrub and desert grass community

i *The forest belt* At the higher and wetter edge of the evergreen forest, there is a zone of bamboo (*Arundinaria alpina*) which often extends to about 10 000 feet (3 040 m). The lower edge of the evergreen forest is drier, and the common trees include a variety of olives (especially *Olea hochstetteri* and *O. chrysophylla*). According to the quantity of moisture available, the mountain forest could be classified as follows.

a A high moisture category with an annual rainfall varying from 55 to 90 inches (1 397 to 2 286 mm). This category thrives best on the eastern slopes of the mountains. While this forest category is characterised by a species of camphor (*Ocotea usambarensis*), and one of podo (*Podocarpus milanjianus*), it lacks cedar.

b A lower-moisture category with an annual rainfall varying from 35 to 55 inches (889 to 1 397 mm). This forest is dominated, at higher altitudes, by a species of cedar (*Juniperus procera*) and that of podo (*Podocarpus milanjianus*). At other levels, however, the two olive species (*Olea hochstetteri* and *O. chryosphylla*) and another species of podo (*Podocarpus glacilior*) dominate.

Fig. 5A Highland grassland and forest

Fig. 5A Mt Kenya, showing giant lobelias

Fig. 5B Aberdares moorland

On Mt Kenya, the upper limit of the forest belt is variable, so that on the west and south sides the forest attains a height of 11 000 feet (3 344 m), whereas on the east and north sides it is limited to 10 000 feet (3 040 m). In the south-eastern parts of the mountain, the temperate rain forest attains its climax development and consists of hardwoods and some conifers. The camphor trees are concentrated on the southern and south-eastern slopes, whilst the cedars and podocarpus do well on the west slopes.

Still in the same belt on Mt Kenya but beyond the temperate rain forest is the bamboo zone, best developed on the south-eastern slopes. The lower margins of the bamboo zone vary from about 8 000 feet (2 432 m) in the south-east, through 7 000 feet (2 128 m) in the south, to 9 000 feet (2 736 m) in the north-west. The bamboo zone is extremely thin in the north-west and disappears altogether on the northern slopes. Within the bamboo belt, especially on the western and southern slopes, there are podocarpus trees. Well above the normal bamboo range, some bamboo may be found growing in sheltered places.

ii *The grassland belt* Red oat grass (*Themeda triandra*) is dominant in the undulating highland grasslands. It never seems to mature to the maximum stage of the succession owing to the regular fires which clear it periodically, hence its common sub-climax status. In certain areas of the grasslands, intensive grazing discourages fires. Consequently, the land becomes covered temporarily by a species of coarse grass, the wire grass (*Pennisetum schimperi*), which is of less value for grazing. The coarse grass species may be substituted, in certain areas, by manyatta grass (*Eleusine jaegeri*). In areas with annual rainfall above 40 inches (1 016 mm), the clearance of the forest results in the dominance of Kikuyu grass (*Pennisetum clandestinum*). At times this

grass grows in a dense association with Kenya white clover (*Trifolium semipilosum*). If the land is managed so that short herbage is maintained and the land's fertility is kept at a high level, both, especially Kikuyu grass, will thrive and maintain their dominance. However, poor management results in the temporary dominance of wire grass (*Pennisetum schimperi*) throughout the area affected.

Those areas lying between 6 500 and 9 000 feet (1 976 and 2 735 m), where the annual rainfall never falls below 40 inches (1 016 mm), are regarded as the possible Kikuyu grass belt. This is the most characteristic highland grassland zone and is comparatively limited in area. Between the highland grassland belt and the adjoining vegetation communities there is a relatively more extensive transitional zone which receives less rainfall. This transitional belt is not a natural habitat for the Kikuyu grass.

Both the highland grassland and the transitional vegetation belts are characterised by numerous constant subordinate grass species not listed here.[1]

Under the influence of man which includes, among other activities, the use of fire and domestic animals, the forest, which originally extended to lower levels now occupied by the highland grassland, has receded to the present higher level.

b *Mountain summit communities*[2-4] The vegetation setting in the Mt Kenya area has been selected for

[1] D. C. Edwards and V. C. Bogdan, *Important Grassland Plants of Kenya*, Pitman, 1951.
[2] B. H. Baker, *Geology of the Mount Kenya Area*, Ministry of Nat. Resources, Govt Printer, Nairobi, 1967.
[3] O. Headberg, 'Vegetation belts of the East Africa mountains', Svensk Botanist Tidskrift, Bd. 45. Ht. 1, 1951.
[4] M. J. Coe, 'The ecology of the alpine zone of Mount Kenya', Junk, Hague, 1967.

convenience as ideal for illustrating the mountain summit communities, and there is a strong tendency for most of the other high East African mountains to show considerable floral similarities to those on Mt Kenya. The higher parts of Mt Kenya consist of the flora called 'Afro-Alpine', which falls into the following vegetation belts.

i *The Hagenia-Hypericum zone* This is the highest part of the montane forest belt, and is typified by *Hagenia abyssinica* and *Hypericum leucoptychodes*. The last named is a giant form of St John's wort. The altitudinal range of this narrow but well-defined zone varies from about 10 500 feet (3 192 m) to 11 000 feet (3 344 m) on the west, and 9 500 feet (2 888 m) to 10 000 feet (3 040 m) on the east. Higher up in the sheltered valleys are to be found limited areas of this community.

ii *The ericaceous belt* This belt has a well-defined lower margin which is marked by transition to several species of giant heather (*Phillipia excelsa*, and species of *Erica*). The ericaceous belt is relatively thin or even absent on the west, while on the east and north sides the belt is wider with considerable quantities of a species of *Protea*. *Erica* and *Protea* forest, with trees up to 20 feet (6 m), covers the north-eastern and Ithanguni slopes between 10 000 feet (3 040 m) and 12 000 feet (3 648 m). The ericaceous belt is poorly defined on its upper margin, so that patches of heather persist, especially in sheltered slopes, up to 13 500 feet (4 104 m). Notable interfingering between the ericaceous and the alpine belts is common. Except in the north-east constant fires have affected the inflammable heather plants on all sides of the mountain. Thus the upper limit of the heather zone has been unduly lowered except in sheltered areas where the limited *Erica* forest enclaves occur.

iii *The alpine belt* This is the moorland, which is practically open and quite often marshy. It is dominated by tussock grasses. *Helichrysum*, giant groundsel and *Alchemilla* shrubs. Although certain plant associations are typical of each zone, the divisions of the alpine belt are gradational.

The lowest division of the alpine belt is dominated by *Senecio brassica* and *Lobelia keniensis*. These occur with the tussock grass (*Festuca pilgeri*) especially in damp ground. In drier and better drained areas *Alchemilla* occurs.

The upper division of the alpine belt is dominated by the tree-like *Senecio keniodendron*. Its highest limit is about 14 700 feet (4 469 m). Solifluction and frost-heaving together with the extreme climate control the characteristic flora of this zone of the alpine belt. Some of the common plants are species of *Carex* sedge and *Agrostis* grass, *Arabis alpina*, *Carduus platyphyllus*, *Senecio keniophytum*, two species of *Helichrysum*, and the apparently sterile *Lobelia telekii*.

This community found in the upper division of the alpine belt extends up to about 15 200 feet (4 621 m) on

the old weathered moraines at the base of Mt Kenya's main peaks. Most of the weathered rock surfaces are also covered by lichens and mosses. However, at the outer edge of a group of recent moraines about 300–900 feet (91–274 m) below the present ice margins, there is a sharp floral boundary. The recent moraines are sparsely colonized by *Arabis alpina*, stunted *Senecio keniophytum*, and *Agrostis trachyphylla*. Occurring sparingly on the virtually unweathered rocks within these recent moraines are mosses and lichens.

c *Coastal forests and associated grassland and other communities* The description of the coastal vegetation which follows the detailed classification of coastal vegetation belts given in Table 5.2 is merely a summary of the complex vegetation patterns found there.

In the coastal region, the nine sub-ecological units comprise some thirty distinctive vegetation zones. Moreover, there are good examples of interfingering and the invasion of the *acacia*-thornbush and the vegetation types found in the hinterland by the lowland dry forest and the coppice and scattered tree grassland formation at the edge of the lowland tropical rain forest vegetation types. According to Moomaw, the composite plant communities on which the above nine sub-ecological units are based may be tabulated as on Table 5.2 (p 78).

In the following brief description of coastal vegetation, the first four vegetation types are included under the various kinds of coastal forest. The next two vegetation types are included under the high grass-bush. Both *acacia*-thornbush land and sand-beach and dune communities belong to the semi-desert vegetation types. It is also important to observe that the coastal vegetation, especially the forests, has been greatly reduced by man's activities. Certain areas once noted for their luxuriant forests have now been almost completely cleared.

The narrow Kenya coastal strip has an annual rainfall varying from 50 inches (1 270 mm) at its highest, to about 38 inches (965 mm) or lower along the drier inland margins. Much of the area averages less than 1 000 feet (304 m) in height. Because of the distinctly humid climate during certain parts of the year, rainfall figures alone give a poor impression of the moisture conditions at the coast. It is important also to consider the coastal mist belt which extends over a considerable distance inland, as evidenced by the occurrence of lichens on trees and bushes. These humid coastal conditions affect a narrow strip of land of about 15 miles (24 km) maximum width. Rapidly decreasing moisture inland beyond the 10 to 15 miles (16 to 24 km) coastal strip results in a transitional belt which separates the vegetation of the humid coastal strip from those of the interior semi-desert and desert regions.

The interrelation of climate and soils is very close, and this has a far-reaching influence on the vegetation, especially in terms of available water. Areas of deep sand, such as those to the south, have low water retention capacity, whereas in the transitional zone there is shale underneath a shallow top soil, which holds water well.

Table 5.2

Main plant communities	Constituent plant communities
1 Forests	i Lowland rain forest *(Stercula-Chlorophora/Memecylon)*
	ii Lowland dry forests (such as: *Manilkara-Diospyros; Cynometra-Manilkara; Manilkara-Dalberga/ Hyparrhenia)*
	iii Lowland dry forest on coral rag *(Combretum schumannii-Cassipourea)*
	iv Mangrove swamps and saline margins
2 Mainly grasslands	v Lowland woodland *(Brachystegia-Afzelia)*
	vi Low moist scattered-tree grassland *(Afzelia-Albizia/ Panicum)*
3 Semi-desert and sea-shore	vii Acacia-thornbush land *(Acacia-Euphorbia)*
	viii Sand, beach and dune communities
	ix Pan and pond communities

i *Coastal forests* Towards the north, the forests are limited by desiccating climatic conditions. Elsewhere, soil types control available water and thus the distribution of forests.

The lowland rainforest includes:

a Witu forest in the north;
b Mida-Gedi forest;
c the forest areas near Malindi and along the River Sabaki;
d the Kayas and adjacent areas near Chonyi, Rabai, Ribe and Jibana;
e Gongoni forest;
f the Shimba Hills forest remnants;
g Ramisi river valley forest including those of Mrima and the eastern slopes of the Jombo Hill; and
h the forest found in parts of the Umba river valley.

Many of these forests have been reduced considerably by lumbering and replaced in most places by scattered-tree grasslands dominated by species of *Andropogon* and *Hyparrhenia*.

The lowland dry forest consists of:

a the lowland dry forest *(Manilkara-Diospyros)*;
b the lowland dry forest *(Cynometra-Manilkara* Sokoke);
c the lowland cultivated scattered-tree grassland, *(Manilkara-Dalberga/Hyparrhenia)*.

These are what Edwards (1956) described as dense, high bush with limited areas of forest and extensive open glades. Many parts of these forests have been cleared. Where the sea fringes this vegetation, mangrove swamps occur in tidal estuaries and lagoons. Coconut palms *(Cocos nucifera)*[1] and whistling pine or mvinje *(Casuarina equisetifolia)*[1] are the dominant trees at high tide line. A narrow belt of doum palm is found near the coastline. *Hyphaene coriacea* (branched stem) is the commonest, and occurs for a considerable distance inland, especially in open areas of high grass subject to seasonal swampy conditions. The lowland dry forest of the first kind

(Manilkara-Diospyros) is found along the entire length of the coast from Boni forest in the Lamu hinterland to the Gonja area near Vanga. The lowland dry forest of the second type *(Cynometra-Manilkara* Sokoke) is best represented by the Arabuko-Sokoke forest. It is also found in the northern (Lungi) areas on the Mundane range and on the Kambe limestone soils behind Kilifi Creek. The lowland cultivated scattered-tree grassland *(Manilkara-Dalberga/Hyparrhenia)* is found between the Magarini ridge and the Shimba Hills. It is confined to the soils associated with Jurassic shale.

The lowland dry forests on coral rag *(Combretum schumannii-Cassipourea)* occupy a small area in and north of Mida. The mangrove and saline margin communities, often referred to as mangrove thickets and adjacent saline areas, fall into two sections, namely:

a the mangrove thickets, swamps or mangrove forests – dominated by *Rhizophora mucronata* (mkoko). Mangroves are confined to tidal estuaries and lagoons along the coast, especially in the Lamu area and in Vanga on the Tanzanian border.
b saline grassland *(Sporobolus virginicus-Arthrocnemum)*. The flats on the landward margins of the mangrove thickets normally support open, low grass and shrub mixture characteristic of saline soils and pond margins.

ii *Coastal grasslands* The coastal high grass-bush described by Edwards (1956) forms a relatively narrow strip of vegetation. It is separated from the semi-desert vegetation of the interior by a wider transitional belt, which is at first moderately productive but which rapidly approaches in nature the adjoining semi-desert vegetation community. The transitional vegetation varies from the lowland woodland *(Brachystegia-Afzelia)* to acacia-thornbush land *(Acacia-Euphorbia)*. Along the coast, sand dunes are a common feature.

Lowland woodland *(Brachystegia-Afzelia)* is found north of Adu, at Marafa, Garashi and around Mangea mountain. A broad band of this vegetation extends

[1] Introduced species.

Fig. 5C Highgrass glade in coastal bush

north of Bamba to Gotani behind the Sokoke forest, and behind Mida Creek on the eastern side of Magarini ridge. Mwachi forest, the forest which covers the Shimba grits on the slopes of the Shimba Hills and that to the west and south of those hills between Kinango and Lunga Lunga, including the western slopes of Jombo, all belong to this vegetation type.

Lowland moist scattered-tree grasslands (*Afzelia-Albizia/Panicum*) is a community also included under coastal high grass-bush by Edwards (1956). The com-

Fig. 5D Mangrove vegetation with aerial roots, Shimoni

munity covers relatively large areas at the coast, and is still being extended by fire and cultivation. Lying between this community and the secondary associations on the coral rag soils is the *Ozoroa-Anona/Hyparrhenia* scattered-tree grassland community. It develops best on a mantle of wind-blown and alluvial sand overlying the coral. As a fire-induced type or because of impeded drainage it may occur on deep sands.

iii *Semi-desert and Sea-shore Communities* These include acacia-thornbush land (*Acacia-Euphorbia*); sand, beach and dune communities and pan and pond communities.

Acacia-thornbush land (*Acacia-Euphorbia*) is equivalent to both Edwards' *Acacia-Themeda* and *Commiphora-Acacia* desert-grass. The community covers a large area at the coast. It is found lying to the west of the Kinango-Samburu areas in the south. It is also found north of the Sabaki River where it swings eastwards approaching the coast between Mambrui and the Tana River. It is also found north of the Mundane range on the Somalia border.

Dune sands are common along the coast north of Malindi and near Lamu. Although many of the plant species from the beaches in the south occur along the fore dunes in the north, most of the associated species in the north are derived from the flora of the more arid areas. The dominant species of plants is *Ipomoea pescaprae*, and is associated with several other minor species. On the second dune from the high-tide mark and in the interdunes a more stable vegetation emerges consisting of the unbranched doum palm species (*Hyphaene parvula*) and several other plants. In places the beach line is marked by the *Casuarina equisetifolia* tree line.

Where clays have accumulated or where the water table is high during some part of the year, areas of impeded drainage called pans form. Since they are dry

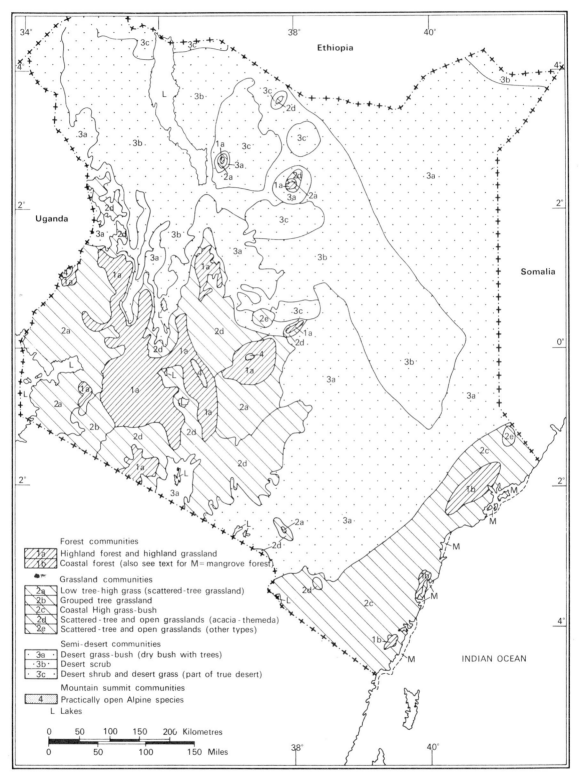

Forest communities

1a	Highland forest and highland grassland
1b	Coastal forest (also see text for M= mangrove forest)

Grassland communities

2a	Low tree-high grass (scattered-tree grassland)
2b	Grouped tree grassland
2c	Coastal High grass-bush
2d	Scattered-tree and open grasslands (acacia-themeda)
2e	Scattered-tree and open grasslands (other types)

Semi-desert communities

3a	Desert grass-bush (dry bush with trees)
3b	Desert scrub
3c	Desert shrub and desert grass (part of true desert)

Mountain summit communities

4	Practically open Alpine species

L Lakes

Fig. 5.1 Vegeto-ecological regions

for long periods during the dry season, pans develop their own kind of flora. The pan flora may consist of a pure grass stand composed of a few species or even of single species occupying several acres. Pond or permanent water sources support a range of sedges, rushes, ferns and lilies. The existence of groundwater is usually indicated by typical shrubs.

2. Grassland Communities[1]

a *Low tree-high grass* (*Combretum-Hyparrhenia*) This community, also popularly known as the scattered-tree grassland, consists of tall grass 5 to 8 feet (1·5 to 2·4 m) high. Densely scattered within it are small trees 10 to 15 feet (3·0 to 4·6 m) high, although in favourable areas where there are better ground water resources, the trees may grow to 30 feet (9·1 m). Considerable though isolated areas support forest trees, some of which may reach a height of 90 feet (27·4 m).

Scattered-tree grassland occupies vast areas in Kenya (Fig. 5.1) both in the Lake Victoria Basin, and south and east of Mt Kenya, where the elevation varies from 3 000 to 6 000 feet (912 to 1 824 m). In these areas the annual rainfall is between 35 and 60 inches (889 to 1 524 mm). There is a strong relationship between forest and the scattered-tree grassland, although the latter, being a fire sub-climax, is kept in its current stage by the frequent fires. Without fire, scattered-tree grassland soon develops thickets instead of grass between the scattered trees.

Protected by the corky bark, the trees composing this community are broad-leaved and deciduous, being dominated by various species of *Combretum*.[2] The most predominant grasses giving rise to the high-grass nature of this community belong to the *Hyparrhenia* and *Cymbopogon* genera. While *Cymbopogon validus*[3] dominates the scattered-tree grassland of the Mt Kenya area, *Cymbopogon afronardus* is predominant in the high-grass area of the Lake Victoria Basin.

b *Grouped-tree grassland* This community is found in the Trans-Mara and Sotik areas. It is a sub-type of the scattered-tree grassland which occupies areas with impeded drainage. The community is park-like, and consists of grouped trees and bushes between which grow coarse tufted grasses. At an altitude of about 6 000 feet (1 824 m) and with rainfall of about 50 inches (1 270 mm), the grouped-tree grassland is practically located in a physical environment akin to that occupied by the main *Combretum-Hyparrhenia* community, with the difference

that the soil occupied by the main community drains freely.

The grouped trees are normally found in raised areas with better drainage. The waterlogging, which typifies the habitat of this sub-type of the scattered-tree grassland, is caused by a hard pan a short depth below the surface. The impervious pan is further underlain by a considerable depth of grey clay.

Most of the species of trees found amongst the grouped trees are similar to those enumerated in association with the main *Combretum-Hyparrhenia* community.[1] They vary in height from about 20 to 50 feet (6·1 to 15·2 m).

Themeda triandra grass dominates the greater part of this sub-type so that periodic fires are common. However, in the waterlogged lower parts comprising the seasonal swamps are found thick growths of either a giant species of *Andropogon* or *kigutu* (*Pennisetum catabasis*). Other finer grasses occur between or intermingled with the higher grasses already mentioned. Most of the finer grasses are practically the same as those of the scattered-tree grassland community already enumerated.

c *Scattered-tree grassland and open grassland* The main community here is the *Acacia-Themeda*. There is, however, a sub-type which is the association of *Tarchonanthus* and *Cynodon*.

i *Scattered-tree grassland and open grassland (Acacia-Themeda)* With an erratic annual rainfall varying from 20 to 30 inches (508 to 762 mm), this drought-prone community covers the intermediate altitudes from 4 000 to 6 500 feet (1 216 to 1 976 m). It consists of a tall uniform grass cover (3 to 4 feet or 0·9 to 1·2 m), with a thin scattering of high flat-topped acacia trees (50 feet or 15·2 m) and much larger numbers of relatively short acacias (6 to 8 feet or 1·8 to 2·4 m), especially *Acacia drepanolobium*.[2]

Themeda triandra is the dominant grass, although it is reinforced in places by various species of each of the following grasses: *Setaria*, *Digitaria*, *Eragrostis* and *Hyparrhenia*.

ii *Other types of scattered-tree grassland and open grassland* The most important of these is the economically recognised *Tarchonanthus camphoratus-Cynodon* association typical of the Rift Valley old lake beds and other favourable areas, where relatively thick scattered bushes of short *Tarchonanthus camphoratus* trees may be seen. However, these trees are uncommon in the recently evolved lake beds, where open expanses of the star

[1] D. C. Edwards, *The ecological regions of Kenya*, Emp. Jnl. of Exptal Agric., Vol. 24, No. 94, 1956.
[2] The other tree associates are species of *Terminalia, Faurea, Erythrina tomentosa, Ficus, Ozoroa, Bauhinia* and *Dombeya*. See I. R. Dale, and P. J. Greenway, *Kenya Trees and Shrubs*, Buchanan's Kenya Estates Ltd., Nairobi, 1961.
[3] D. C. Edwards and A. V. Bogdan, *Important Grassland Plants of Kenya*, Pitman, 1951.

[1] In addition, the sub-type includes such species as *Acokanthera friesiorum, Rhus glaucescens, Pittosporum abyssinicum, Carissa edulis, Olea chrysophylla, Hippocrates* species, and *Teclea nobilis*.
[2] Other acacia species of the community are *Acacia senegal, A. subalata, A. seyal, A. hebecladoides, A. stenocarpa* and *A. drepanolobium*. Where it is drier or in rocky areas plants other than acacia may be found, for instance the *Euphorbia* and aloes of the drier rocky habitats or the *Balanites* occupying the drier fringes of the *Acacia-Themeda* community.

Fig. 5E Scattered tree grassland *(Acacia-Themeda)*

grasses are more common. Throughout the *Acacia-Themeda* community, the *Cynodon* species is found on the more favourable areas such as along streams.

3. Semi-desert and Desert Communities

These communities are often referred to jointly as the thornbush and thicket, and fall generally into two main groups: *Commiphora-Acacia*, including a coastal *Acacia-Euphorbia* sub-group; desert scrub and grass.

The first main group may be sub-divided into several distinctive parts, namely:

a Acacia-thornbush commonly known as *Acacia-Euphorbia*, with relatively higher rainfall;

b the normal *Commiphora-Acacia* also called dry bush with trees (the true *Nyika*);

c Scrub *Commiphora-Acacia*, also referred to as desert scrub (although distinct from the drier desert-scrub and desert-grass which form parts of true desert).

Acacia-Euphorbia vegetation covers some parts of the coastal hinterland. However, inland, where the rainfall is further reduced, semi-desert vegetation (consisting mainly of the two varieties of *Commiphora-Acacia*) occupies about two-thirds of Kenya. In this area, the rainfall is low (usually less than 25 inches, 655 mm) and unreliable. Although the three ecological units above are generally termed the *Nyika*, it is the *Commiphora-Acacia* proper that truly constitutes the *Nyika*.

A direct distance inland of about 20 miles (32·2 km) from the Indian Ocean shores marks the approximate eastern edge of the great *Nyika* wilderness. The Kenya *Nyika* is a hostile thick growth of mostly stunted thorny trees. For much of the year, the *Nyika* is grey, although during the short rainy seasons it becomes green. Many tree species with scaly barks (including several *Acacia* and *Euphorbia* species) thrive in this great plant community.

The joint influence of water, soil and climate is seen at its best in the most complex relationship with the vegetation, so that the latter consists of drought-resisting plants such as the baobab, the *Euphorbia*, the *Commiphora*, the *Acacia* and many others.

During unusually wet seasons, a rich growth of grasses reaches maturity and dies after seeding. The dormant seeds are selectively capable of sprouting for many years provided there is adequate rainfall. Generally, however, this is a vegetation belt for the hardy short and occasional tall trees rather than the grasses.

We now proceed to examine in a little more detail the significant vegetation constituents of the *Nyika*, consisting of the two forms of the *Commiphora-Acacia*. We shall also briefly introduce the desert scrubs and grass, although the two are not strictly part of the *Nyika*. It is, however, an associated drier vegetation type.

a *Desert dry bush with trees (Commiphora-Acacia desert grass or desert grass-bush)* Desert grass-bush and the drier desert-scrub communities cover nearly 70 per cent of Kenya, mainly in the east, north and north-east (Fig. 5.1).

With its unreliable rainfall (10 to 15 inches or 254 to 381 mm) annually, and the generally low altitude (below 2 000 feet or 608 m), this vast area suffers many disadvantages:

i long droughts, made more severe by dry winds;

ii limited durable rivers or complete lack of them; and

iii very high rate of evaporation leaving behind dry water courses.

The *Commiphora-Acacia* desert grass community consists of a wide variety of sparsely distributed deciduous shrubs or bushes varying in height from 10 to 15 feet (3·0 to 4·6 m), with widely scattered taller trees, 30 to 40 feet (9·1 to 12·2 m) in height, especially in more favourable moister southern areas. Much of the ground free of bushes is covered by dispersed bunches of permanent grasses and still lower shrubs. However, these still leave much of the surface comparatively bare, to be covered temporarily by the ephemeral plantlife generated by brief rainy periods. Owing to the long dry periods, most of the permanent grasses are virtually dead and the trees and shrubs are lifeless.

The community's bush dominants are *Commiphora* and *Acacia mellifera*, and its tree dominants the baobab (*Adansonia digitata*), mwangi (*Delonix elata*), and mgunga (*Acacia spirocarpa*). These taller trees are found more towards the fringes of the *Commiphora-Acacia* desert-grass community, (see 'Semi-desert and sea-shore communities' under 'Coastal forest and grassland communities' discussed earlier).

Fig. 5F   Dry bush with trees in the *Nyika*

Fig. 5G   Desert scrub, North Eastern Province

Fig. 5H Open desert grass-shrub

The species common among the lower shrubs include those of *Indigofera, Barleria, Aerva, Sericocomopsis* and *Disperma*. Farther south, a fibre plant called *Sansevieria* is sometimes found thriving thickly in several areas below the bushes. The variant *quinqueplumis* of the grass *Chrysopogon aucheri* is the most predominant in the extensive belt covered by this vegetation community, although to the north of the belt the two species of *Aristida* (*A. popposa* and *A. kelleri*) are the dominant grasses. Because of slightly more rainfall in the south towards the coastal belt, there is scanty though improved development of bush vegetation dominated by the tree species mkupa (*Dobera glabra*). The predominant grasses are the two species of *Chloris* (*C. transiens* and *C. myriostachya*), although there are many other common grasses.

b *Desert scrub (scrub Commiphora-Acacia)* This receives an annual average rainfall of less than 10 inches (254 mm) and covers an area slightly less than the previous community. As it is relatively drier, especially around Lake Rudolf, plant life is much more restricted, and much of the surface is bare with greatly scattered dwarfed trees and low bushes (4–10 feet or 1·2–3·0 m high). All is leafless and in a dormant state, except after the erratic transitory rains. Permanent grasses are virtually absent or trivial. Both the tree and bush dominants of the previous community are also predominant in the desert scrub community, except that they are much dwarfed and scantier here than in the desert grass-bush community. The distinction between these two communities lies in the absence, in the desert scrub, of the typical towering trees and permanent grasses of the desert grass-bush.

c *Desert scrub and desert grass (or part of true desert)* Detached areas of considerable extent occur in the desert scrub community. In these open areas, desert grass and desert scrub vegetation may be found developed especially on red desert sand, but with large areas around them bare and stony. Small scattered shrubs may dominate the scene, although there is usually a very thin and extremely patchy growth of desert grasses and, perhaps, some bushes along dry river margins or dry desert water courses. The more favourable stony ridges (usually consisting of lava) may be colonised by sparse trees of *Acacia* species. While an occasional heavy rain may encourage the rapid ephemeral growth of a number of species of the *Aristida* annuals, the normal significant grasses include various species of *Tetrapogon, Enneapogon, Chrysopogon,* and *Latipes*. The desert scrub and desert grass share the same low shrubs as those of the *Commiphora-Acacia* community.

References

BAKER, B. H. 'Geology of the Mount Kenya area', *Min. of Nat. Resources, Nairobi,* 1967.

COE, M. J. 'The ecology of the alpine zone of Mt Kenya', Junk, Hague, 1967.

DALE, I. R. and GREENWAY, P. J. *Kenya Trees and Shrubs,* Buchanan's Kenya Estates Ltd., Nairobi, 1961.

EDWARDS, D. C. 'A vegetation map of Kenya', *Jnl. of Ecol. Vol. 28,* 1940.

EDWARDS, D. C. 'Horn of Africa: Vegetation', *Dept. of Agriculture, Kenya,* 1945.

EDWARDS, D. C. 'The vegetation in relation to soil and water conservation in East Africa', *Bureau of Pasture and Field Crops, Bulletin 41,* 1951.

EDWARDS, D. C. 'The ecological regions of Kenya', *Emp. Jnl. of Exptal. Agric., Vol. 24, No. 94,* 1956.

EDWARDS, D. C. and BOGDAN, A. V. *Important Grassland Plants of Kenya,* Pitman, 1951.

HEADBERG, O. 'Vegetation belts of the East African mountains', *Svensk Tidskrift, Bd. 45, Ht 1,* 1951.

MOOMAW, J. C. *A Study of the Plant Ecology of the Coast Region of Kenya, East Africa,* Govt. Printer, Nairobi, 1960.

SHANTZ, H. L. and MARBUT, C. F. 'The vegetation and soils of Africa', *Amer. Geog. Soc. Research Series, No. 13,* New York, 1923.

SURVEY OF KENYA, *Atlas of Kenya,* Govt. Printer, Nairobi, 1962.

Chapter 6
Animal Geography

General Comments[1]

It was observed in the previous chapter that plants form the basis of life on the earth; and for animals, the terminal link of the food-chains is in all cases the green plants. It is not easy, therefore, except in very limited cases, to recognise specific animal communities, because all animals are directly or indirectly linked to the plant communities, thus giving rise to plant-animal communities. As the animals are dependent for life upon the vegetation, which in turn is governed in its type and distribution by the physical environment, then the animals, in turn, are also controlled by the physical environment. We notice as a result that, although the structural adaptations of animals (such as the giraffe's long neck) may not have any obvious relation to the prevailing climatic conditions, they are indirectly related to those conditions through the responses of the associated plant communities.

Owing to the close link between animals and plants, the treatment of Kenya's animal geography which follows will draw heavily on the study of Kenya's plant geography. The most striking difference, however, emerges from the fact that, unlike plants, practically all animals are mobile. For many of the animals, however, the mobility is confined to the limits of the associated plant communities in question.

Animals are classified according to their structure (just as plants are) into groups such as *phyla, classes, orders, families, genera* and *species*. Each group (say *class*) consists of animals which possess certain corresponding characteristics not found in any other *class*, and it is these characteristics which distinguish them from animals belonging to other *classes*.

As in plants, some animals are *unicellular* (and are termed *Protozoa*, e.g. amoeba), whilst others are *multicellular* (and are referred to as *Metazoa*, e.g. man).

Some animals in the *Metazoa* group have an internal backbone built up of a number of small bones or *vertebrae*. Such animals are often referred to as *Vertebrata*. All other animals which do not have an internal skeleton are known as *Invertebrata*. Table 6.1 below gives a classification summary of the animal kingdom (Jordaan and Kirsten (1951)).

Although mention is made of some of the invertebrate animals, our study of Kenya's animal geography lays greater emphasis on the vertebrate animals, particularly the mammals. Take the giraffe, for example. This animal belongs to the class *Mammalia*, of the order *Artiodactyla*![1] Its family is *Giraffidae* and its sub-family is *Giraffinae*, whilst its genus is *Giraffa*. In Kenya, there are two well-known species of giraffes, namely *Giraffa camelopardalis* (normally found thriving best within the grassland communities) and *Giraffa reticulata* (found in the drier northern and north-eastern semi-desert areas).

The class *Mammalia* consists of more than eighteen orders, some of them fossilised. Of these various orders, about twelve have representative living members in Kenya as indicated in the non-comprehensive table below (Table 6.2).[2, 3]

A study of the world distribution of animals indicates differences in the location patterns of the various groups of animals, especially in terms of their latitudinal ranges. Thus, the world may be divided into a number of geographical animal regions. According to Wallace, who (in his division of the world into animal belts) considered all the land animals whose ranges were known, there are six zoological or zoogeographical regions. The latter approximately coincide with the continents as follows:

a the Nearctic region–corresponding with North America and Greenland;

b the Neotropical region–including South and Central America and the West Indies;

c the Palearctic region–consisting of Europe (including Iceland and allied northern islands), most of Asia (excluding India, Pakistan and other parts of southeast Asia and southern China), and both the Saharan and Atlas regions of Africa;

d the Ethiopian region–corresponding to Africa, south of the Sahara, but also including the Arabian peninsula, Madagascar and the neighbouring islands;

---

[1] See Newbigin (1950), George (1963) and Beaufort (1951).

[1] The order consists of the mammals which possess even toes.
[2] Cited in W. George, *Animal Geography*, Heinemann, 1963.
[3] See Simpson (1945).

Table 6.1 [1]

Metazoa							Protozoa
Vertebrata (Chordata)	Invertebrata						
	Worms (Vermes)	Arthropods (Arthropoda)	Molluscs (Mollusca)	Sponges	Coelenterata (e.g. sea-anemone)	Echinodermata (e.g. sea-urchins)	
Fishes (Pisces)	Segmented	Insects (Insecta)	Belly-footed (Gasteropoda)				Amoeba Paramoecium
Amphibians (Amphibia)	Unsegmented 1 Round 2 Flat	Crustaceans (Crustacea)	Head-Footed (Cephalopoda)				
Reptiles (Reptilia)		Spiderlike animals (Arachnida)	Bivalve (Pelecypoda)				
Birds (Aves)		Millipedes and centipedes (Myriapoda)					
Mammals (Mammalia)							

[1] Both this and the next table have been modified to suit the text and do not therefore conform to the normal zoological tabulation. Because the vertebrates, especially the mammals, are emphasised in the text, tables 6.1 and 6.2 give the same emphasis.

e the Oriental region–comprising south-east Asia, southern China and the Philippines;

f the Australian region–composed of Australia, New Guinea, Celebes, the Melanesian islands, and all the other islands to the north-east, east and south of Australia.

Kenya is located in the Ethiopian zoogeographical region which, though it resembles the Neotropical region in several aspects, does not extend much into the southern temperate zone as South America does.

The Ethiopian zoogeographical region is perhaps the most varied of the six zoological regions. It ranks second only to the Neotropical region in the number of rare animal families peculiar to it alone. The most widely distributed animals which are also found in the Ethiopian region include dogs, various species of mice, rabbits, squirrels, shrews, mustelids, bovids[1] and cats. It is worth noting that, apart from the scaly anteaters (or pangolins) which belong only to one genus shared in the two regions, all the other families which are shared differ at the generic level in the two regions. Because of this, there is a difference between the Indian elephant

[1] Ungulates.

(Elephas), which is smaller, and the African elephant (Loxodonta africana). In a relative sense, the Ethiopian region appears better endowed with more and larger animals than its oriental counterpart.

The wild animal environment in the African section of the Ethiopian region consists of herds of both small and large herbivorous animals found on the plains. The commonest examples are the various species of antelopes, giraffes, rhinoceroses, zebras and elephants. These herbivorous animals are preyed upon by man and members of the carnivora order, the chief of which are wild dog, civets, hyenas, lions, leopards and cheetahs.

The myriads of birds in the Ethiopian region have many similarities to those found in the oriental region. However, the Ethiopian region has six bird families unique to it. The common birds include woodpeckers, orioles, hornbills, sunbirds, cuckoos, and numerous other birds amongst which are many species of birds of prey such as the vultures and eagles. The region is poorly endowed with parrots, pigeons and pheasants, but is unique in having birds such as mousebirds, ostriches, helmet shrikes, hammer heads, secretary birds and crested touracos.

As for reptiles, there are comparatively few amphibi-

Table 6.2

Order

Chiroptera[1]	Insectivora	Lagomorpha	Rodentia	Pholidota	Tubulidentata	Proboscidea (Proboscidea)	Hyracoidea	Perissodactyla	Artiodactyla	Carnivora	Primates
Pteropodidae (Fruit-eating bats)	Erinaceidae (e.g. hedgehogs)	Leporidae (e.g. hares)	Sciuridae (e.g. squirrels)	Manidae (e.g. pangolins)	Drycteropidae (e.g. ant-bear or aardvark)	Elephantidae (e.g. elephants)	Procaviidae (e.g. hyraxes)	Equidae (e.g. zebra)	Suidae (hogs. e.g. warthog)	Canidae (e.g. dogs)	Tupaiidae (e.g. tree shrews)
Emballonuridae (sheath-tailed bats)	Talpidae (e.g. moles)		Rhizomyidae (e.g. bamboo rats)					Rhinocerotidae (e.g. rhinos)	Hippopotamidae (e.g. hippos)	Viverridae (e.g. civets)	Lorisidae (e.g. lorises)
Nycteridae (Hollow-faced bats)			Muridae (e.g. modern rats and mice)						Camelidae (e.g. camels)	Hyaenidae (e.g. hyenas)	Cercopithecidae (e.g. monkeys, baboons, etc.)
Megadermidae (Big-eared bats)			Thryonomyidae (e.g. cane rats)						Giraffidae (e.g. giraffes)	Felidae (e.g. cats, leopards, lions, etc.)	Hominidae (man)
Rhinolophidae (Horseshoe bats)			Petromuridae (e.g. rock rats)						Bovidae (e.g. antelopes, goats, sheep, buffaloes, cattle, etc.)		
Hipposideridae (Leaf-nosed bats)			Hystricidae (e.g. porcupines)								
Molossidae (Free-tailed bats)											
Rhinopomidae (Mouse-tailed bats)											
Vespertilionidae (Simple-nosed bats)											

[1] Harrison. D. L. (1960) 'A check-list of the bats of Kenya'. *Jnl. E. A. Nat. History Soc.* Vol. 23: No. 7 (104) Dec 1960.

ans, the most common being frogs and toads. The region is, however, heavily populated with lizards, chameleons, turtles and crocodiles. Representing the rich and most diverse fish fauna are characins, catfish, carp, lungfish and several other families.

The country's wild animals may be classified into the following broad and flexible groupings, according to the plant communities with which the animals are associated:

a the highland communities (including those in the forest, grassland and mountain summit areas);

b the grassland communities (comprising all the animals in the various grades of the non-coastal and non-highland scattered-tree grasslands, open grasslands and the allied parts of the Rift Valley;

c the coastal communities (consisting of all the animals inhabiting coastal forest, woodland, scattered-tree grasslands, sand beach and dune habitats, *Acacia-Euphorbia* belt, pan and pond habitats, and the island and marine environments);

d thorn-bush and thicket communities (including all those animals found in the semi-desert and desert areas and the northern part of the Rift Valley).

Highland Communities

Many parts of the Kenya highlands are, in fact, highland grassland plains which range in height from about 4 500 to 8 000 feet (1 368 to 2 432 m). However, several peaks rise above the general grassland plain level, (Fig. 6.1), for instance Mt Kenya, Mt Elgon, the Aberdares and the Mau and Cherangani ranges. Most of these peaks are forest-clad; the peak of Mt Kenya, which is virtually on the Equator, bears some snow throughout the year. Each of these peaks exhibits similar vegetation zones at certain altitudinal ranges, depending on both the prevailing wind direction and slope aspect.

The highland rain forest (often also referred to as mountain rain forest), though much like the true equatorial lowland rain forest in superficial appearance, has different vegetation species and appears to be inhabited by a smaller range of both plant and animal species. Buffaloes, rhinoceroses and elephants are quite commonly found in this habitat, hence the significance of some of the high altitude national parks (Fig. 6.1). Unlike the big game at lower levels, the highland and mountain elephant, buffalo and rhinoceros have everything they need in abundance so that life is comparatively easy.[1] It is no wonder therefore that some of them grow very large. The mountain glades are also noted for their bush babies *(Galago senegalensis)*, colobus monkeys, bushbuck and bongo, while the bamboo zone is frequented by the duiker. The bamboo belt is not as heavily-populated with seed-eating birdlife as would be expected, although various species of francolins find the habitat favourable.

Above the bamboo belt, in the glades found in the

Hagenia and giant or tree heath zones, are such animals as waterbuck, buffalo, eland, forest hogs, bushbuck and bongo. The commonest high altitude predators are the various species of wildcat, leopard and lion.

Most of the larger animals are not found above the tree heath zone. In this higher zone, the commonest animals are steinbok, leopard and duiker. The tree heath, which is, in fact, the beginning of the mountain moor, gives place to the latter. Mountain moor is commonly inhabited by the mountain rock hyrax and a notable variety of small rodents, especially mountain rats. At these levels, a mixture of stray lowland animals and some of the lower level highlands animals such as zebra, buffalo, eland, elephant, leopard and perhaps colobus monkeys may be encountered.

Between 10 000 and 15 000 feet (3 040 and 4 560 m) are found the Alpine meadow lizards *(Algyroides alleni)*. The most characteristic birds inhabiting the Alpine zone include the scarlet-tufted malachite sunbird *(Nectarinia johnstoni johnstoni)*, hill chat *(Pinarochroa sordida ernesti)*, streaky seed-eater *(Serinus striolatus striolatus)*, Alpine swift *(Apus melba africanus)*, and black duck *(Anas sparsa leucostigma)*.[1]

Grassland Communities

Kenya's grasslands, like those of the other East African countries such as Tanzania and Uganda, still support some of the finest wild animal communities in the world. These grasslands, which are dominated by red oat grass *(Themeda triandra)*, support huge herds and varieties of grazing animals, and undoubtedly constitute one of the most important basic elements sustaining large numbers of the ungulates.

In recent years man has caused the destruction of the grassland cover, thereby introducing soil erosion, has killed vast numbers of the wild animals and in so doing has opened up large areas for domestic livestock. In this way the numbers of wild herds have been reduced, and they now tend to be confined to certain protected areas – game reserves, wildlife protected areas, national parks, and so on. Since independence, there have been definite government moves to preserve the remaining wildlife, especially for the tourist industry. These very welcome moves included the setting up of an orphanage for wild animals in the famous Nairobi National Park: this is proving a great attraction to tourists. However, poaching, the greatest menace to wildlife, although considerably lessened by stricter government game hunting regulations, still goes on in many of the remoter protected areas, where law enforcement presents great problems.

In these grasslands purely browsing animals are a minority amongst the predominantly grazing or grazing-cum-browsing animals. The chief large grazing animals are the wildebeest *(Connochaetes taurinus)*, zebra *(Equus*

[1] See Brown (1965).

[1] M. J. Coe, 'The ecology of the alpine zone of Mount Kenya', Junk, Hague, 1967.

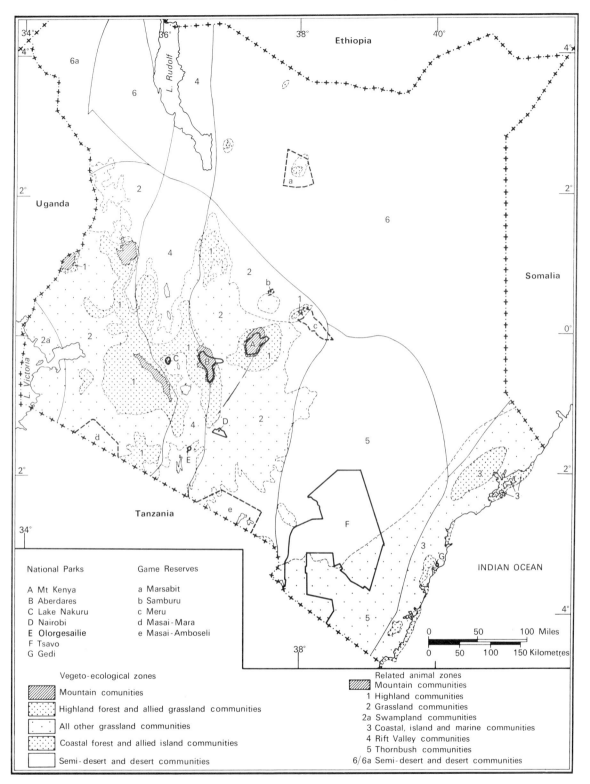

Fig. 6.1 Distribution of animal communities and ecological regions

National Parks

A Mt Kenya
B Aberdares
C Lake Nakuru
D Nairobi
E Olorgesailie
F Tsavo
G Gedi

Game Reserves

a Marsabit
b Samburu
c Meru
d Masai-Mara
e Masai-Amboseli

Vegeto-ecological zones

Mountain comunities

Highland forest and allied grassland communities

All other grassland communities

Coastal forest and allied island communities

Semi-desert and desert communities

Related animal zones
Mountain communities
1 Highland communities
2 Grassland communities
2a Swampland communities
3 Coastal, island and marine communities
4 Rift Valley communities
5 Thornbush communities
6/6a Semi-desert and desert communities

burchelli), and the hartebeest *(Alcelaphus buselaphus)*.[1] Unlike domestic livestock which tends to destroy pastures through over-grazing, the diverse grazing wild animals appear to eat various kinds of grass at different stages of growth, and at certain varying levels. Moreover, unlike domestic animals, wild animals do not confine themselves to certain feeding grounds such as those usually determined by herdsmen. Wild animals move over wide grazing areas, with the consequence that the grazing grounds are unlikely to deteriorate as they do when grazed by domestic livestock. While the various types of grasses are eaten comparatively uniformly by wild animals, domestic animals graze selectively. Consequently, the sweeter grasses and herbs may be over-grazed at the expense of more unpalatable grasses and herbs. The latter are therefore left to grow, thus rendering the feeding grounds worthless for domestic livestock.

A closer study of wild grazing animals indicates that they have many advantages over domestic livestock. Wild animals use more efficiently the food which they derive from the grasslands. Moreover, their resistance to disease and their relatively higher flesh output per acre of grassland in comparison with domestic livestock is significant. Furthermore, wild grazing animals need far less water than domestic livestock; in fact some do not appear to need water at all, since they seem to derive most of their water requirement from the grasses and other herbs they eat.

While wildebeest, zebra and hartebeest are the most numerous amongst the large ungulates, gazelles, especially Thomson's and Grant's gazelles, are the most abundant amongst the smaller ungulates. Although both gazelles are grazing animals, they also browse, especially the larger Grant's gazelle *(Gazella Granti)*. Unlike Thomson's gazelle *(Gazella Thomsoni)*, Grant's gazelle thrives even in the drier north-eastern parts of Kenya. However, the population of Thomson's gazelle is higher in Kenya's high rainfall grasslands than that of Grant's gazelle, hence the tendency for the farmers to complain that they compete for grass with domestic livestock.

Other ungulates found in these grasslands, especially in the fringes of bushy water-courses and near water, are the various impalas *(Aepyceros melampus)* and waterbucks, especially the common waterbuck *(Kobus ellipsiprymnus)*. Such animals as the eland *(Taurotragus oryx)*, warthog *(Phacochoerus aethiopicus)* and, in better sheltered areas, the buffalo *(Syncerus caffer)* also belong to these grasslands. In certain parts of the grasslands are found larger browsers, such as the acacia browsing giraffes *(Giraffa camelopardalis)*, whereas along the watercourses, especially in the hillside thickets, rhinoceroses *(Diceros bicornis)* may be found. Mostly hidden amongst the grazing animals are several carnivorous animals which prey on them, some during daylight and others at night. Some of the flesh-eaters, such as the spotted hyenas *(Crocuta crocuta)*, are also scavengers. The most important carnivorous animal of the grasslands is the lion *(Panthera leo)*. Other flesh-eaters found

[1] See Macdonald (1965).

Fig. 6A Hartebeest (left) and wildebeest

in these vast grasslands include wild dogs *(Lycaon pictus)*, cheetahs *(Acinonyx jubatus)*, leopards *(Panthera pardus)*, jackals *(Canis mesomelas)*, foxes *(Ococyon megalotis)*, and the serval cat *(Felis serval)*.

Lions move in groups or prides whereas leopards are lone killers and eaters. Since lions eat in groups, they prey on the larger ungulates such as zebras, wildebeest, elands and other large antelopes, giraffes and so on. Lions are not, however, limited to preying on the larger ungulates, for they are known to eat the flesh of wart-hogs. Because lions eat at intervals of about a week, taking a heavy meal involving as much as fifty to sixty pounds (23–27 kg) of flesh per adult lion, their rate of reducing the ungulate population is relatively low, so that they cannot be considered as an effective means of controlling the ungulate population. Moreover, despite the existence of such abundant food for the lions, the population of the latter apparently does not seem to increase in any one area. However, a higher hyena population could reduce the ungulate population much faster, especially as the hyenas, which are ruthless killers, may feed on the newly born ungulates. Since hyenas are not fastidious, they both scavenge and kill other animals, particularly the weaker ones, in larger numbers than do lions. Whilst lions hunt by sight for living prey by day, hyenas hunt for carrion at night by smell. Wild dogs are usually found in packs and, like hyenas, are ruthless killers and have been known to eat their prey alive. Like wild dogs, cheetahs hunt by sight during the day. Cheetahs normally kill smaller ungulates such as impalas and Thomson's gazelles.

Other predators of the grasslands include many snakes and predator birds such as vultures, which scavenge on flesh from carcasses left over by lions, hyenas, and allied flesh-eating animals. Other flesh-eating birds are the secretary bird *(Sagittarius serpentarius)*, bateleur eagle *(Terathopius ecaudatus)* and several other grassland species of eagles, kites and owls.

The grasslands also support myriads of seed-eating birds, including pests, such as the grain-eating weaver-birds. A large and specially famous bird found here is the ostrich *(Struthio camelus)*. The grasslands form an important migration route for birds moving north or south to escape adverse winter conditions, especially the northern winters. Birds apart, the grasslands also provide excellent habitats for many species of rats and mice, and numerous other rodents. They also provide a favourable habitat for the various species of baboons *(Papio anubis)*.

In the virtual absence of interference by man, life in these grasslands has a remarkable unity. By functioning according to natural laws, there is a uniformity and agreement which strikes what appears to be a wasteless and stable balance between the intricate plant and animal communities involved.

The eastern fringes of the extensive African scattered-tree grassland belt cover only a small area in western Kenya (Fig. 6.1, 2a). In parts of this fringe zone are tropical swamps maintained by the presence of abundant water and suitable climatic conditions. The courses of many of the rivers which flow into Lake Victoria – particularly in their lower parts nearer the lake – are covered with swamp vegetation dominated by various species of reeds and papyrus. The water below the swamp vegetation is a very poor habitat for both plants and animals; and the dead mass of vegetation only supports a limited range of specialised animals such as the swamp worm. The activities of this worm improve the habitat for other animals and plants, increasing the air content of the wet mass of dead swamp vegetation, which then decomposes faster to enrich the habitat.

In rivers, swamps, and in Lake Victoria itself, lives the hippopotamus *(Hippopotamus amphibius)*, normally found in herds. Their dung fertilises their habitat, thus providing food for certain water plants such as algae on which the lake fish feed. Hippopotamuses are recognised path-makers through the dense lake shore vegetation, and they also keep channels open in the reeds and papyrus-threatened rivers and lakes, thus allowing ease of movement for other less powerful animals in the water and through dense lake shore vegetation. Hippopotamuses breed prolifically in the absence of their enemies, man and some carnivorous animals. Like hippopotamuses, crocodiles *(Crocodylus niloticus)* are found in and by the shores of Lake Victoria, and also in the more accessible parts of the permanent rivers. Crocodiles feed mainly on fish, although they are known occasionally to take human beings and a wide range of other animals, catching these as they come to the rivers or the lakeshore for water. Crocodiles play their part in maintaining the ecological balance of the various fishes in Lake Victoria, and so their greatly reduced numbers (they have been hunted for their skins almost to extinction in recent years) have led to a disturbance of the fish balance. Certain predatory fish have increased in number, consequently reducing the numbers of economically more valuable fish. There is thus a great need to protect crocodiles from further slaughter.

Lake Victoria has a very great variety of fish stock, some of which have been introduced from outside. The two native *Tilapia* species are *T. esculenta* and *T. variabilis*. The introduced species are *T. nilotica*, *T. zillii* and *T. leucosticta*. Another important introduced fish is the Nile perch *(Lates nilotica)*, which is predatory. Other examples of predatory fish in Lake Victoria are lungfish *(Protopterus annectens)*, catfish *(Clarias mozambicus)*, *Bagrus* and *Haplochromis*. The last is important also because it feeds on the snails which carry the bilharzia parasite. It is not possible to give an exhaustive list of Lake Victoria's economically important fish, but the following should be mentioned: *Dogmac, Barbus, Schilbe, Barilius, Mormyrus, Alestes, Labeo, Synodontis, Stolothrissa* and *Engraulicypris*.[1]

The lake swamp area is also known to be an excellent habitat for the python – a giant non-poisonous snake

[1] See Hickling (1961); Morgan (1969); Report on Kenya Fisheries 1956-1970; Review of Kenya Fisheries 1946-1955.

91

Fig. 6B Crocodiles *(Crocodylus niloticus)*

which strangles its prey.

Around Lake Victoria, and on the lake islands, are snake and fish-eating predator birds such as darters *(Anhinga rufa)*, and several species of cormorants,[1] many species of herons, storks, pelicans, and ibis.

Where man has not interfered through settlement, many grazing animals such as the various types of smaller antelopes are found. Elephants may be found in a few areas, especially in parts of south Nyanza. However, they are rarer in the whole of this western area than formerly. In parts of these swamp grasslands of western Kenya, the red antelope (kob) may occasionally also be found.

A significant proportion of the scattered-tree grasslands and the more open grasslands extends into parts of the Kenya Rift Valley. The latter is generally hotter and drier in comparison with the forest-clad high ridges on either side. The comparatively flat floor of the valley is divisible into a number of distinct plains several of which represent the remains of swamps and lakes of the past. Owing to certain physical factors (for example, higher temperatures; much sunshine; and relatively concentrated carbonate content of the waters of some of the Rift Valley lakes, e.g. Elmenteita, Hannington, Nakuru, Magadi, Natron and Rudolf), the waters of some of the lakes form excellent habitats for blue-green algae and diatoms. On multiplying, these organisms turn the waters of these alkaline lakes into a rich green substance on which the millions of Rift Valley flamingoes flourish.

The smaller flamingo species *(Phoeniconaias minor)* occurs in greater numbers than the larger flamingo species *(P. ruber)*, which also inhabits the Rift Valley. It is the lesser flamingo hordes that give such Rift Valley lakes as Natron, Magadi, Nakuru, Hannington and Rudolf much of their magnificent appearance at the peak seasons. Both greater and lesser flamingoes breed in the middle of Lake Natron, where the water is generally hot. However, the mud where the flamingoes build their nest-mounds and rear their young is hotter still. Flamingoes are eaten by most large birds of prey including eagles and vultures, and by other carnivores such as lions, hyenas, leopards, jackals, wild dogs, etc. However, in their breeding habitat in the middle of Lake Natron, they are well protected from most of their enemies.

Between Lake Magadi and the Ngong escarpment, the vegetation consists of sparse pasture and thorns, so that the belt only supports small numbers of rhinoceroses, gerenuks, wildebeest, zebras, oryx[1] and giraffes. In the Ewaso Ngiro swamp hippopotamuses and rhinoceroses are found although, in this belt, the wildlife is normally akin to that of sub-desert steppe.

The water is perhaps too alkaline in many of the present-day Rift Valley lakes, hence normal freshwater fish cannot live in them unless they gradually adapt themselves to living in the alkaline water. This is what has happened in Lake Magadi where an impoverished fish fauna which is relatively adapted to an alkaline habitat is still preserved. The two *Tilapia* species found in Lake Magadi are the dwarf *T. grahami* and *T. alcalica*. They tend, however, to be found in the comparatively fresh water flowing into the lake from the hot springs. During more favourable seasons when rainfall is high,

---

[1] For example, the long-tailed cormorant *(Phalacrocorax africanus)* and the white-necked cormorant *(P. lucidus)* etc.

[1] Fringe-eared oryx *(Oryx beisa callotis)*.

Fig. 6C Lesser flamingoes

thousands of the two *Tilapia* species thrive and are preyed upon by fish-eating birds, such as grebes *(Poliocephalus ruficollis)*, and the great white pelicans *(Pelecanus onocrotalus)*. Where minor fisheries are planned by the Kenya Government in the other alkaline lakes such as Hannington, Nakuru, Elmenteita and Natron, it is most likely that the alkaline-adapted *Tilapia* species will be introduced for future commercial exploitation.

The other Rift Valley lakes such as Naivasha and Baringo are relatively fresh, and even Lake Rudolf's water is less alkaline than the other alkaline lakes listed earlier. Along with these three Rift Valley lakes may be mentioned Lake Jipe in Taita. The only native fish species (which is of little commercial value) found in Lake Naivasha is *Aplocheilichthys*. All the other commercially important fish species of this lake have been introduced from elsewhere. There are at present three species of *Tilapia*, namely *T. leucosticta*, *T. nigra* and *T. zillii*. Another introduced fish is the black bass *(Micropterus salmoides)*. Lake Baringo is noted for its introduced *Tilapia nilotica*, whilst Lake Rudolf is famous for its over-sized *Tilapia nilotica* (measuring 1·5 feet (0·5 m) or more) and Nile perch (weighing 200 pounds (90 kg) or more and measuring 4 feet (1·3 m) or more). The lake also supports other fish species such as the tiger fish *(Hydrocyon lineatus)*, *Citharus* and *Distichodus*. Lake Jipe, which is outside the Rift Valley but within the wooded grasslands in the Taita area, has two native *Tilapia* species (*T. jipe* and *T. girigam*). The introduced fish species include *Tilapia melanopleura*, *T. zillii* and *Ctenopharyngodon idellus*.

Although the Rift Valley floor is normally hotter and has less rainfall than its flanking slopes, the valley bottom often consists of flat floodplains with rich grazing areas supporting far greater numbers of wild animals than the overlooking plateaus and mountains. The Rift Valley acts as a single system which has its own way of life, so that each year, millions of migrant birds use it as the best routeway southwards or northwards. This function of the Rift Valley appears to have evolved probably in pluvial times, when the flanking highlands were perhaps more forested and the plains of the valley floor were possibly richer pasturelands with far more water than is present in our time.

Coastal Communities

Independent of the mainland local climatic and vegetation variations, there is a tendency for the sea coast habitats of Africa to be broadly similar. Some of the common features are the coastal equable temperatures and their usually relatively higher rainfalls than those recorded at the adjoining inland stations. Moreover, the most familiar forms of animal life such as seabirds and marine molluscs are commonly shared by all the African coasts. Along Kenya's short coastline mangrove forests grow in certain parts (Fig. 5.1), whereas other parts are fringed by coral reefs.

Although the offshore islands may have plants and animals which are unique to themselves, they generally also share the same plants and animals as those found on the adjoining mainland areas.

Because mangrove swamps are hot, steamy and rather gloomy habitats they form relatively poor homes for animals. Crabs are normally plentiful, and sponges, barnacles and a variety of other small shellfish are usually found attached to the stilt mangrove roots. Reptiles and mammals are considerably limited in number.

The most characteristic birds of the mangrove swamps are the kingfishers and the small green herons. In the creeks, occasional dugongs still exist; genet cats are more common.

The primitive corals which form reefs are not extensive along the Kenya coast. They flourish best at temperatures ranging between 25° and 31°C, (77° and 88°F) and at depths ranging down to 150 feet (about 46 m). Associated with the corals are the algae, many of which also secrete calcium carbonate. Since the corals are marine animals, their upper limit, unless dead, is determined by low tides. At low tide, the coral surface exposed consists of dead coral, while the living coral is found under the water. The typical Kenya coast coral reefs are the fringing reefs formed around the edges of the stable coastal land masses, which are neither rising nor sinking. There are old reefs along the Kenya coast which resulted from either continental uplift or fluctuating sea level.

Because the water in the coral lagoons is warm, well-lit by the sun, and not unduly exposed to storms, there is a very rich variety of animal life here. The corals themselves are brightly coloured, as are the fish and other animals living around the reef. Since the water is clear and allows the tropical sun to shine through it, the floors of the lagoons are often covered by dense growths of sea-weeds, of which the commonest species along the Kenya coast is *Cymadocea ciliata*–a flowering plant. The seaweeds supply food, but also provide shelter for the smaller animals.

The animals that frequent the coral reefs include starfish and sea urchins, of which the most common is the hatpin urchin (*Diadema*). The urchins move less rapidly than the carnivorous starfish, which eat both the urchins and molluscs. The giant clams (*Tridacna*) are the largest bivalve molluscs found on the Kenya coastal coral reefs. They are protected by strongly-fluted shells meeting in sinuous curves. When feeding or while in shallow water, the clam opens the shell valves and extrudes a colourful flesh mantle which admits sunlight through bright eyelike spots. Within the mantle itself, green algae live. Other sea animals include a variety of univalved molluscs such as the small and large cowries. Several other shelled and non-shelled sea animals in the mollusc group are also found, for example, cameo shells, spiny murex, *Tonna*, *Lambis*, many shell-less molluscs of the sea-slug family, and octopuses.

Among the corals is found an abundant fish life. Amongst the commonest are surgeon fish, butterfly fish (*Chaetodon*), and angel fish (*Plantax pinnatus*). The ornamented moorish idol (*Zinclus cornutus*) and coach man (*Hemiochus acuminatus*) are also found. Moray eels and various rock cods, some very large (e.g. *Promicrops lanceolatus*), inhabit holes and caves in the reef. Various species of parrot fish and numerous kinds of spiny lobsters (*Pannilurus* spp) also live in the reef; and barracuda (especially *Sphyraena jello*) are found in the channels. Marlin (*Makaira herscheli*), sailfish (*Istiophorous gladius*), sharks and rays are also outside the reef. In addition to the last three, other migratory fish species are dolphin, tunny, kingfish, and oceanic bonito.

The inland lagoons and creeks and the reef surface are favourable feeding grounds for migrant temperate birds such as sandpipers (*Calidris testacea*), sanderlings (*Crocethia alba*), and plovers (*Charadrius squatarola*). The permanent seabirds of Kenya's coast include Hemprich's gull (*Larus hemprichi*), and several species of terns, all of which breed in large numbers on the Kiunga islands in northern Kenya and along the Kenya coast.

Although only a few miles wide, the Kenya coastal strip enjoys more rainfall than the adjoining inland area. It is therefore relatively more favourable as a route for the migrant birds such as eagles, falcons, and kites. The most typical Kenya coastal birds are the several species of crows (e.g. *Corvus splendens*), the house sparrow (*Passer domesticus*) and the palm swift (*Cypsiurus parvus*).

With a hotter and relatively wetter climate than the interior, the narrow coastal belt has a mixture of scattered-tree grassland and forest patches, which distinguish it from the drier vegetation prevailing farther inland. The characteristic animal inhabiting the coastal forest is the suni antelope (*Nesostragus moschatus*). However, in the lowland dry forest (*Cynometra-Manilkara* Sokoke), elephant and buffalo may occasionally be encountered.

Thornbush and Thicket Communities

Amongst the acacias may be seen rhinoceroses and elephants, the latter often ploughing the sand for water. Also in the bush are lions, and on the rocky hills dotting the plains are cool patches of forest with leopards and birds. In certain areas of the *Nyika* clear water bursts out in springs, such as Mzima Springs in the Tsavo National Park, which ultimately join to form sizeable rivers. In these springs and rivers are a variety of fish including trout, *Anguilla*, *Barbus*, *Labeo*, *Clarias*, *Tilapia* and *Clarotes*. Sometimes they are also inhabited by crocodiles and hippopotamuses.

With a bark rich in calcium, the baobab tree provides food for the elephant, whereas for man it is the source of fibre. Baobabs are generally focal points, especially favoured by wildlife because of their shade.

Some of the chief animals of the *Nyika* are elephants, rhinoceroses, giraffes, kudus and gerenuks, the last being commoner in the drier northern belt. Herds of impala browse on the bushes and trees and occasionally graze. Most of these animals normally stay near permanent water.

Nowhere in the whole of their huge habitat in Kenya, do elephants so greatly influence both the vegetation and lives of the associated animals, as they do in this thornbush environment. Elephants are here much more destructive in their use of the bush and trees than the other great browsers such as giraffe and rhinoceros. Where they have uprooted bushes and trees, the grass grows dense and, on drying, is easily set on fire. Then huge stretches of thornbush may be destroyed, thus changing it into open grassland. After the fire, grazing animals normally invade the areas affected so as to feed on the grass. In this way, they suppress the dense growth of grass, thereby creating a belt of short grass which discourages the spread of fire. This allows seedling trees to grow and protect themselves from the grazing animals by their thorns. Bushes and trees finally overcome the grass, and the country is once more covered with thornbush vegetation, which elephants and their associates re-occupy. The cycle takes a considerable time, however. It should be observed in passing that elephants not only encourage the growth of grass for the other animals, but also dig wells of water in the sand and make paths in the thornbush, both of which are utilised by other animals.

Throughout the thornbush belt are thousands of lesser kudus (*Strepsiceros imberbis*)[1], which are affected neither by lack of water nor by seasonal changes. They

---

[1] Counterparts of the greater kudus (*Strepsiceros strepsiceros*).

94

are browsers and roam the thin *Commiphora* thorn plains. The other common animal of the thornbush is the dikdik (one of the various species being *Rhynchotragus kirkii*). Both lions and leopards inhabit the *Nyika*, but normally stay near ample water sources. The *Nyika* lions lack the full manes which characterise the lions found in the highland plains. However, they are just as big and as powerful as their highland counterparts. If there is any striking major difference between these two species of lions, it is in their habits. The lions of the highland plains move in relatively large prides. Moreover, they normally tend to leave the carcass of their prey unattended after one satisfactory meal. The *Nyika* lions, on the other hand, are more frugal and therefore far less wasteful. Because suitable large animals on which to prey are not as common in the *Nyika* as in the highland plains, the *Nyika* lions invariably stay near the carcass to protect it from other intruders until they have consumed virtually all.

The *Nyika* also supports a large variety of birds. Many *Nyika* birds (e.g. hornbills) nest on the baobab trees. Birds of prey such as goshawks and the larger eagles (e.g. bateleur) usually nest in the higher parts of the baobabs. At the tips of the baobab branches are built the buffalo weaver-bird nests, which are so delicately balanced as to be inaccessible to all possible predators, including man. These nests are occupied by the buffalo weavers during the rains, and offer favourable shelter to birds such as the superb starling (*Spreo superbus*) and the pygmy falcon.

Many inselbergs occur in the thornbush and thicket belt. At the feet of these hills are found disorderly masses of fallen rocks and boulders. These form excellent habitats for rock hyraxes (e.g. *Heterohyrax brucei* and *H. procavia*). Being very adaptable animals, they live in habitats ranging from sea-level to 15 500 feet (4 712 m) above sea-level. Rock (and other) hyraxes are near-ungulates. They belong to the mammalian order *Hyracoidea*, of the super-order *Paenungulata*. Because the next order in this super-order is the *Proboscoidea* to which the elephant belongs, the hyrax (which weighs only about 2 pounds–1 kg) is the closest relative to the gigantic elephant. Both inhabit the *Nyika*, where the hyraxes are capable of living without water for considerable periods. Many birds of prey and some of the carnivorous animals feed on hyraxes. The latter are also found living deep in the desert.

Much of northern Kenya is semi-desert and, in a few places, desert. The desiccated area is bounded in the south by both the Kenya highlands and river Tana. The latter is a barrier to the southward migration of some of the animal species. Except towards the north-western Sudanese border, which is more associated with the west African faunal zone, (Fig. 6.1, 6a), the remaining large area of northern Kenya has a variety of faunal species with affinities unique to themselves. Unlike the fauna of the north-western Sudanese border, the fauna of the remainder of northern Kenya is much more varied, hence richer, and has links with eastern and southern

Africa rather than western Africa.

The northern semi-arid and arid lands extend westwards, meeting the great Sudanese semi-arid belt along the Uganda escarpment (the watershed between the Nile Basin and the Rift Valley). Thus, there is a mingling of animals and plants typical of each of the two regions in this transitional zone. However, the small portion of the Sudanese belt in north-western Kenya, (Fig. 6.1, 6a), has fewer species of antelopes than the remainder of northern Kenya. While the north-western part of Kenya shares some faunal species with northern Kenya, several species of animals in this corner of Kenya are only found in the western parts of Africa. Thus, this small Sudanese belt in north-west Kenya has no zebras, although it has other species of gazelle such as dorcas, dama and red-fronted gazelles. The hilly areas are excellent habitats for kudus.

Common in northern Kenya are Grevy's zebras (*Equus grevyi*). They are larger than Burchell's zebras (*Equus burchelli*) and have no stripes on the under-belly.[1] Unlike Burchell's zebras, Grevy's zebras do well even by eating only a little dry grass, and are not so dependent on water. Hunter's hartebeest (*Damaliscus hunteri*) and topi (*Damaliscus korrigum*[2]), which are often found in company, are both grazers sometimes found in certain parts of northern Kenya. In this area, all the grazing animals roam in search of food, since the carrying capacity of the area is low. Thus, the concentration of Grant's gazelle, Grevy's zebra and beisa oryx in northern Kenya, which seems to suggest a high grazing potential of this area, is misleading, because these animals tend to converge on different regions which are temporarily the most favourable.

In northern Kenya, a short wet period results in vigorous plant growth. This attracts birds which may consequently breed in such temporarily favourable areas. Slightly higher rainfall results in an outburst of breeding activity in birds, especially weaver birds which nest and breed their young in the acacias. The abundant seeds from a variety of local annual grasses provide food for the following dry season for weavers, guinea fowl, francolin and other birds.

Because much of the semi-arid northern part of Kenya is characterised by bushes and acacia trees (and in drier areas by scrub and shrub), grazing animals are relatively less common: hence the dominance of browsing animals, such as reticulated giraffe (*Giraffa reticulata*), gerenuk (*Litocranius walleri*), and dikdik species (*Rhynchotragus*). In the relatively wetter southern part of northern Kenya elephant and rhinoceros are commoner, especially near rivers during the drier part of the year.

In general, this dry belt does nevertheless support an immense variety of both grazing and browsing animals, on which such animals as lions and cheetahs prey. Lions usually stay in thick bush near the rivers and prey on the larger animals, whereas cheetahs, which prefer either

[1] See Macdonald (1965).
[2] Topi (*Damaliscus korrigum jimela*).

Fig. 6D Cheetah *(Acinonyx jubatus)*

light bushland or the open plains, prey mainly on gazelles. The various birds of prey which inhabit this belt range from the pygmy falcon (*Polohierax semitorquatus*) to the huge vulture (*Torgos tracheliotus*). Hawks, eagles and vultures prey on a wide variety of organisms ranging from insects to the carcasses of large animals.

This is one of the key belts for desert locusts (*Schistocerca gregaria*). Because of modern research and better methods of locust control, most of the area is now spared the locust ravages of the recent past. The regular ravages interfered with agricultural and pastoral activities in the better watered areas such as the river valleys and the highland enclaves, and even the greater part of

populated south-western Kenya. Apart from the inconvenience and great losses the locusts caused to man in his economic efforts, they also caused the deaths of thousands of herbivorous wild animals and the dependent carnivorous animals by eating considerable stretches of the vegetation, especially the grasses, on which the browsing and grazing animals depend.

To the north-west of this dry belt is a portion of the Rift Valley on whose floor is located Lake Rudolf. This lake, about 150 miles (241 km) long and about 20 miles (32 km) wide, was formerly much deeper and covered a much bigger area, and drained through a gorge at its north-western shore into the Nile. Consequently, it was invaded by fish from the Nile. While no longer draining into the Nile, Lake Rudolf still remains an excellent habitat for the Nilotic fish fauna, the best example being the Nile perch (*Tilapia nilotica*). The lake also abounds in crocodiles, which thrive here unmolested for their skins, as these are commercially valueless, because they are covered with 'buttons', due perhaps to the alkalinity of the water. There are also many ducks and geese on the lake shores, and some big white pelicans (*Pelecanus onocrotalus*) in shallow lagoons along the shores. Like crocodiles, pelicans feed on fish. The lake is also a focus for many species of other birds. For instance, on a small volcanic island in the lake, there is a crater with a small lake where lesser flamingoes (*Phoeniconaias minor*) breed. On the other islands are to be found large breeding colonies of spoonbills (*Platalea alba*), ibis (especially *Threskiornis aethiopicus*), herons, (e.g. *Ardea goliath*, etc) and cormorants (e.g. *Phalacrocorax africanus*).

In this belt – dry and rough as it is and apparently unfavourable for dense abundant life – even human beings are migratory livestock herdsmen living in close association with wildlife. Thus lions prey on domestic animals, whilst vultures and hyenas scavenge in the

Fig. 6E White pelicans

96

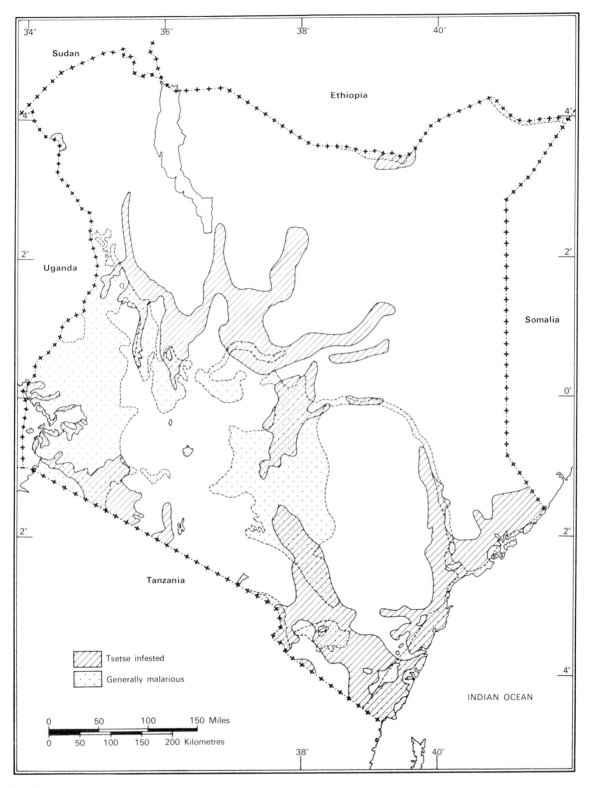

Fig. 6.2 Tsetse-malaria distribution

34°   36°   38°   40°

Sudan

Ethiopia

4°

2°

Uganda

Somalia

0°

2°

Tanzania

2°

Tsetse infested

Generally malarious

0   50   100   150 Miles

0   50   100   150   200 Kilometres

4°

INDIAN OCEAN

38°   40°

vicinities of the temporary human habitations.

The forests that often adorn the mountains located in this belt (Fig. 5.1, especially 1a), consist of cedar and podocarpus trees, beneath which are found, growing from the forest floor, grasses and green glades. These are the grazing grounds for buffaloes and bushbuck. During dry seasons some of the animals from the dry lowlands, such as elephants, migrate to these highland forests.

Distribution of Malarious Mosquitoes and the Tsetse Flies

The accompanying map (Fig. 6.2)[1] shows the distribution of the malaria-spreading mosquitoes, (i.e. various species of *Anopheles*), and a composite pattern of a variety of tsetse flies. The coastal tsetse fly belt, which extends inland for a considerable distance, includes several species, especially the human and animal disease carrying *Glossina pallidipes* which occupy large parts of this belt, and the animal disease propagating *G. longipennis*, *G. austeni* and some sparsely distributed *G. brevipalpis*. In the Embu-Meru area to the east of Mt Kenya, the main tsetse fly species are *G. pallidipes* and *G. longipennis*. Much of northern Kenya appears to be tsetse fly free, although small patches are suspected to contain *G. longipennis* and some *G. pallidipes*, the latter especially to the north and north-east of Kitale and east of the Kapenguria-Eldoret belt. The small isolated boundary patch west of Lake Rudolf harbours the human and animal disease propagating *Glossina morsitans*. Around the Nyanza Gulf, to the north and south, the common tsetse fly species is the human and animal disease carrying type *G. palpalis*, reinforced both to the north and south of the gulf in certain areas by *G. pallidipes*. There are also some animal infecting *G. brevipalpis*. In the Masai area, *G. longipennis* occur in the Amboseli boundary area north of Mt Kilimanjaro. The species is also found in association with *G. pallidipes* immediately west of Lake Magadi. Farther to the west between rivers Kuja and Ewaso Ngiro, the predominant tsetse fly species affecting both humans and animals are *G. pallidipes* and *G. swynnertoni*, but some *G. palpalis* also exist in the extreme west of this belt. There are also some *G. brevipalpis* and another animal infecting fly *G. fulcipleuris* in this area.

The distribution of malaria carrying species of *Anopheles* coincides mainly with the lower areas. Thus, most parts of the highlands are malaria-free. Owing to lack of water for long periods in much of northern and the greater part of eastern Kenya, these areas are also practically free of malaria. During prolonged rainy seasons, however, even these areas become malarious. The map (Fig. 6.2) shows heavy mosquito infestation in Lake Victoria Basin and the area north of it. There is a further malaria belt east of the highlands running from Meru in the north to Taveta in the south. Narrow malarious belts run along both the coastal zone and river Tana. Between the Lake Victoria malaria belt and the eastern Meru-Taveta belt, there is a discontinuous east-west malaria zone north of the highlands, especially along rivers and to the north-west and east of and around Lake Baringo.

References

Atlas of Kenya, Govt Printer, Nairobi, 1962.

BEAUFORT, DE L. F. *Zoogeography of the Land and Inland Waters*, Sidgwick and Jackson, 1951.

BROWN, L. H. *Africa: A Natural History*, Random House, N.Y., 1965.

BURTON, M. *Systematic Dictionary of Mammals of the World*, Museum Press, London, 1962.

COE, M. J. 'The ecology of the alpine zone of Mount Kenya', Junk, Hague, 1967.

GEORGE, W. *Animal Geography*, Heinemann, 1963.

HARRISON, D. L. 'A check-list of the bats of Kenya', *Jnl. of Nat. Hist. Soc.*, Vol. 23, No. 7 (104), Dec. 1960.

HICKLING, C. F. *Tropical Inland Fisheries*, Longman, 1961.

JORDAAN, J. J. and KIRSTEN, L. *Juta's New Biology*, Juta Co. Ltd., Johannesburg, 1951.

MACDONALD, M. *Treasure of Kenya*, Collins, 1965.

MORGAN, W. T. W. *East Africa*, Oxford Univ. Press, 1969.

NEWBIGIN, M. I. *Plant and Animal Geography*, Methuen, 1950.

PRATT, D. J. *et al.* 'A classification of East African rangeland', *Jnl. of Applied Ecology*, Vol. 3, 1966.

Report on Kenya Fisheries 1956-1970, Govt Printer, Nairobi, 1970.

Review of Kenya Fisheries 1946-1955, Govt Printer, Nairobi, 1955.

SIMPSON, G. G. 'The principles of classification and a classification of mammals', *Bull. Ameri. Mus. Nat. Hist.*, Vol. 85, No. 1, 1945.

[1] See *Atlas of Kenya* (1962).

Chapter 7
Ecological Regions

I General Comments

Kenya's main vegeto-ecological regions and their significant sub-divisions have been discussed in Chapters Five and Six. This chapter has as its aim the introduction of the major ecological regions and the associated smaller sub-divisions or ecological units, especially in the light of their utilisation for Kenya's economic development. A special map depicting Kenya's main ecological regions is included in Chapter Six (Fig. 6.1), and it is recommended that reference should also be made to the map showing Kenya's vegeto-ecological regions (Fig. 5.1). The latter indicates all the smaller sub-divisions which are termed ecological units in the current chapter.

Most of Kenya's principal plant communities are products of human influence, superimposed on the effects of climate, soil and animals (both wild and domesticated). Consequently, the present composition and appearance of the vegetation generally give a deceptive picture of possible climax vegetation under undisturbed conditions. Thus an effective ecological classification, in this case, should consist of a system of grouping which emphasises land potentiality, apart from utilising those criteria directly observable in the field.

When the major combinations of climate, soil and topography have been isolated and equated to the basic vegetation types, the resultant ecological units should be ideal. However, owing to lack of the relevant data, such perfect ecological units cannot be fully isolated. The best that can be done at the moment is to give a series of three broad ecological regions based on climate. As a first step towards such sub-divisions, the following aspects deserve closer consideration:

a a distinction between soils of impeded drainage and those that drain freely;

b a more precise definition of climate;

c an extended series of sub-divisions based on soil-type and landform.

In the absence of better and more widely distributed climatic data over Kenya, full use should be made of the vegetation and the existing land-use data as indicators of the climatic conditions. These criteria, especially that of vegetation, can be valuable aids in the objective demarcation of climatic boundaries, provided that:

a it is accepted that vegetation and land-use patterns are true manifestations of total environmental conditions

and not just those of climate;

b sound ecological survey data are available.

In Kenya where the ecological significance of most vegetation types has received considerable attention – see for example Trapnell and Griffiths (1960) – there are few difficulties in applying the above approach.

For purposes of assessing the main problems associated with the development of Kenya's principal plant communities, it is essential to consider current land-use, its influence on vegetation, and the consequent effects of the modified vegetation cover on the associated soils. Since these problems have significant bearing on the corrective measures necessary to take against any impending or existing deterioration, they have important links with conservation, particularly with regard to the knowledge relating to the utilisation of Kenya's grass-land communities.

Given below are the three broad ecological regions of Kenya. These are further sub-divided into six smaller vegeto-ecological units.[1] The three ecological regions coincide with the major plant communities, namely:

a forest and allied communities,

b grassland communities, and

c semi-desert and desert communities.

The smaller sub-divisions or ecological units are portrayed in detail in the vegeto-ecological map (Fig. 5.1).[2] It is these smaller sub-divisions which are stressed in the treatment of Kenya's three principal ecological regions.

In the account which follows, regular reference is made to certain parts of Kenya such as: the Lake Victoria Basin; the Rift Valley and its immediately flanking highlands; the eastern Kenya highlands; the coastal region; and the semi-arid and arid northern, eastern and southern parts of Kenya. The Lake Victoria Basin is assumed to include Nyanza and Western provinces and Kericho District; the Rift Valley and its immediately flanking highlands comprise the existing Rift Valley Province excluding much of the northern half and Kericho District; the eastern Kenya highlands are here regarded as including most of Central Province and those relatively higher parts of both Kitui and Laikipia Districts; the coastal region is defined by the map portraying the main ecological regions (Fig. 6.1), which map also indicates

---

[1] See D. J. Pratt *et al.* (1966).

[2] Based on Edwards (1956).

Table 7.1 *Detailed vegeto-ecological classification*

Principal ecological regions	The six main vegeto-ecological regions	The applied ecological units derived from the six main vegeto-ecological units	Guiding remarks
A Forest and all the allied communities	1 Montane moorland and grassland 2 All forests and allied types and Montane *Acacia* Woodlands	i Mountain summit communities ii Highland a Forest(s) b Grassland(s) iii Coastal forests	Forests i Kikuyu grass zone ii Star grass zone Four forest types

B Grassland communities	3 Evergreen and semi-evergreen bushland, *Combretum* woodland and scattered-tree grassland
	
	4 Dry transitional *Combretum* scattered-tree grassland, upland *Acacia* woodland and several coastal varieties
		iv Low tree-High grass
		
		v Grouped-tree grassland
		
		vi Coastal woodland and scattered-tree grasslands:
		  a Lowland cultivated scattered-tree grassland
		  b Lowland dry forest on coral rag
		  c Lowland woodland
		  d Low moist scattered-tree grasslands
		vii a Scattered-tree grassland and open grassland
		    b Scattered-tree grassland and open grassland
		viii Scattered-tree grassland and open grassland (Coastal variety)
		ix a Sand beach and dune communities
		    b Pan and pond communities
			Combretum-Hyparrhenia (High-rainfall scattered-tree grassland)
			Combretum-Hyparrhenia (impeded drainage varieties)
			
			Manilkara-Dalbergal Hyparrhenia
			Combretum schumannii-Cassipourea
			Brachystegia-Afzelia
			i *Afzelia-Albizia*, and
			ii *Ozoroa-Anona*
			Acacia-Themeda (proper)
			
			Sub-type mainly of the *Tarchonanthus-Cynodon* association
			Acacia-Themeda (and allied types)

C Semi-desert and desert communities	5 Thorn-bush and thicket
	
	6 Desert vegetation
		x a Acacia-thornbush (Coast)
		  b Dry bush with trees (Desert grass-bush extending to parts of the coast)
		  c Desert scrub (extending to parts of the coast)
		xi Desert scrub and grass
			Acacia-Euphorbia
			Commiphora-Acacia
			
			Scrub *Commiphora-Acacia*
			
			Found in patches of true desert in northern Kenya

the extent of the semi-arid and arid northern, eastern and southern parts of Kenya.

It is worthwhile at this point to comment on certain specific ecological characteristics relating especially to agricultural land utilisation, before we proceed to further treatment of the ecological units making up the three principal regions tabulated above.

In the Lake Victoria Basin of Nyanza and Western Provinces, the ecological units differ from one another less sharply than those of both the Rift Valley and the eastern Kenya highlands.[1] Thus in the Lake Basin, there is not such a regular succession of the ecological units from one to the other as is the case in the Rift Valley and the eastern Kenya highlands. Moreover, the greater part of Lake Victoria Basin is of high agricultural potential, so that only relatively small areas (such as those around the shores of Lake Victoria) can be regarded as marginal for agricultural purposes. However, even these marginal areas have far higher potential than their counterparts in the Rift Valley, the eastern Kenya highlands and on the coast. For many years, the agricultural potential of Lake Victoria Basin has been underestimated and should now receive closer attention.

It is not possible to use a single factor for estimating the crop potential of an ecological unit, since the association of animals and plants occupying a given area depends on the interaction of rainfall, temperature, soil, water conditions and many other factors. Apart from its use as a rough guide, altitude is meaningless, as the only effect of variations in height is the alteration of the amount of free oxygen in the atmosphere. Thus all kinds of plant species may become dominant under apparently widely differing conditions. Rainfall by itself, for instance may be misleading, because 45 inches (1 143 mm) of rainfall in Lake Victoria Basin produces a different type of vegetation from that produced by the same amount of rainfall in the Rift Valley, Central and Eastern Provinces. Given any ecological unit in Kenya, it should be possible to deduce the cropping potentiality (or capacity) of the land as follows:

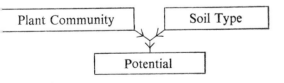

The plant community is by far the more important of the two main factors. From the agricultural point of view, the shrubs and grasses are the most important members of the plant community because they exert the greatest influence. Trees are often able to grow in areas which, though dry on the surface, have deep water supplies accessible to their deep roots. This is one major reason why certain areas may have the same dominant tree species but different grasses growing in association. It is the grasses, in such instances, which are our best indicators of the land potential. The Lake Victoria Basin is a good example, where *Combretum binderianum*[1] occurs over wide areas of the various types of scattered-tree grassland, either as a dominant or as a co-dominant and in association with *Cymbopogon afronardus*[2] and several species of *Hyparrhenia*.[3] Likewise, *Vernonia*[4] grows in both star grass and Kikuyu grass zones. It is significant to bear in mind also that the same tree could grow satisfactorily in a variety of soils. In many such instances, the value of soils may be more as an indicator of minor fertility and textural differences within a wide area. It is even possible to find a very similar vegetative association growing on granitic and volcanic soils adjacent to each other. However, whilst the plant community is the more reliable indicator of the ecological conditions, it should be considered together with the soil type in assessing cropping capacity.

Reference has already been made to the ecological sub-units termed Kikuyu and star grass zones. Opinions of specialists differ slightly as to the virgin vegetations from which these grasses derived as a consequence of man's influence. Indications are that they were derived from either a forest of *Acacia abyssinica-Vernonia-Hyparrhenia cymbaria* associations, or a mixed evergreen forest or a type of *Acacia*[5]-*Hyparrhenia cymbaria* bush (as still occurs in parts of Kericho. Nandi and Sotik). In calling the zones star grass or Kikuyu grass we are referring to man-made communities rather than the original vegetation type. In large areas of the high-rainfall scattered-tree grassland, however, the natural climax occurs much closer to the original state, though influenced by man's burning activities. If fires could be stopped altogether, tree growth would thicken and large areas of the existing grassland would, perhaps, in time be covered with deciduous forest of the type found on the Nandi and Belgut escarpments.

Certain plants are good indicators of local conditions, whilst others are not. In the Lake Victoria Basin, the grass *Loudetia kagerensis*[6] is mostly dominant where there is a hard pan (of either impervious clay, murram or solid rock) a few inches below the surface. Red oat grass (*Themeda triandra*),[7] which often grows in association with *Loudetia kagerensis*, however, merely indicates that the area in question is set on fire from time to time. Red oat grass is a deceptive indicator of the effective cropping rainfall and land potential, since it is found thriving in areas where rainfall varies from 17 to 60 inches (432 to 1 524 mm), and on many differing soil types. Of the various *Hyparrhenia* species, however, *Hyparrhenia cymbaria* indicates the wettest conditions, whereas

---

[1] See Brown (1960).

[1] Synonym: *Combretum populifolium* (Luo: *Keyo*).
[2] *Osinde/Olenge* (Luo).
[3] *Oboro* (Luo).
[4] More than nine species of *Vernonia*.
[5] Perhaps *Acacia lahai*.
[6] *Buoye* (Luo).
[7] *Akwaro* (Luo).

Hyparrhenia filipendula occurs in the driest area. This succession is well represented in the plains below Meru township.

Although animals are poorer indicators of ecological conditions than plants, some species of birds have a comparatively narrow ecological range. However, in the Lake Victoria Basin, bird species which in the eastern highlands would normally be found in semi-arid conditions occur in areas with relatively higher rainfall. Thus they appear to indicate a *relative* succession of climatic conditions more than an *actual* plant succession. A weaver bird known as the red-backed *Anaplectes* (*A. melanotis*) is a simple example of an animal indicator. In the eastern highlands, it inhabits a belt of country where cultivation is marginal or difficult, whereas in the Lake Victoria Basin, it occurs in the lakeshore scattered-tree grassland and the less favourable fringes of the high-rainfall scattered-tree grassland.

It is, perhaps, important to observe here that, although ecology could be used as a basis on which to found agricultural policy, it should not be carried too far. Many of the obvious though unproven associations of plants or animals (such as that between *Coffee arabica* and the Mukumari ·tree *Cordia africaa*[1]) should be regarded rather as weak indicators until more intensive ecological studies have been concluded. What now follows should therefore be regarded only as a rough guide.

II The Ecological Regions and their Economic Potentiality

Forest and all the Allied Communities

Montane moorland and grassland
This is equivalent to the mountain summit communities (Fig. 5.1), also referred to as Afro-Alpine moorland and grassland. It occurs at high altitudes, usually above the forest line, especially in the Rift Valley flanking highlands. However, the high bracken zone on both Mt Kenya and the Aberdares sometimes includes a narrow belt just below the upper forest edge, depending on aspect. The zone is characterised by poor, light, powdery, acidic soil, high rainfall and cold conditions which reduce growth rate. The major controlling factor here is altitude rather than water supply. The normal vegetation consists of bracken and *Triumfetta* bush. In the Aberdares and Mt Kenya areas certain limited parts of the zone support shifting cultivation. There are poor grasses the most prominent of which are *Paspalum scrobiculatum* and a type of couch grass. Kikuyu grass does not thrive at this altitude except under conditions of local fertility. In the Rift Valley flanking highlands, the zone may be used for cattle and sheep ranching. In general, this ecological unit does not appear particularly useful for future development. Those areas suitable for afforestation may, in future, be planted with exotic softwood trees for timber.

All forests and the allied types including montane Acacia woodlands: highland forest/grassland
It was observed earlier that the Kikuyu and star grass zones were perhaps derived from either a forest of *Acacia abyssinica-Vernonia-Hyparrhenia cymbaria* association, or a mixed evergreen forest, or a type of *Acacia lahai-Hyparrhenia cymbaria* bush. The two zones are found in the higher parts of the coastal region (e.g. the Taita Hills), Lake Victoria Basin (in Western Province, Kisii and Kericho-Nandi areas), in the other Rift Valley flanking highlands and in the eastern highlands in Central and parts of Eastern Provinces. In the Lake Victoria Basin, both Kikuyu and star grasses occur together, although at higher altitudes Kikuyu grass becomes dominant. At lower altitudes, it is star grass which dominates. It is incorrect, however, to regard the Kikuyu and star grass zones as always coincidental or even the same. Coffee can be grown, for instance, throughout the star grass zone, although not in the upper more acid parts of the Kikuyu grass zone. In the eastern highlands and the Rift Valley flanking highlands, the Kikuyu grass zone lies typically between 5 500 and 6 500 feet (1 672 and 1 976 m) above sea level, although lower on Mt Kenya. It is heavily populated in parts, but there are large areas of bracken and bush interspersed with patches of poor arable land and belts of grazing land dominated by Kikuyu grass. Throughout Kenya, star grass areas are the most productive and therefore relatively the most populous rural areas. Within the star grass zone, various species of star grasses grow forming excellent pasture for livestock. The star grasses are gradually replaced by Kikuyu grass on the upper fringe and by Guinea grass (*Panicum maximum*) and *Hyparrhenia* species on the lower fringe. The latter fringe probably marks the lower limit of forest within recent times. The star grass zone is heavily cultivated and the areas under cultivation are often re-colonized by the characteristic shrubby bushes including *Lippia* and *Vernonia*, and herbs such as *Wedelia*, *Lantana* and other allied species. A common feature of the star grass zone is the dominance of agriculturally useless tall grasses such as the many species of *Cymbopogon*.

The Kikuyu and star grass zones lie within the highland forest/grassland ecological unit. In many parts of this unit, there still exist natural forests and cultivated forests consisting of exotic softwood trees. The distribution and significance of these forests are discussed later.[1]

The highland forest/grassland ecological unit is generally the agricultural heartland of Kenya. Much that applies to this ecological unit is, to some extent, also true of the *Combretum-Hyparrhenia* scattered-tree grassland (sometimes vaguely referred to as high-rainfall savannah[2]). The highland forest/grassland unit supports large populations based on subsistence agriculture. However, it also supports some of the most important

---

[1] Synonym: *Cordia holstii*.

[1] See also Ogendo (1966).
[2] 'Savannah' is a word to be avoided.

commercial agricultural undertakings in Africa south of the Sahara. The commercial farming carried out here consists partly of extensive ranches, especially in the drier areas (which include the *Combretum-Hyparrhenia* unit), and partly of relatively large farms for cash-crop production, especially in the higher rainfall Kikuyu and star grass zones.

In parts of this ecological unit, soil erosion has precipitated acute conservation problems. Some of the major factors underlying this damage have been intense population pressure on the land, unsuitable methods of agriculture associated with shifting cultivation, sheer carelessness in matters of soil management, and overstocking. In recent years, however, the practice of shifting cultivation has decreased mainly because of shortage of arable agricultural land, but also because of the publicity given to new (though still unexploited) agricultural methods. Consequently, these high rainfall areas have become centres of more stable agriculture with relatively intensive food and cash-crop production, but still with the shortcoming that only slight changes in the original agricultural methods have been assimilated. This new development has destroyed the old ecological balance, which formerly stabilised the human and animal populations, on the one hand, and the vegetation and soils on the other. Furthermore the higher human population densities in the moister areas have resulted in the temptation for the agricultural and semi-agricultural ethnic groups to expand into areas ecologically unsuitable for such demanding agricultural activities. Thus, unfortunately, the destruction of vegetation and the associated soils has been hastened.

Perhaps such surplus populations could usefully be diverted to the new industries whose potential in the high rainfall areas is assured. Kenya's major agricultural policy priorities in the future should be better agricultural methods of land-use and larger holdings. In order to halt soil deterioration, the former bush fallow must be replaced with useful temporary grasses aimed at assisting in the maintenance of soil-water relations, since the effect of water shortage on plant growth (especially crop production) is very marked in Kenya, where the rate of evaporation is accelerated by the relatively higher temperatures.[1] In arable rotation the use of temporary pasture cover would help the soil to recover and attain a good structure. There are several areas in the highland forest/grassland ecological unit, where the characteristics of the terrain together with inadequate water supplies restrict arable agriculture. In such areas, special management of the existing natural grassland is of great importance. Indeed, at the current stage of agricultural development in this ecological unit, the main part of the vegetation consists of natural grassland under extensive (hence light) utilisation.

The chief problem of management in the highland forest/grassland community consists in preventing the advance of mediocre coarse-grass stage dominated by wire grass *(Pennisetum schimperi)* both within the main community and in the vast transitional belt. In the area of the typical community, the preservation of a rich Kikuyu grass-clover sward requires carefully controlled intensive management. In the transitional zone, periodical burning of the herbage usually discourages the coarse-grass stage while promoting the dominance of the useful red oat grass *(Themeda triandra)*. This comparatively moist ecological unit is suitable for a more intensive form of agricultural practice, and its development to the full remains an important future priority.

Coastal forests[1]
This composite ecological unit consists of four subunits:

a lowland rain forest *(Sterculia-Chlorophora/Memecylon)*;
b lowland dry forest *(Manilkara-Diospyros)*;
c lowland dry forest *(Cynometra-Manilkara* Sokoke*)*;
d mangrove swamps and saline margins.

Lowland rainforest (Sterculia-Chlorophora/Memecylon)
The soils associated with this forest are varied, being derived from dune and alluvial sands, the Shimba grits and the 'lagoonal' and wind-blown sands. They are mainly classed as yellow-red loamy sands with a laterite horizon. These soils are generally infertile and may not be successfully cropped for more than a few years after forest clearance without heavy applications of fertiliser. As an exception, the Kambe limestone terra rossa soil is amongst the most fertile soils under natural conditions at the coast. Where this soil occurs, it forms an area of expanding agricultural development, particularly for citrus and coconut cultivation.

In this forest belt, there are three important areas, namely:

a the Kayas which is dependent on the Kambe limestones;
b the Mrima-Jombo volcanic complex of the Ramisi valley; and
c the Sabaki valley.

These three are areas with high potential for agricultural development, and considerable progress is being made there. The cotton crop in the Sabaki valley can be expanded and improved, as can the production of other crops in the Chonyi-Jibana and the Ramisi areas. Unfortunately, owing to the longer wet season which limits cotton ripening and increases the probability of disease, cotton does poorly in the southern districts. However, intensive cultivation of many subsistence crops besides cash crops (such as chillies, cashew nuts, etc.) can be increased in the southern districts, especially downstream and in areas with volcanic soils.

Assumptions about the agricultural development of the rainforest association are based on the fact that timber production is not the most prominent output of the zone. Present timber stands are thin and logging on a

[1] See Woodhead (1968).

[2] See Moomaw (1960).

103

commercial basis has consequently become an expensive undertaking. The only successful and expanding coastal primary agricultural industry is that based on the sugar plantation which is located especially in the southern part of this zone. Sisal is also grown, although high productivity can only be maintained if the crop is not allowed to suffer from the vigorous competition of the shrubs and grasses. Although pineapples can easily be grown, the product is of relatively low quality and not adequately uniform to facilitate mechanised packing. As with so many others of the potential coastal cash-crops, the major limiting factor in the production of high quality crops is the limited industry of the peasant farmer. The latter must endeavour to produce high quality products before a highly developed peasant agriculture can be realised.

Lowland dry forest (Manilkara-Diospyros) This ecological sub-unit is marginal for agricultural purposes, although it has been cropped for a considerable period. South of the Sabaki river it is cropped almost entirely on a shifting cultivation basis, whilst north of the river rapid destruction of the forest is allowing cultivation to be extended into areas without permanent water. In the Boni forest, the shifting cultivation process is of even longer standing, and burning of the forest appears to have been by game and honey hunters rather than by cultivators.

The real danger in the cultivation of this vegetation type lies not so much in possible soil erosion hazards or even in the drying of the general environment, but rather in the possibility that a drought of long duration could lead to starvation or at least the displacement of a large segment of the population. The area involved lies below the 30% rainfall probability isoline for 20 inches (508 mm) so that fewer than 20 inches (508 mm) of precipitation can be expected in three years out of ten. This makes the area a risky proposition even for long-rain maize.

As the rainfall is unreliable, and the original forest and bush vegetation is unproductive and supports little wildlife, it seems advisable to investigate further the grazing potential of this ecological sub-unit. Although our specific knowledge about plant succession (after fire has destroyed parts of this sub-unit) is limited at present it seems that the *Manilkara-Diospyros* association, in its closed form, is quite resistant to fire because it has sparse understory with little inflammable herbaceous material to support fire. Whatever small success is achieved, the best time for firing is during the dry season.

Under this plant association, the soils are mainly coastal sands. Evidence exists that the association is favoured by impeded drainage. Thus, the soils are generally seasonally waterlogged and seem to have high contents of magnesium and calcium.

The forage production that can be attained in the *Manilkara-Diospyros* association with the application of management techniques is to be seen at the Mariakani Livestock Breeding Centre. Here, a pasture has been developed and consists of a number of important grasses.[1] Since 1951 this pasture has been adapted, from a dense *acacia*-thornbush land which was probably invaded due to overgrazing, to a carrying capacity of one beast per four acres (1·6 hectares). The technique has been to use heavy seasonal grazing with supplemental irrigated forage for the dry season, and to follow a programme of manual control of the invading shrubby species. The grass *Panicum maximum* has been increasing, and this is likely to enhance the carrying capacity of the pasture in time. *Cynodon* has also multiplied in areas of heavy use, especially those around water supplies.

The general estimate for the carrying capacity of the surrounding country is approximately one beast per 20–30 acres (8–12 hectares), and in most of the Mariakani areas it is probably much less now. This method cannot be applied universally, although it presents a good example of what can be achieved. Less expensive yet highly efficient methods of bush control must be devised for large areas. The control of livestock numbers and their movement can achieve a three- to four-fold increase in the productivity of the natural pastures of the area without re-seeding once the removal of the bush has been effected.

Lowland dry forest (Cynometra-Manilkara: Sokoke) This ecological sub-unit known as the Sokoke forest community is essentially confined to the Magarini sandy soils or dark loamy sands (latosolic-soils), although some similar development is also evident on soils developed from windblown materials. These soils are extremely infertile, probably excessively drained and laterised throughout the profile. They have the dark red colour of latosolic soils. Fertiliser responses to phosphorus and manure are usual, depending on the crop.

Since 1920, the Sokoke forest community has been exploited for its muhuhu *(Brachylaena hutchinsii),* mugambo *(Manilkara sp.),* and mbombakofi *(Afzelia quanzensis).* Because of negligible planned utilisation or sustained-yield development of the timber, the economic tree species are almost depleted. Thus, sawn timber is becoming more difficult to find, and the resultant output is of poor quality.

The forest does not burn readily and has been relatively well protected from agricultural clearings except on the eastern slopes of the Magarini ridge outside the forest. The forest supports a considerable population of wild animals such as small elephants and buffaloes.

The low productivity of the site of the sub-unit has been adequately tested by the Matuga and Jilore agricultural experimental stations (with mean annual rainfalls of 38·0 inches (965 mm) and 41·0 inches (1 041 mm) respectively). The general nitrogen and phosphorus deficiency can be corrected by applying double super-

---

[1] For example, *Digitaria milinjana, Eragrostis superba, Chloris gayana, Chloris myriostachya, Bothriochloa insculpta, Enteropogon* species and *Cynodon dactylon.*

phosphate. Pulses and sweet potatoes do better with farmyard or green manure than with the phosphate fertiliser. Because of the poor response, cassava cultivation is uneconomic, but tree crops, especially cashews, do fairly well, although citrus fruits such as lime and grapefruit need irrigation. Coconuts do not grow well but groundnuts do, especially in response to fertiliser. On the less fertile soils of the Shimba hills and Duruma sandstones, chillies grow quite well. Sisal is successful as a plantation crop, but pineapples are of poor quality. Most vegetable crops do not seem to survive here. Annatto *(Bixa orellana)*[1] shrub (simply known at the coast as *Bixa*) is successfully cultivated and has a promising future.

Mangrove swamps and saline margins This area has not received closer attention here because it is of little agricultural significance. However, it is of considerable interest to foresters and ecologists. The *Rhizophoraceae* trees such as msindi *(Bruguiera gymnorrhiza)*, mkandaa *(Ceriops tagal)* and mkoko *(Rhizophora mucronata)* thrive in this ecological sub-unit. Msindi has up to 53% tannin in its bark, mkandaa 24–42% and mkoko 12–50%.[2] Mkoko was formerly exploited for the tannin, and is still economically valuable because it produces the best building poles (boriti) used both at the coast and in the Middle East (especially in southern Arabia and the Persian Gulf). The coast supplies the Middle Eastern countries through the dhow export trade.

The soils on the flats on the landward margins of the mangrove thickets are compact lacustrine or lagoonal clays. They are of little use for agricultural purposes except in the areas of rich cultivation along the Tana and Umba rivers.

Grassland Communities

Evergreen and semi-evergreen bushland, Combretum woodland and scattered-tree grassland

Low tree-high grass (Combretum-Hyparrhenia) This is the ecological unit often loosely referred to as high-rainfall savannah, although it is properly known as the *Combretum-Hyparrhenia* scattered-tree grassland. With certain exceptions, much that has been said about the highland forest/grassland ecological unit also applies to the *Combretum-Hyparrhenia* unit. The latter, however, experiences higher temperatures, and receives lower annual rainfalls, ranging from about 60 inches (1 524 mm) down to about 35 inches (889 mm), as compared with the higher annual rainfall range of about 90 inches (2 286 mm) to about 55 inches (1 397 mm) in the highland forest/grassland unit. It is the highland grassland portion of the latter unit which, because it receives an intermediate annual rainfall of never less than 40 inches (1 016 mm), compares more favourably with the high-rainfall parts of the *Combretum-Hyparrhenia* unit.

In the *Combretum-Hyparrhenia* scattered-tree grassland unit (especially those parts of it where relatively intensive agriculture is currently practised), the prevalent method of regular burning of the natural grassland to discourage the recolonisation of the man-made open grasslands should be replaced by better methods. Despite the higher temperatures and comparatively lower rainfall characteristics of this unit, the *Combretum-Hyparrhenia* association still provides suitable conditions for the successful introduction of temporary grass in the normal rotation associated with farming practice in these parts of Kenya. Furthermore, in order to encourage the growth of the more readily utilisable herbage species, the high-grass constituent of this unit could easily be suppressed by controlled use of fire, and by the introduction of both intensive natural grassland management and fencing.

The best example of the *Combretum-Hyparrhenia* unit is in the Lake Victoria Basin, where it occupies about 3 000 sq miles (7 770 km²). It is probably derived from an originally denser scattered-tree grassland type than exists nowadays. Although it has been modified in most parts of the basin by clearing, cultivation and by constant fires, it is much nearer the normal natural climax vegetation than either the star or Kikuyu grass vegetation types. The dominant trees are the various species of *Combretum, Bauhinia, Erythrina, Terminalia* and *Vitex,* whereas the most predominant grasses consist of the various species of *Cymbopogon*[1] and *Hyparrhenia.*[2] Other associated grasses are sword grass *(Imperata cylindrica)* and, in certain places, red oat grass *(Themeda triandra)*. The latter is not, however, a characteristic grass of this zone. Although much of the zone has considerable agricultural potential, it is inferior to the highland forest/grassland ecological unit. Consequently, it has attracted a thinner population. In fact, a proportion of it is useless for arable agriculture, because of the existence of either stones or murram from latosolisation. Much of the grassland is currently poor and coarse. However, the *Combretum-Hyparrhenia* ecological unit is capable of great development.

The grass woodland zone of the Rift Valley and the eastern highlands are transitional and not typical, and hence are discussed elsewhere (under *dry transitional Combretum scattered-tree grassland, etc.*).

Apart from the *Combretum-Hyparrhenia* unit of the Lake Victoria Basin, there are areas where the community has been modified mainly by impeded drainage or by seasonal swamps. These are briefly introduced below.

The impeded drainage sub-zones Poor drainage affects possibly 1 000 sq miles (2 590 km²) in the Lake Victoria Basin. Although the areas affected may have equally favourable rainfall to those already discussed above,

---

[1] See McIlroy (1963).
[2] See Dale and Greenway (1961).

[1] cf: *C. afronardus* and *C. validus.*
[2] cf: *H. Rufa* and *H. filipendula.*

they require a different treatment from that applicable in the mixed farming zones. In general, the impeded drainage sub-zones have small pockets of good arable land surrounded by large areas of land which are either completely useless or only of little use. The typical examples of such sub-zones are:

a Sotik vleiland,
b Butende and Trans-Mara grouped-tree grassland, and
c *Pennisetum catabasis* seasonal swamp area of south Nyanza.

In Butende, Trans-Mara and Sotik areas the impeded drainage is characterised by grouped-tree grassland vegetation. However, the final sub-zone is simply a grass plain dominated by *Pennisetum catabasis*.

Sotik vleiland consists of the Sotik Highlands and part of the Sotik division of Kipsigis. The hill pockets originally supported the *Acacia abyssinica-Hyparrhenia cymbaria* association. Indeed, parts of this can still be seen in Sotik, although it has been heavily cultivated in Kipsigis. Were this zone covered with thick free-draining soil, it would support cedar and olive forests similar to those of the Chepalungu area. However, owing to impeded drainage, the zone is characterised by groups of small trees perched on ant hills or hummocks with lower areas of relatively wet grassland between the tree clumps. The grasses are dominated by species of both *Setaria* and *Andropogon*, and by *Pennisetum catabasis* and *Exotheca abyssinica*. Some of the treeless hilltops are relatively stony and are favourable for grasses such as *Themeda triandra* and *Loudetia kagerensis*. The drainage difficulty is caused by a heavy impervious clay a few inches below the surface. At the present stage of technical development, this type of country has limited agricultural usefulness. Hilltops are poor and the flats have little value for stock rearing unless the drainage problem is solved.

In Butende and Trans-Mara country, about 150 to 200 sq miles (388·5 to 518·0 km²) to the Tanzanian border are involved. This area is similar to the Sotik vleiland type except that it is flatter with no sharp hills. The patches of potential arable land carry similar vegetation to that of the Sotik vleiland and occur on ridges where the soil is deeper. The impeded drainage conditions have resulted in grouped-tree grassland dominated by *Themeda triandra* and *Loudetia kagerensis*. This sub-zone is noted as an important stock country, with patches suitable for arable agriculture. In parts of this sub-zone, the impeded drainage is due to an impervious layer of clay, whilst in other parts it is caused by a murram layer. Somewhat similar impeded drainage conditions occur in the western parts of Western Province. These are, however, caused by murram below the surface.

The *Pennisetum catabasis* seasonal swamp country occurs over 400 sq miles (1 036·0 km²) in south Nyanza. It is a virtually treeless grass plain on black cotton soil, with an almost uniform association of *Pennisetum catabasis* and star grass, but with some couch grass. *Pennisetum catabasis* is relatively dominant. The impeded

drainage is caused by the soil type rather than by the presence of a hard pan just below the surface. This sub-zone differs from the other two in that it is probably cultivable and appears to have a high sugar cane production potential.

Coastal woodland and scattered-tree grasslands

Lowland cultivated scattered-tree grassland (Manilkara-Dalberga/Hyparrhenia) The shale soils underlying this vegetation type consist of brown clay (or grumosolic soils).[1] The brown clay develops a distinct calcium carbonate horizon. It is therefore in a lower effective moisture category than the neighbouring soils. The surface heavy clay is very slowly permeable to water once it is wetted. Moreover, it is quite easily eroded, and produces a high amount of run-off water. It is also of low to moderate fertility. An important factor which limits the cultivation of this soil is the high power requirement for cultivating it effectively. This involves work beyond what an individual can do without a plough, and this factor tends to overshadow the already confirmed reasonable productivity of the soil.

The scattered-tree grassland found on the shales supports goats and a few cattle. For the most part, surface water is unavailable except for springs at the boundary of the shales and the overlying materials. Cultivated pockets located within the area of this vegetation community are usually confined to the drainageways and valleys, where more water is available from both run-off and seepage. Consequently, this leads to the dense secondary bush in the drainageways and valleys, whenever cultivation is abandoned for some time.

Lowland dry forest on coral rag (Combretum schumanii-Cassipourea) This site is characterised by coral rag soils, which resemble the soils in the Kambe limestone area, except for the lower rainfall in the coral rag forest area.

When the forest is cleared, the characteristic and widespread coastal bush quickly dominates. This is the same dense thicket found both on the Kambe limestone soils in the rain forest and on the shale soils. It also occurs in the scattered-tree grassland formation at an early stage after cultivation.

Soil fertility in the lowland dry forest on coral rag is relatively high, and it has been used by indigenous cultivators for many years, even where the coral outcrops very near or at the surface. Maize, beans, cassava, and a wide variety of vegetable crops are raised with little effort. Moreover, the association provides one of the best sites for coconut growing.

Lowland woodland (Brachystegia-Afzelia) This community is an edaphic type and develops only on freely drained sands. Its climatic limits are consequently relatively broad, ranging from suitable areas with 25 inches (635 mm) to those with 40 inches (1 016 mm) of

[1] See Scott (1959).

rainfall. The soils under this community are deep, loose, light grey to buff, medium to coarse sands. They often exceed 10 feet (3·0 m) in depth, although in most situations there is evidence of groundwater at depth for part of the dry season. To the north of Kilifi district, this ecological sub-unit is normally confined to the stream bottoms, where the alluvial sands are deep. However, in the country south of Bamba, the sands overlie the fine-textured materials derived from the Mariakani and other sandstones; consequently, these finer materials develop an impervious layer. The sands are slightly acid and, being very infertile, are low in organic matter and easily eroded, especially where there is any slope. In parts of the Gotani area, for instance, a considerable depth of sands seems to have been eroded. In general, these soils have poor prospects for agricultural development, and are rarely cultivated by the local inhabitants.

After a fire, the understory of the community consists of solid grass (dominated mainly by *Digitaria mombasana* and a species of *Panicum*) which is considerably productive for grazing. However, stocking of the area should be kept much below the apparent carrying capacity, because of the danger of damage from trampling. In areas north of Gotani, it seems that even relatively light grazing is detrimental to the forage and only results in the exposure of loose sand. Lowland woodland is semi-tolerant of fire, although late burning may destroy it. Hence fire should be directed towards the preservation of the canopy of trees, whilst destroying the shrubby understory. This procedure allows the grasses to increase.

Low moist scattered-tree grasslands (Afzelia-Albizia and Ozoroa-Anona) Studies of a few stands in the *Afzelia-Albizia* and *Ozoroa-Anona* scattered-tree grasslands indicate that the forage production in one season lies between 10 and 15 tons per acre (25·1 and 37·7 tonnes per hectare), on a dry-weight basis. This amount of forage will provide one animal unit of grazing per acre (0·4 per hectare) per year, even if only utilised at 50 per cent by local cattle. Unfortunately, the entire association is heavily infested with tsetse fly, and the pronounced seasonal fluctuation in production limits the carrying capacity to a very low figure.

Because soil fertility is generally low, cultivation is intermittent and the population is sparse. In part this is the result of a high elephant population which damages cultivation. When the forest patches are cultivated, they quickly regenerate with shrubs and grasses which, if not burnt, soon return to forest. Parts of the more heavily forested areas are being cleared for plantations. Tree crops are especially well-adapted to the conditions prevailing in this area, although forestry is not as productive as might be expected. Coconut, citrus, cashew, mango and kapok are some of the many tree crops grown. It is possible, by means of fertilizers, to grow an additional range of cash and food crops.

Dry transitional Combretum scattered-tree grassland, upland Acacia woodland and coastal varieties

Scattered-tree grassland and open grassland The main ecological unit here is the *Acacia-Themeda* scattered-tree grassland which, in certain areas, is represented by or associated with open grassland. However, there is also a sub-type of the 'scattered-tree grassland and open grassland', which is essentially an association of the short tree *Tarchonanthus camphoratus* and species of star grass (*Cynodon*) popularly referred to as *Tarchonathus-Cynodon*. This ecological sub-unit is normally found in old lake beds, especially in the Rift Valley. The sub-unit consists of densely scattered bushes which are dominated by the Ol'leleshwa (*T. camphoratus*). The low trees and the bushes are in turn strongly dominated by the two species of star grass.[1] The low trees and bushes do not readily colonise the areas from which the existing lakes have recently receded. In such habitats, it is common to find almost pure stands of the two star grass species. The same star grasses are also common in favourable areas throughout the *Acacia-Themeda* community, especially along the margins of streams.

In the *Acacia-Themeda* unit proper, the chief constituents of the vegetation are very much influenced by both fire and impeded drainage. The wide areas of virtually open grassland (sometimes with thinly scattered dwarf *Acacia*) are mainly the result of impeded drainage. In such instances, the characteristic soil is the poor draining tropical black earth. However, the general dominance of the red oat grass (*Themeda-triandra*) in the community is due to the frequent fires, mostly started by the indigenous pastoralists who like this community best. It is these fires that discourage the recolonisation of parts of this ecological unit by the characteristic bushes and low trees.

The *Acacia-Themeda* community, on the average, receives relatively unreliable rainfall varying annually from about 20 to 30 inches (508 to 762 mm). It is normally suitable for light pastoral utilisation, except at its wetter transitional fringes with the higher rainfall communities, where limited arable agriculture may be practised. Although the greater part of this community is inhabited by subsistence pastoralists, commercial beef cattle ranching of considerable significance to Kenya's beef industry is already located here. The chief drawback of this ecological unit is its inadequate water supplies; thus the first signs of vegetation degeneration are usually noticeable near the perennial water supply points. The following are some useful lines of approach towards success in agriculture in the area covered by this community:

a the control of livestock numbers;

b increased and improved well-distributed water supplies; and

c the initiation of rotational land-use based on seasonal migrations from one part of the unit to the other.

[1] Namely *C. plectostachyus* and *C. dactylon*, the Naivasha star grass and the common star grass respectively.

Perhaps the discreet use of fire aimed at improving the red oat grass constituent of the community is to be recommended. Since the community is generally unsuitable for arable agriculture, the migration of crop-cultivating ethnic groups into the areas occupied by the community (owing to the population pressures and the resultant land hunger in the higher rainfall ecological units) should be discouraged.

Several significant differences in the various parts of this extensive community call for brief comments on the characteristics that typify the specific constituent parts. The latter include portions of the Lake Victoria Basin, the Rift Valley, the eastern highlands and the coastal region.

In the Lake Victoria Basin the relevant areas include the lakeshore scattered-tree grassland extending to the Kano plains. This area is not referred to as marginal for agriculture, since the rainfall is nowhere so low that cultivation under a reasonable agricultural system could be really precarious, as is the case in the drier parts of Kenya.

The lakeshore scattered-tree grassland (composed of *Acacia, Balanite, Combretum, Albizia, Euphorbia* and *Bothriochloa* of the various species) is somewhat similar to the eastern Kenya highlands scattered-tree grasslands in their potentiality. The dominant grasses are red oat grass *(Themeda triandra)* and sweet pitted grass (*Bothriochloa insculpta* and other *Bothriochloa* species). The stony grounds are dominated mostly by grasses such as sour grass *(Loudetia kagerensis)* and various species of *Hyparrhenia*. The major trees are various species of kudho *(Acacia)* and otho *(Balanites)*. There are patches where impeded drainage occurs in slight degree, and these (as is typical in Uyoma) are indicated by an association of the various species of the grass *Setaria* with *Acacia seyal*. The entire lakeshore zone has been considerably modified by man, especially through the use of fire. It is possible that it developed from patches of scrubby forest and dense bush interspersed with sections of open grassland.

With some care this zone can support a balanced agriculture, provided that the importance of fodder feeding is appreciated and allowed for by growing suitable fodder crops.

The Kano plains extension of the foregoing community experiences similar rainfall conditions, except that it has a variety of alluvial soils. It suffers from some impeded drainage, although this is not as severe as in the other areas of impeded drainage discussed earlier. This area has a very characteristic vegetation association in which large scattered otho *(Balanites)* and kudho (especially *Acacia seyal*) trees occur, along with sweet pitted grass,[1] red oat grass[2] and *Setaria sphacelata*. Parts of this area are swampy and/or subject to flooding by rivers. These conditions prevail also beyond the Kano plains in several places in the vicinity of the lakeshore

(cf: Lambwe valley in South Nyanza).

Because the impeded drainage in the Kano plains is not too severe in most places, practically the whole of this zone is cultivable. Indeed, the area has a high agricultural potential under irrigation, with rice as the most favourable crop. However, a farming system should be possible for the non-irrigable areas (similar to the lakeshore scattered-tree grassland zone examined earlier) with slight variations. In the two zones, the importance of fishing as a source of protein should be recognised.

The Rift Valley Masai grassland is also in this category. This is, in fact, a small corner of a much larger zone of country extending along the southern side of the Mau hills. The vegetation consists of *Acacia* and shrubs[3] with such grasses as star grass *(Cynodon dactylon)*, red oat grass, *Sporobolus fimbriatus* and various species of *Eragrostis, Bothriochloa* and *Digitaria*. The Masai grassland zone is marginal for arable agriculture and is good mainly for ranching (see further under *Commiphora-Acacia*).

In the eastern Kenya highlands are considerable areas of grass plains, and scattered-tree grassland or grass woodland. The communities cover most of the lower areas lying partly on metamorphic rocks and partly on both granitic and volcanic soils. Although there is considerable variation, much of this area usually lies below 4 500 feet (1 293 m) on gentle sloping land. There appear to be two main ecological extremes of the scattered-tree grassland, namely:

a an association of plants indicating a definite seasonality of rainfall, the characteristic plant association consisting of various species of trees[1] and grasses;[2]

b an association of plants indicating a very poor rainfall, possibly worse than that in the better parts of the *Acacia-Combretum* zone described below. This is the *Combretum-Themeda* association and appears to be sub-marginal especially for arable agriculture.

Considerable parts of the eastern highlands also support the *Acacia-Combretum* community. The soils found in this zone are derived from metamorphic rocks and are particularly important in Machakos and Kitui. The zone appears to have a lower water availability than the better parts of the above scattered-tree grassland zone. The latter merges with the *Acacia-Combretum* community very gradually where slopes are gentle. However, where the slopes are steep (such as near the base of hills), the two communities merge relatively suddenly. There are many minor ecological variations within the *Acacia-Combretum* zone among the tree and shrub growth. The grasses are the most useful climatic indicators here, and the typical species are the African fox tail *(Cenchrus ciliaris)*, *Eragrostis superba* and spear grass *(Heteropogon contortus)*. Although both red oat grass *(Themeda triandra)*[1] and Guinea grass *(Panicum*

---

[1] *Bothriochloa insculpta.*
[2] *Themeda triandra.*

[3] Mainly small tree species of *Olea* and *Acokanthera*.
[1] e.g. *Terminalia, Dombeya, Cussonia, Faurea, Combretum* and *Acacia*.
[2] *Hyparrhenia, Digitaria, Panicum* and *Themeda*.
[1] *Akwaro* (Luo).

maximum) also occur, they are not useful indicators.

What is now Machakos badlands was probably occupied by the *Acacia-Combretum* community at one time. At present this community affects a large number of people, and is notorious for semi-permanent famine problems. Only drought resisting crops do well here and irrigation would be a great relief, especially in parts of Kitui, since the annual rainfall range in this relatively hotter area is about 25 to 35 inches (635 to 889 mm).

Considerable parts of the coast region are also under scattered-tree grassland and open grassland (mainly *Acacia-Themeda* and allied types). In the main ecological unit, two factors exercise an important influence upon the chief vegetation constituents. The two factors are impeded drainage and fire. The former tends to inhibit tree growth and is probably responsible for the wide tracts of practically open grassland. The main soil type in such open grassland country is the tropical black earth found under conditions of seasonal flooding. Fire, on the other hand, is closely associated with the dominance of red oat grass *(Themeda triandra)* throughout the belt. This grass is effectively maintained by the frequent dry season fires, which have a marked effect in retarding the advance of tree and bush constituents. Broadly speaking, man, acting either as a cultivator or as a pastoralist, has been responsible for the fires, at least, in recent years. In the geological past, however, the fires were probably caused by volcanic activity.

Along the coast are found sand, beach and dune communities. As these communities do not furnish any agricultural potential, they are insignificant. However, some of the more stable ancient dunes are cultivated by the coastal peoples.

The pan and pond communities, on the other hand, furnish considerable grazing facilities during the dry season. They are also sometimes cultivated and planted with rice or other cereals.

Semi-desert and Desert Communities

Because true desert is relatively limited in Kenya, and also since desert ecology, as such, is insignificant for the present study, the account which follows is wholly confined to one of the two ecological regions, namely: the thorn-bush and thicket zone. Thus only the semi-desert parts of the above communities are examined.

Thorn-bush and thicket
This zone consists of three ecological units:
a acacia-thornbush *(Acacia-Euphorbia)*;
b dry bush with trees *(Commiphora-Acacia)*; and
c desert scrub (scrub *Commiphora-Acacia*).

In the following discussion, the above three units are first examined together except where special differential treatment is essential. The individual units are then introduced after the general treatment.

Semi-desert vegetation occupies about two-thirds of Kenya. In this vast area, the rainfall is usually less than 25 inches (655 mm) and unreliable. Consequently, the high temperatures cause very rapid evaporation.[1] These areas are mostly occupied by the nomadic pastoral peoples. Although the mode of land-use and the resultant effects are akin to those in the *Acacia-Themeda* areas, the paucity of water supplies is greater, thus producing more marked effects, especially where animals concentrate near the permanent water supply points.

In areas remote from water, and these are practically negative for the customary land-use practised in the neighbouring ecological zones, the vegetation cover is inadequate to stop wind erosion. Moreover, under such desiccating atmospheric conditions the more obvious instability which characterises the vegetation and soil relationship is prone to be tipped on the side of deterioration. It is this delicate balance, which is easily upset if there is any slight concentration of the ungulates in such areas, that should be improved substantially where possible, or, at least, maintained.

Apart from improving both the distribution and output of the permanent water supply points, better utilisation calls for a carefully controlled population of the animals which inhabit these areas, particularly the domestic animals. Moreover, the seasonal migration of the animals between the *Commiphora-Acacia* and the scrub *Commiphora-Acacia* belts should be encouraged, so that the former is utilised during the dry season, whilst the scrub variety is reserved for wet season utilisation.

Provided water supplies are improved, what we presently regard as semi-desert in Kenya could, in fact, form a major beef cattle reservoir for the future. A further problem to be solved is that of the disease transmitted by the tsetse flies. Large parts of the semi-desert are infested with these flies, especially those parts of *Commiphora-Acacia* which are adjacent to the coastal region, and also those in the vicinity of riverine vegetation in the northern and eastern parts of Kenya.

Coast region Acacia-Euphorbia The soil types found in this large ecological unit are numerous and varied. They include soils derived from the Basement Complex system of gneisses and schists, from Taru grits, from Duruma sandstones, and from various sands and alluvial materials over a large part of the semi-arid areas of Kenya.

The following soil categories, amongst others, have been observed, many of them being components of catenary complexes:[2]
a yellow-red loamy sands (podzolic soils);
b dark-red sandy loams (latosolic soils): these are the low humic derivatives of Basement Complex and volcanic rocks, and are probably relic soils developed under a more humid climate;
c light-yellow brown sandy loams with latosolic horizon;
d seasonally waterlogged very pale brown mottled loamy sands with latosolic horizon; and
e brown clay with impeded drainage (grumusolic soils).

[1] See Woodhead (1968).
[1] See Moomaw (1960).

This vegetation covering vast parts of the coastal hinterland is principally useful for grazing and for wildlife purposes. However, research in wildlife land management should be carried out first in the ecological unit. Water is an important limiting factor in the development of much of the belt for ranching. In areas where water is available (e.g. Taita Hills, Vugurungani, etc.) the development of substantially better utilisation of both the forage and water could be undertaken.

Tsetse fly infestation is from low to moderate, and is controllable by using drugs and insecticides. Even in areas which are heavily infested, the fly could probably be reduced by controlling the vegetation. The information obtained by conducting experimental work on drug regime, ranching, bush control and 'grazing stocking rates' in this belt has proved basic to sound development of the ecological unit. What is urgently required is a detailed study using quantitative methods by field officers trained in range ecology and/or forage crops in close co-operation with the staff of the tsetse fly control and veterinary departments.

Estimates of the carrying capacity of the ecological unit have been made, and a value of 30 to 50 acres (12·1 to 20·2 hectares) per head of cattle is considered realistic for most of the parts, where fire and other factors have controlled the bush to some degree. It would, however, approach 100 acres (40 hectares) per head on an annual basis in the areas of dense bush. Thus vast areas must be controlled and watered, if substantial livestock populations are to be produced in competition with the grazing species of wildlife.

Eastern Kenya highlands Commiphora-Acacia *and its scrub variety*
Commiphora-Acacia zone: the *Acacia-Combretum* belt gradually gives place to the *Commiphora-Acacia* community as the climate becomes hotter and drier. There may be very little difference in total rainfall, but higher temperatures and greater evaporation may render the climate so unsuitable that arable agriculture becomes impracticable except by irrigation. Once *Commiphora* has become dominant, a sub-marginal level of agriculture has been reached and cultivation should be discouraged except under special conditions such as irrigation.

Scrub *Commiphora-Acacia-Sansevieria* zone: this comprises a large area of practically useless country, which receives less or about 20 inches (508 mm) of rain annually. The belt experiences much higher temperatures, and much of it is low-lying. It is frequently heavily infested with disease-transmitting tsetse flies.

The *Commiphora-Acacia* and its scrubby variety are widespread both in the eastern and northern parts of Kenya. The Rift Valley variety, which is located in Masailand, is introduced below.

Southern Rift Valley Commiphora-Acacia and associated varieties

The southern part of the Rift Valley Province is mostly occupied by Masailand, and involves some 15 000 sq miles (38 850 km²). It is bordered in the east by the Chulu Hills and the Kenya-Uganda railway, thus separating it from the Machakos and Kitui counterparts described above. In the west, its borders are demarcated by the Mau Escarpment, Kipsigis, Kisii and Kuria land units, and by the 250 miles (402·3 km) of the Kenya-Tanzania boundary. In the extreme south-east, the zone is bordered by the Tsavo National Park.

The Great Rift Valley divides it into two dissimilar parts:
a the western section, which is more varied and includes some relatively well-watered country suitable for intensive forms of agriculture: this portion has already been discussed either under the Lake Victoria Basin or under the Rift Valley and the associated highlands;
b the eastern section, where the landscape consists of a series of plains interspersed with hill remnants.
Thus Masailand exhibits, in its ecology, a variety of habitats ranging from limited areas of dense highland forest to bush, open grassland, and hot low-lying semi-desert areas.[1] The account which follows is confined to the semi-desert zone, which is under *Commiphora-Acacia* and its scrubby variety with *Sansevieria*.

Apart from the above pockets of high potential, the greater part of Masailand is *Commiphora-Acacia* with or without *Sansevieria*. This is low potential land, where physical difficulties and pastoral traditions of the occupants only allow very sparse population. Arable agriculture has been introduced in a few ecologically suitable areas; however, subsistence livestock keeping remains the principal economic activity. In general, Masailand is vital to the future of Kenya's economy because of its wildlife and the associated tourist industry.

Conclusion

From the viewpoint of economic development, it has been observed that the major plant communities react differently to the various forms of utilisation. Thus any progress made towards vegetation management requires separate treatment for each of the principal plant communities.

Each of the main ecological regions requires a research station for investigating its agricultural problems and potentialities. From the findings of such researches, it would then be possible to see more clearly the relationships existing between the ecological regions and both the human activities (ranging from intensive land cultivation to pastoral nomadism) and the distribution of domestic and wild animals. Moreover, the above patterns of people and the animals (wild or domesticated) are also relatively closely associated with the various development-limiting patterns of diseases, since the

[1] See Ominde (1968).

110

disease insect vectors (such as tsetse flies, etc.) are, generally, closely related to certain plant communities.

Owing to the significance of the revenue derived from tourism (based on wildlife), the environmental requirements of many of the wild animals could best be satisfied using knowledge derived from local ecological studies.

It is obvious from the above discussion that there are close links between the ecological regions of Kenya (as defined by the principal plant communities) and the country's economic activities, which have their bases mainly in agriculture. It would therefore be more realistic if future development plans relating to agricultural and other allied resources could recognise the significance of the ecological regions. The objective of this chapter has been to assist both planners and users, to utilise the ecological regions as important bases for the conservation and development of the rich organic natural resources of forestry, agriculture and wildlife.

References

BROWN, L. H. 'Agricultural policy for Central and Nyanza Provinces', unpublished manuscript, *Min. of Agric. and Animal Husbandry*, Nairobi, 1960.

DALE, I. R. and GREENWAY, P. J. *Kenya Trees and Shrubs*, Buchanan's Kenya Estates Ltd, Nairobi, 1961.

EDWARDS, D. C. 'The ecological regions of Kenya', *Emp. Jnl. of Exptal. Afric.,* Vol. 24, No. 94, 1956.

EDWARDS, D. C. and BOGDAN, A. V. *Important Grassland Plants of Kenya*, Pitman, 1951.

MCILROY, R. J. *An Introduction to Tropical Cash Crops*, Ibadan University Press, Nigeria, 1963.

MOOMAW, J. C. *A Study of the Plant Ecology of the Coast Region of Kenya, East Africa*, Govt. Printer, Nairobi, 1960.

OGENDO, R. B. 'Industrial significance of the Kenya forests'. *Cahier d'Études Africaines*, Vol. 6, Mouton, 1966.

OMINDE, S. H. *Land and Population Movements in Kenya*, Heinemann, London, 1968.

PRATT, D. J., *et al.* 'A classification of East African rangeland', *Jnl. of Applied Ecol.*, Vol. 3, 1966.

SCOTT, R. *Second Provisional (Kenya) Soil Map and Key,* unpublished manuscript, 1959.

TRAPNELL, C. G. and GRIFFITHS, I. F. 'Altitude-rainfall relation and its ecological significance in Kenya', *E. A. Agric. and Forest Jnl.,* Vol. 25, 1960.

WOODHEAD, T. 'Studies of potential evaporation in Kenya', *Water Development Department, Min. of Nat. Resources*, Nairobi, 1968.

Part 2

Chapter 8
Population Geography

Major Demographic and Social Features

The main aspects of human population which the geographer is most interested in knowing include: the total
number of people in the particular country or place,
the spatial distribution of that population including
density per unit area, pattern of settlement including
rural and urban proportions, age-sex pyramids, growth
rates and population mobility. Because of the approach
of his discipline, the geographer usually tries to discover
the inter-relationship between these aspects of population and the physical environment. In the circumstances
of Kenya, we must include in our study the composition
of the population including its racial complexity.

In comparison with other aspects of its geography,
Kenya's population has received fairly detailed study:
first by Blacker (1962), then by Morgan and Shaffer
(1966), whose monograph is certainly the most detailed
study of the subject to date. More recently, Ominde
(1968) has examined the mobile section of this population mainly in terms of causes and consequences of the
movements.

Total Population and Growth Rate

Only three nation-wide censuses have been carried out in
Kenya: in 1948, 1962 and 1969. Prior to 1948, therefore,
demographic statistics in Kenya were scanty and of
extremely doubtful accuracy, partly because the then
administration was primarily interested in knowing the
number of African tax-payers. The 1948 census was a
result of the formation of the East African Statistical

Department in the same year. It was a hut-to-hut count
which covered the whole country except the then
Northern Frontier District, East Suk and Samburu,
where the exercise was again confined to estimating only
the tax-payers.

In 1926, the non-African population stood at 53 669
people made up of 29 324 Asians (Indo-Pakistan), 12 529
Europeans, 10 557 Arabs and 1 259 others. We may note
also that the 1962 figure for Asians represented a rate of
growth of 4·32% per annum for the period 1948 and
1962. The rate of growth for the European population
over the same period is nearly the same, being 4·5% per
annum for the inter-censal period. The average rate of
growth for the African population can not be determined
so easily as there are many difficulties, but when allowance has been made for these it appears to be around
2·8% per annum. The difficulties are to do with the lack
of reliable statistics, in that African births/deaths have
not been recorded in the past, and even now a start is
only being made to cover some urban areas.

The non-African Population in Kenya

We have already noted the historical circumstances that
encouraged Europeans and Asians to come to Kenya. In
terms of numbers, they comprise a very small fraction of
the total population and are better known in most works
as the *minority community* although their contribution
to the national development has been far out of proportion to their meagre number. The other minority element
is the Arabs. This group is now part of the Kenya
population, and following Independence a number of

Table 8.1 *Estimated population growth in Kenya by race*

Year	African	Non-African	Total	European	Indo-Pakistan	Arab	Others
1948	5 252 753	154 846	5 407 599	29 660	97 687	24 174	3 325
1962	8 365 942	270 321	8 633 634*	55 759	176 613	34 048	3 901
1963	8 575 000	272 000	8 847 000	53 000	180 000	35 000	4 000
1968	9 941 000	268 000	10 209 000	42 000	182 000	40 000	4 000

¹ This figure excludes the 2 629 people who were grouped as being in transit in the census.

Table 8.2 *Comparison of Kenya's mean population density with that of other countries*[1]

Country	Area		Population	Density	
	sq miles	km²		sq miles	km²
Kenya (1962)	219 789	569 250	8 636 263	39	15
Tanzania (1962)	342 170	886 220	9 927 000	29	11
Uganda (1962)	74 748	193 783	7 016 000	94	36
Ghana (1962)	92 100	238 538	7 148 000	78	30
Zambia (1963)	288 055	746 062	3 409 110	12	5
India (1961)	1 175 846	3 045 429	435 511 606	370	143
USA (1960)	3 348 974	8 673 800	179 323 175	51	20
United Kingdom (1961)	93 024	240 931	52 708 934	567	219

Table 8.3 *Mean population density by provinces, 1962*

Province	Area		Population	Density	
	sq miles	km²		per sq mile	per km²
Nairobi EPD	227	588	314 760	1 386·6	535·3
Central	11 043	28 602	1 925 365	174·3	67·3
Coast	25 712	66 594	727 844	28·3	10·9
Nyanza	9 607	24 882	3 012 468	313·6	121·1
Rift Valley	17 007	44 048	1 049 136	61·7	23·8
Southern	32 727	84 763	1 013 977	30·9	11·9
Northern	123 466	319 774	590 084	4·8	1·86

[1] From *Kenya Population Census* 1962. Vol III

Europeans and Asians have also become Kenya citizens. At the 1962 census the Asians (Indians and Pakistanis), Europeans (white, irrespective of continent of origin), and the Arabs, comprised 2·0%, 0·6% and 0·4% respectively of the whole population of Kenya.

The bulk of this minority population live in the urban centres where much of their business is also found. In 1962 93% of the Asian population and 62·6% of the European population was urban, while the corresponding Arab figure was 76·5%. Of the Arabs 89% are found in the Coast Province where the former 'coastal strip' had been the main area where the then Sultan of Zanzibar had nominal political control.

Absolute Distribution and Density Pattern

Kenya's population is very unevenly distributed. In 1948 the mean density was 33 persons per sq mile (13 per km²) which by 1962 had risen to 39 per sq mile (15 per km²). In these terms Kenya is a country of low population density and Table 8·2 gives a comparison with some other countries.

A breakdown of provincial densities into district and location levels is necessary to gain further details on distribution variations. In 1962 six rural districts, Fort Hall (492 per sq mile, 190 per km²), Kiambu (559, 216), Nyeri (428, 155), Kisii (691, 266), North Nyanza (507, 196) and Central Nyanza (366, 141), had mean densities

of more than 350 persons per sq mile (136 per km²). A further breakdown into division level showed that four divisions, Vihiga (1 196 per sq mile, 462 per km²), Limuru (1 228, 474), Kikuyu (1 525, 589) and Kiambaa (1 704, 658), had more than 1 000 people per square mile (386 per km²). In the whole of Kenya, 11 locations had more than 1 000 people per sq mile (386 per km²).

Absolute Distribution

Fig. 8.1 is a dot map showing the absolute distribution of population in Kenya as per the 1962 census. The value for each dot may appear a little too large but this is necessitated by the very uneven distribution of the country's population.

Factors which have influenced the present distribution
There is a close relationship between areas of adequate rainfall (30–70 inches, 760–1 780 mm, per annum) and population, with the highest density being found in areas which receive 40–45 inches, 1 020–1 140 mm, per annum. The general absence of people in much of northern and north-eastern Kenya is due to the aridity of the area. The detailed distribution of the few who live in this dry north shows an obvious preference for river valleys, permanent water borehole sites, and the occasional rainfall islands in the area. The same lack of surface water explains the sparse population between Mac-

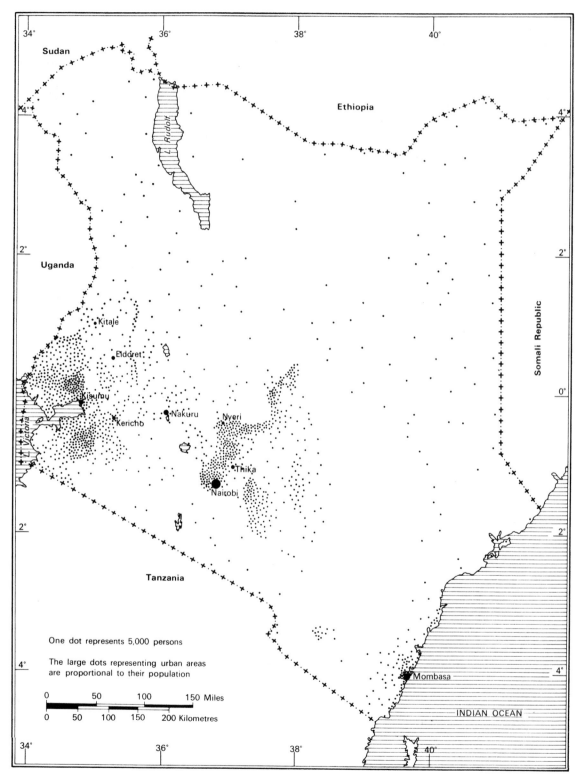

Fig. 8.1 Population distribution, 1962

kinnon Road and Kibwezi and in much of southern Kenya including parts of Serengeti, Kajiado and Narok.

The other factors affecting distribution are: altitude, administrative policy, soils and occurrence of tsetse fly. Altitudinal control places the limit of normal human settlement at about 9 000 feet (2 700 m). Beyond this height, cold, severe soil erosion, and dampness keep man away. Note the sharp boundary on Mt Kenya, the Aberdares and the Mau Hills in connection with this.

Most authors have explained the high density in Kikuyuland and parts of Maragoli and Bunyore in terms of high soil fertility. While this may be so in the case of Kikuyuland, it is not the sole factor. For instance, in Kericho the soil has always been rich, but it is only recently that agriculture has been accepted by the Kipsigis people, who formerly preferred to rear cattle. Neither can the very high density in Vihiga Division be explained in terms of rich soils, since much of North Maragoli (413 per sq mile, 160 per km²) and South Maragoli (1 252 per sq mile, 483 per km²) is in a rocky granite area. What can be the important and the more significant explanation? The answer, it would seem, lies in political factors. The British administration in Kenya was based on tribal areas, and where the different tribes used to clash with each other over land or cattle, buffer non-African settlements were started. Many of the white farms in marginal areas of Kenya can be explained in this way. The most important result of this policy is that various tribal lands or tribal territories were firmly fixed and any increase in population in any tribe had to be absorbed and contained within that tribal territory. The idea of natural population adjustment and spread

within the country as a whole was not open to the various tribal groups, and this restriction was still effective up to the time of independence. Since then there have been some outlets, such as were provided by the purchase of former European farms, especially in the Rift Valley Province and in the former 'buffer zones'.

The above considerations lead us to an important conclusion: that the whole provincial or district administrative system based on tribal areas is a retrogressive practice. A modern, forward looking Kenya nation must allow free domicile for its citizens in any part of the country. This is the only approach that can allow free and sound population adjustments. In the same manner, the soundness of the practice of a man going into town for a couple of years to work and then returning to his family in his tribal area is to be questioned. This leads to unnecessary tribal fears and mistrust. Provincial or district developments might wrongly be interpreted as being motivated by tribal preferences rather than sound economic reasoning and planning.

Tsetse fly Infested Areas and Trypanosomiasis

Several species of tsetse flies with a number of disease-bearing trypanosomes have either together or singly been a major limiting factor in the distribution of population in Kenya. The trypanosomes are the carriers of both the human sleeping sickness and the animal trypanosomiasis. For many decades this peculiar relationship between man, his stock and the fly (the vector of the disease) has been an important link. Areas affected with the trypanosomes of sleeping sickness have been unsuitable for

Table 8.4 *Kenya population by race, sex, and five-year age groups (in thousands)* [1]

Age Group	African and Somali		Asian		European		Arab		Others		Total	
	Male	Female	Male	Female	Male	Female	Male	Female	Male	Female	Male	Female
0–4	708·1	737·8	12·2	11·8	3·3	3·1	2·8	2·7	0·3	0·3	726·6	755·6
5–9	662·8	656·0	14·0	13·3	2·6	2·4	2·7	2·6	0·3	0·2	682·4	674·5
10–14	601·5	501·0	13·2	12·3	2·0	1·9	2·0	1·7	0·3	0·2	619·1	517·3
15–19	424·1	405·6	8·7	8·5	1·8	1·5	1·6	1·5	0·2	0·2	436·5	417·3
20–24	271·6	392·3	7·3	8·3	3·4	1·8	1·3	1·4	0·2	0·2	283·8	404·0
25–29	275·8	372·1	7·4	7·3	2·6	2·2	1·4	1·3	0·1	0·2	287·2	383·0
30–34	227·3	285·2	6·5	6·0	2·8	2·4	1·2	1·1	0·1	0·1	238·0	294·8
35–39	200·3	216·3	5·0	4·8	2·5	2·3	1·0	0·8	0·1	0·1	208·9	224·3
40–44	166·0	171·2	5·0	3·8	2·3	2·1	1·0	0·8	0·1	0·1	174·5	178·0
45–49	149·0	128·2	4·0	2·9	2·0	1·6	0·7	0·5	0·1	0·1	155·8	133·2
50–54	114·9	102·2	3·4	2·0	1·6	1·3	0·7	0·5	0·1	0·1	120·6	106·1
55–59	76·0	58·5	2·1	1·1	1·1	1·0	0·3	0·2	—	—	79·5	60·8
60 and over	228·5	178·7	3·2	1·8	1·8	1·9	1·2	0·8	0·1	0·1	234·9	183·4
Not stated	28·5	26·2	0·3	0·3	0·3	0·4	0·1	0·1	—	—	29·2	26·9
TOTAL	4 134·6	4 231·3	92·4	84·2	29·9	25·8	18·1	15·9	1·9	2·0	4 277·0	4 359·3

[1] From *Statistical Abstracts*, Republic of Kenya, 1968, p. 16.

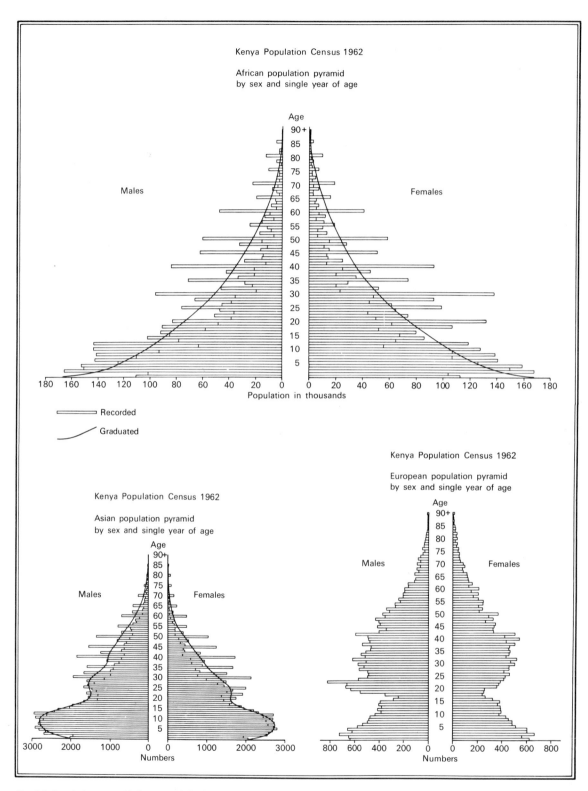

Fig. 8.2 Population pyramids by sex and single year of age for the three racial groups in Kenya, 1962

human habitation. Similarly, areas carrying bovine trypanosomiasis have kept stock away, and so have not been settled by the pastoralists. Human alterations to the ecological equilibrium, for example large-scale clearing of forests or introduction of large-scale farming, create a new habitat which is inhospitable to the fly and so enable man to colonise at its expense.

Age and Sex Distribution

It is important that the composition of population of any country be known in terms of age and sex ratios, for it is on this knowledge that sound national planning can be formulated. The age and sex ratios of the African population are not known exactly as no records have been kept and the desire to start keeping records was only partially established by the Government on 30 October 1964. Notwithstanding these difficulties the 1968 Kenya Statistical Abstract gives a breakdown of the 1962 population as summarised in Table 8.4.

In Fig. 8.2, we give the age/sex pyramids of the African, Asian and European populations. Certain salient features of much interest emerge. The high proportion of children in the African population is particularly outstanding. Over 50% of the African population were under 16 years old. This is because of the high national birth rate (the crude birth rate being about 48%). In this respect, the percentage of Kenya's youth is even higher than in most tropical developing countries. Note also the low proportion of old people amongst the African population in Kenya. This is also characteristic of developing countries. For the Asian and European groups, the two pyramids are almost true representatives of Indo-Pakistan and British patterns. The sex ratio of the African population works out at 96·9 males per 100 females.

Tribal Distribution

In the 1962 census, the indigenous African population was grouped into forty-two different tribes. The basis of this was rather unscientific using ethnic, linguistic and supposedly geographical considerations.

Space does not permit a detailed discussion on the prob-

Table 8.5 *Tribal distribution*

Major group	Tribes
Central Bantu	Kikuyu, Embu, Meru, Mbere, Kamba and Tharaka
Western Bantu	Luhya, Kisii and Kuria
Coastal Bantu	Mijikenda, Pokomo/Riverine, Taveta, Taita, Swahili/Shirazi, Bajun and Boni/Sanye
Nilotic	Luo
Nilo-Hamitic (Kalenjin speaking)	Nandi, Kipsisgis, Elgeyo, Marakwet, Pokot, Sabaot and Tugen
Other Nilo-Hamitic	Masai, Samburu, Turkana, Iteso, Nderobo and Njemps
Eastern Hamitic (Somali speaking)	Gosha, Hawiyah, Ogaden, Ajuran, Gurreh, Degodia and other Somali
Western Hamitic (Rendille and Galla speaking)	Rendille, Borana, Gabbra, Sakuye, Orma

Table 8.6 *Population of major tribes as per 1962 census*

	Male	Female	Total
Kikuyu	810 756	831 209	1 642 065
Luo	561 721	586 614	1 148 335
Luhya	533 180	553 229	1 086 409
Kamba	455 215	478 004	933 219
Kisii	266 978	271 365	538 343
Meru	214 991	224 930	439 921
Mijikenda	199 587	215 300	414 887
Kipsigis	170 447	171 324	341 771
Nandi	83 535	86 550	170 085
Masai	75 002	79 007	154 079
Ogaden	66 507	55 138	121 645
Tugen	54 934	54 757	109 691
Elgeyo	51 310	49 461	100 871
All Others	500 398	482 836	983 234
Total	4 134 634	4 231 208	8 365 942

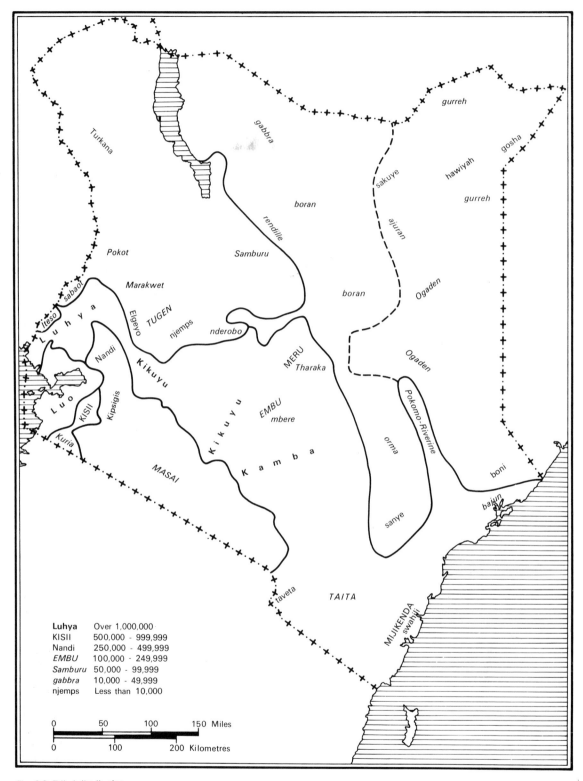

Fig. 8.3 Tribal distribution

118

lems and errors of the above classification of tribes, but many contemporary scholars would not agree with it (see Sutton 1968).

It is doubtful that tribes should be emphasised in a 'modern' Kenya. Kenyans should begin to abandon tribal differentiation in their vocabulary. This must be an urgent prelude to a strong, forward looking Kenya people with a united purpose.

The distribution of the main tribal groups is shown in Fig. 8.3. The totals of the large tribes as by the 1962 census are set out in Table 8·6.

Population Density Region

The aim in delimiting population density regions is to identify broad variations in population distribution. The method also allows for a more sympathetic appreciation of population pressure in terms of unit areas from medium or low population areas. The vital link between the physical landscape and man's response to it is brought out and factors at work identified. This aspect of Kenya's population was first examined by Morgan and Shaffer (1966) and then by Ominde (1968). This study accepts the units as recognised by Morgan and Shaffer with only minor differences in terminology brought about by emphasis of the factors involved. We believe that the population regions emphasise the fact that it is *people* and not relief which is the subject matter.

Four main population density regions can thus be recognised in Kenya (see Fig. 8.4). The best map from which to delimit these is the 1:1 000 000 dot map of 1962 Kenya population-distribution by Morgan and published by Oxford University Press with Morgan and Shaffer's 1966 monograph. The regions are:

1 *Very high–high density regions* Two areas fall in this category:

a *The Lake Basin* This embraces more or less the Old Nyanza Province as at the 1918 or the 1924 declaration. Denstities here average nearly 340 persons per sq mile (131 per km²).

b *Kiambu–Nyeri–Embu and Meru Belt* This includes the very high population zone of Kikuyuland (averaging 610 per sq mile (236 per km²) which continues through the eastern foothills of Mt Kenya to include the Nyambeni area of Meru. Densities in this latter zone average about 600 people per sq mile (232 per km²).

2 *Medium density regions* Three zones have this category:

a *Kamba Hills Cluster* This embraces (i) the fairly dense population of Machakos, Kilungu and Mbooni; (ii) the higher parts of Kitui District and northwards to include Tharaka; (iii) the Kiboko-Makindu and Masongaleni areas of Machakos District.

b *Coast Belt* Two belts in the Coast Region belong to this category: (i) Vanga to Kilifi area; (ii) Malindi Cluster.

c *Kitale–Cherangani–Nakuru–Naivasha Zone* This is a vast sub-region but one with more or less equal population density. Any significant variations occur on the eastern edge of the Cherangani and on the Tugen Hills. Readers should also note the concentrations in the more or less evenly spaced out farming-based towns in the area such as Kitale, Eldoret, Nakuru, Thomson's Falls and Naivasha.

The density in this sub-region is very different from that found in the Kiambu-Nyeri-Embu and Meru Belt and there does not seem to be any good reason for lumping these two together.

3 *Population islands* These are small concentrations in the otherwise almost unpopulated and unfavourable plains. They are thus due entirely to localised favourable conditions such as an island of high rainfall due to relief features or to the availability of ground or surface water. Thus we may differentiate three sub-groups here:

a *High rainfall population islands* These include: Marsabit, Moyale, Taita Hills, Kasigau, Taveta, Oloitokitok.

b *Available groundwater population islands* These include: Wajir, El Wak, Lokitaung, Lamu and Faza areas.

c *Water-course population islands* These include: Turkwel Valley, Kerio Valley, Daua Valley, Mid-Ewaso Ngiro up to Habaswein and Lower Tana (from Saka through Garissa to the coast).

4 *Low density region* This includes the vast dry plains of the interior of Kenya. Here the average density is about 6 persons per sq mile (3·7 per km²). Lack of water is the main factor limiting settlement. This very extensive region covers nearly 77% of the country. Regrettably, it is an area in which very little research is being directed so far.

1969 Census

The 1969 census showed that there were 10 942 705 people in Kenya, 5 482 381 males and 5 460 324 females. This represented an average population density of 49 people per sq mile (19 per km²) and an annual growth rate of just over 3·3%. To the above totals should be added the 13 796 people (6 821 males; 6 975 females) who lived in the Karasuk (now Karapokot) area and who during the census night were not included with Kenya because the area was still being administered from Uganda. Thus on the night of 24/25 August 1969, there were 10 956 501 people in Kenya. The provincial and district spread of this population is as shown in Table 8·7.

The above breakdown of the population by provinces and districts shows that west Kenya (the old Nyanza Province) has the highest population with over 3·3 million people (or 30% of the national total. Kisii district with an average density of 788 per sq mile (304 per km²) was the most densely peopled district. The next three most densely peopled districts were Kisumu (497 per sq mile, 192 per km²), Kiambu (476 per sq mile, 184 per km²) and Murang'a (456 per sq mile, 176 per km²).

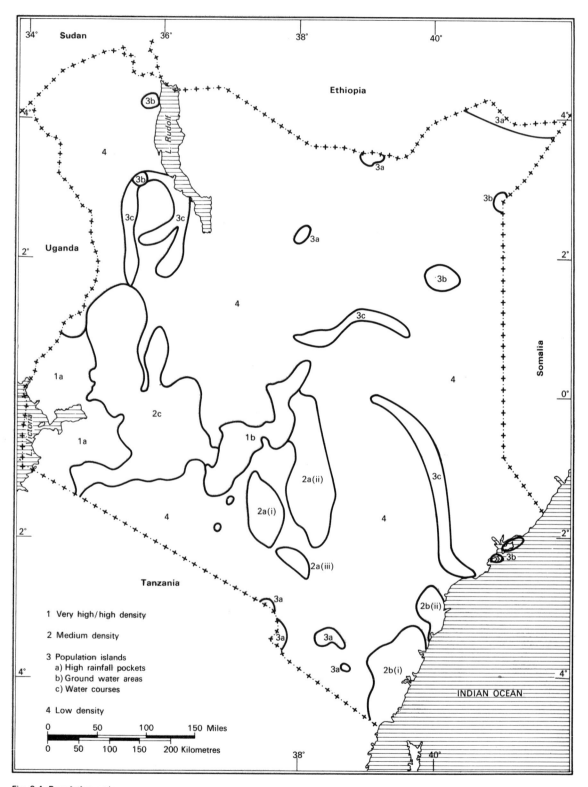

Fig. 8.4 Population regions

Table 8.7 *Population of Kenya by province and district*

Province	Districts
Nairobi Extra Provincial District Total 509 286 Average density 1 903 per sq mile 734 per km²	This population now represents the new enlarged city boundary which covers 268 sq miles (694 km²). Of this population 303 219 were males
Central Total 1 675 647 Average density 328 per sq mile 127 per km²	Kiambu 475 576; Kirinyaga 216 988; Murang'a 445 310; Nyandarua 176 928; Nyeri 360 845
Coast Total 944 082 Average density 29 per sq mile 11 per km²	Kilifi 307 568; Kwale 205 602; Lamu 22 401; Mombasa Island 247 073; Taita 110 742; Tana River 50 696
Eastern Total 1 907 301 Average density 31 per sq mile 12 per km²	Embu 178 912; Isiolo 30 135; Kitui 342 953; Machakos 707 214; Marsabit 51 581; Meru 596 509
North-Eastern Total 245 757 Average density 5 per sq mile 2 per km²	Garissa 64 521; Mandera 95 006; Wajir 86 230
Nyanza Total 2 122 045 Average density 435 per sq mile 168 per km²	Kisii 675 041; Kisumu 400 643; Siaya 383 188; South Nyanza 663 173
Rift Valley Total 2 210 289 Average density 32 per sq mile 12 per km²	Baringo 161 741; Elgeyo Marakwet 159 265; Kajiado 85 904; Kericho 479 135; Laikipia 66 509; Nakuru 290 853; Nandi 209 068; Narok 125 219; Samburu 69 519; Trans Nzoia 124 360; Turkana 165 225; Uasin Gishu 191 036; West Pokot 82 458; The Karapokot, 13 796 people, should be added to West Pokot
Western Total 1 328 298 Average density 416 per sq mile 161 per km²	Bungoma 345 226; Busia 200 486; Kakamega 782 586

The racial and tribal composition of the population as revealed by the 1969 census is as shown in Table 8.8.

The most significant point in the above figures is the number of Europeans, Asians, Arabs and other nationalities who have taken up Kenya citizenship since Independence. The rather high numbers of non-Kenyan Africans are mainly from the neighbouring states of Tanzania (26 360), Uganda (17 232), Rwanda (4 855), Somalia (3 519), Sudan (1 944) and Ethiopia (851). These figures also show that at least 37 700 Asians had left Kenya between 1962 and 1969. This post-Independence departure of Asians from Kenya formed part of the much publicised Asian exodus from East Africa.

We have already noted the rather high population rate of growth in Kenya especially since 1962. The numerical breakdown of the Kenya African population by tribal groups would appear to indicate that the rate of increase is higher in some tribes. The population totals of the main tribes as revealed by the 1969 census are as shown in Table 8.9.

While rural conditions still show little of the modern essentials of livelihood, towns like the City of Nairobi and Mombasa Municipality have a standard very much comparable to that of any European city or town of their sizes. This is to be regretted as it can give a false picture of the standard of living or development attained by a

Table 8.8 *Racial composition of Kenya's population as per 1969 census*

	Total	Males	Females
A: KENYANS (i.e. citizens)			
Africans	10 687 566	5 345 636	5 341 930
Asians	60 994	32 052	28 942
Europeans	3 889	2 168	1 721
Arabs	24 199	12 432	11 767
Others	339	159	180
Total	10 776 987	5 392 447	5 384 540
B: NON-KENYANS			
Africans	59 432	35 090	24 342
Asians	78 043	39 547	38 496
Europeans	36 704	18 961	17 743
Arabs	3 687	2 341	1 346
Others	1 648	816	832
Total	179 514	96 755	82 759

Table 8.9 *Population of major tribes as per 1969 census*

Tribe	Total	Males	Females
Kikuyu	2 201 632	1 091 413	1 110 219
Luo	1 521 595	763 080	758 515
Luhya	1 453 302	723 071	730 231
Kamba	1 197 712	592 889	604 823
Kisii	701 679	356 730	344 949
Meru	554 256	276 325	277 931
Mijikenda	520 520	255 508	265 012
Kipsigis	471 459	237 578	233 881
Nandi	261 969	131 001	130 968
Turkana	203 177	107 249	95 928
Masai	154 906	77 745	77 161
Tugen/ Cherangani	130 249	66 461	63 788
Embu	117 969	58 223	59 746
Elgeyo	110 908	57 002	53 906
Taita	108 494	52 501	55 993
Pokot	93 437	45 606	47 831
Ogaden	90 118	48 729	41 389
Iteso	85 800	42 703	43 097
Marakwet	79 713	41 187	38 526
Degodia	62 425	33 901	28 524
Kuria	59 875	30 570	29 305
Samburu	54 796	27 989	26 807
Tharaka	51 883	25 159	26 724
Mbere	49 247	23 166	26 081
Gurreh	49 241	26 443	22 798
Sabaot	42 468	21 196	21 272
Pokomo/ Riverine	35 181	17 110	18 071
Boran	34 086	17 472	16 614
Bajun	24 387	11 808	12 579
Nderobo	21 034	10 741	10 293

people. The concept of 'back to the land' may offer a partial solution, but what is really needed is to encourage the district headquarters to grow faster with investment incentives. Sound rural development programmes including more medical, educational and employment facilities are urgently needed.

The Origin of Towns in Kenya

Urbanisation in Kenya is a creation of the colonial administration. The only near exceptions to this are the urban settlements found along the coast which were founded by the Arab and other foreign traders. These early towns included Mombasa, Gedi, Malindi, Pate, Kilwa, Zanzibar, Shungwaya, Barawa, Merka and Mogadishu. As the list suggests, they spread almost from the southern tip of the Red Sea to Mozambique, that is, along the entire length of the east African seaboard.

One result of this early contact is that Kenya's coastal population is still more urbanised than the interior population, with 32% of its population living in urban areas. In the 1969 census the urban centres with over 2 000 inhabitants each are as shown in Fig. 8.5. They are also shown in Table 8.10.

These figures indicate a marked increase in the urban population which rose to 10% of the national population. The list also shows the dominating position of Nairobi which has become East Africa's first half million city. Mombasa has also shown considerable growth over the 1962 census of 179 575.

Urbanisation in the Interior of Kenya

This is entirely the result of colonial rule. The primarily subsistence economy of the African population with its

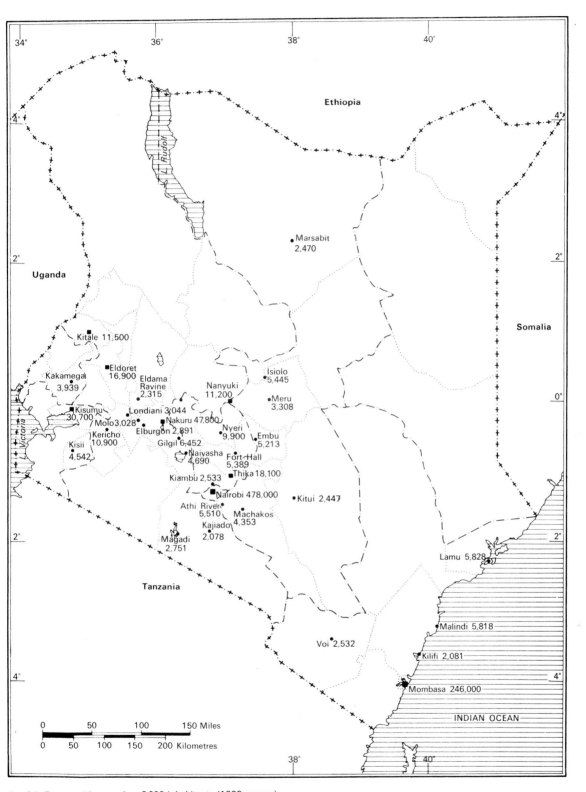

Fig. 8.5 Towns with more than 2 000 inhabitants (1969 census)

Table 8.10 *Population of urban centres as per 1969 census*

City of Nairobi	509 286
Municipality of Mombasa	247 073
Municipality of Nakuru	47 151
Municipality of Kisumu	32 431
Municipality of Thika	18 387
Municipality of Eldoret	18 196
Lodwar Rural	12 201
Nanyuki	11 624
Kitale	11 573
Malindi	10 757
Kericho	10 144
Nyeri	10 004
Isiolo	8 201
Thomson's Falls	7 602
Lamu	7 403
Naivasha	6 920
Marsabit	6 635
Machakos	6 312
Municipality of Kakamega	6 244
Kisii	6 080
Athi River	5 343
Elburgon	5 343
Voi	5 313
Fort Hall	4 750
Meru	4 475
Bungoma	4 401
Wundanyi	4 385
Molo	4 240
Gilgil	4 178
Lokitaung	4 090
Embu	3 928
Maralal	3 878
Galole	3 609
Homa Bay	3 252
Kitui	3 071
Njoro	3 037
Londiani	2 994
Kiambu	2 776
Eldama Ravine	2 692
Kilifi	2 662
Wamba	2 650
Narok	2 606
Lumbwa	2 577
Magadi	2 529
Kinango	2 450
Karatina	2 436
Baragoi	2 383
Migori	2 066

emphasis on pastoralism did not lend itself to urban living. Also many of the tribes were mobile and in conflict for tribal lands.

The colonial government was based on administrative *bomas* spread throughout the country, and it was these administrative centres which formed the nuclei of the urban development of the interior.

The creation of the White Highlands created a second type of urban centre. The farmers soon formed small local clubs and hotels, and these again formed the nuclei of urban centres where the farmers bought and sold their equipment, provisions and farm commodities. Such towns as Nakuru, Nyeri, Kitale, and Eldoret have this origin.

Purely industrial towns are few in Kenya. The main one is Magadi, although Athi River and Thika are sometimes classed as industrial towns. Magadi, started and run by the Magadi Soda Company Limited, is a mining town. Athi River, besides its cement and meat factory, has a greater diversity, as has Thika.

In conclusion, we note that our urban centres serve the various needs of the people. There are the administrative towns headed by the City of Nairobi, and followed by the provincial centres led by Mombasa, which is also the major port. Other coastal towns are ports and holiday centres. Inland, most towns serve the large farming communities as centres for selling and collecting. We should note also the inland lake port of Kisumu, while distant centres such as Mandera, Moyale and Namanga also serve as border posts. The physical layouts of the four largest towns in Kenya are shown in Figs. 8.6 to 8.9.

Population Mobility [1]

The 1962 census indicated considerable African population movements between the provinces. These movements had various causes, of which one of the leading was employment opportunity.

The movement of people into the former Northern Province, as indicated by the 1962 population census, was relatively restricted owing to the unattractive nature of the province.

During 1962 the total number of Africans who had moved to the six provinces – Rift Valley, Nairobi, Coast, Central, Nyanza and Southern – was 604 675 persons, or about 7% of the total 1962 population. Out of the 604 675 persons, about 43·6% moved into the Rift Valley Province, 25·7% entered Nairobi Extra-Provincial District, and 12·8% moved into Coast Province. Central and Nyanza Province attracted 11·2% and 4·6% respectively, whilst Southern Province accounted for the remaining 2·1% since movement into the former Northern Province was negligible.

Most of the people who entered Nyanza Province came from Nairobi Extra-Provincial District and from Central Province. A small but consistent stream came all the way from the Coast Province, whereas the bulk of the remaining immigrants into Nyanza Province (which then included most of the present Western Province) came from the Rift Valley Province. Both Northern and Southern Provinces contributed very little to the incoming population of Nyanza Province. The main

[1] See Ominde (1968) pp. 122–35.

centres of attraction in Nyanza to the incoming population were the Kericho tea producing belt, Kisumu township and the Miwani sugar belt. Still the province lost more people than it gained.

The Rift Valley Province had the largest incoming population, mainly from Nyanza, Central and Nairobi Provinces. A significant number of people came from Northern Province, and a few also entered from the former Southern Province. Coast Province made a negligible contribution to the total Rift Valley incoming population. The Rift Valley towns such as Nakuru, Eldoret, Kitale, Naivasha, Gilgil and Thomson's Falls were centres of great attraction. However, the commercial agricultural districts such as Nakuru, Uasin Gishu, Naivasha, Trans Nzoia and Laikipia also absorbed large numbers of the immigrants. The incoming population showed a surplus over the outgoing population.

Central Province attracted most of its incoming population from Nyanza, Rift Valley and Nairobi Provinces. Some immigrants came from Southern Province, but both the Coast and Northern Provinces had very small contributions. Central Province is noted for its commercial agriculture, which is based on a variety of cash crops such as coffee, tea, sisal, pineapples, and pyrethrum. Other sources of employment are its forests and dairy cattle. Its towns such as Thika, Nyeri, Limuru, Uplands, etc. are extremely attractive owing to their labour and capital intensive industries. Despite heavy losses via its high outgoing population, Central Province gained through a huge incoming population. This gain is concentrated more in the southern part of the province.

After Rift Valley Province, Nairobi Extra-Provincial District is the second most important focus of African immigrant population. The centre of attraction is, of course, Nairobi, with its many industries and commercial and administrative activities. Nairobi's population hinterland is enormous, and extends beyond Kenya. Internally, however, its incoming population comes from Central, Nyanza, Rift Valley and Southern Provinces. There are also a few people coming from the Coast and Northern Provinces, Nairobi's gains from the incoming population are in excess of the outgoing population,

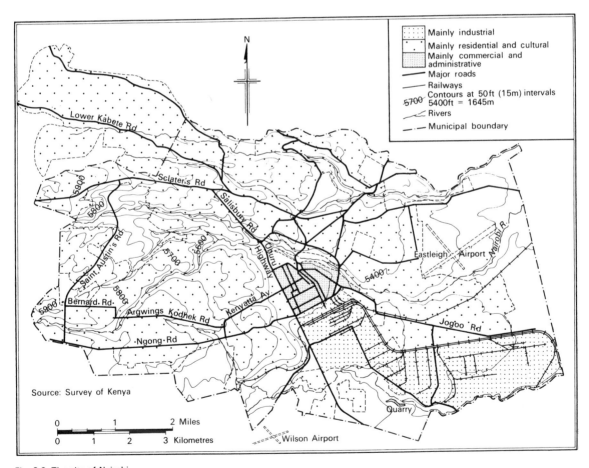

Fig. 8.6 The city of Nairobi

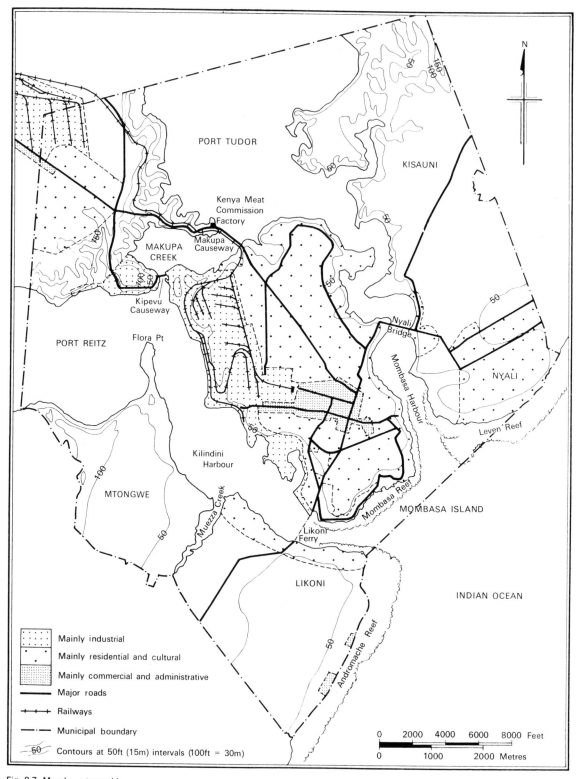

Fig. 8.7 Mombasa township

126

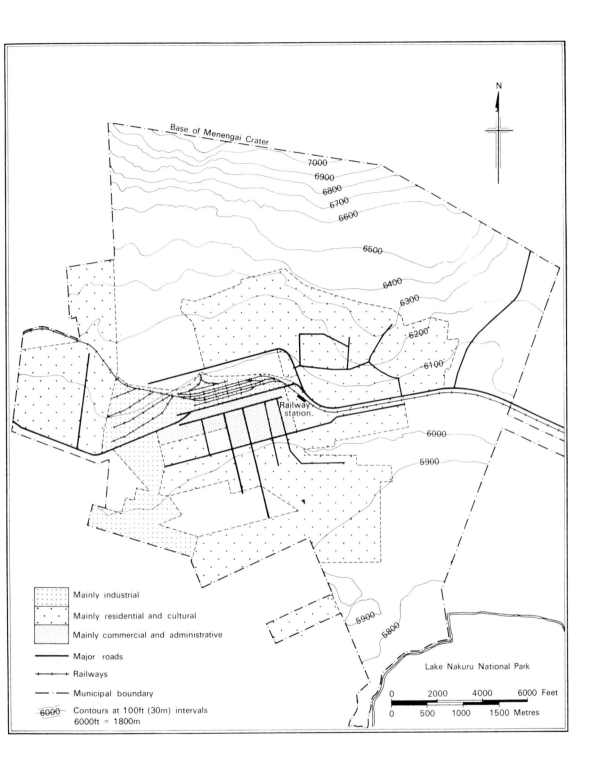

Fig. 8.8 Nakuru township

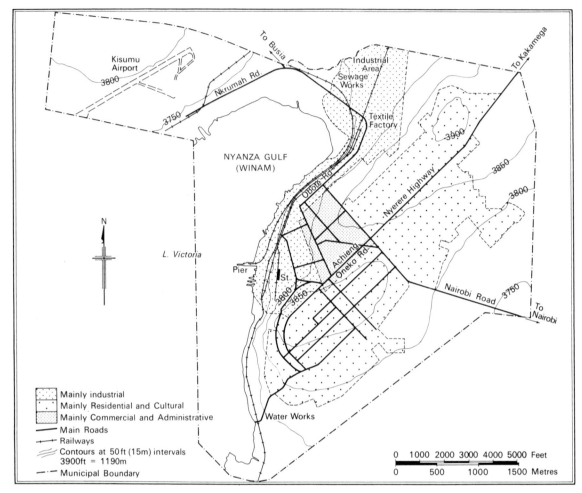

Fig. 8.9 Kisumu township

hence the district suffers acute unemployment problems.

The former Southern Province attracted most of its immigrant African population from Nairobi, Rift Valley, Nyanza and Central Provinces, in that order. Its main centres of attraction were the Magadi Soda complex, the Athi River meat and cement factories, the sisal and fruit and vegetable factories, and the town of Machakos. In general, the province lost rather than gained in population as a result of attractions to the other provinces.

The main focus of attraction of Coast Province is Mombasa District, especially Mombasa municipality, although the many large sisal farms and factories, the sugar plantations and allied factories, the cashew nut industry, and the many other varied coastal economic activities are the basic cause of the population flow. People have come mainly from Nyanza,[1] Rift Valley, Nairobi, Central and Southern Provinces and there is a surplus of incoming population over outgoing popula-

tion. Mombasa municipality experiences considerable unemployment problems as a result of this surplus influx of up-country people.

Taking into account the 34 Kenya towns, each with total population of over 2 000 inhabitants, the 1962 Kenya census of population indicates that about 93·1% of the population was then rural, and only 6·93% was urban. Of the largest towns 7 had population totals of over 10 000, ranging from 266 794 in Nairobi to 10 448 in Nanyuki. These seven towns[1] shared between them about 5·56% of Kenya's total population. A further 11 towns,[2] with population totals between 5 000 and 10 000, ranging from 9 342 in Kitale to 5 213 in Embu, accommodated another 0·80% of Kenya's total population.

---

[1] Nairobi (3·09%); Mombasa (1·25%); Nakuru (0·44%); Kisumu (0·27%); Eldoret (0·23%); Thika (0·16%) and Nanyuki (0·12%).
[2] Kitale (0·11%); Nyeri (0·09%); Kericho (0·09%); Gilgil (0·07%); Lamu (0·07%); Malindi (0·07%); Athi River (0·06%); Isiolo (0·06%); Fort Hall (Murang'a, 0·06%); Thomson's Falls (0·06%); and Embu (0·06%).

---

[1] Now split into a smaller Nyanza Province and Western Province.

The remaining 16 towns[3] had population totals ranging from 4 690 in Naivasha to 2 078 in Kajiado. However, they only housed about 0·57% of Kenya's total population. These towns are most unevenly distributed, so that much of western and northern Kenya is without towns.

Two forces are exerted on the rural population by the urban centres. In the first instance, there is the normal urban attraction of better economic conditions and higher wages. However, the better wages have forced the employers to engage fewer workers and increase mechanisation for greater productivity. The result has been acute unemployment. In the second instance, people are being forced to move to the urban areas owing to lack of employment opportunity in the rural areas. In those rural areas with very high population densities some people have no land, and the great temptation has been for the able-bodied youths to move to the towns and the richer rural areas (such as the Kiambu coffee and sisal areas, the Kericho tea areas and the coastal sisal and sugarcane areas) to search for employment.

At present, the primary and secondary school leavers are, in fact, creating a further unemployment category, since they prefer urban office employment to the more demanding physical or agricultural employment. It seems likely that, unless more industries are decentralised to the rural areas from the urban centres, there is bound to be greater population movement from the rural to the urban areas in the future. This will inevitably cause considerable urban over-crowding, as urban council authorities are most likely to be overtaken in their plans to provide housing and other social amenities.

References

MORGAN, W. T. W. and SHAFFER, N. M. *Population of Kenya: Density and Distribution*. Oxford Univ. Press, 1966.

BLACKER, J. G. C. 'The demography of East Africa', in *Natural Resources of East Africa*, ed. E. W. Russell, East African Literature Bureau, 1962.

OMINDE, S. H. *Land and Population Movements in Kenya*, Heinemann, 1968.

EAST AFRICAN HIGH COMMISSION *African Population of Kenya Colony and Protectorate, 1953 Reprint.*

EAST AFRICAN COMMUNITY *Economic and Statistical Review*, No. 27, 1968.

J. BEAUJEU-GARNIER *Geography of Population*, Longman, 1966.

GOVT OF KENYA *Kenya Statistical Abstracts*, Govt Printer, Nairobi, 1968.

GOVT OF KENYA *Kenya Population Census, 1962, Vol. III– African Population and Vol. IV–Non-African Population*, Govt Printer, Nairobi, 1966.

SUTTON, J. E. G. 'The settlement of East Africa', in *Zamani: A Survey of East African History*, EAPH/ Longman, 1968.

CHITTICK, N. 'The coast before the arrival of the Portuguese', in *Zamani: A Survey of East African History*, EAPH/Longman, 1968.

[3] The 16 towns were in order: Naivasha, Kisii, Machakos, Kakamega, Meru, Londiani, Molo, Elburgon, Magadi, Kiambu, Voi, Marsabit, Kitui, Eldama Ravine, Kilifi and Kajiado.

Chapter 9
Agricultural Economy

General Comments

Kenya is primarily an agricultural country and agriculture continues to play a leading role in her domestic exports. Up to 1967, agricultural crops accounted for an average of 70% of her total exports by value. In 1962, the figure was 80·9% but in 1967 it·was 60·3%. If the animal products are included then the annual average between 1961 and 1967 inclusive is 81·6% of the total value of the exports. This situation has occurred partly because Kenya has not found large quantities of important minerals and partly as a result of governmental agricultural policies (including land ownership).

Agriculture in Kenya has always brought to mind the policy of the White Highlands, or 'a European tribal reserve', as Morgan (1963) has termed it, on the one hand, and the 'African Land Units' on the other. Following the attainment of independence, important changes in the land ownership and use of the former White Highlands are taking place. The transformation is a gradual dismantling of the White Highlands by re-settlement of African farmers in some of the former European farms.

In this chapter we examine the soils, subsistence (including the distribution of some of the main subsistence crops), peasant cash crops and plantation and large-scale commercial production. The government efforts being made to transfer the means of production to the hands of citizens are also examined. In Kenya this latter point is important since the old policy confined much of the production in the hands of non-Africans, a situation which gave rise to some of the most outstanding and immediate complaints against the then colonial regime.

Land Tenure and Land Use Categories

The physical landscape in Kenya is such as to give it tremendous ecological extremes. There is a bewildering variety of local conditions even within very short distances. This situation is always a blessing to agriculture in Kenya since most crops can therefore be grown. Kenya thus need not depend on a single crop and land

use changes can easily be effected in response to the price dictates of the various crops.

Agricultural expansion is mainly limited by lack of sufficient rainfall. So far the dry zone can only support poor stock under nomadism. Only one-fifth of the country is high potential land (categories 1 and 2), with adequate rainfall for cultivation. Four-fifths of this high potential land has always been in the 'African Land Units' and only the other one-fifth in the formerly 'alienated land'. The African sector was however handicapped by population pressure, lack of modern farming expertise and by being treated merely as a pool of labour supply. It is clear though that before this area can be made to produce to its full capabilities, the population must be redistributed since the present dispersed pattern does not permit the best use of the land. The alienated land, which was under modern farming methods (with government assistance with loans, marketing and transport), has been responsible for nearly 85% of the agricultural exports of the whole country and about two-fifths of the total agricultural production.

Table 9.1 gives a summary of land potential and land use categories by provinces and districts. Note that only 11·9% of the country is in category 1 and 5·5% in category 2. The table also clearly illustrates the necessity for a more careful use to be made of the limited good land, as well as the need for research into what the category 3 land (74·2% of the total) is being used for and could be used for. With regard to this point, some of the suggestions made by David Hopcraft (1969) should be investigated.

The Old Practices: Subsistence Economy and Shifting Cultivation

Within the country, many old farming practices can still be noted. On the whole the cultivated fields are very small (averaging half an acre, 0·2 hectare, each), and cultivation tends to go on, side by side, with some degree of pastoral activity except with the purely nomadic tribes where little, if any, cultivation is undertaken. The plots for cultivation were usually prepared by burning before cutting the unwanted trees from the plot. Burning

Table 9.1 *Categories of agricultural land in Kenya* (Simplified) '000 hectares·

Province and District	High potential*	Medium potential	Low potential	Total	All other land	Total land area
Central						
Murang'a	157	—	—	157	30	187
Kiambu	127	—	5	132	132	264
Kirinyaga	98	10	—	108	35	143
Nyandarua	265	—	5	270	83	353
Nyeri	160	—	12	172	157	329
Thika	102	5	19	126	—	126
Total Central	909	15	41	965	437	1 402
Coast						
Kilifi	104	247	851	1 202	39	1 241
Kwale	126	162	508	796	29	825
Lamu	7	319	321	647	4	651
Mombasa	21	—	—	21	—	21
Taita	42	10	590	642	1 054	1 696
Tana River	73	58	3 393	3 524	354	3 878
Total Coast	373	796	5 663	6 832	1 480	8 312
Eastern						
Embu	66	186	—	252	19	271
Isiolo	—	—	2 560	2 560	—	2 560
Kitui	67	1 137	1 078	2 282	657	2 939
Machakos	125	771	454	1 350	69	1 419
Marsabit	4	—	7 045	7 049	224	7 273
Meru	241	95	315	651	342	993
Total Eastern	503	2 189	11 452	14 144	1 311	15 455
Nairobi—Total	16	—	38	54	14	68
North-Eastern						
Garissa	—	—	4 393	4 393	—	4 393
Mandera	—	—	2 647	2 647	—	2 647
Wajir	—	—	5 650	5 650	—	5 650
Total North-Eastern	—	—	12 690	12 690	—	12 690
Nyanza						
Kisumu } Siaya }	432	29	—	461	—	461
Kisii	220	—	—	220	—	220
South Nyanza	566	5	—	571	—	571
Total Nyanza	1 218	34	—	1 252	—	1 252
Rift Valley						
Baringo	166	84	751	1 001	66	1 067
Elgeyo-Marakwet	104	—	92	196	77	273
Kajiado	22	—	1 760	1 782	314	2 096
Kericho	380	—	—	380	109	489
Laikipia	130	—	768	898	74	972
Nakuru	291	39	231	561	141	702
Nandi	234	—	—	234	40	274
Narok	908	—	704	1 612	240	1 852
Samburu	140	—	1 612	1 752	329	2 081
Trans Nzoia	208	—	—	208	39	247
Turkana	12	—	6 070	6 082	—	6 082

Province and District	High potential*	Medium potential	Low potential	Total	All other land	Total land area
(Rift Valley cont.)						
Uasin Gishu	327	—	—	327	51	378
West Pokot	103	—	365	468	39	507
Total Rift Valley	3 025	123	12 353	15 501	1 519	17 020
Western						
Bungoma	253	—	—	253	55	308
Busia	163	—	—	163	—	163
Kakamega	325	—	—	325	27	352
Total Western	741	—	—	741	82	823
Total Kenya	6 785	3 157	42 237	52 179	4 843	57 022
Percentage of total land area	11·9	5·53	74·07	91·5	8·5	

*High potential land for agriculture or forestry with not less than 35" (889 mm) annual rainfall (40" (980 mm) in the Coast Province)
Medium potential land for agriculture suited to stock raising and limited cultivation (though some areas are densely populated). Annual rainfall as follows: Coast Province 30"–40" (762–1 016 mm), Eastern Province 25"–35" (635–899 mm), Nyanza and Rift Valley Province 30"–35" (762–889 mm).
Low potential land has less than 25"–30" (635–762 mm) annual rainfall, suited exclusively to stock raising and/or wildlife, with the exception that sisal does well in areas near upper rainfall limit.

Source: Statistical Abstracts, Republic of Kenya, 1970, p. 76, and other sources.

was also a natural method of getting rid of dry turf grass that could not be eaten by the animals so that fresh soft, juicy grass could grow.

Soil erosion and soil exhaustion were solved by the well known practice of *shifting cultivation*. This is the method of resting an exhausted piece of ploughed field that had been subjected to continuous cropping for some time. The cultivator would leave the field to rest and lie fallow for a number of years during which time he moved on to fresh ground. Some writers have noted that 'the memory of the old cultivation is lost'[1], but in Kenya this was not the case. In fact amongst most African land tenure and land ownership systems, once someone had cultivated a piece of ground for the first time he could always claim the right of ownership over it. Fragmented plots owned by one farmer thus were the result of this method of farming, as after a number of years the farmer who had at different times tilled, say, six different plots, would have the right of ownership over these. The right definition as practised in Kenya is the one given by O'Connor (1966) that 'over most of the region (East Africa) shifting cultivation is practised only in the sense that the farmer cultivates a plot for a few years and then allows it to rest while he tills another patch'.

Shifting cultivation is a large consumer of space and a very primitive form of land use, and with the increase in population, only those with a lot of land could afford to continue the practice.

In many parts of the country the hoe is the standard

digging tool, but in Kikuyuland the *panga* is more evident. When the ox-drawn plough came into use it considerably increased the efficiency of many farmers who also kept cattle. The plough has spread amongst most cultivators although it is particularly widespread in west Kenya. The kinds of crops grown were mainly for immediate consumption by the family and the only estimation of how much to grow depended on the resourcefulness of the particular family. In most places, digging was left to females while men acquired the land and cleared it. The erection of homesteads was the work of men but in Central Province the women were also involved in this task.

The Main Subsistence Crops

There are many different types grown all over the country, the main determining controls being rainfall and soil fertility. The peasant farmers appear to have been able to tell soil fertility and the suited crops for the different ecological zones by certain plants which they were able to identify as 'safe tellers' for the crops to be grown in the particular area. The main food crops are millet, cassava, sweet potatoes, maize, bananas, beans, peas, groundnuts and vegetables of which there are numerous wild varieties.

Cash crops were not important and in the event of a serious famine, those who had spare food could usually exchange it for animals or for work done. Neighbours also lent their friends spare food to be repaid in kind during the following harvest season.

[1] e.g. de Schlippe (1956).

132

Sorghum, Finger Millet and Bulrush Millet

These are *Sorghum vulgare, Eleusine Coracana* and *Pennisetum typhoideum* respectively. These can be treated together because they tolerate nearly similar conditions. They can withstand fairly poor soils but *E. Coracana* does better on well-drained soils. They do not require much rainfall, about 15 inches (381 mm) during the growing season being sufficient. They can also withstand fairly high temperatures. Sorghum is particularly widespread around the Nyanza Gulf, in Ukambani, Embu, Meru and parts of the Coast Province. It seems to be a declining crop. Its place is being taken over by maize which is more liked. These crops are also widely used by the different tribes to make local beer.

Cassava *(Manihot utilissima)*

This root crop came to East Africa from South America. It is an important crop in the marginal areas where it does very well and where it has been encouraged by the Government as a 'reserve crop' in the case of famine. It is easy to grow and easily gives high yields even without much attention. It is estimated that there are some 350 000 acres (240 000 hectares) of the crop in Kenya, the main area being western Kenya, Coast Province, Kitui and Machakos Districts.

Sweet potatoes *(Ipomoea batatas)*

This is the next most important root crop and it also reached Africa from Latin America. It requires more rainfall but is also grown as a reserve crop. It is grown widely in the whole country especially in western Kenya, Central Province and the coast. It gives very high yields but it presents considerable problems with storage.

Maize

This is now the most extensively grown food crop in Kenya. It is eaten by more people in the country than any other crop. It also reached Africa from America and its historical development in Kenya is rather unusual for a staple food crop. It was grown on a commercial basis by European farmers in the highlands where the peak period was 1929 when nearly 3 million acres (1 214 000 hectares) of the crop was grown especially in Trans Nzoia, Nakuru, and Uasin Gishu areas. Taking the whole country, it probably occupies half of the cultivated land and in Kericho District and parts of the Rift Valley it is practically a monoculture amongst the peasant farmers. Also it is very widely grown in Eastern, Central and Western Provinces.

The price offered to growers is unfortunately very low and the marketing of the crop is done by a Government-backed Maize Board. It seems to be an assured crop in the country and recently a hybrid variety (Katumani Maize) has been evolved which does very well in certain marginal areas.

Bananas *(Musa spp.)*

This is another main staple food amongst some Africans but not as significant as in parts of Uganda or Tanzania. It is estimated that some 180 000 acres (73 000 hectares) of land are under the crop in the country, mainly in Western Province, Kisii District, parts of Central Province and in the Tana-Galana areas. The crop now has a considerable demand as a fruit in the urban areas and production in Kisii and parts of the wetter Luo areas of south Nyanza could certainly supply the market. Unfortunately, a proper marketing organisation has not been established by the growers.

Beans, Peas and Other Pulses

These are fairly important in most areas, where they are usually planted with other main crops such as maize or millet. In fact, they provide the only source of protein for many people. Their main advantage is their short growing season. They are most important in Central Province and among the Kamba people. In Machakos nearly half the land under cultivation is under the crops and they have second place in Kiambu. Kirinyaga, Fort Hall, Meru and Embu. But we must emphasise that beans are widespread throughout the country. Chick peas and field peas are better suited to wetter areas, generally above 6 000 feet (1 800 m), while cow peas on the other hand do better in the coastal zone. In Ukambani, Embu and Meru, pigeon peas are the dominant pulse crop.

Groundnuts and Sesame *(simsim)*

Groundnuts came from America but Sesame is thought to be an East African crop. Groundnuts are important particularly in Nyanza Province and especially along the shores of the Nyanza Gulf.

Cash Economy and Principal Crops

The British government, as the colonial power, encouraged her citizens between 1902–59 to come and live in Kenya, supporting themselves mainly by farming the land that was specially preserved for their exclusive use in the highlands (see Fig. 9.1a). These farmers were encouraged to live very much as they would live back in Britain or in other European countries. These circumstances made possible rapid development in agriculture involving large farms in which heavy machinery and many modern techniques were applied. To ensure quality and to free the necessary cheap labour, certain cash crops could only be grown by the European farmers. This also meant that the indigenous population could only develop small farming plots. The large-farm sector (controlled by Europeans and Asians) and the small-farm sector (managed by Africans) are now a well-established feature of our agricultural landscape. Large farms are found in former scheduled areas while small farms are found in

Fig. 9.1a The 'White Highlands'

Fig. 9.1b Geographical regions of the 'White Highlands'

the former non-scheduled areas (the African Land Units).

In 1968 the large farm sector totalled 6·5 million acres (2·6 million hectares) of which nearly 14% has now been transferred to African ownership. The actual size of individual holdings varies a great deal. The 1967 picture was as shown in Table 9.2 below.

The growing role of the African farmer and his participation in the cash economy is receiving ever-

Table 9.2 *Size of holdings in Kenya's large farms in 1967*

Size of holdings		Number of holdings
acres	hectarés	
20— 499	8·1— 201	1 165
500— 999	202— 404	477
1 000— 4 999	405— 2 022	866
5 000— 9 999	2 023— 4 046	106
10 000—49 000	4 047—19 830	117
50 000—and over	20 234 and over	14
	Total	2 745

increasing governmental encouragement.

The principal cash crops are: coffee, tea, pyrethrum, sisal, wattle, maize and other cereals (mainly wheat, barley and oats), cotton, pineapples and cashew nuts. From 1961 to 1967 inclusive, coffee exports accounted for 29·6% of the country's total export by value (they earned Kenya £K15·6 million), and tea accounted for 13·2% (worth £K7·3 million). Sisal and pyrethrum have shown a steady decline. In 1963 sisal fibre and tow represented 17·2% of the total exports but in 1967 the figure declined to 3·9%. Between 1958 and 1967 the value of pyrethrum extracts and flowers exports have also varied from 8·7% of the total exports in 1961, to only 4·7% in 1965.

Coffee

This crop has dominated the country's exports list since its introduction as a cash crop in 1900. Its cultivation was confined to Europeans until the early 1950s. Its peak year was probably 1936 when some 100 000 acres (40 469 hectares) were planted. It has continued to receive close governmental support and there are a number of well-established research foundations in the country to serve the farmers in every way. In Kenya it is the *Arabica* coffee which is planted. This variety, despite its lower

Fig. 9A Young coffee plants protected by a covering of grass

yields, maintains a higher price than *Robusta*, which is the main variety grown in Uganda and Tanzania.

Coffee does better on well-drained soils in cool upland areas between 5 000 and 7 000 feet (1 520 and 2 128 m). It needs at least 30 inches (762 mm) of well-distributed rainfall without excessively high temperatures. In addition to the above requirements, rich volcanic soils are excellent for the crop. The main areas, therefore, are Kiambu, Thika, Embu and Meru. Other fairly important localities include the higher parts of Machakos, Fort Hall, Kitale, Solai, Mt Elgon, Kisii and Taita Hills. Production in 1967 came to 47 300 tons (48 059 tonnes) of which small farms accounted for 28 500 tons (28 957 tonnes). The average price to producer was £K296·19 per ton (£K291·5 per tonne) (cf. the 1959 price of £K399·39 per ton, £K393 per tonne).

The main problem which has bedevilled the crop is that to avoid flooding the world market with excess production, the International Coffee Agreement now has to fix annual export quotas for each country. In 1967 Kenya was allocated 42 330 tons (43 000 tonnes) which meant that the rest of the coffee had to be sold to non-quota markets. More recently (following the 1961–2 floods), an imperfect fungus *(colletotrichum Coffeanum)* attacked the plants. The disease, better known as *Coffee Berry Disease (C.B.D.)*, has damaged many crops since and caused many hundreds of trees to be uprooted. The disease spreads very rapidly during high moisture conditions and although a little more is known about it, no definite control has been found.

Tea

The growing of tea is one of the best success stories in

Fig. 9B Tea picking at Limuru, near Nairobi

135

Kenya and a large estate such as can be seen in Kericho presents one of the most refreshing man-made landscapes that can be seen anywhere. Kenya is now Africa's leading exporter of tea and in 1966 tea earned Kenya more than £K8 million. It was brought to Kenya from China in 1903 but steady development did not start until 1924.

The plant grows best in tropical highland areas at altitudes between 5 000 and 7 500 feet (1 520 and 2 280 m). It needs usually not less than 50 inches (1 270 mm) of rain which should also be evenly distributed throughout the year, and a deep, loamy, friable and acidic soil. The main areas which meet the above requirements, and in which tea is grown, are the Kericho area, which has nearly half the total acreage, Nandi Hills, Limuru, Sotik, Nyeri, Murang'a, Meru, Kisii and Trans Nzoia. During the first quarter of 1969 these areas produced 21 465 829 lbs (9 736 000 kg) of manufactured tea leaves.

Tea growing is an expensive occupation, needing considerable initial capital as the young plants are ready for first plucking only after four years. Full yields per acre are not expected until after seven years. For this reason the growing of tea was confined to estates, mainly under the monopoly of the Brooke Bond Tea Company with its headquarters in Kericho. When the bush has matured it can be plucked at 10–14 day intervals for

nearly fifty years. In January 1969 there were some 82 920 acres (33 554 hectares) under tea in Kenya and of these the small farm sector (African growers) acreage was 30 220 (12 229 hectares). The African growers joined the industry in 1957 and by the beginning of 1969 there were 38 000 growers, each having about 0·70 acre (0·28 hectare). The small farm production is under the overall supervision of the Kenya Tea Development Authority which is a government statutory body. So far the African contribution has been excellent. The quality of their tea has been even better than the estate produced and the industry appears to have a bright future. The only worry appears to be the fluctuating world market price. The tea industry (large farm sector) employs nearly 10% of the working labour force in Kenya, which makes it one of the largest employers.

Pyrethrum *(Chrysanthemum cinerariaefolium)*

Pyrethrum is a perennial herb which is grown for its daisy-like flowers which contain a substance known as pyrithrin. The pyrithrins are used to manufacture insecticides which are particularly convenient because they are not harmful to man or to his food. Pyrethrum was introduced as a commercial crop in Kenya in the

Fig. 9C Pyrethrum picking in the Kenya Highlands. The gathering of the flowers is commonly done by women

Fig. 9D Stripping wattle bark

early 1950s and for a while could only be grown by Europeans. However, by 1964, African growers were producing nearly one-third of the total production.

The plant requires a cool tropical highland region at an elevation of between 6 000 and 8 000 feet (1 824 and 2 432 m). The main producing areas are therefore the Kinangop Plateau, Limuru, Molo, Ol Joro Orok, Kipkabus and Kisii Highlands. The flowers are picked every two to three weeks throughout the year for about four years. Since being introduced to African growers the plant has proved very popular because of the quick return (picking can be within one year), so that it is very suitable as a filler crop for tea growers, especially in Kisii. The price to producers in 1967 was shs 180/- per pound weight (shs 73/- per kg). Nearly 11 800 acres (4 484 hectares) were planted in the large farm sector and the total export was worth £K2·699 million of which £K2·275 million was paid to small farm growers.

The main threat facing pyrethrum growers is the danger from world overproduction and competition from synthetic pyrethroid. For these reasons the growing is closely controlled by the Pyrethrum Board of Kenya and the Pyrethrum Marketing Board, the two government statutory bodies in the trade. Each cooperative society or individual grower is allocated a quota by the Board after surveying the market potential, so that any slight overproduction in one year is off-set by a lower yield the next year. The other main producing countries are Tanzania, Ecuador, Zaire and Japan.

Sisal *(Agave sisalana)*

Sisal is valued for its fibre which is used for rope and twine making. The crop was introduced to Kenya fairly early during the beginnings of European settlement. It was successful partly due to its broad degree of tolerance to various conditions, including areas of impeded drainage and marginal rainfall, and because cheap labour was abundant. The main producing areas are shared between the Coast Province (at Voi, parts of Kilifi), the poorer parts of Thika and the adjoining parts of Machakos, Murang'a (Maragua Ridge) and the drier parts of the Rift Valley especially Rongai. The African production is mainly from small shamba fences and hedges around homes, especially in Nyanza.

In 1967, 51 000 tons (51 818 tonnes) were produced and sold at an average price of £K44·61 per ton (£K43·90 per tonne). Large farms (some 255 400 acres, 103 357 hectares) produced 50 000 tons (50 800 tonnes). This shows clearly that sisal is essentially a large farm crop. However, it is rapidly declining because of rising labour costs, poor prices paid to producers (in 1963 the price was £K112·09 per ton, £K110·4 per tonne), and because of severe competition from synthetic fibre and from other producing countries including Tanzania.

Wattle

The wattle tree is indigenous to Australia. It is grown primarily for its bark which is the chief source of tannin, a chemical used in the manufacture of leather. The tree was introduced to the cool highlands of Kenya in the early 1940s mainly as a cash crop for the Kikuyu peasants and a factory was built near Muguga Station. The crop was popular despite its long growing season because the people valued its firewood (a by-product here). Later

137

large plantations were set up, mainly in the Uasin Gishu Plateau, by large commercial companies and in 1959 there were 85 700 acres (34 681 hectares) in large farms in the country. By 1967 the acreage had fallen to 45 900 (18 574 hectares) which earned the country some £K861 000 in the year, with India as the main market. Indications are that the crop is on the decline.

Cotton

Cotton has always been a small growers' crop in Kenya where it has done fairly well although lack of enthusiasm on the part of the growers has been evident. For it to grow well, cotton needs high temperatures (over 18°C, 65°F), plenty of sunshine during the growing season, which lasts five to six months, and 20–40 inches (508–1 016 mm) of rain.

The main growing areas are confined to the shores of Lake Victoria and the Coast Province, but the crop also does well in the dry parts of Central Province and Meru. In 1968, 174 819 acres (70 748 hectares) were planted throughout the country which the Cotton Lint and Seed Marketing Board broke down by provinces as follows: Nyanza (60 366 acres, 24 429 hectares), Western (55 834 acres, 22 595 hectares), Coast (27 700 acres, 11 110 hectares) and Eastern/Central (30 919 acres, 12 512 hectares). From these areas the value of Kenya cotton in 1968 was £K398 134. The growing and marketing is supervised by the board, which is a government statutory body.

The aim of the government was to raise production to 100 000 bales by 1970. Towards the attainment of this end the board started in 1968 an ambitious pilot project at Wamumu in Kirinyaga, which aims at planting 1 000 acres (405 hectares) of cotton as a demonstration scheme. The board hopes that when it is fully producing (after about three years), it will be divided out to the original tenants. From the scheme the board hopes to obtain some useful experience in large farm cotton production. It may be too early to judge the project, but three years may be too short a time for an agricultural experiment of this kind and the poor yield in the first year might be said to confirm this view.

Indications are that cotton growing should expand especially if the hoped-for textile mills to be built in Western Province become a reality. The danger from cotton pests, particularly the American boll worm, continue to worry growers. The board must put more emphasis on seeking a control to these pests if the crop is to have a firm foundation.

Sugar

Sugar cane growing for milled sugar and jaggery has in the past been almost wholly a plantation activity by Asian growers in some 15 000 acres (6 073 hectares) in the foothills of the Nyando Escarpment near Kisumu and 14 000 acres (5 669 hectares) at Ramisi some 80 miles (129 km) south of Mombasa. In both these localities conditions are ideal for mechanised production. However, since 1965 considerable additional production has been achieved by African growers in the government-backed settlement schemes at Muhoroni, Songor and Koru. As a result of these, two additional factories have been erected. Total production in 1967 was 695 200 tons (706 737 tonnes), which earned the growers £K1 598 000 out of which £K85 292 was paid to the small farm growers.

Considerable expansion can certainly be achieved in Nyanza but only if all those concerned can cooperate and provide an efficient system between the growers, transporters and millers.

Fig. 9E Harvesting sugar cane, Muhoroni

Fig. 9F Arable farming at Molo in the heart of the Kenya Highlands. Note the terracing lines to check soil erosion, and the indigenous highland forest

Fig. 9G Boran bullocks at a borehole water trough in the Thomson's Falls area

Wheat, Maize and Other Cereals

Wheat was one of the main cash crops in the former White Highlands above 6 500 feet (1 976 m) where there was not sufficient rainfall for other crops. The main producing areas are Uasin Gishu, Nyandarua, Nakuru, Molo and Thomson's Falls. In 1967, some 328 900 acres (133 100 hectares) were planted (mainly in large farms) and earned the growers £K4 575 000.

Maize we have already mentioned, but it should be added here that in 1967 142 300 acres (57 586 hectares) were planted and earned the large farm sector £K2 872 000 while the small growers earned £K1 346 000. Barley is confined to large farms and earned the growers only £K242 000, but rice has expanded lately due to irrigation projects which the Government has introduced. In 1967, the small growers, mainly from Mwea and Tebere, earned £K387 000 from this much-liked crop.

Coconuts and Cashew Nuts

These two crops are found together along the coastal belt where they have proved to be extremely popular. In fact the palm tree is now almost a near-natural plant along the coastal belt where it provides food, coir, toddy and thatching material. In 1967 small farm growers earned £K450 000 and large farmers £K30 000 from coconuts.

Cashew nuts are a more recent innovation on the coast, but, like coconuts, are very popular because of the little work which growing them involves. In 1967, small growers earned £K392 000 and the large farmers £K30 000.

Other Cash Crops

Pineapples, fodder crops and grass leys are the most important here. Pineapples, from Machakos and Thika in particular, are now an important export item. Other crops include tobacco from Kitui and Embu and kapok from the coast. Carnations and sunflowers should also be noted, and bixa, which is used in the manufacture of lipstick, was becoming important along the coast as a peasant cash crop until its market price fell.

Pastoralism

As in crop husbandry, pastoralism in Kenya shows two sharply contrasting stages of development. There is the traditional nomadism on the one hand, and, on the other, the modern commercial farming for dairy, beef, and other animal products such as hides and skins and wool. In the traditional set-up many tribes carried on pastoralism hand in hand with cultivation, but amongst the Nilo-Hamitic peoples, the Masai, Kalenjin and Somali, pastoralism was almost a monoculture and livestock for generations provided almost all the diet.

Many authors have emphasised that Africans kept animals mainly for social prestige and as a symbol of wealth. While this might have been the case, it should be remembered that these animals could always be exchanged for many other immediate or unforeseen family needs, for example, the well known bride price. Before a money economy developed, the keeping of animals was a means of storing resources, and looked at in this light it is easier to understand why everyone tried to increase his herd.

Fig. 9H Flock of Corriedale sheep on one of the college farms, Egerton Agricultural College, Njoro. Menegai Crater is in the background

There are not statistics to show clearly the total number of animals in Kenya. The estimates at the end of 1968 of the Head of the Animal Husbandry Division of the Ministry of Agriculture were:

Cattle—Dairy grade		491 000
Beef cattle		6 752 000
Camels		1 200 000
Sheep—Wool sheep		569 000
Hair sheep		3 667 000
Goats		5 400 000
Pigs		37 000
Poultry (about)		10 000 000

Statistics are particularly lacking in the African areas. In 1966, O'Connor published a choropleth map which related the number of cattle to human population (Fig. 9.2). The map thus gives a generalised impression of the number of cattle per unit area besides giving the high density areas, although the latter is marred by the fact that human population density is so low in the dry areas of the country.

The cattle are mainly *Zebu* and *Sanga* types which are said to have originated in Asia and Ethiopia respectively. In northern Kenya, camels are more important.

Livestock in Large Farms

Statistics are more readily available in the former White Highlands where the exotics from Europe are

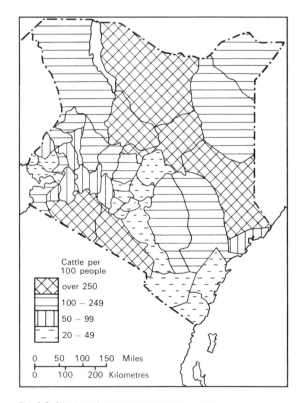

Cattle per
100 people

	over 250
	100 – 249
	50 – 99
	20 – 49

0   50   100   150   Miles
0   100   200   Kilometres

Fig. 9.2 Number of cattle per head of population

141

most important. More recently cross-breeding with the local types has achieved considerable success. We should also point out here that it is this section of the husbandry that accounts for nearly 80% of the 11·9% of the total share of the domestic export which was accounted for by animal products during the seven years between 1961 and 1967.

The numerical breakdowns of the animals by type and purpose in 1960 and 1967 are compared in Table 9.3. Fig. 9.3 is a simplified sketch to show the main agricultural regions (land use) in the former White Highlands, which during the colonial period amounted to 7·5 million acres (3 million hectares).

Table 9.3 *Large farm livestock numbers in 1960 and 1967*

Type of animal	1960	1967
Dairy cattle		
Cows	241 700	144 500
Heifers	163 400	89 100
Bulls and bull calves	7 600	11 600
Total	412 700	245 200
Beef cattle:		
Cows	134 700	126 500
Bulls and bull calves	12 600 }	
Other	419 600 }	358 000
Total	566 900	484 500
Sheep	582 600	477 700
Horses	4 600	—
Pigs	50 500	35 600
Poultry	255 800	207 600

[1] *Statistical Abstracts*, Republic of Kenya, 1968.

Cash revenue to producers in the large farm category during 1967 was £K7 480 000, with the value of dairy and livestock being nearly equal.

The future of this section of Kenya's farming economy is probably secure and promising. It is clearly tied up with the country's stability which will determine the future participation and contribution of people who are not Kenya citizens. The transfer of these farms to African ownership might also be expected. The danger in this case is that the new African owners might fail to maintain full production because they are absent in other full-time senior positions in the cities.

Government Assistance to African Agriculture

The historical development of commercial agriculture in Kenya, including the fact that this sector of the nation's participation was largely in the hands of non-Africans (who were mostly non-Kenyans), necessitated the independent Kenya Government to encourage its citizens to break through into this occupation. We have already

noted that by about 1958 most cash crops could be grown by Africans and that by 1959 the White Highlands had technically ceased to be a 'European reserve'. However, lack of capital was such a limiting factor that Africans could not be expected to buy off some of the European farmers who might have been willing to sell their farms to Africans. This is the background against which the involvement of the Kenyan Government must be seen. In what follows in these pages we are not concerned with the economic or political soundness of the methods used by the government to achieve its goals. We must add though that it has represented a major operation and the fact that it has been so smooth is clearly a credit to the government although it has cost a great deal of money.

Government assistance to farmers has included the establishment of settlement schemes, cooperative societies, and credit facilities through the establishment of para-governmental statutory bodies such as the Agricultural Finance Corporation, the Kenya Tea Development Authority and the Pyrethrum Board of Kenya. There are other credit facilities in range management and advice services on such items as artificial insemination. Also farmers can obtain short term crop finance through the Minimum Financial Returns (MFR) while those in the settlement schemes have fairly elaborate credit facilities. More recently a cooperative bank has been set up. The government also has tractor unit facilities in at least eight districts in the country. In other directions the government has also embarked on irrigation projects to aid production and provide employment facilities in certain suitable localities. It is necessary to examine the settlement schemes programme and the irrigation projects in a little more detail.

Settlement Schemes

This is the method which the Kenya Government has used to accelerate African participation and ownership of land in the former 'White Highlands'. It should also be pointed out that it was a convenient way of ensuring that the outgoing settlers were given fair prices for their land and the improvements that they had made.

The Kenya Government obtained financial assistance from the British Government, the International Bank for Reconstruction and Development (IBRD), the Commonwealth Development Corporation (CDC) and the West German Government, amounting to £K25 091 000 for the operation. This money was on long term loan save for the £K9 649 000 from Britain, which was a grant.

The farms were either given to individual settlers or were farmed by large groups as cooperative schemes. There are two types of schemes for the individual farmer, the *high density schemes* and the *low density schemes*. The former are for small farmers who had no land before or had been dispossessed by land consolidation or as squatters, and who had no capital of their own. Plots in this category are usually small: 10–15 acres (4–6 hectares) or 27–48 acres (11–19

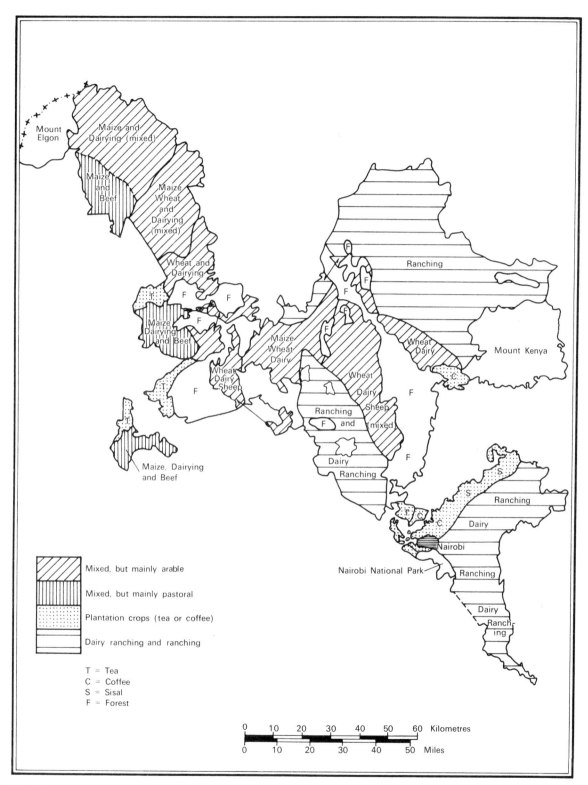

Mount
Elgon

Maize and
Dairying (mixed)

Maize
and
Beef

Maize
Wheat
and
Dairying
(mixed)

Wheat and
Dairying

T   F   F

Maize
Dairying   F
and Beef

Ranching

F

F

F

F

F

T

Wheat
Dairy

Mount Kenya

Maize
Wheat
Dairy

Wheat
Dairy
Sheep

C

F

F

F

Wheat
Dairy
Sheep
(mixed)

T

Ranching
F   and

Dairy

Ranching

F

Maize, Dairying
and Beef

S

S

Ranching

Dairy

T C

C

Nairobi

Nairobi National Park

Ranching

Dairy

Ranch-
ing

Mixed, but mainly arable

Mixed, but mainly pastoral

Plantation crops (tea or coffee)

Dairy ranching and ranching

T = Tea
C = Coffee
S = Sisal
F = Forest

| 0 | 10 | 20 | 30 | 40 | 50 | 60 | Kilometres |

| 0 | 10 | 20 | 30 | 40 | 50 | Miles |

Fig. 9.3 Land use in the former 'White Highlands'

143

hectares) on the not so rich sections, and were expected to give incomes of £K25–70 per year. The low density schemes were intended for those Africans who were experienced in farming and had some capital of their own. They include some of the larger farms which were bought by Africans prior to the scheme. The size of the plots in this category vary from 50–250 acres (20–100 hectares).

The high density schemes eventually became known as the 'Million Acre Scheme' because that was the acreage involved. The low density scheme was to include an additional 180 000 acres (72 844 hectares) and the target date for the completion of the transfers was between 1961 and 1966.

The Cooperative Settlement Schemes were necessary in the cases where farms did not lend themselves to fragmentation on ecological or economic considerations. These were to be given to people who came together and formed farming cooperative societies. They included ranching areas, as in Machakos; a special type is the Ol Kalou Salient which is a sort of super-co-

operative society but with the Government having a strong say and interest in its running because of large financial backing to the society. Table 9.4 gives a progress report on this unique venture.

The information given in Table 9.4 involved some 135 settlement schemes throughout the country. The individual schemes are shown in Fig. 9.4.

Irrigation in Kenya

The Government with the assistance of the United Nations and other agencies has plans for irrigation in six areas of the country. Two of these, Taveta and Lower Tana Basin, are still not yet started but feasibility work is in progress. The actual schemes are shown in Fig. 9.5 with the state of what has been achieved and what can be expanded. However, we must comment here that lack of capital makes the realisation of the Tana Basin Scheme still look far away. It is an expensive scheme in a difficult environment but given the development of the Seven

Table 9.4 *Progress of land settlement schemes in 1964–5 and 1967–8*[1]

Province and type of scheme	1964–5			Total at end of 1968		
	Area planned		Plots allocated	Area planned		Plots allocated
	acres	hectares		acres	hectares	
Eastern						
High Density	5 648	2 286	143	32 974	13 344	768
Low Density	—	—	—	—	—	—
Total	5 648	2 286	143	32 974	13 344	768
Central						
High Density	74 332	30 081	3 957	378 828	153 306	13 319
Low Density	30 947	12 524	317	65 563	26 532	1 411
Total	105 279	42 605	4 274	444 391	179 828	14 730
Nyanza						
High Density	9 666	3 912	483	44 509	18 912	1 617
Low Density	25 532	10 332	1 200	43 724	17 694	1 796
Total	35 198	14 244	1 683	88 233	36 606	3 413
Western						
High Density	43 292	17 519	2 250	167 325	67 714	6 716
Low Density	—	—	—	21 107	8 442	489
Total	43 292	17 519	2 250	188 432	76 156	7 205
Rift Valley						
High Density	31 564	12 773	1 070	203 824	82 484	4 452
Low Density	15 700	6 354	262	48 569	19 655	1 121
Total	47 264	19 127	1 332	252 393	102 139	5 573
All Schemes	236 681	95 781	8 682	1 006 423	408 083	31 689

[1] *Statistical Abstracts* Republic of Kenya, 1968; Ministry of Lands and Settlement; etc.

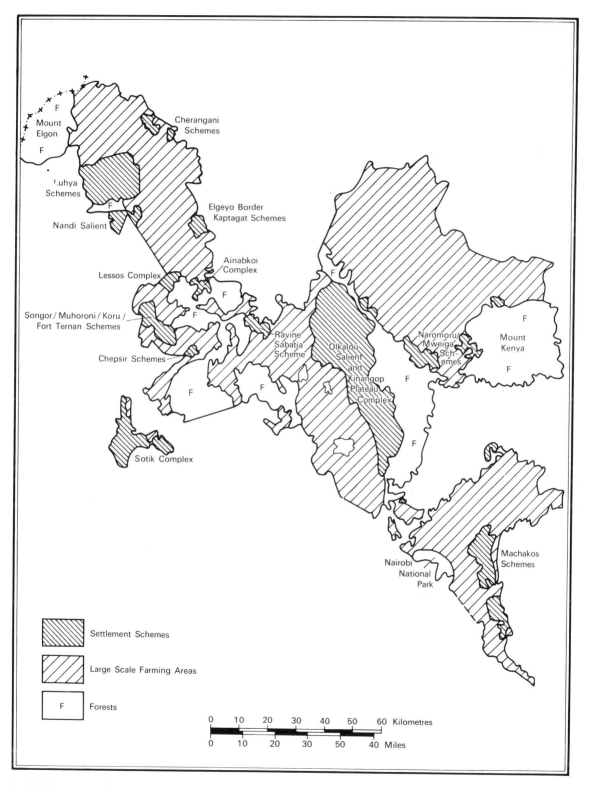

Mount Elgon

F

F

F

Cherangani
Schemes

Luhya
Schemes

Nandi Salient

Elgeyo Border
Kaptagat Schemes

Lessos Complex

Ainabkoi
Complex

F

Songor / Muhoroni / Koru /
Fort Ternan Schemes

F

Ravine
Sabatia
Scheme

F

F

Olkalou
Salient
and
Kinangop
Plateau
Complex

F

Naromoru/
Mweiga
Schemes

Mount
Kenya

F

F

F

Chepsir Schemes

F

F

Sotik Complex

Nairobi
National
Park

Machakos
Schemes

Settlement Schemes

Large Scale Farming Areas

F   Forests

0   10   20   30   40   50   60   Kilometres

0   10   20   30   50   40   Miles

Fig. 9.4 Settlement schemes

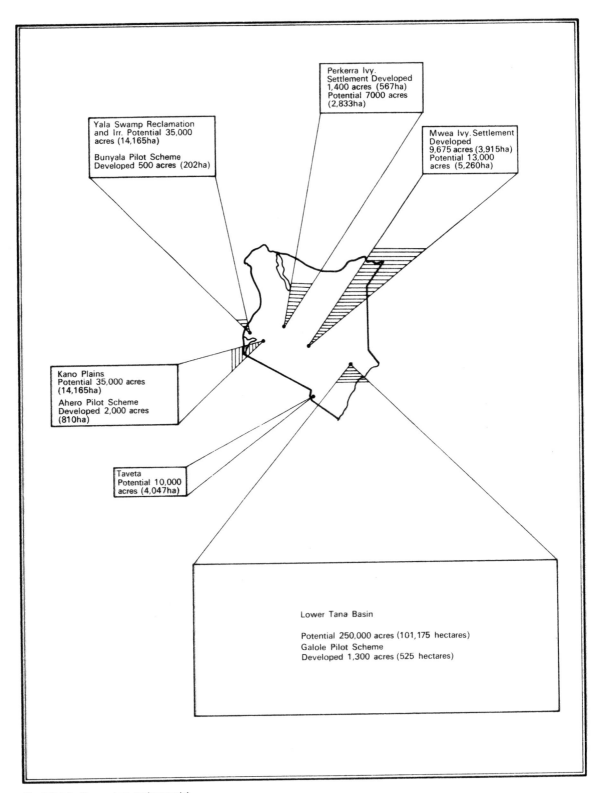

Perkerra Ivy.
Settlement Developed
1,400 acres (567ha)
Potential 7000 acres
(2,833ha)

Mwea Ivy. Settlement
Developed
9,675 acres (3,915ha)
Potential 13,000
acres (5,260ha)

Yala Swamp Reclamation
and Irr. Potential 35,000
acres (14,165ha)

Bunyala Pilot Scheme
Developed 500 acres (202ha)

Kano Plains
Potential 35,000 acres
(14,165ha)

Ahero Pilot Scheme
Developed 2,000 acres
(810ha)

Taveta
Potential 10,000
acres (4,047ha)

Lower Tana Basin

Potential 250,000 acres (101,175 hectares)
Galole Pilot Scheme
Developed 1,300 acres (525 hectares)

Fig. 9.5 Irrigation projects and potential

146

Forks water storage facilities it should not prove impossible.

The Perkerra Scheme, which produces onions, is at some disadvantage as compared with other areas since it is rather remote. Mwea, with its adjoining Tebere Scheme, is already producing rice and is essentially a success story. The Tana Basin is suited for cotton, kenaf, sugar and groundnuts. So far only a pilot scheme involving 1 300 acres (526 hectares) at Galole is operating and if money is found then a pilot of 10 000 acres (4 047 hectares) to the west of the river bank between Funi, Ingille and Galole will be started. The Kano Scheme has been discussed by Odhiambo, Ominde and Ojany (1968). Again the pilot project is now completed but there do not appear to be funds for the intended extension. All told, the Kano Plains is the one best suited for immediate development. The Yala and Bunyala Schemes are still in their early stages of investigation. At the end of the 1967–8 Financial Year all these irrigation schemes had cultivated 9 568 acres (3 871 hectares) and settled 2 330 plotholders, and those in production produced £K485 243 from the crops planted.

It is difficult to see much development beyond the present stage achieved in the irrigation programmes in the country. The main limitation is clearly lack of funds although the problem of personnel is also there. If Kenya can persuade one of the friendly developed countries to assist in this then, as has been said, the Kano Plains is the area most naturally suited to irrigation.

References

MORGAN, W. T. W. 'The "White Highlands" of Kenya', *The Geog. Journal*, Vol. 129, part 2, 1963, pp. 140–155.

BROWN, L. H. 'Agriculture and land tenure in Kenya Colony', in *The Natural Resources of East Africa*, ed. E. W. Russell, East African Literature Bureau, 1962.

O'CONNOR, A. M. *An Economic Geography of East Africa*, Bell, 1966.

COTTON LINT AND SEED MARKETING BOARD (KENYA). *Fourteenth Annual Report and Accounts for the Year ended 31st October 1968*, 1969.

Wamumu Cotton Pilot Project Operations Review 1968–9 Season, Unpublished.

THE PYRETHRUM BOARD OF KENYA AND THE PYRETHRUM MARKETING BOARD. *Annual Report and Accounts for the period 1st October 1967 to 30th September 1968*, 1969.

THE KENYA TEA DEVELOPMENT AUTHORITY *Annual Report and Accounts for the Kenya Tea Development Authority for the period 1st July 1967 to 30th June 1968*, 1968.

THE TEA BOARDS OF EAST AFRICA 'Tea', Vol. 10, Number 7, April 1969.

HOPCRAFT, D. 'Wildlife and land-use in Africa', *African Scientist*, No. 1, August 1969, pp. 21–26.

ODHIAMBO, T. R., OMINDE, S. H. and OJANY, F. F. 'The Kano Plain: A geographical challenge', *African Scientist*, Vol. 1, August 1969, pp. 7–20.

ODINGO, R. S. *The Kenya Highlands: Land Use and Agriculture Development*, East African Publishing House, 1971.

Chapter 10
Forestry, Fisheries and Mineral Resources

Forest Resources

Present Extent

At the end of 1967 about 5·2% of the land surface of Kenya was covered by various types of forest. Of the total forest area of 11 406·3 sq miles (29 542·2 km²), 41·6% was not analysed into the various forest types. The remaining 58·4% consisted of: 31·7% closed forest, 12·4% woodland, 5·5% bamboo forest, 7·4% grassland forest, and 1·4% mangrove forest. Forests owned privately covered 39·9% of the total forested area, whilst central government and county council authority forests accounted for 34·9% and 25·2% respectively of the remaining forested areas.[1]

Afforestation Programme

Extensive afforestation has been going on in Kenya since 1946. About 7 710·9 sq miles (19 971·2 km²) of forested land was registered at the end of 1963, and of this approximately 4·1% was under plantation forest mainly of exotic trees. From 1953 to the end of 1963 there was an increase in the plantations area from about 178·1 to 315·6 sq miles (461·3 to 817·4 km²).[2] At the end of 1967, the total afforested area was 376·6 sq miles (975·4 km²). The annual afforestation rate in Kenya is scheduled at 23·4 sq miles (60·7 km²), including the Turbo special scheme plantation[3] for future Broderick Falls paper mill supplies.

Forest Production

The accompanying Table 10.1 shows forest production, 1958–67.

Other forest products are: mangrove poles, power and telegraph poles, bamboos, fence posts, mangrove bark and withies.

Location

Apart from the forest patches at the coast and elsewhere (Fig. 10.1), the principal Kenya forests are located in the highlands flanking the Rift Valley. The greater acreages lie to the east of the Rift Valley.

The forest belts coincide with those zones which receive relatively higher rainfalls (50 inches – 1 270 mm, or more annually). Some of Kenya's forests are, however, located in areas receiving annual rainfalls varying from 30 to 50 inches (762 to 1 270 mm). The Kenya forests do not thrive in localities which receive annual rainfalls below 30 inches (762 mm), except in areas either where the water-table approaches the surface or along permanent river courses.

Future Forecast

Although the indigenous forests are limited in extent in relation to Kenya's total area, they still contain moderately large quantities of industrial and domestic raw materials. Considerable quantities of the indigenous softwoods (especially podo and cedar) have already been cut, with the result that a decline in saw-log supplies of these species seems imminent. Failure to improve the situation may result in the disappearance of the podocarpus timber, perhaps by the end of this century.[1] Similarly, sawn cedar may also be available only in reduced quantities.

It is likely that by about 1980 the Kenya Government will have planted about 550 sq miles (1 424·5 km²) or more with the exotic softwoods. The chief areas scheduled for exotic commercial tree plantations are in Kitale, Eldoret and Kisumu areas, Londiani, Thomson's Falls, Elburgon, Nairobi and Nyeri areas.[2] Other lesser areas earmarked for afforestation are at the coast and in southern parts of Eastern Province. The present 376·6 sq miles (975·4 km²) of exotic commercial tree plantations in Kenya are made up of about 80·8% softwoods (42·8%

---

[1] *Statistical Abstracts*, Republic of Kenya, Government Printer, 1968.
[2] R. B. Ogendo, 'Industrial significance of the Kenya forests', *Cahiers d'Etudes Africaines*, Vol. 6, 1966.
[3] This scheme is being increased at the rate of 4·7 sq miles (12·1 km²) per annum.

[1] F. T. Henson, 'The future of the timber industry in Kenya', *East Africa Economic Reviews*, (old series), vol. IV, No. 2, 1958, pp. 75–89.
[2] Daily Nation, 'Forest development in Kenya', 30 April 1969, Nairobi, pp. 12–13; see the accompanying map.

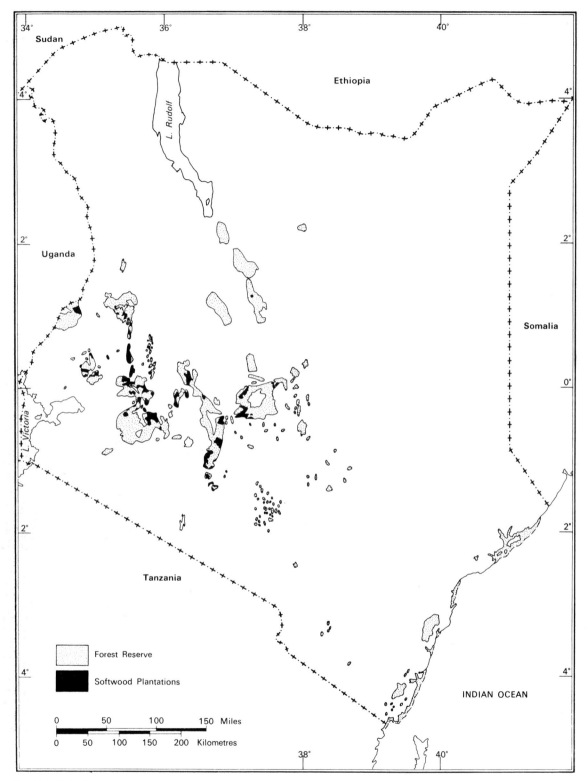

Sudan

Ethiopia

L. Rudolf

Uganda

2°

Somalia

L. Victoria

Tanzania

INDIAN OCEAN

Forest Reserve

Softwood Plantations

| 0 | 50 | 100 | 150 | Miles |

| 0 | 50 | 100 | 150 | 200 | Kilometres |

Fig. 10.1 Major forests

149

Table 10.1 *Forest production*[1]

Year	Thousands of cubic feet and m³ (round timber true volume)						Fuel sales (thousands of stacked cu feet and m³)	
	Total softwoods		Total hardwoods		Total hard and softwoods			
	cu feet	m³	cu feet	m³	cu feet	m³	cu feet	m³
1958	6 010	170	1 298	37	7 308	207	6 987	198
1959	5 784	164	1 133	32	6 917	196	6 459	183
1960	6 105	173	1 485	42	7 590	215	7 210	204
1961	3 418	97	649	18	4 067	115	6 386	181
1962	4 309	122	585	17	4 894	139	7 621	216
1963	4 243	120	496	14	4 739	134	5 867	167
1964	4 449	126	577	16	5 026	142	5 858	166
1965	6 929	196	602	17	7 531	213	6 725	190
1966	5 512	156	487	14	5 999	170	8 966	254
1967	7 690	218	626	18	8 316	236	6 157	174

[1] *Statistical Abstracts*, Republic of Kenya, 1968. Source: *Statistical Abstracts*, 1968.

of various species of pine and 38% of cypress) and 10·1% hardwoods. Indigenous softwoods only make up about 5%, whilst the indigenous hardwoods account for another 4·1% of the total area afforested to date.

The indigenous softwoods are being used at the moment but will in time be replaced by the cheaper exotic softwoods such as pines and cypresses, as these become available. As a result, the demand for both podo and cedar will invariably decline. Because the indigenous species either do poorly or are unsuccessful in plantations, the very slow process of natural regeneration is now largely relied upon. However, there remains a large quantity of over-mature cedar which is unsuitable as sawlogs but invaluable for the manufacture of fabricated timber products such as hardboard, fibre-board, blockboard, and other products. Provided they are properly utilised and the demand does not increase suddenly, the over-mature cedar supplies are probably sufficient for approximately another 70 to 90 years.

Estimates of sawn timber to be expected from a given plantation or natural forest are difficult to arrive at, although in recent years some forest experts[1] have given such estimates as the possible quantities of exotic timber for the years indicated in the accompanying table.[2]

[1] 'Future importance of Kenya's timber industry', *E. A. Trade and Industry*, Vol 1, No. 8, 1954, pp. 16 and 55.
[2] F. T. Henson, 'The future of timber industry in Kenya', *E. A. Economics Review*, (old series), Vol. iv, No. 2, 1958, pp. 75–89.

From about 1970 onwards, the Kenya afforestation programme should begin to yield an increased volume of available exotic softwoods. Moreover, since the conifers cultivated in Kenya grow twice or thrice as fast as those cultivated in Scandinavia, and reach comparatively great heights (80–120 feet, 24·3–36·5 m), and fair diameters (1–2 feet, 0·30 to 0·61 m) in about 20 years, the planned big increases in exotic softwoods, particularly pines and cypresses, should ultimately provide about 50% of all exotic softwood supplies. If the present annual rate of afforestation (23·4 sq miles or 60·7 km²) is either maintained or increased, the forest-based industries are unlikely to run short of raw materials in the foreseeable future. However, it is difficult to be absolutely certain because there is always the possibility that exotic softwood timber demand development, especially in Uganda, may be faster than the estimates, with consequent higher demands on Kenya's timber output. In a normal year, the output from the forest is about 7 million cu feet (198 100 m³), excluding some 1·5 million cu feet (42 450 m³) from private forests.

Timber Trade

General

In Kenya, the marketing of wood and wood products is

Table 10.2 *Sawn timber production*

		Estimated	
	1970	1975	1980
Logged weight of exotic softwood logs tons	258 000	338 000	429 000
tonnes	262 141	343 425	435 885
Expected recovery true from the logs	55%	55%	60%
Sawn timber (in tons of 50 cu feet)	142 000	186 000	257 000
(in tonnes of 1·415 m³)	144 279	188 985	261 125

Fig. 10A Felling indigenous forest

practically a monopoly of the private sector. Exports of all types of timber fall into two general categories:
a exports to Uganda and Tanzania, and
b exports to countries outside the Community.

There has been a steady improvement on the total value of exports, especially to Uganda and Tanzania. Exotic softwoods are now more popular than the indigenous podo and cedar softwoods. In 1965 total exports of exotic softwoods was 284 900 cu feet (8 062·7 m³), whilst in 1967 the exports had increased to 467 000 cu feet (13 216·1 m³). During the same period podo and cedar exports combined decreased from 337 800 to 175 000 cu feet (9 559·7 to 4 952·5 m³). Between 1966 and 1968 the sale of cypress timber to Uganda and Tanzania together nearly doubled.[1]

In the international market several countries are involved. Whilst Reunion normally purchases the unsorted grade, European sales consist mainly of prime and selected grades of softwoods.

The other major exports comprise wood carvings and charcoal. The local demand for charcoal, fuelwood and sawn timber continues to be favourable and brisk.

Sawn timber

In the field of sawn timber[2] nearly 3 million cu feet (85 000 m³)[3] of sawn wood was sold by the 35 licensed sawmills. Although the following trade analyses are based on the 35 sawmills they are not the only producers of sawn timber in Kenya. There are over 200 other sawmills of various sizes which process the raw materials from private forests. It is these other sawmills which supply most of the timber consumed by the African household sector, and their combined output is considerable. It would seem that apart from approximately 2·2 million cu feet (62 260 m³) sold by the licensed sawmills in Kenya, a further 800 000 cu feet (22 600 m³) which is put on the rural market comes from these other sawmills.

The quantities of sawn timber sold during 1967 are given in Table 10.3 below.

[1] *Progress Report (1966–68) for the African Forestry Commission (Second Session)*, Govt Printer, Nairobi, 1969.
[2] F. D. McLearon, 'Where does the timber go?' *Asili*, Min. of Nat. Resources publication, No. 1, Jan. 1969, pp. 9–12.
[3] To be exact: 2 916 203 cu. ft. (6 882·2 m³).

Fig. 10B A Forestry Department nursery

Table 10.3 *Sawn timber production 1967, by species*

Species/group	Volume		% Volume of total	Value £K
	cu feet	m³		
Cypress	1 758 730	49 772	60·3	525 268
Pine	23 261	658	0·8	5 598
Podo	711 773	20 143	24·4	288 009
Cedar	274 927	7 780	9·4	118 673
Total softwood	2 768 691	78 354	94·9	937 548
Total hardwood	147 512	4 175	5·1	82 648
Grand Total	2 916 203	82 529	100·0	1 020 196

The 2 916 203 cu feet (82 529 m³) produced by the licensed mills was sold as follows:

a about 5% to countries outside the East African Community,

b 20% transferred to Tanzania and Uganda, and

c the remaining 75% sold locally in Kenya.

The European market for Kenya timber is restricted to the first and second grades of cypress, cedar, podo and a few choice hardwoods. This is due to the relatively high milling charges in Kenya and the high transport costs. The principal European timber importers interested in Kenya sawn timber are Norway, UK, Belgium, Netherlands, Denmark and Germany.

The only large export market for unsorted grades is Reunion in the Indian Ocean. In 1967 this island bought 21 000 cu feet (594 m³) of cypress. The possibilities for extending cypress export sales to the North African countries and the Persian Gulf area are at present under investigation.

Although the exported sawn timber is small in proportion to what is consumed in East Africa, the 151 181 cu feet (4 278 m³) exported in 1967 earned Kenya £K94 637 worth of foreign currency. However, the quantity exported annually has been decreasing in recent years owing to increased demand within East Africa. The increased sales of cypress sawn timber to Uganda and Tanzania since 1964 have been close on 400%. However, the effect of these transfers is offset somewhat by the movement of timber from the neighbouring states into Kenya. For instance, while 43 000 cu feet (1 217 m³) of hardwoods went out from Kenya to Uganda and Tanzania in 1967, 181 000 cu feet (5 122 m³) were brought into Kenya from the two neighbouring states. On the other hand, more than half a million cu feet (over 14 150 m³) of softwood timber was exported to Uganda and Tanzania in 1967 and earned Kenya almost £K200 000.[1]

[1] J. E. M. Arnold, 'Present wood consumption and future requirements in Kenya', F.A.O. Report to E.A. High Commission, 1962.

The Uganda forest industry is based on the indigenous species, so it relies on Kenya to supply softwood construction timber. Tanzania also relies on Kenya for similar timber because most of her industrial plantations are still immature and cannot, like those of Kenya, supply all her internal softwood timber needs. However, as the internal softwood supplies in the two countries become more adequate, the market for Kenya cypress in the two countries will ultimately disappear.

In considering the home market for sawn timber the segments enumerated below are worth studying:

a urban users, including
   i public agencies;
   ii main towns;
   iii other towns, settlements, etc.;
   iv large industrial units;
   v the more densely settled areas around Nairobi.

b rural areas, including
   i African households;
   ii capital-intensive farms;
   iii non-household units;
   iv mining industries.

The African household category contains most of the population, has the largest consumption of any sector of sawn timber and poles, and also has the greatest prospects for increased consumption. Much of the 2·2 million cu feet (62 250 m³) of sawn timber absorbed internally by Kenya is consumed in the 'urban sector'. Only the lowest grades of the softwoods end up in the rural market.

Fishery Resources

Kenya's forests have been developed and exploited to a much greater extent than her fishery resources. The future industrial activities dependent on fishing will continue to rely both on the inland fisheries and the sea fisheries.

Fig. 10C Turkana fishermen, Lake Rudolf

Inland Fisheries

The inland fisheries are of two major types:
a those of Nyanza, Western and Central Provinces, and
b those located in the Coast Province.

The inland fisheries of Nyanza, Western and Central Provinces comprise the following:
a Lake Victoria fishery,
b Lake Naivasha fishery,
c Lake Baringo fishery, and
d Turkana fishery at Ferguson's Gulf of Lake Rudolf. However, if the fish culture farms and/or hatcheries are also included amongst these sources, then the smaller sources may be considered to consist of:
a the fish ponds of Nyanza, Central and Western Provinces;
b the river fisheries, especially the trout fisheries;
c the fish culture farms at Sagana and Homa Bay; and
d the trout hatchery at Kabaru.

The fresh water fisheries of the Coast Province consist of the following:
a the Tana and Sabaki river fisheries, centred on Lakes Balisa and Shakababo and other smaller lakes in the two rivers;
b the Lake Jipe fishery in Taveta district;
c the Lake Chala fishery–a volcanic crater lake near Taveta in the same district;
d Tsavo National Park fish resources (especially those of Aruba Dam, the Galana area of Galana River and the Lugard Falls area).

Sea Fisheries

These fall into the following principal divisions:
a Lamu and the north coast fishery (the most productive);
b Malindi fishery;
c Mombasa and the south coast fishery.
Apart from these three major areas, there are others, such as:
a sedentary fisheries (based on bêche-de-mer, oysters and green turtles); and
b sport fishing (an important tourist attraction), centred especially on Malindi, but also developed in Mombasa, Kilifi and Shimoni.
There are also the two fish reserves at Watamu and at Malindi's Casuarina Point. The two fish reserves are a great attraction to many tourists and local residents. They are especially noted for their great variety of fish life.

Production and Miscellaneous Aspects of the Fisheries

Owing to the delay in the publication of the 1967 and 1968 reports on the Kenya fisheries, considerable use has

153

Table 10.4 *1966 fish production*

Location and/or fish type	Quantity		Gross retail value
	long tons	tonnes	£K
Freshwater fish			
Lake Victoria	15 200	15 444	2 042 880
Lake Baringo	600	610	94 080
Lake Rudolf	1 500	1 524	234 000
Lake Naivasha	900	914	140 400
Other lakes	950	965	148 200
Fish ponds	200	203	22 400
Rivers	1 500	1 524	185 600
Total	20 850	21 184	2 867 560
Marine fish			
Lamu and N. Coast	3 055	3 104	Not available
Malindi area (and Kilifi)	1 305	1 326	Not available
Mombasa and S. Coast	2 045	2 078	Not available
Total	6 405	6 508	789 059
Other marine products			
Crustacea	138	140	105 712
Oyster (meats and grit)	90	91	6 526
Bêche-de-mer	22	22	2 406
Green turtle	9	9	870
Total	259	262	115 514
Grand total	27 515	27 954	3 772 133

been made of the out-dated 1966 report. The figures quoted from the report should be regarded therefore as more of an indication of exploitation activities taking place and their relative importance than as an accurate quantitative picture.

In 1965 the total production of fish and other marine products by the Kenya fishing industry was 23 018 tons (23 392·3 tonnes), or about 83·7% of the equivalent total of 27 514 tons (27 961·4 tonnes) for 1966. The gross value of the 1966 output was about £K3·7 million, of which the 12 300 fishermen were paid £K1 443 203, or £K52·5 per ton (£K51·7 per tonne).

In Nyanza a broadening of statistical coverage and exploratory fishing indicated the expansion of the work on the Lake Victoria fishery, and the actual start of the implementation of the first development projects for the area. Total landings for the Kenya waters of the lake increased to 15 200 tons (15 477·2 tonnes). During 1966, a new fishery station was opened at Homa Bay.

In 1966 there was no major expansion of the domestic fishpond scheme in Nyanza, Western and Central Provinces. However, satisfactory progress was noted, especially in the improvement of pondfish farming techniques. There are more than 22 000 ponds at present

in use and total fish production from them has increased to about 200 tons (203·3 tonnes) valued at £K22 400.

In northern Kenya, a significant expansion of the Lake Rudolf fishery at Ferguson's Gulf has been achieved. Towards the end of the year, new markets for salted Lake Rudolf fish were established in Uganda and Zaire (Congo); consequently, production in this area has increased to about 1 500 tons (1 524·4 tonnes). A new Fisheries Department station was established here in 1966.

From the fish culture farm at Sagana Station, about 100 000 tilapia and black bass fingerlings were distributed to be stocked in dams and ponds throughout Kenya. A small proportion was also exported to Tanzania, Uganda and Ethiopia.

At the Kabaru trout hatchery, the production of rainbow trout and brown trout fingerlings totalled 84 999 fish. Altogether, 119 062 trout fingerlings were distributed for stocking in public, private and allied waters, and a few were retained and reared for breeding purposes. The Kabaru trout factory has recently been enlarged.

On Lake Naivasha and also in Kampi-ya-Samaki on Lake Baringo, new fisheries stations have been established. Lake Baringo's output during 1966 was about 600 tons (609·8 tonnes), whilst Lake Naivasha's output was slightly higher, at 900 tons (914·6 tonnes).

Production of sea fish, including molluscs, crustacea, turtles and bêche-de-mer has increased further, and totalled 6 664 tons (6 722·4 tonnes) with a gross value of £K904 573. Owing to improved marketing facilities[1] and fair weather conditions at sea, especially in Lamu area,[2] it was possible to raise the sea fish output for 1966.

In 1966, big-game fishing had a record sailfish catch of 2 417 fish, 94·3% of which were caught in the Malindi area. About 49 marlin and 9 423 other sport fish species were also recorded during the year.

Kenya Fish Trade

At the side, and overleaf, are given three tables illustrating the Kenya fish trade.

Tables 10.5 and 10.6 indicate that Kenya still imports more fish than it exports. The value of Kenya's fish exports is only about 11% of that of its fish imports. In East Africa Kenya's fish imports from Uganda and Tanzania are almost four times as great in value as Kenya's own fish exports to the two members of the Community. Thus Kenya needs to produce more fish for its internal market and should therefore encourage the budding fishing industry.

Surveys of the Kenya Fisheries

Four important surveys have been carried out on the potential of the Kenya fisheries, and the findings of the surveys have been published in the form of reports. The latter have been studied and accepted by the Kenya Government and are as follows:
1. UNDP/FAO Report No. TA.2144. 'Report to the Government of Kenya on Kenya Fisheries Development possibilities'.
2. Sparks A. K. 'Report to the Government of Kenya on Shell-fish Survey', US Agency for International Development.
3. UNDP/FAO Report No. TA.2191. 'Report to the Government of Kenya on Long-line Fishing Resources in East African Waters'.
4. ASMIC 'Report to the Government of Kenya on the Possibility of Establishing a Deep-sea Fishing Industry in Kenya'. French Govt Technical Co-operative Agency in association with Promopeche.

1 The fish report on 'Fisheries Development Possibilities'[3] deals with the whole range of fisheries activity throughout Kenya, and emphasises the need for the development of the Rift Valley fishery resources of

folio 253 – galley 58

1 These resulted largely from the establishment of the government-sponsored fishing company called 'Kenya Inshore Fisheries Limited'.
2 The sea adjoining the Lamu district is the most productive on the Kenya Coast.
3 Based on D. H. Rhodes' work.

Table 10.5 *Fish imports*

Year	Dried, salted or smoked			Fresh or frozen			Canned			Crustacea			Fish-meal			Fish-oil			Total		
	tons	tonnes	£K	tons	tonnes	£K	tons	tonnes	£K	tons	tonnes	£K	tons	tonnes	£K	tons	tonnes	£K	tons	tonnes	£K
1964	667	678	45 101	49	50	16 408	288	293	62 617	15	15	4 585	240	239	13 451	46	47	4 959	1 301	1 322	147 121
1965	407	413	34 358	32	32	11 339	219	222	54 182	10	10	4 212	591	600	40 125	622	632	58 620	1 882	1 912	202 836
1966	1 268	1 288	95 481	48	49	18 647	217	220	54 709	9	9	3 569	398	404	28 455	33	33	4 260	1 973	2 003	205 121

Table 10.6 *Fish exports*

Year	Fresh and frozen fish			Other fish			Dried bêche-de-mer			Crustacea			Miscellaneous			Total		
	tons	tonnes	£K	tons	tonnes	£K	tons	tonnes	£K	tons	tonnes	£K	tons	tonnes	£K	tons	tonnes	£K
1964	22·1	22·4	3 908	25·8	26·2	8 192	9·6	9·7	1 493	13·5	13·7	6 175	0·2	0·2	16	71·2	72·3	19 785
1965	28·0	28·4	5 116	37·5	38·1	16 071	14·1	14·3	2 437	7·0	7·1	3 116	—	—	—	86·6	88·0	26 740
1966	35·4	36·0	5 595	24·3	24·7	8 675	4·0	4·1	768	13·4	13·6	7 014	—	—	—	77·0	78·2	22 052

Table 10.7 *East African Community fish trade*

Fish types	Imports from Uganda and Tanzania			Exports to Uganda and Tanzania		
	tons	tonnes	£K	tons	tonnes	£K
Fresh, chilled or frozen fish	331·3	336·6	62 306	57·0	57·9	14 328
Salted, dried or smoked fish	77·6	78·8	7 126	73·0	74·1	5 751
Crustacea	45·9	46·6	16 779	4·0	4·1	1 559
Total	454·8	462·0	86 211	134·0	136·1	21 638

Lakes Rudolf, Baringo and Naivasha. Apart from confirming the need for the development of the fisheries listed in the Revised Kenya Development Plan, the report also recommends additional fishery projects for implementation in the very near future. It is forecast in the report that when all Kenya's fish resources are fully exploited, the eventual annual fish output will amount to 250 000 tons (254 000 tonnes). The 1966 output, for example, is about 11 % of this estimated total.

In order to achieve even the lesser targets proposed in the Revised Development Plan, a considerable increase in the Fisheries Department staff is essential, especially in the specialised fields such as quality control, planning, training, statistics and marketing, etc. Already many of the recommended projects have been implemented, and some specialist staff have also been recruited.

2 The second report is based on Professor A. K. Sparks' work relating to the shellfish survey which took place between February and July of 1965. Although the report emphasises the commercial development of the lobster and prawn fisheries, it also deals, in general, with both crustacea and mollusc resources.

Perhaps the most valuable contribution of the survey and the report was the programme of experimental fishing designed to assess the extent of the prawn stocks of the Malindi/Formosa Bay area. This apart, the report also contains a useful summary, and attempts to consolidate the findings of various experimental programmes and other work on the shell fisheries of Kenya.

3 The Long-line Fishing Resources Report (published by FAO in 1966) summarises the results of the investigations into the possibilities for long-line fishing undertaken during 1964 and 1965 by both the Fisheries Department and the East African Marine Fisheries Research Organisation (EAMFRO). The report also analyses the catch records of a number of Japanese commercial fishing vessels which became available on their call in Mombasa.

A considerable amount of information was gained by concentrating the Fisheries Department vessel[1] on the

inshore waters up to 30 miles offshore, whilst the EAMFRO research vessel[2] tackled the middle-distance operations from 30 to 150 miles (48 to 240 km) offshore. Coverage of the more distant fishing grounds was achieved by collecting data and fishing logs from the Japanese commercial fishing boats whenever they visited Mombasa. The information synthesised from these three sources was sufficient to allow for a detailed analysis of the fish resources, and to provide a guide for the future management of the sea fishing industry.

It is obvious that the available fish stocks justify the establishment of a modest deep-sea fishing industry in the Mombasa area. However, further investigation should be carried out into the costs of establishing and running such an industry.

Both the Fisheries Department and the EAMFRO have continued to carry out regular long-line cruises as part of the normal exploratory fishing programme with the aim of achieving more accurately plotted seasonal variations in catch composition, better knowledge of the fishing grounds, and the effectiveness of different baits. All these items of information are bound to prove invaluable to the industry when it is finally established.

4 The Long-line Fishing Resources Report resulted in the posting of D. Charbonnier, a French fisheries expert, to Kenya in order to investigate costs and profitability of the proposed deep-sea fishing industry. His work was published as a report by the French Government Technical Co-operation Agency in association with an organisation called Promopeche set up by a number of French industrial concerns.

Although the proposed deep-sea fishing industry would face many problems, such as the lack of trained manpower and direct competition from well-established overseas companies, etc., the report concluded that the establishment of such an industry in the Mombasa area was economically feasible. In order to achieve economic viability, at the necessary scale of operation, the cost of establishing the industry would be £K1 845 000. Such an organisation could expect an annual turnover of

---

[1] *Menika II.*

[1] *RV Manihine.*

£K968 260, with working expenses totalling £K843 500. It would thus produce a gross profit before taxation of £K124 760. There seem to be good prospects, on this basis, for such an industry being established in the foreseeable future.

Mineral Resources

For any country water and building materials are the two most basic mineral requirements. The sources and the hydrological problems associated with the availability of water for domestic and industrial use have been mentioned elsewhere. A note on the building materials will be added here, but otherwise in what follows we aim at examining the more usual mining minerals.

Mining is a skilled operation requiring detailed geological information and considerable initial financial backing and for these reasons has tended to be the monopoly of a few large international companies.

Kenya, however, is not one of the main mineral producing countries because none of the world's major minerals has been found in large quantities in the country. The country has thus not attracted enough of the foreign capital necessary for detailed prospecting. Also, geological mapping of the country is still incomplete and as more detailed information accumulates new finds may well be possible.

Despite the above limitations traces of more than one hundred different useful minerals, ranging from gold to such little known minerals as anglesite and villiqumite (sodium fluoride) have been found. The full list of these minerals has been pleasantly presented by Du Bois (1966), and readers are recommended to look at this source. In the Geological Survey of Kenya bulletin Du Bois gives the uses (as far as known) of all the minerals concerned and the geographical localities of their occurrence. Some of the minerals appear to have limited uses at present but, as Du Bois also points out, as the more popular minerals get exhausted and as industrialisation develops, new uses are likely to emerge for the rarer minerals. Such a change could considerably alter the picture of our mineral potential.

Trona

Large quantities of this mineral occur in Lake Magadi, where it is mined by the Magadi Soda Company, which was formed in 1911. The trona is formed from intense leaching of the basic volcanic ash, which then collects at the bottom through spring seepage. The high rate of evaporation (due to high temperatures in an enclosed depression) further helps to create a situation suited for trona precipitation. The ash is almost pure sodium carbonate. Crude trona is also present on the floor of Magadi Crater near Chanler's Falls. The soda ash is used mainly in glass industries and for making soap and other cleansers. Another important use is in the chemical industry where it is refined into bicarbonate, caustic soda, drugs, dyestuffs and other chemicals for paper and rayon manufacture. It is also used for softening water, in oil refineries, and desulpherising steel. The main importers have been South Africa, Japan and India.

Gold

This was probably first discovered in Kenya in 1893 at Jombo in the Coast Province. A minor gold rush into Nyanza and Western Provinces occurred between 1922 and 1932. The main rock formation concerned is the gold-bearing Nyanzian and Kavirondian rocks. The Kakamega goldfield was discovered in 1931 and like the South Nyanza goldfield was associated with an intrusive granite. In these goldfields mineralisation has produced chiefly auriferous quartz veins, but at Macalder Nyanza Mine the type is auriferous sulphide.

Other localities which have produced or are still producing gold are at Lolgorien, Kihancha, Nandi, Sigalagala and Port Southby, while along the Turkwel River alluvial gold has been produced for some time. But the future of the mineral in Kenya is uncertain. Further efforts may be concentrated in modernising the mining companies to enable them to work at greater depths than has been achieved in the Nyanza mines.

Diatomite

Diatomaceous earth is formed by the accumulation of siliceous skeletons of freshwater organisms, diatoms and algae. Large deposits are found in Pleistocene lakebeds in the Rift Valley. Kariandus, Elementaita, Gicheru, Eburu, Legemunge and Koora are the main localities, with the Kariandus deposit being the one worked to the greatest extent; the Legumunge deposit near Olorgasailie has also been worked since 1956, and the Soysambu deposit has also been worked to some extent.

The main uses for diatomite depend on the size and shape of the diatoms. It is used as a filtering agent in the clarification of fruit juices, soft drinks, and sugar. It is also used in heat and sound insulation, in lagging compounds, as a flatting agent in some paints, as a dusting agent to prevent the caking of fertilisers, and in the drycleaning of fabrics.

Carbon Dioxide

This gas was first found in 1918 in fault fissures near Mt Margaret in the Kedong Valley. The main commercial discovery was made in 1946 at Esageri near Eldama Ravine. Production commenced in 1951 and another borehole was sunk at Kerita near Uplands in 1957. These holes produce the natural gas at the considerable pressure of 35 to 80 lb per sq inch (2·5 to 5·7 kg per cm^2). The gas is sold in steel cylinders and in solid state, when it is known as dry-ice.

The dry-ice is particularly well-suited for refrigeration in the transportation of meat, fish and other perishable foodstuffs such as vegetables.

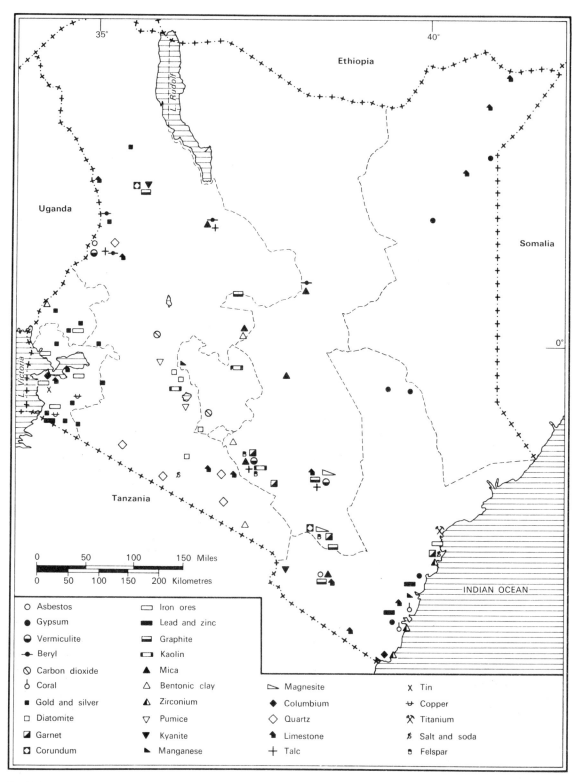

Fig. 10.2 Minerals of economic and potential economic importance

Silver

In Kenya this mineral occurs naturally alloyed with gold as electrum. It is found in the Marun river in West Pokot, although in 1962 99% of Kenya's production was found as a by-product of the Macalder Copper Mine. It has also been produced from manganese ore from Mrima. Silver is used as an alloy with copper for coinage, plate and jewellery. It is also used extensively for the silver salts used in photographic films and papers.

Asbestos

The main producing area is in Kaptumet in West Suk. It is used chiefly as an ingredient in insulated boiler-coverings, fireproof paints and, more extensively, it is mixed with cement to produce asbestos-cement roofing-sheets, pipes and other similar products.

Gypsum

The main producing areas are near Garissa and Malindi. It is used for cement manufacture, building and the manufacture of plaster of Paris and chalks. Other localities where this mineral is known are at Roka and Gongoni (both near Malindi) and in other parts of semi arid eastern Kenya at El Wak, the Daua Valley, and near Wajir and Konza.

Copper

Production in Kenya started in 1951 at the Macalder Mine in South Nyanza. Other localities where the mineral is known include the Gori River, Makuru, Oganga, Kitere and near Oyugis, all within the same rock system (Nyanzian and Basement). Other sites are in Tharaka, the Tsavo-Athi confluence, Vitengeni (near Mombasa), in the Karasuk hills and at Kipkomo near Kapenguria.

Copper is used mainly in the electrical industry owing to its excellent conductivity. Other uses are in alloys and in 'copper' coinage, while powdered copper is also used in metallurgical work; copper compounds (e.g. copper sulphate) are used as insecticides and fungicides.

Meerschaum

This clay was discovered in commercial amounts in 1953 in the Sinya Beds in the Lake Amboseli Basin. It is used to make smoking pipes and pipe bowls where its lightness and absorbent nature are ideal.

Kaolin

This substance occurs in the Basement rock especially near Opete in the Kilungu Hills of Machakos, and in the Rift Valley, where the mineral formed as a result of the action of steam through obsidian country rock, and near Karatina, where it is found in weathered felspathic gneiss. Kaolin is used chiefly to make fine porcelain and china, rubber and paint, and as a filler in paper.

Pumice

This is a very cellular glassy lava, and occurs widely in the Naivasha-Longonot areas as a result of the volcanic activities of recent times. The main uses are in polishing compounds and in electroplating for cleaning metal surfaces.

Graphite

This is a crystalline variety of carbon and is found mainly in the Basement system rocks. Isolated outcrops have been worked in Kanziku (Kitui), Ol Doinyo Nyiro (near Nanyuki), the Taita Hills, near Oyugis, in the Karasuk Hills and in Baragoi, etc.

The mineral is used mainly in foundry facings, graphite crucibles, dry batteries, brushes, electrodes and pencils.

Kyanite

This is a silicate of aluminium which when heated to 1 450°C becomes mullite, a much more valuable compound used in the manufacture of heat resistant articles. The main producing area is Murka Hill near Taveta which was the biggest producer in the world from 1947 to 1949. High costs have completely stopped production although evidence from other parts of the world (such as Baker Mountain, USA) shows that the Kenya deposits should still be profitable.

Magnesite

This mineral is used to make magnesium salt and metal, refractory bricks, crucibles and furnace linings. It occurs mainly at Kinyiti Hill (near Mtito Andei), parts of Baragoi, in Mwingi, and in other parts of Kitui, south Embu and Namanga-Bissel areas.

Vermiculite

Being chemically inert, rot-proof, fireproof and a non-conductor of electricity, this substance is very suitable as an insulator of heat and sound. It is also used in lightweight building construction materials and it has been worked from Kinyiki Hill (near Konza), Lodosoit (in Samburu) and at Kapoponi Hill (in south Kitui).

Mica

Interest in mica started in Kenya in 1911 mainly in Machakos and Embu-Meru areas. Good production has come from Boji (near Archer's Post) and from Nachola (near Baragoi). The future of this mineral is affected by changing prices in world market as well as methods of mining.

159

Table 10.8 *Summary of mineral production in Kenya*[1] Value in £K

	1957	1958	1959	1960	1961	1962	1963	1964	1965	1966	1967
Salt (crude and refined)	179 053	146 810	146 398	166 772	183 492	150 497	278 053	420 299	528 009	555 121	494 598
Soda ash	1 339 201	1 275 826	1 743 201	1 410 238	1 584 938	1 346 470	1 283 602	887 883	895 806	1 183 677	1 093 521
Gold	92 168	97 269	114 290	108 143	153 964	116 632	128 900	168 552	150 126	149 490	420 118
Diatomite	80 467	60 044	57 209	51 674	47 584	41 080	71 039	71 913	49 228	33 826	27 840
Carbon dioxide	47 022	48 629	50 714	47 677	38 037	30 603	54 219	59 239	60 530	68 814	70 115
Silver	6 947	13 940	15 275	11 935	14 122	20 938	25 151	22 261	12 121	8 602	1 821
Asbestos	1 987	2 795	1 275	3 481	4 525	6 129	1 919	6 516	3 329	1 790	1 671
Beryl	500	423	217	147	66	50	—	64	—	—	2 163
Columbite	726	388	376	—	—	5	—	—	—	—	nil
Copper	344 020	383 684	458 174	412 660	583 043	505 033	504 652	654 662	868 281	426 270	5 500
Felspar	600	127	—	—	—	—	—	—	—	—	1 940
Graphite	39 847	32 987	28 024	—	—	—	—	—	—	—	—
Gypsum	29 076	44 089	7 194	2 590	426	63 031	20 810	60 874	8 608	81 026	97 749
Kaolin	4 562	4 740	3 729	3 506	2 437	2 387	5 203	2 899	5 241	16 126	22 512
Kyanite	—	15 076	22 641	9 966	4 308	—	—	—	—	—	—
Magnesite	538	2 460	9 998	75	166	—	643	611	332	5 332	3 690
Meerschaum	2 375	4 605	2 850	3 300	57	—	1 020	871	889	295	62
Mica	—	503	1 040	544	—	573	500	—	—	—	—
Pumice	7 248	2 564	4 557	1 644	1 236	278	68	351	279	194	30
Quartz	2 006	5 670	3 508	8	—	—	381	663	250	226	741
Vermiculite	900	259	1 427	2 530	—	70	319	—	—	—	—

[1] 'Minerals of Kenya'. Mines and Geological Dept Annual Report, 1966.

Table 10.9 *Other mineral production*
Value in £K

Mineral	1965	1966	1967
Barytes	3 329	2 261	2 550
Corundum	—	—	960
Guano	—	5 951	—
Limestone products	109 905	126 992	128 420
Sapphires	630	8 030	2 706

Table 10.10 *Cement production*

Year	Production		Domestic consumption		Value in £K
	long tons	tonnes	long tons	tonnes	
1963	338 300	343 724	115 600	117 456	2 542 357
1964	330 983	336 289	82 700	84 027	3 243 185
1965	497 204	505 189	96 600	98 150	3 793 192
1966	476 773	484 424	143 500	145 803	3 774 756
1967	471 398	478 963	182 200	185 124	4 190 178

Other minerals which are being worked have earned the country money as shown in Table 10.9.

The limestone products (calcite from Basement rocks and later carbonatites) are used to make cement and lime. The main firms currently engaged in the production of limestone products are Homa Lime, at Koru; Lime Burners (Msa) Ltd, at Mombasa; and Kenya Marble Quarries Ltd, at Nairobi. Corundum is vital because of its hardness (after diamonds it is the hardest substance) and Kinyiki Hill has been the main producer.

Conclusions

The above summary has covered only the more important minerals known and worked in Kenya. Prospecting is continuing especially for oil in the sedimentary north-eastern part of the country. The overall picture suggests that Kenya may depend mainly on the lesser known minerals. The main gold mine at Macalder Mines in Nyanza has now closed down because gold is no longer available in economic quantities, but other minerals, especially wallastonite from Turoka and the radioactive minerals, appear to show much promise for future development. More detailed mineralogical investigations, preferably with United Nations or other foreign assistance, will still be needed before the full natural mineral potentiality of Kenya can be said to be known.

Trona is Kenya's most valuable mineral and the next best, at present, appears to be carbon dioxide. The total value of mineral production from 1964 to 1967 was respectively £K2 575 388, £K3 096 394, £K3 043 270 and £K2 697 619.[1] Future growth in mineral production is now pinned on wallastonite, which has been discovered in large amounts near Kajiado, and on the radioactive and rare earth minerals from Mrima Hill in the Coast Province. At present, private firms have been licensed to do further prospecting on these minerals. Wallastonite is a metasilicate of calcium and is thought to be very suitable for use in quick-firing ceramics.

Building Materials (Cement and Building Stones)

In the production of these two basic requirements Kenya is relatively fortunate. Cement is easily manufactured at Bamburi from the coral rock along the coast and from Kunkur limestone, volcanic ash, and former lake deposits at Athi River. The potential reserves from these sources appears to be considerable, but weathered sand from the instrusives and other Basement system rocks also appears to be readily available in most places.

Building stone has been obtained mainly from volcanic materials especially trachytes, phonolites, ash and near-similar rocks in the volcanic areas. With the availability of more cement, concrete blocks are now gaining over quarried building stone because they are more economical to produce.

In Table 10.10 we give a summary of cement production and consumption from 1963 to 1967.

[1] These figures are for both minerals and building materials but excluding cement.

Fig. 10D Bamburi Portland Cement bulk handling silos, Mombasa

These figures suggest an upward trend in building construction since 1964. Their main limitation is that they only show what might have been recorded for the urban centres which are far from being representative of rural life or development.

References

ARNOLD, J. E. M. 'Present wood consumption and future requirements in Kenya', FAO Report to the EA High Commission, 1962.

'Forest development in Kenya', *Daily Nation,* Nairobi, 30 April 1969.

DU BOIS, C. G. B. 'Minerals of Kenya', *Geol. Surv. of Kenya, Bulletin No. 8,* 1966.

'Future importance of Kenya's timber industry', *E. A. Trade and Industry,* Vol. 1, No. 8, 1954.

GOVT OF KENYA 'Report on Kenya fisheries', *Min. of Tourism and Wildlife,* Govt Printer, Nairobi, 1966.

GOVT OF KENYA 'Forest Department annual report', *Min. of Nat. Resources,* Govt Printer, Nairobi, 1966.

GOVT OF KENYA *Statistical Abstracts,* Govt Printer, Nairobi, 1968.

GOVT OF KENYA 'Progress Report (1966–1968) for the African Forestry Commission, (Second Session)', *Min. of Nat. Resources,* Govt Printer, Nairobi, 1969.

HANSON, F. T. 'The future of timber industry in Kenya', *E.A. Economics Review,* (old series), Vol. 4, No. 2, 1958.

MCLEARON, F. D. 'Where does the timber go?' *Asili,* Min. of Nat. Resources Publication, No. 1, January 1969.

OGENDO, R. B. 'Industrial significance of the Kenya forests', *Cahiers d'Etudes Africaines,* Vol. 6, 1966.

'Report to the Government of Kenya on Kenya fisheries development possibilities', *UNDP/FAO Report* No. TA.2144.

'Report to the Government of Kenya on long-line fishing resources in East African waters', *UNDP/FAO Report,* No. TA.2191.

'Report to the Government of Kenya on the possibility of establishing a deep-sea fishing industry in Kenya', French Govt Technical Co-operative Agency in association with Promopeche.

SPARKS, A. K. 'Report to the Government of Kenya on shell-fish survey', US Agency for International Development.

GOVT OF KENYA 'Minerals of Kenya', *Mines and Geological Dept. Annual Report, 1966,* Govt. Printer, Nairobi. (See also other annual reports.)

Chapter 11
Manufacturing and Service Industries

Introductory Comments

The extractive organic and inorganic industrial activities have been examined in detail in the previous chapters, and it is clear that agriculture is still the mainstay of the Kenya economy. Thus, most of the country's processing and fabricating industries, which are discussed in the present chapter, derive their raw materials from agricultural sources.

The distinguishing criteria of manufacturing are as follows:[1]

a the activity must change the form of the assembled raw materials into more useful commodities. True manufacturing is not concerned with the provision of services;

[1] H. H. McCarty and J. B. Lindberg, *A Preface to Economic Geography*, Prentice-Hall, 1966, p. 176.

b it normally takes place in special establishments known as factories and not in the open air as in the construction of a building. The latter activity is therefore not manufacturing;

c it requires special equipment called machinery, which is operated by a definite source of power;

d as well as the powered machinery there must be human labour. The manufacturing process is normally divided into a number of distinct activities and the workers are assigned to these;

e the finished product should normally be uniform and not heterogeneous.

Kenya's manufacturing and service industries may be grouped very broadly into three main classes:

a the agricultural manufacturing industries,

b the non-agricultural manufacturing industries, and

c the service industries.

Fig. 11A Processing of edible oils at East Africa Industries, Nairobi

Fig. 11B Biscuit manufacture at the House of Manji, Nairobi

The agricultural manufacturing industries fall into two further smaller classes:
i the food processing industries, and
ii the non-food manufacturing[1] industries.

Qualitative and Quantitative Industrial Analyses

Qualitative Analysis

Kenya has 39 individual groups of processing, fabricating and service industries, and according to the International Standard Industrial Classification of All Economic Activities (ISIC),[2] these may be tabulated as in Table 11.1.
The qualitative map (Fig. 11.1) which shows the patterns of the agricultural manufacturing industries clearly portrays three main generalised industrial distributions, namely:
a the location of the agricultural food processing industries,
b the location of the agricultural non-food manufacturing industries, and
c the location of the principal industrial centres, including a number of minor and potential industrial centres, all of which are suitably differentiated.
  Hydro-electricity generation, cement and lime processing and some of the basic (non-vegetable) industrial chemical products processing industries are, perhaps, good examples of the few non-agricultural manufacturing industries located, to a considerable extent, in the rural areas. It should be noted that the industrial centres shown on the accompanying map (Fig. 11.2) vary so that some cater for the agricultural manufacturing in-

dustries only and others, especially the smaller ones, for specific non-agricultural manufacturing and/or service industries. Most of the main urban centres, however, are multi-industrial and accommodate most of the manufacturing and service industries, and the best examples are: Nairobi, Mombasa, Kisumu, Nakuru, Thika, Eldoret, Kitale and Nanyuki. Out of the 39 individual groups of manufacturing and service industries surveyed in the 1964/5 research project, 37 were located in Nairobi, 33 in Mombasa, 30 in Kisumu, 24 in Nakuru, 21 in Thika, 19 in Eldoret, 21 in Kitale and 11 in Nanyuki. Other less important multi-industrial smaller towns are: Athi River (4), Machakos (9), Malindi (8), Nyeri (10) and Naivasha (5).

Industrial Concentration

Kenya's industrial concentration is best studied qualitatively and quantitatively. The qualitative approach uses the distribution of the industrial towns and centres (Fig. 11.2), and the density of factory sites (Fig. 11.3). It should be observed that at any factory site, one or more factories may be located. The quantitative approach uses the 1964/5 total manufacturing and service manpower figures and the district industrial units (see Fig. 1.3). Two quantitative features are examined on the basis of the above district industrial units, namely:
a the distribution of Kenya's industrial work force for 1964, and
b the district index of industrial concentration.

Qualitative Features of Industrial Concentration

The location pattern of the industrial towns and centres (Fig. 11.2) differentiates towns and centres of great importance to the country, those of considerable significance, those of a minor category and, finally, those likely to have considerable potential for future industrial location. When all the towns and centres shown on the map are closely considered, thirteen stand out as much more significant than the rest. Five of the thirteen are classified as important; these are in order: Nairobi, Mombasa, Kisumu, Thika and Nakuru. Four others which are significant although relatively inferior to the above five are, in order: Eldoret, Kitale, Athi River and Machakos. The last four, Nanyuki, Nyeri, Malindi and Naivasha are the most important of the minor industrial towns. All thirteen industrial towns enumerated above are specifically shown in the map which portrays the areal density of factory sites (Fig. 11.3). This map is derived from a detailed large scale field map which shows the sites of practically all the mechanised factories outside the thirteen industrial towns mentioned earlier. Note the qualitative factory site density grades varying from areas where the density is high, through those where it is moderate or low, to those areas which have practically no factories.

---

[1] Wherever the word 'manufacturing' is used, it means processing or fabrication or both.
[2] Published in the series M, No. 4, by the UNO Statistical Bureau, July 1953.

Table 11.1

Quantitative Analysis

Group, index number and name of the industry	ISIC Code	Percentage of national total
a *Agricultural food processing industries*		
1 Meat products processing	201	1·5
2 Dairy products processing	202	0·9
3 Fruit and vegetable canning and soft drink processing	203; 214	2·0
4 Grain milling	205	2·5
5 Miscellaneous food products processing	204 and part of 209	1·1
6 Bakery products processing	206	1·7
7 Chocolate and sugar confectionery processing	208	0·1
8 Sugar processing	207	2·9
9 Tea processing	part of 209	3·0
10 Coffee processing	part of 209 (200)	4·6
11 Brewing and blending of alcoholic beverages	211–213	1·7
		Total = 22·0
b *Agricultural non-food manufacturing industries*		
12 Tobacco processing	220	1·2
13 Soap and edible oils processing	312; (315)	1·1
14 Miscellaneous vegetable chemical products processing (mainly pyrethrum)	316; part of 319	0·5
15 Footwear fabrication (including repair)	241	1·7
16 Tanning extract, leather tanning and non-footwear leather goods fabrication	291; 299; (314)	2·5
17 Fibre processing (and sisal fibre fabrication)	231; 233	11·9
18 Textile processing	232; 234; 239	2·1
19 Clothing fabrication	243; 244	3·0
20 Sawmilling	251	6·7
21 Miscellaneous wood products manufacture	259	1·4
22 Furniture and fixtures fabrication	260	3·6
23 Pulp, paper and paper products manufacture	271; 272	0·6
		Total = 36·4
c *Non-agricultural manufacturing industries*		
24 Basic (non-vegetable) industrial chemical processing	311	2·9
25 Misc. (non-vegetable) chemical products processing	313; part of 319; (354) and 356	1·5
26 Clay and concrete products manufacture	331; 333; 339	2·3
27 Cement, glass and allied products manufacture	332; 334	2·3
34 Motor vehicle assembly	383	0·9
38 Electricity generation	511	0·7
39 Water processing	521	0·4
		Total = 11·0
d *Service industries*		
28 Printing and publishing	280	2·5
29 Electrical machinery and repair (mainly maintenance)	370	0·8
30 Rubber products manufacture (mainly tyre retreading)	300	0·4
31 Non-electrical machinery and repair (mainly maintenance)	360; 386; 389	1·7
32 Boat, steamer and ship repair assembly and building	381	1·0
33 Railway services (and allied manufacturing)	382	7·1
35 Motor vehicle repair	384	7·7
36 Metal products servicing (and manufacture)	350	3·0
37 Miscellaneous service industries (and manufacturing)	(390); 391–399	6·4
		Total = 30·6
39 National manufacturing and service industries	—	Total national industrial operatives = 95 692

Quantitative Analysis (refers only to those establishments employing more than five operators)

165

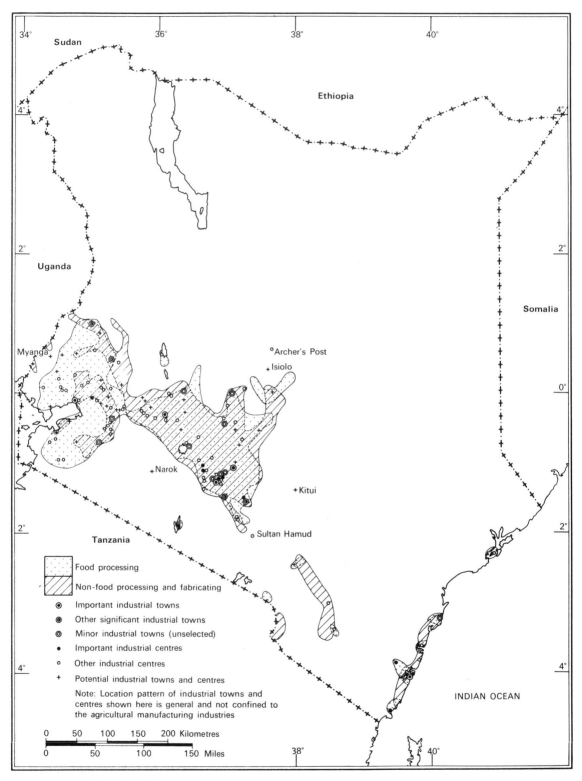

Fig. 11.1 Agricultural manufacturing industries

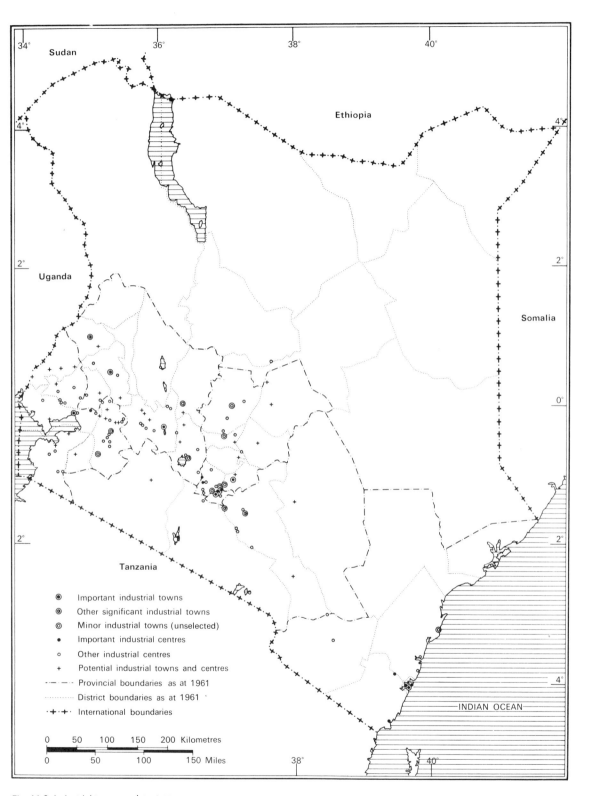

Legend:
- ◉ Important industrial towns
- ◎ Other significant industrial towns
- ⊚ Minor industrial towns (unselected)
- • Important industrial centres
- ○ Other industrial centres
- + Potential industrial towns and centres
- —·—·— Provincial boundaries as at 1961
- ············ District boundaries as at 1961
- ·+·+· International boundaries

Scale:
0 50 100 150 200 Kilometres
0   50   100   150 Miles

Fig. 11.2 Industrial towns and centres

167

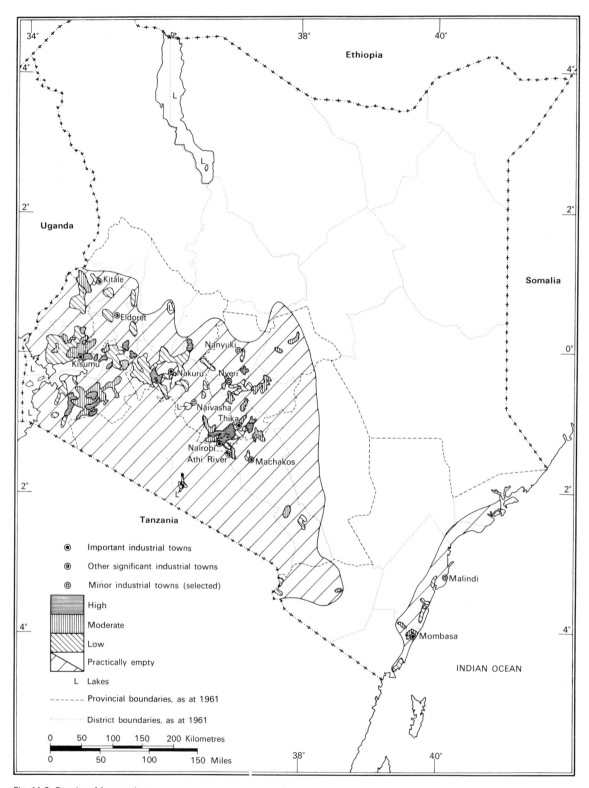

Fig. 11.3 Density of factory sites

Quantitative Features of Industrial Concentration

The distribution of Kenya's 95 692 manufacturing and service industrial operatives for 1964 in the 41 district industrial units is shown on the accompanying map (Fig. 11.4). Considering only those district industrial units each employing more than 3% of the national manpower total, it is to be noted that up to 81% of the operatives worked in factories located in the eight district industrial units of Nairobi (34·1%), Mombasa (14·2%), Thika (8·1%), Nakuru (7·1%), Central Nyanza, although mainly in the present Kisumu district (see Fig. 1.3, Chapter 1) (about 5·5%), Uasin Gishu (4·3%), Kericho (4·2%) and Kiambu (3·5%). The map indicates that the other 25 district industrial units shared in varying and certainly smaller proportions the remaining 19% of the work force, and that 8 districts were industrially empty.

It should also be observed that the map shows the internal district industrial unit composition of the industrial work force. Each district industrial unit's share, where relevant, falls into four segments consisting of the workers in:

a agricultural food processing industries,
b agricultural non-food manufacturing industries,
c non-agricultural manufacturing industries, and
d service industries.

Clear distinction is also made, in each case, of the urban and rural shares of the operatives.

The map demonstrates the overwhelming significance of at least two of the thirteen industrial towns enumerated earlier, Nairobi, with 28·9% of the industrial work force,

and Mombasa, with 11·1%. The remaining eleven towns shared the 14·0% of the national industrial operatives jointly employed by them as follows: Kisumu (3·4%), Thika (2·7%), Nakuru (2·4%), Eldoret (1·8%), Kitale (1·1%), Athi River (1%), Machakos (0·6%), Nanyuki (0·4%), Nyeri (0·3%), Malindi (0·2%), and Naivasha (0·1%). Altogether the thirteen main industrial towns of Kenya jointly shared 54% of the national industrial operatives. The map also reveals the relative industrial insignificance of most of Kenya's rural areas.

According to the index of industrial concentration,[1] the detailed pattern of concentration by district industrial units is portrayed in Fig. 11.5. The map deals with all the manufacturing and service industries.

The map shows that three district industrial units (namely AI; DI; and BI, Fig. 1.3, Chapter 1) jointly employed more than 50% of the industrial work force. However, the 1964 population estimates give the combined population total for the 3 district industrial units as only 5·9% of Kenya's total population of 9 162 000 at the time. Therefore, the 3 district industrial units had a high joint index of industrial concentration of 94·1. Moreover, more than 75% of the industrial labour force was concentrated in 10 out of the 41 district industrial units (Figs. 11.5 and 1.3,): A1, D1, B1, C2, C1, F2, C4, B3, C9, and D7. The ten district industrial units had a joint population total of 15% of Kenya's estimated total

[1] R. B. Ogendo, 'The significance of industrial zoning to rural industrial development', *Cahiers d'Etudes Africaines*, Vol. 7, 1967, pp. 476–81.

Fig. 11C Mombasa's industrial area

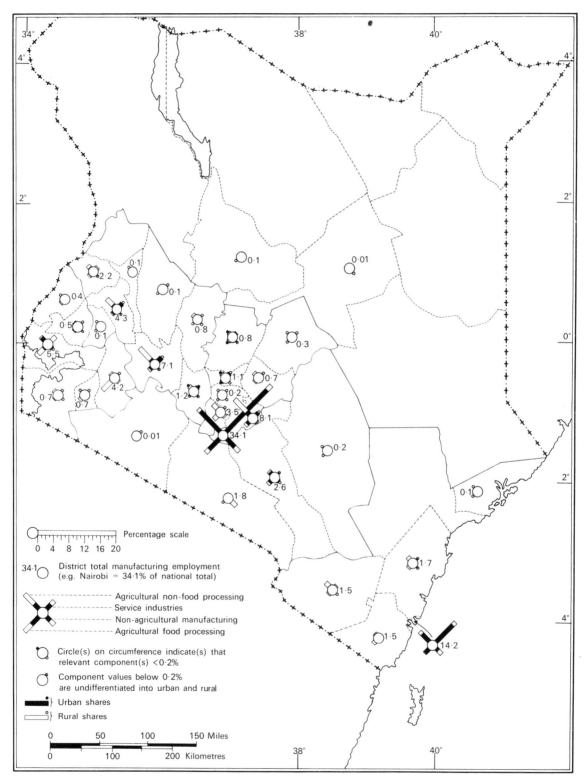

Fig. 11.4 Distribution of manufacturing operatives in 1964 (national total: 95 692)

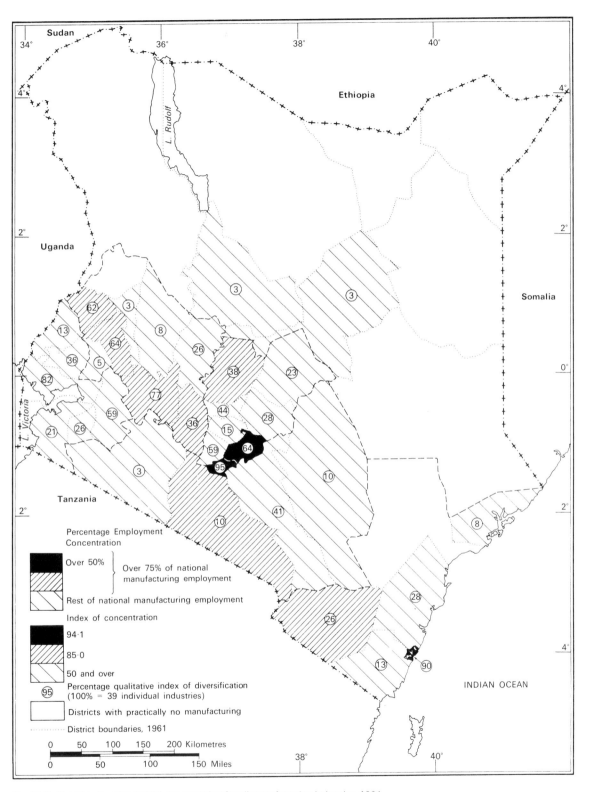

Fig. 11.5 District index of industrial concentration for all manufacturing industries, 1964

171

population quoted earlier. Thus, the 10 districts had a joint index of industrial concentration of 85·0. Whilst 23 of the remaining 31 district industrial units shared less than 25% of the national industrial operatives, the last eight district industrial units (C5, G1, G2, G5–G8 and B5) were practically empty. Two of the three district industrial units constituting the Nairobi Area (A1 and D1, but not D2) had a very high quantitative industrial concentration (Fig. 11.5). The Nairobi Area is the industrial core of Kenya, and in 1964 accounted for 45·8% of the industrial work force.

Industrial Diversification

In considering Kenya's industrial diversification, two indices are involved:
a qualitative index of diversification, and
b quantitative index of diversification.

Qualitative Index of Industrial Diversification

In order to derive the qualitative index of industrial diversification for any district industrial unit, the number of individual groups of industries located in the particular district is divided by the total number of individual groups of industries for Kenya (i.e. 39) and the quotient so obtained is multiplied by 100 to give a percentage figure. The figures enclosed in circles in Fig. 11.5 are, in fact, the percentage qualitative indices of diversification for the relevant district industrial units. The district industrial units having the best percentages are, in order: Nairobi (95%), Mombasa (90%), and Central Nyanza (mostly the present Kisumu administrative district, 82%). Other district industrial units, such as Nakuru (77%), Thika (64%), Uasin Gishu (64%), Trans Nzoia (62%), Kiambu (59%), and Kericho (59%) have moderate percentage qualitative indices of industrial diversification. The remaining district industrial units which have any significant development have low and therefore poor qualitative indices of industrial diversification.

The percentage qualitative index of industrial diversification relies on individual groups of industries without considering their size, either in terms of value added by manufacturing or, as in the present case, the industrial labour force. Thus district industrial units with small individual industries which employ few people are consequently given undue recognition. Whilst noting this weak feature of the qualitative approach the index is useful for rapid isolation of those district industrial units which are likely to have better quantitative indices of industrial diversification.

Quantitative Index of Industrial Diversification

If most of the industrial workers in a given district, province or the entire state are concentrated merely in one individual industrial group then, obviously, that area has a much lower quantitative industrial diversi-

fication than another in which the operatives are spread out relatively evenly among many different industries. This aspect of industrial structure is measured by the quantitative index of industrial diversification, as devised by E. C. Conkling.[1]

In the accompanying triple-curve diagram (Fig. 11.6), the numbers given in the three rows below the X-axis are the industrial index numbers introduced earlier in this chapter.

The Y-axis is devoted to cumulative percentages of the national industrial operatives. Take, for instance, the N row which shows all the 39 individual groups of industries in Kenya, arranged in ascending order of magnitude of the industrial operatives in each individual industrial group. Thus the chocolate and sugar confectionery processing industry (index number 7) was Kenya's smallest individual industrial group in 1964, whilst the fibre processing and fabricating industry (index number 17) was Kenya's largest individual industrial group during that year.

In order to obtain the cumulative percentages, the number of operatives in each individual industrial group is expressed as a percentage of the national total. Take again the chocolate and sugar confectionery processing industry (index number 7). The percentage value of its operatives is only 0·12%. This value is plotted as shown on the diagram. Next the sum of the percentage values for industries numbers 7 and 39 (0·12% plus 0·37% equals 0·49%) is plotted immediately above the industry number 39. Further the sum of the percentage values for industries numbers 7, 39 and 30 (0·12% + 0·37% + 0·41% = 0·90%) is plotted immediately above the industry number 30. This process is continued till the cumulative percentage values for all the other industries have been plotted on the graph. A smooth curve is then drawn through the plotted points and the result is the continuous curve shown in the diagram immediately below the 100% diagonal line. The area below this curve, marked by the X-axis and the vertical line in the extreme right of the diagram, is a quantitative measure of industrial diversification for all the manufacturing and service industries in Kenya. To express this index as a percentage, we proceed as follows:
a Take x to be the area defined above.
b Take y to be the area of the triangle bounded by the diagonal, the X-axis and the vertical line in the extreme right of the diagram. The area of this triangle represents 100% diversification.
c Now divide area x by area y and multiply the quotient by 100. The result obtained from the diagram is 54·4%.
If the above procedure is adopted for all the thirteen main industrial towns considered together, and then the rural areas only excluding the above towns, two other curves may be drawn. Similar calculations result in 46·3% diversification for the urban areas considered

[1] E. C. Conkling, 'South Wales: A case study in industrial diversification', *Econ. Geog.*, Vol. 39, No. 3, 1963, pp. 258–272.

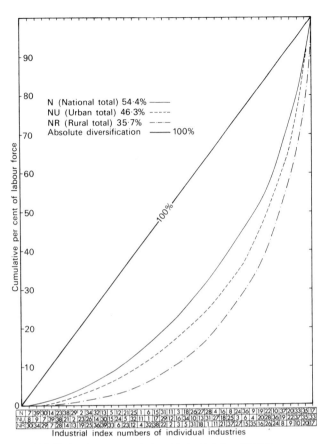

Fig. 11.6 National percentage index of industrial diversification in all manufacturing industries, 1964

jointly, and 35·7% diversification for the joint rural areas.

It can be seen from the above results that Kenya industries are better diversified at the joint national level, and that the diversification in towns, considered jointly, is better than in the rural areas.

References

ALEXANDER, J. W. *Economic Geography*, Prentice-Hall, 1964.

CONKLING, E. C. 'South Wales: A case study in industrial diversification', *Econ. Geog.*, Vol. 39, No. 3, 1963.

MCCARTY, H. H. and LINDBERG, J. B. *A Preface to Economic Geography*, Prentice-Hall, 1966.

OGENDO, R. B. 'The significance of industrial zoning to rural industrial development', *Cahiers d'Études Africaines*, Vol. 7, 1967.

OGENDO, R. B. *Industrial Geography of Kenya*, East African Publishing House, 1972.

Chapter 12
Infrastructure

Preliminary Considerations

Infrastructure includes a wide variety of facilities such as:

a electricity generation and supply network,

b water collection, processing and supply,

c various types of transport goods and services, for instance:
  1 waterways, docks complete with cargo-handling equipment,
  2 roads, including bridges, associated ferries and parking facilities,
  3 railways, rolling-stock and allied equipment,
  4 airports and the essential navigation equipment,

d sewerage systems and allied waste disposal facilities,

e the other communication systems such as radio, television, and telecommunication network including telephone, telegraph and postal systems.

During the initial stage of Kenya's industrial development many companies provided their own infrastructure. Today this approach still exists in certain situations. Even when public infrastructural facilities exist they are not always used. For example, water is taken from privately owned boreholes in the Nairobi area, and privately generated electricity is used in the Kericho tea area. As a rule, however, those industries which provide or partly provide their infrastructural needs are large and tend to be isolated from infrastructurally developed areas, for example, the Magadi soda factory in Kajiado and the Macalder mines in South Nyanza. Most Kenya industries, however, do depend on others for their infrastructure requirements, although it is true that in some instances certain industries located in areas which are infrastructurally well-provided for establish part of their infrastructural needs because this has been imposed on them by the need to reduce costs or to provide continuous service to the public.

It is the responsibility of the government of any country to provide the necessary infrastructure either directly, or, as in most countries of the world today, indirectly by guaranteeing franchises to privately operating companies, and this too is the case in Kenya with regard to such facilities as power and water supplies, telecommunications, postal and air services, rail trans-

port and many other infrastructural facilities. Roads, radio and television communications and several other allied infrastructural facilities are at present controlled by the government, which may in the future also assume direct responsibility for many more of the infrastructural facilities at present provided by private companies. By so doing the government will have accomplished one of its primary tasks, i.e. the creation of conditions attractive to the growth and development of the economic activity upon which the future prosperity of the country depends. This infrastructure should constitute part of the public sector because, as service facilities are in many instances monopolies by nature, it would be possible for the public to be exploited if such facilities were owned privately. Such a situation would prevent the proper development of the economy.

Very careful planning of infrastructural facilities is essential to avoid wastage of scarce capital in providing facilities not required. But the provision of these facilities should not be regarded as a panacea for all problems of industrial development. It is rarely true that industrial development in an area is imminent simply because the infrastructural facilities are available, although the absence or paucity of such facilities will often prevent the establishment of industry. It should also be observed that the infrastructural constituents rarely form a major part of the production costs of a manufacturing operation. Notwithstanding the few exceptions, such as aluminium refining, the availability, even at extraordinary low costs, of infrastructural facilities will hardly make the difference between feasibility and unfeasibility for a new industry. The availability and cost of transport, electricity, and other facilities will only lead an *entrepreneur* to prefer one location to another, in his attempt to find the most economic location for the industrial plant.

Fig. 12.1 gives a fairly well-graded infrastructural density from which the infrastructural regions can be derived. The National Atlas of Kenya[1] gives all the details relating to road, rail, air and waterway networks. It also gives the patterns of several other infrastructural

[1] *The National Atlas of Kenya*, Public Map Office, Nairobi, 3rd ed., 1970.

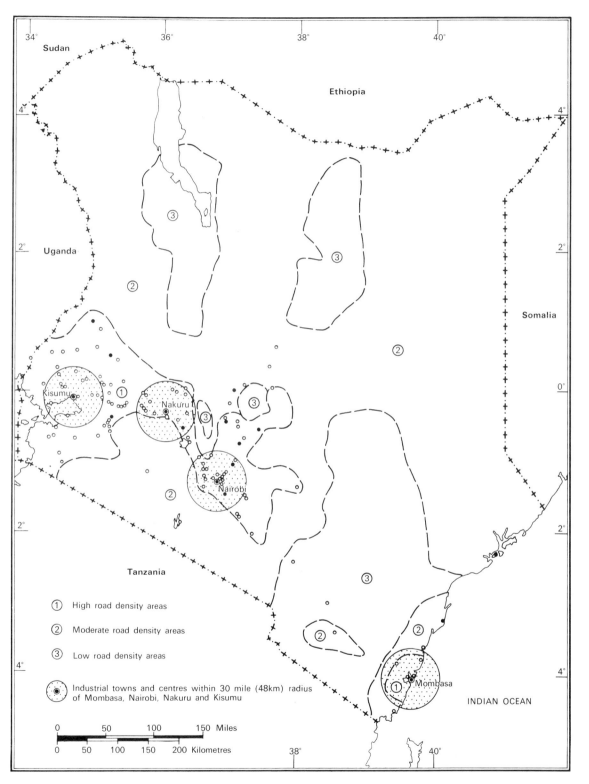

Fig. 12.1 Road network regions and 30-mile (48-km) radius urban spheres of influence

175

Fig. 12A An East African Railways Corporation diesel locomotive hauling a goods train near Equator Station

features such as water supplies, the electricity supply pattern and postal facilities.

Transportation

Railways

The main railway line runs from the coast at Mombasa through Nairobi and Nakuru to Eldoret, and from there into Uganda to its old terminus at Kampala. It has several branches:

a From Voi through Taveta into Tanzania,
b Konza to Magadi,
c Nairobi to Nanyuki,
d Gilgil to Thomson's Falls,
e Nakuru to the Nyanza lake port of Kisumu and thence to Butere,
f Rongai to Solai, and finally
g Leseru to Kitale.

The main line from Mombasa to Kampala originated from the British desire to stop the slave trade in the interior of this part of Africa. However, it soon became an important transport route for the export and import of goods from and to Uganda and Kenya. Today the hinterland of Mombasa is extensive and includes not only Uganda and Kenya but also northern Tanzania.

Unlike the railway line in Tanzania from Dar es Salaam to Mwanza, whose alignment was from the beginning greatly influenced by the 1914–18 military needs rather than economic considerations, the main line in Kenya was constructed to pass through some of the richest farming areas in the country. Moreover, it was also provided with a link between Voi and the

Moshi-Arusha area, which is one of the richest agricultural parts of Tanzania.

As the only reliable medium of land communication in the early parts of the twentieth century the railway system controlled the development of the road pattern for a considerable period. At this early stage the policy was for the road pattern to feed the railway network and not compete with it. Thus roads running parallel to the railway network, such as that from Mombasa to Nairobi, were considered competitive and therefore unfavourable to the profitable performance of the railway system. Such roads were either developed by the government relatively slowly or, like the section of Sclater's Road which was parallel to the railway in western Kenya, were neglected and returned to bush because the government would not allocate funds for their maintenance.

This unfortunate policy was changed, especially after Kenya's independence, and the railway system has increasingly suffered losses at the expense of the expanding and constantly improving road pattern which now includes the tarmac Mombasa-Nairobi highway. A further factor which has favoured the recent road network expansion since independence is that the railway system was mainly designed to serve the former White Highlands rather than the African areas. Hence emphasis on road expansion in the needy African areas has been necessary to rectify the imbalance caused. The role of the railway system may be increased in the future by branch extensions into feasible African areas. A potentially good example is a branch-line through Kericho, Sotik, Kisii to the high potential sugar cane area of South Nyanza.

Although at present road transport is more hazardous, it is faster than rail transport and has therefore captured much of the passenger traffic and a significant part of the goods traffic which formerly went by rail. Because of this trend the railways may, in the long run, rely more on the transport of bulky non-urgent goods. However, there are areas, for example Magadi, where rail transport is still paramount or, at least, more important than road transport.

The greatest disadvantage of our roads at present is the fact that many of them have sub-standard surfaces, which become impassable during the rainy seasons. However, much improvement is in progress and they will inevitably be an even greater threat to the railways in the future, especially when most of the murram and dirt roads are converted to all-weather roads.

In 1964 the railway income from passenger traffic was only £K1 174 400 compared with £K13 008 400 from goods traffic. The corresponding figures for 1967 were £K1 143 900 and £K15 491 700.

Roads

Fig. 12.1 shows the high, medium and low density road network distribution in Kenya.

In 1968, Kenya had about 27 623 miles (44 197 km) of various types of roads. About 6·3 % of the total distance consisted of metalled roads and the remaining 93·7 % were gravel and earth. The total length of roads classified under the primary road system during the year was 3 827 miles (6 123 km), whilst the secondary road system totalled 6 535 miles (10 456 km). There were 15 523 miles (25 837 km) of other reasonable but unclassified roads, with minor roads, mostly tracks, totalling 1 738 miles (2 781 km). Most of these roads have very little traffic, but a few such as the trunk roads and those roads in and around the main urban centres carry a great deal of traffic. The main trunk roads with considerable traffic are: Mombasa-Tororo, Nakuru-Kisumu, Nairobi-Nanyuki and Nairobi-Namanga roads. Heavy to moderately heavy traffic are also experienced in and around Nairobi, Mombasa, Nakuru, Kisumu, Thika, Eldoret, Kitale, Kericho and Nyeri.

In 1964 income from passenger road traffic was £K5 391 200 compared to £K6 589 200 for goods traffic, giving a total of £K11 980 400. By 1967, the corresponding figures were: passenger traffic income £K7 376 100 and goods traffic income £K7 303 500, giving a total of £K14 679 600. This is an increase in income of 22·5 % over the three years as compared with an increase in the railway traffic for the same period of 17·3 %.

Although income from railway traffic is still higher than that from road traffic, the latter has increased slightly faster between 1964 and 1967 than the former. This illustrates clearly the growing preference for road traffic.

Water Transport

Apart from lake transport centred on Kisumu and other smaller lake ports such as Kendu, Kusa, Karungu, Asembo Bay, etc.,[1] the main water transport focus is Kilindini Harbour in Mombasa. Other smaller sea ports along the Kenya coast are Lamu, Malindi, Kilifi and Shimoni, but Mombasa is of overwhelming significance, due to its extensive deep water facilities which make it pre-eminent among all East African ports.[2, 3]

In 1959 Kilindini Harbour handled 1 787 ships (14·8 % of which were sailing ships) as compared with the 1967 total of 2 354 (of which only 5 % were sailing ships). Passengers handled in 1959 were 80 321, and of these 48·8 % embarked for destinations outside Kenya. In 1967 the corresponding figures were 44 119 persons and 48·1 % embarking passengers.

Exports for 1959 amounted to 993 000 long tons (952 041 tonnes) whilst imports were 1 564 000 tons (1 595 918 tonnes). In 1967 the corresponding figures were: exports 2 432 000 tons (2 481 633 tonnes) and imports 3 497 000 tons (3 568 367 tonnes).

During 1964 the income from water transport in Kenya totalled £K9 412 100 excluding charges for storage facilities. In 1967 income increased by 45 % to £K13 292 100.

The three component parts of Kilindini harbour are as follows:

a the slipways, lighterage wharves and other minor port establishments situated on the south-west shore between Likoni Ferry and Ras Kilindini on Mombasa island;

b the first nine deep-water berths (1–5 and 7–10) and the Shimanzi oil jetty on the north-west shore between Makupa Creek and Ras Kilindini, on the island;

c a further four deep water berths (11–14) located at Kipevu, and connected to Mombasa island by a causeway carrying both rail and road. Note that Kipevu is situated on the mainland north of the entrance to Port Reitz.

Apart from the thirteen deep-water berths with a total length of 7 690 feet (2 338 m), there are two lighterage wharves about 1 125 feet (410 m) in total length. The 16 transit sheds together with extensive stacking grounds provide a total ground space of about 1 528 193 sq feet (141 230 m²). This extensive area along the deep-water quays is served by the railway. The 31 cargo lighters and pontoons have a capacity of about 7 295 tons (7 444 tonnes). The port is also equipped with excellent cargo handling equipment such as cranes, forklift trucks, etc. Kilindini harbour has facilities for ships up to 65 000 tons (66 326 tonnes) dead weight and is capable of accommodating 50 ships at a time.[4] Despite all these facilities and advantages of deep-water berths, Kilindini Harbour still experiences severe congestion at certain times of the year which indicates the need for further expansion for which there still exists ample room.

[1] V. C. R. Ford, *The Trade of Lake Victoria*, E.A. Literature Bureau, Nairobi, 1955.

[2] *Statistical Abstracts*, Republic of Kenya, 1968.

[3] *Economic Survey*, Govt Printer, Nairobi, 1968.

[4] B. S. Hoyle, *The Seaports of East Africa*, East African Publishing House, Nairobi, 1967.

Fig. 12B Kilindini Harbour, Mombasa

Air Transport

Nairobi international airport (at Embakasi) is the largest and best equipped East African airport. Other important Kenya airports are: Port Reitz at Mombasa, Wilson airport at Nairobi, Eastleigh military airport at Nairobi and Kisumu airport. Wilson airport (for light aircraft) is perhaps the busiest airport in Africa. Other significant airports are located in Kitale and Malindi, and Magadi also has an aerodrome.

Because of its international status, Nairobi airport is served by more than twenty airlines. The most important airline centred on Nairobi (and owned by the East African Community) is the East African Airways. Seven other African airlines also call at Nairobi (United Arab Airlines; Air Congo; Ethiopian Airlines; Ghana Airways; Sudan Airways; Zambia and Somalia Airways). Eleven European airlines also call at Nairobi. They are: BOAC, BUA, Air France, KLM, Sabena, SAS, Swissair, Lufthansa, Olympic, Alitalia and Aeroflot. Air India also has routes through Nairobi, as have the two American airlines of Pan American and TWA. A further link with the Middle East is provided by the Israeli's El Al Airline, whilst Madagascar is connected to Nairobi by Air Madagascar.

During 1964 there were 14 191 aircraft movements at Nairobi Airport as compared with 8 548 at Mombasa's Port Reitz airport, and 96 463 at Wilson Airport.[1] During the same year 485 000 passengers passed through Nairobi airport, 123 000 through Mombasa airport and

10 200 through Wilson airport. Freight handled by Nairobi airport in 1964 totalled 8 173 long tons (8 340 tonnes); Mombasa handled 894 tons (912 tonnes). The 1964 figure for Wilson airport is unavailable but in 1965 it handled 16·9 tons (17·3 tonnes).

In 1967 there were 16 650 aircraft movements at Nairobi airport, 7 477 at Mombasa airport and 149 306 at Wilson airport. The total number of passengers through Nairobi airport was 734 000, and those through Mombasa and Wilson airport were 131 000 and 14 500 respectively. Nairobi airport handled 10 118 tons (10 325 tonnes) of freight, Mombasa airport 782 tons (798 tonnes) and Wilson airport 26·7 tons (27·3 tonnes).

At the end of 1964 income from air transport, excluding transport incidental charges and those for storage, was £K5 187 600, compared to £K8 626 600 for 1967, an increase of about 56%.

Nairobi is the centre of air traffic in Kenya and the detailed air network based on Nairobi can be seen elsewhere.[1]

Other Forms of Communication[2]

Posts and Telecommunications

The area of greatest concentration of postal facilities as shown in the *National Atlas of Kenya* tapers south-

[1] *Economic Survey*, Govt Printer, Nairobi, 1968, p. 103.

[1] R. B. Ogendo, (Adviser), *The New Kenya Atlas*, Collins-Longman, 1971, p. 5, 9, 18, 41 and 49.
[2] E. W. Soja, *The Geography of Modernisation in Kenya*, Syracuse University Press, 1968, chapter 4, p. 27–47.

eastwards from the Kitale-Yala baseline, a short distance east of the Uganda-Kenya border, to the coast at about the Mombasa-Malindi line. The facilities are very scanty in the vast area of the south-western Kenya-Tanzania border and in north, north-east and eastern Kenya. The rail-road-postal facility association is very close.

Apart from the internal postal services, the East African external telecommunications facilities, now supported by satellite communication, are closely associated with Kenya's postal services. In 1967 Kenya had 332 post offices with 40 188 private boxes.

During 1964 73 653 000 letters and 693 000 parcels both external and internal were handled by the Kenya postal system. In 1967, the respective figures were: 83 882 000 letters and 389 000 parcels. In 1964 there were about 50 850 telephones as compared with 60 521 in 1967. About 536 000 articles of telegraphic traffic were handled in 1964 and 545 000 in 1967.

Income from all types of postal and allied communications amounted to £K5 760 900 in 1964, and £K6 684 500 in 1967. The postal system has now reached the stage of automatic trunk dialling between many leading urban centres in East Africa, with the consequent cheapening of this service.

Radio and Television

These mass communication media, provided by the government through the Voice of Kenya, have their headquarters in Nairobi and a well-developed network (for the radio only) throughout the country.

The television network is still limited in extent, and the numbers viewing are severely restricted by the high cost of television installation.

During 1964 about 89 032 radio licences were issued, as compared with 135 486 for 1967. In 1964, however, only about 8 655 television licences were issued,[1] although this number rose to 10 179 by the end of 1967.

Other Selected Public Utilities

Electricity[2]

This account excludes the many small private diesel and hydro-electric sources of power found throughout the country. To date there are ten hydro-electric power stations of importance in Kenya. These are: Kindaruma (40 mw), Low Tana (14·4 mw), Wanjii (7·4 mw), Liki, Sagana, Mesco, Ndula 1 and 2, Selby Falls and Gogo Falls. Each of the latter seven power stations has an installed capacity of 4 mw or less. The Gogo Falls station was privately owned by the Macalder Mines Company, now dissolved.

[1] More radios and televisions than this are certainly being used in Kenya as there is a large number of unlicensed appliances.
[2] R. B. Ogendo, 'Some aspects of the geography of electricity in Kenya', *Proc E. African Academy*, Vol. 3, 1965, p. 15–34.

Fig. 12C The new Mt Longonot Satellite Tracking Station, which provides Kenya with worldwide telecommunications

Fig. 12D Kindaruma hydroelectricity generating dam, at Seven Forks on the Tana River, Eastern Province

There are also eight functioning thermal stations, located at Kitale, Nanyuki, Gogo Falls, Mbaraki, Kipevu, Meru, Homa Bay and Lamu. The Gogo Falls thermal station was privately owned and supplemented the Gogo Falls hydro-electric station. The capacity of the Kipevu thermal station is about 30 mw, whilst that at Mbaraki is about 7·2 mw. The remaining thermal power stations have an installed capacity of 4 mw or less each. Eight thermal power stations at Sagana Falls, Malindi, Kericho, Kisumu, Nairobi, Ruiru, Nakuru and Eldoret, are also maintained for standby duties in case of power failure.

In 1964 Kenya had a total installed capacity of 101 414 kw, of which 73 514 kw were thermal and 27 900 kw hydro. During 1967 the installed capacity was increased by 12 213 kw to 113 627 kw. Meanwhile, the installed capacity of the thermal stations rose to 85 537 kw and that of hydro stations totalled 28 090 kw.

Whilst 323 170 000 kw hours of electricity were generated in Kenya during 1964, a further total of 183 286 000 kw hours (5 655 000 from Tanzania and 177 631 000 from Uganda) were imported. In 1967, 339 365 000 kw hours were generated and 241 982 000 kw hours imported from Uganda. Thus power consumption rose from 506 456 000 hours in 1964 to 581 347 000 kw hours in 1967. Owing to transmission losses and use at the power station of some of the electricity, actual power consumption in Kenya during 1964 amounted to 425 676 000 kw hours as compared with 485 562 000 kw hours in 1967.

There are seventeen electricity distributing areas. Most of these are concentrated in south-western Kenya and along the coast.[1, 2] The latest areas to be connected to public supplies are Homa Bay, Kisii, Kitui, Lamu, Kwale, Kapsabet, Mweiga, Githunguri and Molo townships.

The installation at Kindaruma is the first phase of development of the hydro-electric potential of the Seven Forks Scheme. This will include further power stations at Gtaru and reservoir sites apart from others along the Tana.

A source of relatively cheap and reliable power is essential for the rapid economic development of Kenya, because without such power the foreign capital much needed for the many new industrial projects would be difficult to attract. Nairobi and Mombasa were the first places to be supplied with electricity and consequently received the bulk of the early industrialisation.

In the course of time, however, it was strongly felt that the distribution areas should be expanded to encourage economic (especially manufacturing) development in a larger part of the country. There has been a great upsurge in the demand for electricity since Independence to supply agricultural and village needs and for a greatly expanding manufacturing activity.

Although it is bound to take time before supplies can be extended to farms throughout the economically viable

[1] National Atlas of Kenya, Public Map Office, Nairobi, 3rd ed, 1970.
[2] R. B. Ogendo, Industrial Geography of Kenya, East African Publishing House, Nairobi, 1972.

parts of Kenya, electricity is already supplied to many of the larger commercial farms and plantations. Further extensions to important centres and/or areas of agricultural development in the more densely populated areas are also being undertaken.

Since the question of power supply to new areas involves careful surveys based both on the short and long term financial returns and the extent to which the existing customers are likely to be involved in subsidising the new users, it is obvious that the new consumers closer to the existing distribution areas can be supplied more cheaply than those located farther out. Thus the power tariffs are regulated from time to time in accordance with the balance between the interests of the consumers and the financial stability of the supplying organisation.

Demands backed by sound economics are being met as can be observed in those areas supplied by the Lessos and Lanet sub-stations. The ever expanding area of power supply in the Nairobi district is constantly being reviewed. Meanwhile further extensions to the tea, coffee and other high value commercial plantation crop areas in parts of the Rift Valley, Central, Nyanza and Western Provinces are under consideration. Moreover power extension to cater for the greater needs of Coast Province has been completed from the Nairobi power nucleus.

Fuel Oils

These include: motor spirit, aviation spirit, turbo fuel, lighting and power kerosene, light and heavy diesel fuel and furnace oil. In 1964 Kenya consumed a total of 189 568 000 gallons (861 776 128 litres) of the above fuel oils, and in 1967 the corresponding amount consumed was 229 451 000 gallons (1 043 084 246 litres). The principal lubricants consist of: branded and unbranded motor oils, aviation lubricants, motor greases, industrial and railway oils, industrial greases, petroleums and bitumen.

The East African Oil Refinery started operating at Changamwe in Mombasa in December 1963, during which month it processed about 34 619 330 gallons (156 192 274 litres) of crude petroleum. During 1964, it processed 392 577 500 gallons (1 784 657 315 litres). By the end of 1967, the quantity of crude petroleum processed that year was 504 428 900 gallons (2 293 133 779 litres).

The output of the refinery consists of such products as: Mogas, LPG, kerosene, gasoil, diesel, fuel oil, bitumen, and export residue. Taken together, the refinery's total output of the above products in 1964 was 370 064 800 gallons (1 682 314 580 litres) and in 1967 the total was 483 063 900 gallons (2 196 008 489 litres).

Pattern of Water Supply Source

The higher rainfall in much of south-western Kenya is the basis of the abundant good water supply in the area.[1]

[1] National Atlas of Kenya, Public Map Office, Nairobi, 3rd ed, 1970.

Fig. 12E The East African Oil Refinery, Changamwe, Mombasa

The rest of Kenya, including the coast, is poorly provided for by nature. Because of this poor distribution some areas obtain their water from distant sources, for example, the Ngong Hills supply for the Magadi soda complex.

In the urban areas the water supplies are obtained from central government, local authorities and approved private suppliers.

The main consumers are Nairobi and Mombasa. However, all the urban centres together require larger and more regular supplies, although the absolute needs of the rural areas are yet to be gauged in order to attempt a reasoned comparison.

Nairobi's main water supply sources are the Sasumua and Ruiru dams in the Aberdares, whilst Mombasa gets its water from the Mzima Springs in the Tsavo National Park. Extensions to both the Nairobi and Mombasa water supply sources are in progress and surveys are underway in connection with the proposed dam site on the Chania River on the slopes of the Aberdares. Two further supply projects for Mombasa are also under construction by the Mombasa Pipeline Board.

Because the distribution of rainfall in Kenya is uneven and grossly inadequate and unreliable in certain areas, water supply development, especially in the rural areas, is of major importance. The government therefore plans to encourage such development within its financial limits, provided the projects so created are run on an economic basis. This government assistance leans heavily on several attractive incentives and also outright financial commitments such as:[1]

[1] D. R. L. Prabhakar, *Kenya's Water Resources*, Ministry of Agriculture and Animal Husbandry, Nairobi, 1970.

a the provision of technical service and advice,
b full grants in poor areas for small scheme water supplies,
c half grants in low and medium potential areas for small basic supplies,
d loans for larger supply schemes,
e subsidies for dam construction,
f partial insurance against borehole failure.

In the development of new rural water sources, the procedure of the government has been:
a to use all the existing surface water,
b to reinforce the above by the use of dams, tanks and/or reservoirs fed from catchment areas and the exploitation of weirs,
c to develop shallow wells or drill boreholes where the above two approaches are inapplicable.

The ultimate aim of the Government in its policy of rural water development is as follows:
a in the areas with high agricultural potential each farm or smallholding should be supplied with water, and
b in those areas with medium potentiality and with an annual rainfall ranging from 20 to 30 inches (510 and 760 mm) and growing subsistence crops in association with ranching activities, the water would be provided at intervals of 2 miles (3·2 km),
c finally in the semi-arid and arid areas, where the main economic activity is ranching, water would be supplied at intervals of 5 miles (8 km).

Kenya's water resources are influenced by its geology, relief and rainfall patterns and not by its industrial pattern, although the pattern of the supply points is closely related to the industrial location pattern. The source pattern of Kenya's major water resources is

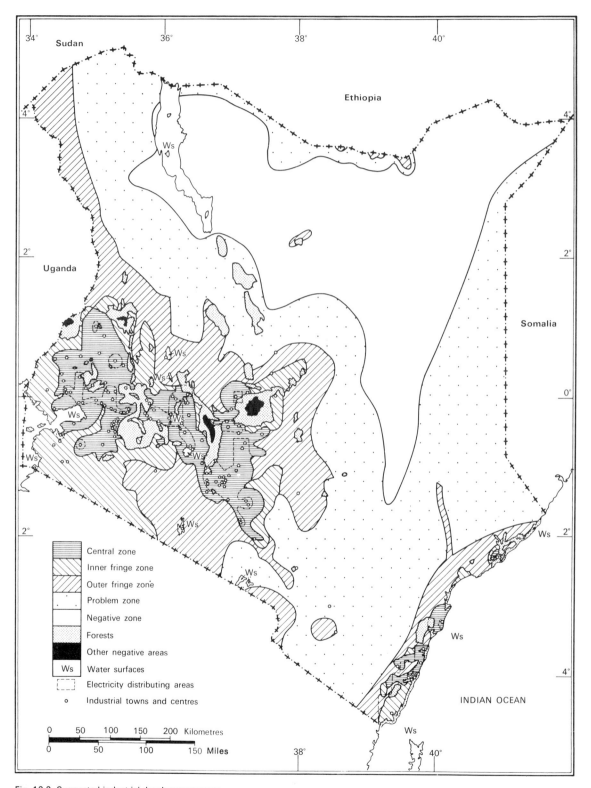

Fig. 12.2 Suggested industrial development zones

practically confined within the belts where the prospect of receiving twenty or more inches (508 mm) of rainfall per annum is 20% or more.[1]

Sewage Pattern

Very few of the smaller towns have sewerage systems. However, larger urban centres are partly provided for in this respect. In many cases the main sewers only serve limited areas of the urban centres, while the remaining areas rely either on septic or conservancy tanks. In the more enlightened rural areas pit latrines are prevalent. The smaller towns and the centres rely either on septic tanks, pit latrines or on the removal of night soil.

The collection and disposal of garbage, waste paper and other refuse is well organised in most urban areas. This is also true in many of the larger centres and the larger of the markets.

Generally speaking, however, much still remains to be done in this field.

Infrastructural Zoning

The closest and most systematic approach to infrastructural zoning is portrayed in Fig. 12.2.

Most of the central zone, especially the core demarcated by electricity distributing areas, is the best provided for infrastructurally, and the rest, excluding the forest areas which are relatively poorly provided for, has many facilities, although it does lack public supplies of both electricity and water. Transportation and other forms of communication are, generally, good in practically the whole of the central zone. Those sections of both the inner and outer fringe zones which are contiguous with the central zone have comparatively better facilities than the remaining sections remote from the central zone. However the inner fringe zone is better provided for than the outer fringe zone.

Both the problem and negative zones have much poorer infrastructural facilities. In the negative zone such infrastructural facilities as exist are rudimentary and are unreliable. The roads, for instance, are more like tracks in many parts, and are thus impermanent. There are no water supplies here comparable to those in parts of the central zone. The problem zone has a better network of roads. Although the water resources are poor they are more abundant than those in the negative zone. The infrastructure development in this zone is bound to be slow, owing to the presence of human and livestock diseases, especially those propagated by tsetse flies and mosquitoes. However, this zone has great potentiality, for tourism and livestock ranching. Its future development is therefore very much bound up with: tsetse fly and mosquito eradication; improvement of the skeletal road network; provision of better water supplies; and expansion of both education and medical facilities.

References

FORD, V. C. R. *The Trade of Lake Victoria*, East African Literature Bureau, Nairobi, 1955.

GOVT OF KENYA *Economic Survey*, Republic of Kenya Govt Printer, Nairobi, 1968.

GOVT OF KENYA *Statistical Abstracts*, Republic of Kenya, Govt Printer, Nairobi, 1968.

HOYLE, B. S. *The Seaports of East Africa*, East African Publishing House, Nairobi, 1967.

OGENDO, R. B. 'Some aspects of the geography of electricity in Kenya', *Proc. East African Academy*, Vol. 3, East African Publishing House, Nairobi, 1965.

OGENDO, R. B. *Industrial Geography of Kenya*, East African Publishing House, Nairobi, 1972.

PRABHAKAR, D. R. L. 'Kenya's water resources', *Min. of Agriculture*, Nairobi, 1970.

SOJA, E. W. *The Geography of Modernisation in Kenya*, Syracuse University Press, 1968.

GOVT OF KENYA *The National Atlas of Kenya*, Public Map Office, Nairobi, 1970.

---

[1] R. B. Ogendo, *Industrial geography of Kenya*, East African Publishing House, Nairobi, 1972.

Chapter 13
Location Factors, Industrial Orientation, Density and Zoning

Location Factors

Definition and Classification

In the geography of manufacturing the term *location factor* refers to any phenomenon which exerts an influence on the location of a factory. Some of the leading industrial location factors in Kenya are indicated below:

a The physical factors consisting of:
    i the combined influence of topography and geology,
    ii the influence of both total annual rainfall and its reliability,
    iii the importance of industrial water supplies, and
    iv the ecological influence on the organic raw material potential;

b the human factors such as:
    i demographic and the allied social factors,
    ii the historical, political and administrative factors,
    iii the economic factors including, among other things:
        1 capital and managerial skill,
        2 industrial raw materials of various types,
        3 industrial interdependence,
        4 market attraction,
        5 the influence of infrastructure.

Brief Sample Assessment of Location Factors

It is obvious that the requirements of the various factories depend first on the purpose of each factory and secondly on the factory size or the size of the firm running the business. Whilst some entrepreneurs are very systematic in their investigations to find the best place for a factory, others appear to pay little attention to these considerations. The latter's approach seems to go against the theoretical arguments which normally assume that the first aim of all industrialists is to make maximum profits by rationally deciding on the best location possible. Experimental research in this field indicates that the personal considerations of certain industrialists have greatly influenced final location decisions. But generally speaking, however, despite apparently irrational location decisions the long-term pressures of the economic system appear to exercise a sufficiently powerful influence on the seemingly non-economic motives of individuals thereby creating a rational economic pattern.[1]

Government influence[2]

Since Independence the government has taken much more interest in matters affecting the location of manufacturing activities. But much still remains to be achieved through careful planning, especially for the benefit of the depressed rural areas. At present, general government influence affects industrial activity through the laws which govern such things as:

a minimum wages and hours of work,
b insurance, safety and health requirements,
c minimum age of the labour force, and
d other legal requirements in organisation.

Government intervention in the function and location of manufacturing can be direct or indirect, and some of the main reasons likely to precipitate such intervention include the need to:

a protect national industries from external competition,
b alleviate high and persistent unemployment,
c decentralise industries, especially from large urban industrial agglomerations, to the poor rural areas in order to discourage both rural depopulation and urban overcrowding,
d diversify the industrial structure of the provincial industrial units, and
e stimulate the general process of economic growth.

Some methods which the government can use for indirect influence include: the introduction of tariff barriers, and application of import quota systems directed against external competition likely to interfere with local industries. The location of industry may also be affected by the government unemployment policies (such as the Kenya 10% to 15% compulsory increase in employee numbers during 1964). By prohibiting industrial location in certain areas, the government influences location through land use control.

Location decisions may also be affected by budgetary controls such as credit restrictions, differential taxation

[1] J. Rutherford, *et al., New Viewpoints in Economic Geography*, Harrap, 1967.
[2] R. C. Estall and R. O. Buchanan, *Industry Activity and Economic Geography*, Hutchinson, 1962.

and government expenditure. Differential taxation in Kenya is imposed by local authorities rather than central government. Although such taxes do not form a highly important proportion of total costs, they can make industrialists locate their industries in areas with comparatively lower local taxes.

The government can also influence industrial location directly by providing inducements such as:

a low interest rate loans, tax exemption, low or subsidised rents,

b provision of factories in certain areas thereby deciding on the location beforehand,

c the development of the infrastructure in selected areas, thus increasing their attraction as possible sites,

d the provision of research information to industrialists on the location and site advantages and disadvantages of various areas regarding specific industrial enterprises,

e government purchase of the manufactured products, etc.

Influence of raw materials

The degree of attraction exerted by raw materials varies considerably according to:

a the nature of the raw materials,

b the various processes for which such materials are used, and

c the available distribution and utilisation techniques.

It is important to observe that, whilst some manufacturing industries have as their raw materials the products of the primary extractive industries, others use, as their raw materials, the finished products of yet other manufacturing industries. Thus, raw materials supplies in the two instances differ considerably. Further, each of the two types of industry require more than one kind of raw material.

The influence which the procurement of raw material exerts on location decisions depends on the following aspects:

a Whether the material loses or gains weight or bulk in undergoing the manufacturing process,

b whether the material's value per unit weight is high or low,

c whether the relevant material is perishable and/or fragile, and

d the number of raw materials needed for the process, the proportions necessary, and hence the relative importance of each material item.

Certain industries, such as the processing of sugar cane, tea, coffee, fibres (especially sisal) and dairy products, etc., are strongly raw material orientated, although owing to technological advances, there is a universal tendency for raw materials to become less significant in location decisions. Whilst some raw materials lose heavily in weight or bulk on being processed (for instance, about ten tons of sugar cane yield about one ton of mill-white sugar), others gain weight or become bulkier (for example, the brewery and bakery products). The orientation of an industry towards raw materials tends to be related to the ratio of raw material weight to finished product weight. In the case of cane sugar this ratio is 10:1, whilst for beet sugar it is about 8:1. This ratio is often referred to as the material index of the relevant industry.[1] The cane sugar industry, therefore, has a material index of ten whilst that of beet sugar industry is eight. As a general guide, those industries with high material indices are usually raw material orientated.

In cases where the material is highly perishable, especially when industrial businesses serve distant markets, processing may also be raw material orientated (for instance, Thika's Kenya Canners factory is conveniently located in the fruit and vegetable growing area of Central Province). In such instances, manufacturing may be broken into two stages consisting of a simple processing operation which is raw material orientated aimed at removing bulk or perishability (cf: coffee pulping and sisal decortication), and a final processing stage normally taking place near or at the market.

Owing to the fact that a material of high value per unit weight bears transport costs better than one of low value per unit weight, location decisions are often based on raw material value per unit weight. Despite higher freight rates charged by the railways and other forms of transport on the more valuable than the less valuable materials, transport costs ultimately add less, proportionately, to the cost of a higher value material than to one of lower value. In other words, the more highly-priced the material is in relation to the value added by manufacturing, the greater is the possibility of its being carried over long distances with a fair profit margin.

Where one material can be substituted for another, the attraction exerted by each is thereby reduced. Both the number of materials required for a process and their relative proportions and individual costs affect the degree of their location attraction. Unless one of the raw materials loses weight heavily on processing, the location influence of each material in such a combination tends to decline as the number of the various raw materials needed for the process increases. If only very small quantities of the various raw materials are used and if very little or no loss of weight of such materials occurs during processing, then the influence of the materials on the location decisions becomes negligible.

Sometimes the structure of freight rates increases or decreases the influence of the raw materials. The structure of freight rates depends on both the distance covered and the nature of the transport facility. Where the production sites can take advantage of sea transport, remote manufacturers stand to gain through the relatively low sea freight rates over long distances (for instance, Mombasa Oil Refinery).

The influence of materials on location decisions also varies in accordance with the technological status of distribution and utilisation. Despite a strong material

[1] A. Weber, *Theory of the Location of Industries*, Univ of Chicago Press, Chicago, 1929.

attraction, industrial location may not be orientated towards the material source, owing to other even stronger location forces[1] militating against such orientation thereby rendering production at the material source uneconomic.

Influence of transfer costs[2]

Considered in terms of either raw materials or the finished products, industries which either process bulky raw materials or manufacture bulky finished products of low value per unit weight normally experience relatively high transport costs. The cost of materials, and the procurement of power and fuel may be regarded as part of transport costs. However, it should be noted that the structure of freight rates, owing to its complexity, may have a far reaching influence on industrial location. Transport should thus be considered as an integral part of the productive process, because the cost of assembling materials and that incurred in distributing the manufactured products together may vary from a small to a fairly large fraction of total costs. For this reason, varying transport costs in different areas, if not overshadowed by other more powerful location factors, tend to focus industries in areas where such costs are least. The actual costs incurred in moving the goods.[3] and the other indirect costs add up to the total transfer costs. Reflected in the indirect costs are such things as the reliability of the services, their speed and regularity. In general, transfer costs are influenced by the distance to be covered, the character of the land surface traversed and the type of transport medium and carrier. Lower freight rates also are charged where they are return cargoes. Other important considerations affecting costs are: quantities of goods to be transferred, whether they are liquid or solid, and also whether fragile and/or perishable. Broadly speaking, there is a tendency for transport costs per ton to decrease, as the hauling distance increases. Terminals, however, absorb a relatively high fraction of the total transfer costs owing to such special features as loading, storage and unloading. Thus, whilst the adverse effects of actual length of distance may be lessened by the special long distance haul reduced rates, it is the necessity to break bulk (involving transfer of the goods from one type of carrier to another) or to cross national frontiers that tends to increase the transfer costs comparatively steeply.

Transport-orientated industries are best located where the costs of raw materials assembly and that of distributing the finished products, taken together, is least.

However, a compromise is essential where the market to be served is extensive or scattered, and/or the industry concerned uses several raw materials whose locations are widely scattered. But although transport costs may be least at a given location, the final siting decisions can be influenced by other factors such as low processing costs rather than low procurement and distribution costs.[1,2]

Influence of processing costs

Processing costs include all the costs other than those incurred in transporting both the raw materials and the finished products. They therefore consist of: labour costs, costs of administration, interest paid on capital, rents and royalties, taxes, costs of services (including insurance), maintenance and depreciation of building and capital equipment.

Transfer costs in certain industries may vary so little from site to site that processing costs emerge considerably higher and therefore more influential in determining the location decisions. The best examples of this are provided by those industries which utilise compact materials[3] and manufacture equally compact finished products. Such industries have complex production processes although the associated transfer operations, even to distant markets, are simple.

The factors of production include capital, enterprise[4] and labour. Whilst capital and labour involve the payment of interest and wages, respectively, enterprise is associated with profits.[5] However, the price paid for using the factors of production is regarded as a constituent part of the total costs of production. Amongst other reasons, the above price is geographically variable owing, especially, to the imperfect mobility of the production factors.

The variations in production factor prices can be offset to some extent by varying the proportions in which the factors are used. For instance, if labour is the most costly input, the entrepreneur could replace it with another relatively cheaper input such as capital: thus a higher degree of mechanisation would reduce costly labour. On the other hand, if capital is more costly than labour, it can be used more intensively by employing more labour and, through several shifts, ultimately using expensive equipment for longer periods per day. The ability to substitute an input such as labour with another such as capital in order to offset locational variations in costs results, for the businessman, in substantial freedom in location decisions.

---

[1] For instance, lack of labour, high transport costs or lack of transport facilities, remote markets, etc.

[2] It is assumed here that transfer costs are not exactly identical with transport costs. The latter phrase refers to actual freight costs of goods movement. Transfer costs include both transport costs and other indirect costs such as goods and materials, insurance, interest charged on capital invested in the goods and materials, damage and/or deterioration, clerical costs, etc.

[3] Properly called transport costs.

[1] E. M. Hoover, *The Location of Economic Activity*, McGraw-Hill, 1948.

[2] M. L. Greenhut, *Plant Location in Theory and in Practice*, Chapel Hill, 1956.

[3] Materials which have high value in comparison to their weight or their bulk.

[4] Willingness to undertake bold projects.

[5] And losses.

Whilst geographical variations in the prices of production factors are worth close attention, similar variations in the efficiency of the production factors should be considered, since they determine the ultimate processing costs. In other words, an entrepreneur is satisfied only when he gets a profit on his expenses, and not when the business is run at a loss. For this reason, a businessman will continue substituting one factor of production for another until a point of optimum net profit is attained.

Because labour is a fundamental requirement in practically all the manufacturing activities, it is one of the most important constituent parts in the cost structure of all such activities. In certain industries,[1] labour costs form a substantial part of the 'value added by manufacturing'.[2] In their attempt to cut down labour costs, entrepreneurs concerned with labour intensive industries normally locate such industries in areas where labour is cheap and plentiful. However, in order to reduce production costs caused by rapid turnover of trained operatives, such industrial concerns prefer or are more successful if their trained labour is less mobile and the annual turnovers are minimal. To avoid possible industrial decline adverse trade union influence and negative workers' attitudes[3] should be discouraged through sound industrial relations. In Kenya trade unionists who indulge in unnecessary strikes are dealt with by stringent labour laws whilst in Tanzania strikes are illegal. A further deterrent to strikes in Kenya is the unemployment problem.

In Kenya, perhaps the major problem in industrial development is the widespread lack of technical skills necessary for running the modern equipment which is constantly being introduced with the expansion of manufacturing activities. As the general levels of skill increase, and also as mechanisation and standardisation in production become significant, a higher level of productivity will be attained.

Although capital is perhaps the most mobile of the factors of production within Kenya, its free movement is apparently centralised in those areas with the most attractive investment conditions. Large urban foci, especially Nairobi and Mombasa, have become sources of capital and, consequently, influence the spatial pattern of industrial investment. Nairobi, in particular, serves as the best location for the headquarters of most of the leading industrial firms in Kenya (and used to be so for East Africa until recently, when inter-territorial independence forced decentralisation to Dar es Salaam and Kampala).

Mobility of capital, on an international level, is much more complex and involves a number of important considerations. For a developing country like Kenya, aid capital takes the form of money or capital goods. Sometimes the foreign cash loans which Kenya negotiates are actually received in the form of equipment. Thus, though the money and capital goods are closely related forms of capital, they differ in their mobility. Capital equipment[1] is immobile and therefore encourages geographical inertia. In general, since the risks involved in money capital are greater than those in capital equipment, it is not surprising that the mobility of money capital across international boundaries is much less than theoretically believed. Overseas investments in developing countries are also affected by political instability and the developing countries' suspicion of possible strings attached to such capital. Some developing countries experience retarded foreign investment in the industrial sector owing to poor infrastructure.[2] Perhaps the best solution for overcoming the difficulty of the immobility of foreign capital across national boundaries is to devise effective methods, within the state, for raising local low interest capital[3] which the government could then invest in more decentralised industrial development, aimed especially at stabilising the rural population.

To succeed in the above, however, capital and labour must be applied efficiently, and such productive enterprises as are established must be based on the highest possible level of modern business organisation and management. The country must train, without delay, its own cadre of managers for future economic growth, since imported personnel are usually in inadequate supply. However, the necessary skills cannot be imparted all at once, or else poorly trained local personnel who have been hurried through training are more likely to wreck well-established enterprises. Importation of skilled personnel is therefore likely to continue, especially for purposes of cross-fertilisation. Inefficiently managed enterprises could in future survive in Kenya if protected against foreign competition, but this is not a good policy in the long term. This can, however, be avoided by gradual progress, always looking for the highest quality personnel. If circumstances compel us to import or retain foreign managers and executives, it is important to bear in mind that a hostile attitude towards such personnel is incompatible with their continued supply, and if we fail, as a country, to attract such international higher forms of skilled labour, the consequences are bound, in the long run, to retard our economic growth.[4-6]

[1] Such as the textile, leather and clothing industries.

[2] This is defined as 'the difference between the cost of materials (including power and fuel used) and the value of the finished product at the factory'.

[3] Involving work stoppages.

[1] Especially if the equipment is heavy, e.g. sugar cane processing equipment.

[2] For instance, insurance, stock markets and banking facilities.

[3] Such as a more widely based national social security fund or more attractive conditions for insurance with government sponsored schemes, etc.

[4] M. L. Greenhut, *Plant Location in Theory and in Practice*, Chapel Hill, 1956, p. 123–139, 140–162.

[5] J. Rutherford, *et al.*, *New Viewpoints in Economic Geography*, Harrap, 1967, p. 278–280.

[6] E. C. Estall and R. O. Buchanan, *Industrial Activity and Economic Geography*, Hutchinson, 1962, p. 80–101.

Influences of markets

In the processing of glass or the making of pots, the finished product is fragile and transport losses could be high if great care is not taken, especially where haulage over long distances and a lot of handling are involved. Factories which manufacture such fragile finished products are best located in or near the main markets for their products. Certain manufacturing processes, for example baking and brewing, have finished products which are substantially bulkier and more awkward to handle than their constituent materials. All such industries tend to be located in or close to their main markets because of the transport costs of the finished products are greater than those of the raw materials. The baking industry has also to cope with the perishable nature of its product, and this is a further factor which influences the location of industries near their markets.

Many industries in Kenya are thus attracted to the larger towns, such as Nairobi, where there are big markets. However, certain industries, such as soft drinks processing, have widely scattered markets and in such cases, an attempt to derive the maximum economies of large-scale production by serving an extensive market becomes impracticable owing to the steep rise in transport costs. This problem is partly solved in Kenya by establishing branch plants in smaller towns. For instance, the soft drinks processing factories in Kisumu and Eldoret are intended for most of western Kenya and the Mombasa brewery supplies coastal beer requirements. In cases where only single plants operate for the whole country, the best nodal location is normally some significant town, for instance, Nairobi, Mombasa, Nakuru, Thika, or Kisumu. There is, however, need to balance the internal scale economies gained through serving a large market area against the allied extra transport costs.

Influence of power and water supplies[1]

Because Kenya lacks coal and natural gas resources, it relies heavily on electricity and fuel oil for industrial power. The details of electricity generation and supply and oil fuel have been discussed under infrastructure. Unless abnormally large supplies are required neither electricity nor water are important factors in the location of industry as both of these can be transported with relative ease. Fuel oil, through the increased use of motor vehicles for transport has actually encouraged the spreading of industrial sites throughout the country.

Influence of personal considerations[2]

This factor is complex and appears to share many features with the cost and demand factors. It may affect location decisions in several ways. For instance, it may
a indirectly influence the cost factor,

b partly control demand, or
c provide rewards which are non-pecuniary.

At this point, it will be useful to differentiate between the two sets of factors (namely, 'cost and revenue' factors and 'cost-reducing and revenue-increasing' factors) because they have important bearing on the personal considerations factor. Those gains which arise from agglomeration or scattering of industries (see below) constitute the cost-reducing factors, although it should be observed here that the advantages of agglomeration consist of a mixture of cost and cost-reducing factors. As distinct from a cost factor, a cost-reducing factor emphasises the relationship between the physical distance and costs other than in terms of transportation and labour costs. Whilst the price of raw material, for instance, is a cost factor, the availability of the raw material (apart from its price) is a cost-reducing factor.

The agglomerating-scattering types of forces (such as the need for quick delivery) affect sales, and are therefore regarded as revenue-increasing factors. The importance of personal cost-reducing and revenue-increasing factors in Kenya is quite obvious, especially in and around the larger urban centres. Cost savings based on personal relationship between the seller and the customer are regarded as personal cost-reducing factors. Because a businessman is aware that friendship between him and a material supplier and/or a banker will influence the availability of materials and/or funds, he may decide to locate his industrial establishment close to the raw material supplier and/or the banker. Personal contact is hereby emphasised. From the revenue-increasing viewpoint, most businessmen know that the already existing contacts with their customers promote sales.

Several instances in Kenya point to the fact that businessmen are often limited in their selection of plant location because there is a strong preference for a familiar, more neighbourly environment. Over and above this consideration, instances could be cited where the businessmen's physical income apparently determines the location decisions. Such personal considerations are indirectly related to the cost and demand factors provided they affect either the finished products sales or the purchase of production factors through their influence on the businessman's service. The connection between price and the personal considerations factor lies, therefore, primarily by way of imputed cost. It should also be observed that personal contentment at a given location may boost the entrepreneur's sales ability. Such a factor is basically non-pecuniary, however.

The influence of home environment in Kenya is quite strong. A large number of Kenya's manufacturing and service industries are owned or controlled by Asian businessmen who, in most cases, located their industries in the towns where they lived. Initially, many Kenya Asians were engaged in commercial activities, although some, such as those in the Kibos-Miwani-Chemelil-Muhoroni sugar belt of Kisumu District, took part in agricultural production. Once capital had accumulated or become available and the decision had been taken to

[1] R. B. Ogendo, *Industrial Geography of Kenya*, East African Publishing House, Nairobi, 1972.
[1] M. L. Greenhut, *Plant Location in Theory and in Practice*, Chapel Hill, 1956, p, 163–177.

go into manufacturing, a given Asian businessman almost invariably established his manufacturing enterprise in the town where he lived. Thus it seems that personal considerations involving cost-reducing and revenue-increasing factors of location were of great importance. Some of the best examples of industrial activities much influenced in this fashion include the manufacture of soft drinks, bakery products, soap and edible oils, clothing, chocolate and sugar confectionery, leather goods, miscellaneous food products, furniture and grain milling products.

Owing to the fact that many of the founders of these industrial enterprises already had excellent commercial contacts with the leading local wholesalers and retailers or were themselves engaged in such commercial activities, they easily became well-established industrialists. Generally speaking, such businesses were characterised by small beginnings and therefore benefited little from the economies of large-scale operations. On the other hand, the finished products from such small-scale enterprises satisfied the then limited local market. In the course of time, however, there were created sales networks sufficiently strong to be the basis for the expansion of the industrial enterprises. Because of personal relationships credit facilities were more easily available. The main issue thus became 'what to manufacture' rather than 'where to manufacture it'.

The above analysis gives a clearer picture of the location factors responsible for the present, mostly urban-orientated, industrial pattern, with special reference to Asian and European owned or controlled businesses. African industrial enterprises are practically all post-independence and relatively rudimentary.

Influence of agglomerating economies and/or industrial interdependence

The economies of agglomeration seem to be closely related to the concentrations of labour supply and markets. New industries are attracted to these centres and this tendency becomes perpetuated by being reinforced by fixed capital investments and sooner or later geographical inertia.

In the whole of East Africa the Nairobi district industrial unit benefits most by the agglomerating economies. Out of a total of thirty-nine individual groups of manufacturing and service industries in Kenya, this district industrial unit houses thirty-seven. This significant industrial agglomeration, especially within Nairobi city (and also to a lesser extent in such other towns as Mombasa, Nakuru and Kisumu), promotes industrial interdependence.

The leading agglomerative advantages that Nairobi enjoys include:
a a large range of insurance facilities;
b good commercial facilities;
c readily available service facilities and spare parts;
d an international airport; and
e excellent communication links with its principal port of Mombasa.

These agglomerative advantages also explain the de-

Fig. 13A Pineapple canning at the Kenya Canners, Thika

Fig. 13B Tin cans being made at the Metal Box Company, Thika

veloping cluster (near Nairobi) of such industrial estates as Ruaraka, Kassarani and Kahawa, and several small industrial towns such as Athi River, Limuru, Thika and Uplands.

Certain industrial enterprises benefit considerably by locating close to other industrial establishments, either because they obtain their raw materials from such factories and hence reduce transport costs or owing to easy access to service industries. This interdependence of industries makes industrial decentralisation to the rural areas difficult, because efficiency would inevitably suffer. Moreover, the small towns in the rural areas do not offer the economies of scale in electricity supplies, transport, insurance and other protective and maintenance services as are offered in Nairobi and Mombasa and, to some extent, in Kisumu, Nakuru, Thika and Eldoret.

Industrial interdependence may reach such a stage that some firms may even function as units in a production sequence, so that the materials pass from one firm to the other. In such cases each firm within the chain benefits from the agglomerating economies of the entire complex. On the other hand, a take-over bid may occur, so that a given industrial firm may grow larger by absorbing all the other smaller firms, thus incorporating all the manufacturing activities originally forming the production sequence. Such a firm would benefit considerably by internal economies of scale.

Apart from numerous other examples to be found in large urban areas such as Nairobi, Mombasa, Kisumu and Nakuru, perhaps the best two examples of industrial interdependence are those in Thika township. The first example is that between the Kenya Canners factory and Metal Box Company which are located next door to each other. The Kenya Canners factory uses large quantities of tins for its tinned fruit and vegetable industry, and the tins are conveniently fabricated in the immediate vicinity by the Metal Box Company factory. This is an excellent example of industrial linkage, where one industry uses the finished products of another industry in its manufacturing activity. The second example of industrial interdependence in Thika is that between Bulleys Tanneries which uses substantial quantities of the production of the Kenya Tanning Extract factory which is located close by.

Closing Comments on Industrial Location Factors

The study of the entire range of location factors, rather than the selected sample of factors discussed above, points to the fact that no single factor on its own completely determines the best location for an industry. Moreover, the industrial circumstances in Kenya have tended to change relatively rapidly during the life of an industrial plant so that, in practice, it is virtually impossible to know what the optimum location is. Con-

190

sequently, the concept of an optimum location has little significance at present.

It should also be observed that personal consideration factors are of great significance in location decisions in Kenya, especially from the viewpoint of our imperfect knowledge and the uncertainty observed in many of the businessmen. Furthermore, when an industrial firm investigates alternative locations at its disposal, it incurs extra expenses which vary directly according to the thoroughness of the investigation. Because such expenses have to be set against the capitalised benefits expected to accrue from the choice of the best location available, these benefits must be large in comparison to the cost of ascertainment. In Kenya, such benefits are, in many cases, not large, so that many industrial firms do not normally press their researches far, and are satisfied with semi-optimal locations, or they prefer to locate in areas where industrial concentration is already high and the agglomeration economies are obvious. This has resulted in considerable industrial centralisation in a very small part of Kenya.

A further decisive element is that of time. Any investigation of alternative locations may require more time than can be allowed in the circumstances or under the conditions laid down by the government. As a result, it seems that in a country such as Kenya location considerations based on the geographical limits within which industrial enterprises could be successful may be more fruitful than the search for near-perfect industrial locations. In the application of this method it should be borne in mind that in East Africa where new products are continuously being introduced and are being given a relatively short time to spread and where competitive conditions are changing radically, the correspondence between economic margins and geographical limits may be hard to reconcile.[1]

For purposes of isolating location factors the concept of geographical limits is widely applied. Along with the main industrial location factors are a number of secondary factors whose effects are felt through the more important factors discussed above. From the viewpoint of the principal factors, the following composite groups of factors emerge:

a historical, geological-topographical and ecological influences, including those of raw materials;

b the combined influence of transfer and processing costs, with special emphasis on availability and cost of capital, managerial and other industrial skills and transport costs;

c the influence of personal consideration factors and their interaction with governmental industrial location directives;

d the influence of the distribution of infrastructural facilities and markets; and

e the influence of economies of agglomeration and/or industrial linkage.

---

[1] M. Chisholm, *Geography and Economics*, Bell, 1966.

General Industrial Orientation

The following Table 13.1 divides the 39 national manufacturing and service industries of Kenya into three classes: 'market-orientated', 'material-orientated' or 'market-cum-material-orientated'. When examining this classification it is important to bear in mind the earlier discussion on the various industrial location factors.[1] In the case of the market-cum-material orientated industries, market attraction within the raw material areas seems stronger. For instance, the major dairy factories in the dairy farming areas of Kenya are located in or close to the principal urban markets.

Out of the 39 individual groups of industries 25 (64·1%) are market-orientated, 9 (23·1%) are market-cum-material-orientated and the remaining 5 (12·8%) are material-orientated.

Industrial Orientation, Density and Zoning

Preliminary Comments

This final section has two aims:

a to present the existing qualitative and quantitative industrial density patterns, and

b to utilise location factors to derive the industrial development zones.

The study of (a) industrial density patterns; (b) classification of Kenya's agricultural land[2]; (c) the distribution pattern of the exploitable minerals[3]; the suggested industrial development zones; and (d) the natural regions of Kenya, and the correlation of the five should lead to a better understanding of Kenya's economic potentiality, on which more convincing development planning for the future could be based.

Industrial Density

This feature is better appreciated when examined both qualitatively and quantitatively, as in the former case the distribution is not quantified, and thus gives an incomplete picture.

Qualitative industrial density
The simplest and most generalised approach to qualitative industrial density was introduced earlier under industrial location. Fig. 11.3 indicates clearly that practically the whole of northern and eastern Kenya are industrially empty. The map also shows that much of the former Southern Province and Coast Province (except for the narrow coastal belt from Ramisi to

---

[1] See also R. B. Ogendo, *Industrial Geography of Kenya*, East African Publishing House, Nairobi, 1972.

[2] L. H. Brown, *A National Cash Crops Policy for Kenya*, Ministry of Agriculture, Nairobi, 1963.

[3] An important part of this industry is soon to become material-orientated, and is to be located probably at Broderick Falls in Western Province.

Table 13.1

	ISIC Code
a *The market-orientated industries*	
i *Agricultural food processing:*	
Grain milling	205
Miscellaneous food products processing	204; part of 209
Bakery products processing	206
Chocolate and sugar confectionery	208
Brewing and blending of alcoholic beverages	211–13
ii *Agricultural non-food manufacturing:*	
Tobacco processing	220
Soap and edible oils processing	312; (315)
Miscellaneous vegetable chemical products processing (mainly pyrethrum)	316; part of 319
Footwear fabrication and repair	241
Textile processing	232; 234; 239
Clothing fabrication	243; 244
Furniture and fixtures fabrication	260
Pulp, paper and paper products manufacture[1]	271; 272
iii *Non-agricultural manufacturing industries:*	
Basic non-vegetable industrial chemical products processing	311
Miscellaneous non-vegetable chemical products processing	313; part of 319; (354); 356
Motor vehicle assembly	383
iv *All service industries:*	
Printing and publishing	280
Electrical machinery and repair (mainly maintenance)	370
Rubber products (mainly tyre retreading)	300
Non-electrical machinery and repair (mainly maintenance)	360; 386; 389
Boat, steamer and ship repair (including assembly and/or building)	381
Railway services (including some manufacturing)	382
Motor vehicle repair	384
Metal products (including some manufacturing)	350
Miscellaneous service industries (including manufacturing)	(390); 391–399
b *The material-orientated industries:*	
i *Agricultural food processing:*	
Sugar processing	207
Tea processing	part of 209
Coffee processing	(200), or the rest of 209
ii *Agricultural non-food manufacturing:*	
Fibre processing (including sisal, cotton, socfinaf, coir, flax, etc)	231, 233
Sawmilling (soon to be associated with items 271 and 272)	251
c *The market-cum-material-orientated industries:*	
i *Agricultural food processing:*	
Meat products processing	201
Dairy products processing	202
Fruit and vegetable canning and soft drinks processing	203; 214
ii *Agricultural non-food manufacturing:*	
Tanning extract processing; leather tanning and fabrication of non-footwear leather goods	291; 299; (314)
Miscellaneous wood products manufacture	259
iii *Non-agricultural manufacturing industries:*	
Clay and concrete products manufacture	331; 333; 339
Cement; glass and allied products manufacture	332; 334
Generation (and supply) of electricity	511
Processing (and supply) of water	521

---

[1] An important part of this industry is soon to become material-orientated, and is to be located probably at Broderick Falls in Western Province.

Malindi, especially around Mombasa) have no significant industries, apart from the few at Magadi, Athi River and Machakos townships. Most of Kenya's industries, therefore, are located in the highlands where their distribution is influenced by the railway and road networks.

A fairer view of the qualitative industrial density introduced above is better portrayed in the map which shows the distribution of factory sites (Fig. 11.3). In the construction of this map, all the factory sites known in 1965 are indicated in terms of varying density rather than by the absolute dot method. The varying density map was, however, derived from the absolute dot map not included in this volume.[1]

Fig. 11.3 shows that nearly 60% of Kenya's surface is industrially empty. About 75% of the remaining 40% of the surface is very scantily dotted with industrial establishments, while the remaining 25% (of the 40% of Kenya's surface) accommodates most of the industrial plants.

Note the location of the thirteen main industrial towns. There are five important industrial towns, Nairobi, Mombasa, Kisumu, Thika and Nakuru. Other significant industrial towns are Eldoret, Kitale, Athi River and Machakos. Minor industrial towns include Nanyuki, Nyeri, Naivasha and Malindi. The rest of the minor towns are shown in Fig. 11.2, which depicts the principal industrial towns and centres.

Apart from the Kisii-Kericho rural clusters, the other major industrial concentrations are associated with towns such as Nairobi and Thika, Mombasa, Nakuru and Kisumu. Industrial towns such as Kitale, Eldoret, Nanyuki, Nyeri, Athi River, Machakos and Malindi stand out either as isolated industrial areas, or in proximity to other purely rural industrial islands.

Quantitative industrial density
To place the above qualitative industrial densities in their proper perspective, two quantitative methods of measurement have been used:
a the percentage distribution of Kenya's 95 692 manufacturing and service workers in 1964 (Fig. 11.3), and
b the district index of industrial concentration, including the qualitative index of diversification, for all the manufacturing and service industries for 1964 (Fig. 11.5).

The first map (Fig. 11.4), indicates the percentage share of the national manufacturing and service workers of each district industrial unit. According to the map, the qualitatively high and moderate densities of Mombasa, Nairobi, Thika, Nakuru, Kericho, Uasin Gishu and Central Nyanza district industrial units are quantitatively significant. The map also indicates the overwhelming industrial importance of towns such as Nairobi and Mombasa.

Quantitatively, the more favourable qualitative in-

dustrial densities in the other district industrial units (other than those enumerated in the above paragraph) are not as significant as they appear to be.

In terms of industrial concentration, the map showing the district index of industrial concentration for all the manufacturing and service industries (Fig. 11.5), speaks for itself. It clearly isolates the three district industrial units A1, D1 and B1, (Fig. 1.3, Chapter 1) which jointly employed more than 50% of the 95 692 national manufacturing and service work force for 1964. However, the 1964 population estimates give the combined population total for the three district industrial units as equivalent to only 5·9% of Kenya's total population of 9 162 000 at the time. Thus the three district industrial units had a high (94·1) joint index of industrial concentration.

The map also indicates that more than 75% of the national manufacturing and service labour force were concentrated in 10 of the 41 district industrial units (Figs. 11.5 and 1.3, that is, A1, D1, B1, C2, C1, F2, C4, B3, C9 and D7). The ten district industrial units had a joint total population equivalent to 15% of Kenya's estimated total population for 1964. The ten districts, therefore, had a joint index of industrial concentration of 85·0.

Whilst 23 of the remaining 31 district industrial units shared less than 25% of the national manufacturing and service workers, the last 8 district industrial units (C5, G1, G2, G5–G8 and B5; Figs. 11.5 and 1.3) had almost no manufacturing and/or service industries at all.

Industrial Zoning

Qualitatively, about 60% of Kenya is industrially empty. Of the remaining 40% only a small part is, quantitatively, developed. However, the country has considerable industrial raw material potential (both organic and inorganic) for future development.[1] It is estimated that 60% of Kenya's land surface has a potential of one sort or another. The country can be divided into a number of industrial zones according to the density of distribution of industrial activity. To do this the following location factors have to be considered:
a positive and negative ecological influences[2] and the effects of history;
b influence of raw materials;
c combined influence of the former colonial government attitude towards industrial development, especially from the viewpoint of the alienated land (particularly the former 'White Highlands'), and the African reserves;
d joint influence of transfer and processing costs;
e influence of infrastructural networks of electricity, railways, roads, telecommunications, piped water supplies, waste disposal, etc.;

---

[1] R. B. Ogendo, *Industrial Geography of Kenya*, East African Publishing House, Nairobi, 1972. (See Fig. 8 'Composite pattern of factory sites', and also Figs. 5 to 7).

[1] R. B. Ogendo, *Industrial Geography of Kenya*, East African Publishing House, Nairobi, 1972. See Figs. 66, 67, 75 and the agricultural-industrial raw materials location table.
[2] Including rainfall distribution and reliability, the effects of varying altitude, and the influence of disease carrying organisms.

f influence of personal consideration factors, main urban spheres of influence, the agglomeration economies and industrial interdependence.

The five principal industrial development zones emerging from the combined influence of the above factors are as follows (see Fig. 12.2):

a the Central Zone;
b the Inner Fringe Zone;
c the Outer Fringe Zone;
d the Problem Zone; and
e the Negative Zone and other negative areas.

The Central Zone

This is the most favourable industrial belt in Kenya. Its core, which is demarcated by the electricity distributing areas, has all the attractive location forces, and because of this it has attracted most of the industrial towns and centres in Kenya, resulting in considerable industrial concentration in parts of the core areas (Fig. 12.2). The rapid development of the remainder of the central zone depends to a large extent on the expansion of the electricity distributing areas. It will be noted that, although the greater part of the central zone coincides with the former White Highlands, parts of the zone are located discontinuously along the Indian Ocean seaboard, especially in and around Mombasa district.

The Inner Fringe Zone

Because of its location mainly outside the former White Highlands (with its capital, managerial skill and govern-ment assistance), the inner fringe zone is relatively inferior to the central zone. It also lacks some of the attractive location forces, or else such forces as exist are weakly developed. It is also comparatively more exposed to some of the negative ecological factors such as disease-carrying tsetse flies and mosquitoes.

A further cause of retarded industrial growth of both the inner fringe zone and parts of the central zone has been the labour drain from these areas to the more prosperous parts of the central zone where the original European enterprises created added attraction in the form of a money economy and a large residential labour market. Also, the inner fringe zone has not attracted foreign development capital owing to its comparatively poorly developed infrastructural facilities and the few small scattered markets. The zone, therefore, shares few of the industrial towns and centres with the more prosperous parts of the central zone. A small part of it is found along the coast.

The Outer Fringe Zone

This is a large zone which almost completely envelops both the central and inner fringe zones. It is in two parts, the northern more extensive and continuous section, and the smaller discontinuous southern part centred on the Magadi area, but also found in the vicinity of Mt Kilimanjaro, in the Taita Hills area and along the coast. It is at present poorly endowed with organic industrial raw materials, but by introducing irrigation and other improved agricultural methods the organic resources of

Fig. 13C Meat inspection at the Athi River Kenya Meat Commission factory

the zone could be greatly improved. Irrigation is already profitably used in the Perkerra area of Baringo, Mwea Tebere in Embu and Galole along the Tana.

The biggest potential of the outer fringe zone is beef cattle ranching, provided the cattle and human disease-carrying tsetse fly species are eliminated. The zone is already supplying a substantial part of the requirements of both Athi River and Mombasa Kenya Meat Commission factories. Because of the wildlife of the zone it has important tourism potential.

The Problem Zone
This is the largest of the five development zones, and resembles the outer fringe zone in many of its characteristics. However, the problems experienced in the outer fringe zone are severer in the problem zone. The latter could be a source of great wealth to Kenya if it were freed of the disease-transmitting tsetse flies, provided with more water and a better infrastructure network and reinforced educationally. The problem zone is a possible high potential area for beef cattle ranching, especially in conjunction with the maize belt in the Rift Valley for fattening. Its other important potential lies in its wildlife for the tourist industry. Many of Kenya's major game parks and reserves lie in this zone (Figs. 6.1 and 12.2).

The southern part of the zone has higher agricultural potential than the northern section. It is therefore more likely to be developed first, especially in view of the present plans to improve its infrastructure.

The Negative Zone
Owing to its poor communication network, the negative zone is at present the remotest of the five zones. It also experiences desiccating climatic conditions. Furthermore the zone has very limited known natural resources and consequently is the most backward area in Kenya. Other areas not physically located in the negative zone proper are to be found on the peaks of the high mountains such as Mounts Kenya and Elgon, the Aberdares and the Cherangani and Mau Hills.

The five development zones are referred to further in the final chapter both in terms of their potentialities for future economic development and in relation to the natural regions of Kenya.

References

CHISHOLM, M. *Geography and Economics*, Bell, 1966.

ESTALL, R. C. and BUCHANAN, R. O. *Industrial Activity and Economic Geography*, Hutchinson, 1962.

GREENHUT, M. L. *Plant Location in Theory and in Practice*, Chapel Hill, 1956.

HOOVER, E. M. *The Location of Economic Activity*, McGraw-Hill, 1948.

OGENDO, R. B. *Industrial Geography of Kenya*, East African Publishing House, Nairobi, 1972.

RUTHERFORD, J., *et al. New Viewpoints in Economic Geography*, Harrap, 1967.

Chapter 14
Tertiary Industries and Tourism

Tertiary Industries

Tertiary industries are primarily service industries. They form the backbone upon which other essential services draw their trained manpower. The concerns and operations that are commonly embraced under this category of activities are commercial activities (particularly retail trade), banking, professional (including medical) and educational facilities. Tourism is strictly speaking an industry in its own class. The unifying theme of the tertiary industries is that they provide an important backbone to the quality of the human resources which form the basis of the manpower, the backbone to economic performance, industrial development and growth. The tourist trade too can be included, being itself a substantial earner of foreign capital.

Kenya's commercial activity is mainly concentrated in the larger urban centres with Nairobi as the commercial capital. Mombasa, Nakuru and Kisumu, in that order, follow in importance, and it might be noted that the relative importance of each centre is a function of the size of its population. The historical development of this commerce has been mainly in the hands of the Asian traders who managed to penetrate into rural trading centres and established cordial relationships with the local inhabitants.

Recently the Government, in its efforts to transfer this activity into the hands of its citizens, has deliberately enacted certain trade licensing laws intended 'to help African businessmen to enter wholesale and retail trading' by restricting certain trading areas to citizens alone.

Banking and Other Financial Institutions in Kenya

Before Independence the East African Currency Board (founded in 1919) was responsible for the supply and the control of currency in Kenya and Uganda. Later, when Tanganyika became a British Mandated Territory, the Board extended its services to cover that Territory, Zanzibar and Aden. For many years the board had its headquarters in London, but in 1960 it moved to Nairobi although it still maintained much of its assets in London.

Apart from this currency board, all the normal banking facilities were provided by the commercial banks, building societies, hire-purchase financial houses and a few government-backed organisations such as the Land Bank and the Post Office Savings Bank. Up to the time of independence, there were nine foreign commercial banks operating in Kenya. These banks provided the normal banking facilities and formed the main source of money in the country. It is noteworthy that, in the history of Kenya, a number of these banks contributed significantly to national development by providing credit facilities for industry and agriculture as well as for other short-term credit facilities to their customers. Many of the British banks, for instance, provided financial support for many European farmers in the 'scheduled' areas until farming was well established. As is shown in chapter nine (Agriculture) the Board of Agriculture, the Land Settlement Board, the Land and Agricultural Bank and the ALDEV (the African Land Development Board) also provided credit facilities to farmers particularly prior to independence.

The Central Bank

Since Independence each of the three East African governments has established a Central Bank which took over its share of the functions of the East African Currency Board. The establishment of the Central Bank of Kenya was certainly a sound decision, as it should give the Government much useful advice and should also function as the Government's link with other world financial institutions. It should also be able to set up other local financial institutions more relevant to the national needs. It might even discourage certain established mortgage houses and hire-purchase firms which do not show sufficient interest in helping the people. But above all, the Central Bank must ensure that some of the earnings of foreign based firms are ploughed back to help in developing the country. In this respect, the recent inauguration of a Commercial Bank of Kenya was another healthy action by the Central Bank. The Central Bank also holds, on behalf of the Government, a foreign exchange which at the end of 1969 stood at £K62 million.

Other Financial Institutions

The oldest of these is the Post Office Savings Bank which is operated by the East African Posts and Telecommunication Administration. It has played a useful role in encouraging the local inhabitants, even in remote areas, to take to the habit of saving and to place their money in safe custody.

There are also some five building societies in the country (mainly in the big towns) which have been willing to make mortgage loans available to their approved customers for residential and commercial buildings. The history of the operation of many of these financial institutions does indicate that the local Africans did not benefit very much from their facilities because the prevailing circumstances were such that the 'African' could not provide the expected 'security'. It also appears that some of these institutions helped to inflate the price of property and now Kenya is in a situation in which houses cost as much as similar houses in some of the most highly developed cities in the developed countries. We believe that this state of affairs should be checked. Another important source of finance in Kenya comes from insurance funds. At the end of 1968 insurance houses held nearly £K28 million. This sum was invested in local securities.

Health Services in Kenya

Service industries which go to make up the tertiary industries also include, of course, the social services of health and education.

Because of its special topographical circumstances, Kenya does not suffer unduly from the numerous tropical and sub-tropical diseases. A number of endemic diseases, some of which occur in epidemic form, are present in Kenya. The great contrast in relief has also produced large regional variations in the occurrence of diseases over the country. Respiratory diseases are, for instance, more widespread in the highlands especially in Central Province. Likewise, tropical diseases including leprosy, malaria and bilharzia are more common in the low-lying parts of the Coast and Nyanza Provinces.

The provision of medical facilities in Kenya is the responsibility of the Ministry of Health. In 1967, these facilities consisted of the following and were spread throughout the country as shown in Table 14.1.

The above facilities were supported by 13 608 hospital beds of all categories. Of this number, 7 928 beds were in government hospitals, 1 590 in private hospitals and the remaining 4 090 beds were in mission hospitals. It should also be noted that most of the private beds are in the main urban centres while it is the mission hospitals which really penetrate into the interior of rural communities. Thus, apart from their evangelical aims, the missionaries have played a vital pioneer role in getting medical facilities to the rural inhabitants, just as they also played, and still play, an extremely important part in the country's education structure.

Against the above picture, the supporting professional

Table 14.1 *Number of medical facilities in Kenya 1967*

Province	Hospitals	Health centres	Dispensaries
Nairobi	22	—	47[1]
Central	35	32	80
Coast	23	13	60
Eastern	25	23	91
Northeastern	3	—	9
Nyanza	26	29	56
Rift Valley	50	44	144
Western	15	21	13
Total	199	162	500

Source: *Statistical Abstracts*, Republic of Kenya, 1968.

[1] Includes maternity and child welfare clinics of which there were 26 in 1967.

staff in the country during the year 1966 was as follows: 820 registered doctors, 90 licensed doctors, 49 dentists (only one African of Kenyan origin), 2 332 registered nurses, 3 182 enrolled nurses, 1 067 registered midwives and 1 217 enrolled midwives. The main limitations placed on the Government are limited finance and, indeed, trained personnel to man adequately existing facilities. In its efforts to tackle the problem the Government recently introduced free outpatient treatment for all citizens, and a National Hospital Insurance Fund which gives all contributors free treatment at government hospitals, or a large bed-subsidy in non-government hospitals for those who can afford the private doctor's charges.

In the 1970–4 Development Plan the Government hopes to add 2 000 extra hospital beds. This will provide a bed for 1 250 people in each district. The plan also envisages 475 more doctors, 1 800 nurses and 750 midwives, and an addition of five new health centres each year in the country.

Education

Education is the foundation of modern development both intellectually and economically, and is therefore one of the areas that takes a large share of the Government's revenue. In 1966–7 some £K7·92 million were spent on education and this over the years is nearly twice the amount which goes to the health department. There is now such a desire for education that government efforts are inadequate and since Independence a number of self-help schools by local communities (harambee schools) have sprung up. Secondary education is now a government priority, as this is looked on as the source of semi-skilled and skilled manpower which will help the Kenyanisation programme.

In the ten years following 1959 the number of schools and the pupils have increased considerably as shown in Tables 14.2 and 14.3.

The enrolment of pupils into these schools has been as follows:

Table 14.2 *Number of pupils enrolled in schools by type of school*[1]

	1959	1961	1963	1965	1968
Primary	719 510	870 448	891 553	1 014 719	1 209 680
Secondary	19 239	22 167	30 120	47 976	101 361
Teacher training	3 867	3 897	4 119	5 355	6 634
Trade	1 228	2 094	1 202	1 247	2 036
Total	743 844	898 606	926 994	1 065 467	1 319 711

[1] *Statistical Abstracts*, Republic of Kenya, 1968.

Table 14.3 *Number of schools by type 1959 – 68*[1]

	1959	1961	1963	1965	1968
Primary	4 876	5 725	6 058[2]	5 078	6 135
Secondary	98	105	151	336	601
Teacher training	48	45	37	33	28
Trade	5	21	7	8	11
All schools	5 027	5 895	5 415	5 455	6 775

[1] From 1963, primary and intermediate schools have been amalgamated into full primary schools.

Teaching this number of pupils during 1968 were: primary schools – 27 485 trained and 10 438 untrained teachers; secondary schools – 2 743 trained and 1 902 untrained teachers; teacher training colleges – 468 trained teachers; trade schools – 123 trained and 7 untrained teachers. Thus, altogether, there were 43 166 teachers in service in Kenya as shown by the official records in the Ministry of Education. The number of Kenya students attending full courses in the then University of East Africa rose from 536 in 1963/4 academic year to 1 297 in the 1967/8 academic year.

The government plan as advanced in the 1970/4 Development Plan anticipates that by 1974 about 75% of all the children of primary school age will be in school (the 1968 enrolment was 60%). It also envisages that of this number, the proportion attending school free will double. It does not envisage total free education but aims at enabling those who would otherwise be deprived to receive education.

The number receiving secondary education will be about 135 000 during 1974, with the emphasis on science and mathematics in order to meet the increasing demand in these areas. More lower secondary schools will be geared to offer practical courses in agriculture, commerce, industrial arts and home science.

Fig. 14A The University of Nairobi

Fig. 14B A herd of zebras in the Nairobi National Park

At university level, the intention is to double the enrolment at the University of Nairobi from 822 Kenya students in the 1967/8 session to about 4 400 by 1974. It also envisages that instead of students getting grants to enable them to complete their university education they will get loans which will have to be repaid when they enter salaried employment. The success of the above plans will of course depend on sound planning at all stages and in all areas. As Kenya approached its 1970/4 development plan its long term policy on higher education and technical institutes did not seem to be sufficiently clear.

Tourism

The tourist industry is Kenya's number two foreign currency earner (after coffee), the most important invisible export and fastest growing industry. Unfortunately it is also an industry which is very sensitive to political or administrative inefficiencies.

Together with Tanzania and Uganda, Kenya is magnificently endowed with the richest and largest animal fauna in the world. The magnificent scenery, climate and beaches draw the tourist to Kenya. The factor of natural habitat is of crucial importance. Many who live in large conurbations and cities in developed countries where nature has largely been subdued and polluted by man are moved by the spectacle of vast stretches of bush and tropical forest where the environment is virtually untouched and wildlife, big and small (including birds), can still be viewed in their natural habitats. It is here that wildlife conservation becomes so important for it is essential that the national parks

be protected from human depredation. The money that accrues from visitors to game reserves also makes this an economic and sound form of land use. The National Park Trustees are charged with the maintenance of the habitat and all forms of life, plants and animals, and 'to conserve them for posterity with all the means at its disposal'. Its second duty is to provide facilities to enable visitors to see, study and enjoy this untouched wilderness.

Tourism as an industry thus involves careful preservation of game in their natural homes and the provision of facilities to enable the visitor to reach the wildlife and other places of scenic charm in a reasonable amount of comfort, speed, and in maximum safety.

Historical Development of Tourism in Kenya

On 8 May 1969 East African tourism celebrated its twenty-first anniversary. Back in 1948 a few far-sighted concerns including the East African governments foresaw the tourist potential in the area and formed the East African Tourist Travel Association. Its aim was to develop and encourage tourism in the region. The Association was a small affair, limited by lack of finance, but with a strong purpose. In 1949 it managed to persuade the *Alliance Internationale de Tourisme* to choose Nairobi for its annual conference. The 100 delegates who attended gave East Africa and Nairobi (which has since continued to be the centre for tourism in East Africa) the much needed international advertisement. From that conference the East African tourist industry has mushroomed. In 1950 BOAC also helped by bringing out to East Africa 50 journalists and travel agents to see for themselves the potential of the area. By 1965 the

199

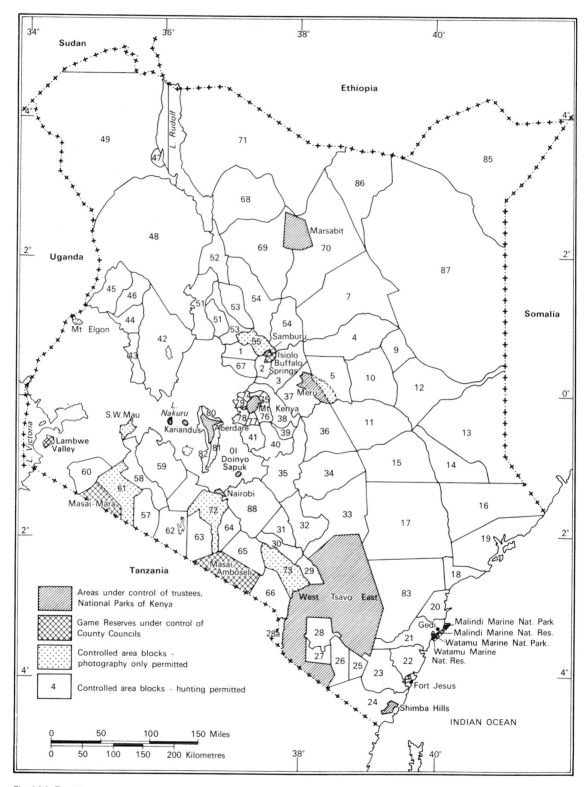

Fig. 14.1 Tourist areas

200

Fig. 14C Treetops Hotel in the Aberdare Forest, near Nyeri. Wild game frequent the waterhole in front of the hotel

industry had grown so big that the Association could not operate the whole management and planning and as the East African scene had also undergone many changes, including political independence, it went into voluntary liquidation and was replaced by national bodies with strong government backing and direction.

The Kenya Tourist Development Corporation was thus formed in 1965. Its main duty is to develop tourism by providing accommodation and transport facilities. The Corporation thus works closely with the National Parks Trustees, although a more definite relationship between the two bodies might be an advantage.

Kenya's tourist attractions are:

a Major national parks which possess a tremendous amount and variety of wildlife. Excellent facilities are available, including the world famous Treetops Hotel in the Aberdare National Park.

b Great scenery and superb climate. Scenery includes the Great African Rift Valley and Africa's highest mountains for mountaineering, big game hunting, trout fishing and motoring for sport.

c Excellent beaches along the coast for quiet holidays and big game fishing. These are served by hotels and beach cottages for all tastes. Two unique attractions in this area are the marine parks (see Fig. 14.1).

Tourism as an Industry

The income from tourism comes from a number of sources. The Government benefits from the balance of payments derived from the foreign exchange which the tourists bring to meet their holiday expenses. From 1961 to 1967 the income from tourism (net balance on foreign travel) grew very rapidly from £K0·8 million to £K9·8 million. The Government also benefits from the sales of

licences to tour operators, who are also taxed on their profits, sales of hunting licences and from entrance fees to national parks. The local authorities in the rural areas also levy hunting fees on hunters in their respective game-controlled areas.

The private sector benefits from the money tourists pay to hotels and tour operators. The tourists also spend money equipping themselves with appropriate clothing before they begin their safaris, and the many shops that specialise in these safari outfits and photographic goods in Nairobi and Mombasa, in particular, confirm the magnitude of the business. The tourists also buy souvenirs and other locally made goods to take back with them to their homes.

It is therefore evident that it is the service industry that really benefits. Indirectly, the agricultural sector also benefits from the sale of more food products to hotels to feed the tourists. Finally, it should also be noted that the whole operation is one of the important sources of employment in the country.

Home Origin and Number of Tourists

Table 14.4 gives a breakdown of the visitors who arrived in Kenya during 1966 and 1967. Note also Fig. 14.2 for a summary of the purpose of trip of visitors.

National Parks, Game Reserves, Conservation Areas, and Controlled Area Blocks

National Parks

We have already stated that the principal tourist attraction is Kenya's wildlife. The preservation of this

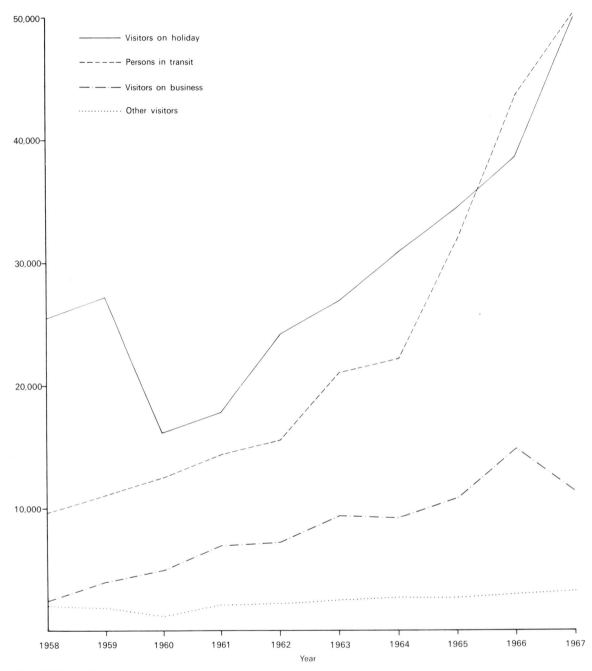

Fig. 14.2 Tourists by purpose of visit

national and natural resource, including places of pre-historic importance, has been placed in the care of the Kenya National Parks Trustees. This body was formed in 1945 following the National Parks of Kenya Act of that year and the establishment of the first national park in East Africa, the Nairobi National Park. The country's national parks in 1969 are shown in Table 14.5.

The Nairobi National Park is the park for the city of Nairobi, and its being practically within the city enables residents and business tourists who have not much time to make a quick tour through it. Between 1963 and 1967 it had an average of 100 000 to 120 000 visitors per year, which makes it the most visited park in the country.

Tsavo Park is divided in two by the main road to

Table 14.4 *Visitors to Kenya by nationalities during 1966 and 1967*[1]

Country of nationality	Visitors on holiday		All visitors	
	1966	1967	1966	1967
Europe				
United Kingdom	18 501	18 562	39 204	43 516
West Germany	6 125	8 408	8 203	11 400
Italy	1 718	1 782	3 878	4 955
France	1 851	2 408	3 547	3 990
Switzerland	3 524	2 990	4 084	3 729
Other	3 407	4 546	6 721	9 387
Total	35 126	38 786	65 637	76 977
USA	10 484	14 472	17 050	24 168
Canada	715	876	1 633	2 085
Asia				
India	1 379	1 648	3 877	6 029
Israel	414	351	1 638	1 803
Japan	276	396	1 026	1 298
Pakistan	275	364	737	1 054
Other	330	373	1 094	1 487
Total	2 674	3 132	8 372	11 671
Africa				
South Africa	405	215	3 594	3 186
Zambia	115	211	1 269	1 663
Other	671	1 012	4 354	5 540
Total	1 191	1 438	9 217	10 389
Australia and New Zealand	383	585	1 022	1 623
All other countries	230	270	652	851
All visitors	50 802	59 559	103 583	127 764

[1] *Economic Survey*, Republic of Kenya, 1968, p. 90.

Table 14.5

Name of Park	Size	
Nairobi National Park	44 sq miles	114 km²
Tsavo National Park (East)	5 000 sq miles	12 950 km²
Tsavo National Park (West)	3 024 sq miles	7 832 km²
Mount Kenya National Park	240 sq miles	621 km²
Aberdare National Park	293 sq miles	759 km²
Meru National Park	336 sq miles	870 km²
Marsabit National Park	360 sq miles	932 km²
Ol Doinyo Sabuk National Park	4 550 acres	1 841 hectares
Mount Elgon National Park	41 800 acres	16 916 hectares
Shimba Hills National Reserve	47 550 acres	19 243 hectares
Lake Nakuru National Park	22 sq miles	57 km²
Fort Jesus National Park (Mombasa)	5·7 acres	2·3 hectares
Gedi National Park	—	—
Olorgesailie National Park	—	—

Fig. 14D Gedi, near Malindi. The ruins of a sixteenth-century Arab settlement. The photograph shows the Sultan's Palace, with the Audience Hall on the left

Mombasa, hence the east and west parts. This is Kenya's largest park and the main stronghold of big game. The Aberdare Park is now world famous for its Treetops Hotel built on the branches of Cape Chestnut trees. From this unforgettable viewpoint the visitor can watch during daylight and at night (floodlit) hundreds of elephant, buffalo, rhino and many other wild animals which visit the pool that the hotel overlooks. This is the rich man's hotel and certainly most memorable.

Ol Doinyo Sabuk Park has also the advantage of being near Nairobi besides having the additional interest of providing some fairly difficult climbing. Mount Elgon Park includes one of 'the finest stands of podo trees in the world' besides providing an exerting climb. The two marine national parks should preserve the marine life and add much to the variety of attraction to those fond of the coastal resorts. As we have said, by starting the marine national parks, Kenya is giving a lead to the rest of the world. The main attractions of Lake Rudolf Park will be Central Island which is a breeding area for crocodiles, and its desert-type ecosystems.

Fort Jesus, Gedi, Olorgesailie and Kariandus Parks are different from the others. They have pre-historic and historic value of extreme importance to Kenya. Olorgesailie Pre-historic Sites which was made a National Park in 1947, is perhaps the best preserved example of pre-historic remains. It shows conditions during the early part of the Stone Age, which in this region is thought to be at least 100 000 years old. Hundreds of stone tools belonging to the Acheulian culture here suggest that the people were mainly hunters. Fort Jesus, in Mombasa, was built by the Portuguese in 1593 to keep this 'best

harbour' in the east coast safe from their enemies. Gedi, best known for its great mosque, has the ruins of a twelfth century Arab settlement. It was rebuilt during the fifteenth and sixteenth centuries but the building of Fort Jesus deprived it of its dominant role along the coast.

Lake Nakuru Park is famous for its ornithological interest. It is a bird sanctuary and its millions of flamingoes provide an exciting and unique spectacle. It gives Nakuru people what the Nairobi Park gives to those who live in Nairobi.

The total number of visitors to the parks during 1966–7 were: Nairobi 116 531, Tsavo 61 770, Aberdare and Mt Kenya 8 835, Gedi 12 424 and Fort Jesus 45 834.

Game Reserves

Game reserves are similar to game parks. The only difference is that they are under the control of the country councils in which they are situated. There are such areas in Kenya, namely:

a Masai-Amboseli Game Reserve (area 1 250 sq miles, 2 237 km²).

b Masai-Mara Game Reserve (area 650 sq miles, 1 683 km²).

c Samburu Game Reserve (area 60 sq miles, 155 km²).

d Lambwe Valley Game Reserve (area 46 sq miles, 119 km²).

There are also two National Reserves under the control of the Trustees of the National Parks of Kenya:

a Shimba Hills National Reserve (area 74 sq miles, 192 km²). This Reserve is famous for its sable antelope, and makes a pleasant half-day outing for

Mombasa tourists and residents.

b Marsabit National Park (area 806 sq miles, 2088 km²).

Conservation Areas

These are areas specially set aside within the controlled area blocks for photography. They are managed by the Game Department where permits are sold to would-be photographers. In Fig. 14.1 they include blocks 55, 61, 72 and 73 but are also known as:

a Samburu Game Conservation Area (Block 55).

b Mara Triangle (Block 61).

c Kitengela Game Conservation Area (part of Block 72).

d West Chulu Game Conservation Area (part of Block 73).

Controlled Area Blocks

The rest of Kenya with the exception of Nyanza and Western Provinces and parts of the Rift Valley and Central Provinces is divided into area blocks (see Fig. 14.1). These are the places where hunting is permitted to those who purchase hunting permits from the Game Department. The permits are £50 to visitors and £5 to residents. There are separate fees to hunt specific animals. This money goes to the central government but the hunter also has to pay controlled area fees which go to the county council concerned.

National Museum and Snake Park

The National Museum (formerly the Coryndon Museum) and the adjoining snake park are run by the Director of the Museum. The present spectacular success of these two places is really due to the personal efforts of Dr L. S. B. Leakey and Mr James Ashe respectively. The country gets considerable revenue from the tourists who visit these two sites, which are located in Nairobi.

The Future of the Tourist Industry in Kenya

The wildlife, scenery and beautiful coastal resorts continue to attract visitors from all parts of the world. But the tourists are people who will come only if the organisation and facilities are good and their safety assured. Any signs of political uncertainty or instability will quickly scare them. The Congo (Zaire) troubles of 1960 are said to have cost East African tourism 10 000 visitors during that year! The fact that the tourist trade is so very sensitive to changes and minor considerations is also its weakness. However, given stability, good management and a coordinated system involving tourist planning, park and coastal resort administration and tour operators, Kenya's tourist potential should continue to expand to become her greatest national asset.

References

KIRKMAN, J. S. *The Arab City of Gedi*, O.U.P., 1954.

LAMPREY, H. F. 'East African wild life as a natural resource', *The Natural Resources of East Africa*, ed. E. W. Russell. East African Literature Bureau, 1962.

'East African tourism's 21st anniversary: A look at our fastest growing industry', *Reporter*, 16 May 1969.

GOVT OF KENYA, *Statistical Abstracts*, Govt Printer, Nairobi, 1968.

GOVT OF KENYA, *Economic Survey, Chapter 6*, Govt Printer, Nairobi, 1968.

GOVT OF KENYA, 'The economic development of Kenya', *Report of Economic Survey Mission*, Govt Printer, Nairobi, 1962.

GOVT OF KENYA, *Development Plan 1970–74*, Govt Printer, Nairobi, 1969.

Chapter 15
Trade and Markets

General Remarks

To try to ensure surpluses with trading partners most countries make vigorous efforts to promote and to advertise their produce in other countries. In Kenya this is carried out by a government department which is much too small and lacks proper scope for its operations. A young developing country such as Kenya must embark on a vigorous advertising campaign to make known to the world, especially beyond the ex-colonial power, what she can sell them. In this respect such functions as the annual Agricultural Shows in Kenya are to be encouraged but with a slightly different emphasis. The show must aim especially at advertising and selling Kenyan products to potential buyers from abroad and one way of doing this is to try and obtain more foreign participation by the Agricultural Society of Kenya in foreign trade fairs. The show, as it is, is very well-known locally, but the emphasis must shift from mere records in terms of total gate entrants to new and more important records in terms of foreign visitors who place orders for Kenyan products as a result of having seen these products on display at the Nairobi Show. The activities of the Export Promotion Council and the trade attachés in foreign missions could be greatly expanded, for it must be remembered that the success the tourist industry is now enjoying is to a considerable extent the result of good advertising. Similarly vigorous advertising has obtained London markets for Kenyan pineapples and carnations. Perhaps the Agricultural Society of Kenya and the Export Promotion Council could together promote annual trade exhibitions in selected foreign capitals, or alternatively, this might be done on an East African Community basis. There does not seem to be sufficient emphasis in the 1970–4 Development Plan on the vital issue of the export promotion drive. Production must be directly related to the vigorous search for markets especially as new markets may well offer higher prices.

Having stated these preliminary observations, we must now turn and look at Kenya's trading position in a little more detail. We have already noted that the internal trade of one province with another will not be examined in this study partly because it is not carried on in any organised form.

Kenya's most favourable trading is with the other members of the East African Community, especially with Tanzania, and this should encourage Kenyan respect for the provisions of the East African Treaty of Co-operation.

While the external state of Kenya's trading shown below is generally an unfavourable one, it should also

Table 15.1 *External trade* (in £K'000) [1]

Type of trade	1960	1961	1962	1963	1964	1965	1966	1967
Net Imports								
Commercial	65 023	61 988	63 801	70 251	68 024	80 507	92 428	88 424
Government	5 046	6 949	5 694	3 438	8 571	8 530	19 968	18 172
Total	70 069	68 937	69 494	73 688	76 595	89 037	112 396	106 596
Exports								
Domestic	35 191	35 326	37 913	43 832	47 115	47 173	58 073	53 519
Re-exports	5 006	6 418	7 235	7 147	6 434	4 869	4 235	6 071
Total	40 197	41 744	45 148	50 979	53 549	52 042	62 308	59 589
Visible								
Balance	−29 872	−27 193	−24 347	−22 710	−23 046	−36 995	−50 088	−47 007
Volume	110 266	110 681	114 642	124 667	130 144	141 079	174 704	166 185

[1] Source: *Statistical Abstracts*, Republic of Kenya, 1968, p. 41.

Table 15.2 *East African trade* (in £K'000) [1]

Type of trade	1960	1961	1962	1963	1964	1965	1966	1967
Tanzania (mainland)								
Imports	1 875	1 844	1 954	2 915	4 110	4 570	3 806	3 288
Exports	7 608	8 901	10 017	10 365	13 299	14 087	13 282	11 382
Balance	+5 733	+7 057	+8 063	+7 450	+9 189	+9 517	+9 475	+8 094
Uganda								
Imports	5 120	5 152	5 386	6 248	7 244	7 135	7 317	10 165
Exports	6 163	7 047	7 303	9 425	12 581	15 339	15 619	14 796
Balance	+1 043	+1 895	+1 917	+3 177	+5 337	+8 204	+8 302	+4 631

[1] Source: *Statistical Abstracts*, Republic of Kenya, 1968, p. 41.

Table 15.3 *Value of Kenya's exports by geographical areas* (in £K'000) [1]

Area	1960	1961	1962	1963	1964	1965	1966	1967
Western Europe	20 820	19 573	23 208	26 242	25 616	25 844	30 868	26 609
Eastern Europe	51	16	52	484	1 534	1 005	1 549	884
The Americas	4 909	6 331	4 852	4 808	6 720	4 483	7 376	5 718
Africa	3 309	3 287	3 553	4 605	3 837	3 769	5 401	5 442
Middle East	858	1 047	1 252	1 464	1 946	1 933	2 273	2 493
Far East and Australia	4 600	4 357	4 092	5 088	6 013	6 127	6 208	5 660

[1] Source: *Statistical Abstracts*, Republic of Kenya, 1968, p. 47.

be pointed out that invisible trade (mainly from tourism) is helping to improve the position. In 1967 income from tourism (net balance on foreign travel) was worth £K9·8 million. The growth of this source of income has been examined in Chapter 14.

Exports

Kenya's principal export commodities reflect her essentially agricultural economy. Figures for the volume and value of this trade have already been given, so the more important commodities only will be examined here. In 1967 coffee (unroasted) led the list, and made up 29·3% of the total value of the exports. Tea and petroleum products (both at 13·8%) came jointly in second place. The others were pyrethrum extract and flowers (5·4%), meat and meat preparations (5·3%), sisal fibre and tow (3·9%), hides, skins and furskins (undressed) (3·3%), maize (unmilled) (2·6%), cement and related building materials (1·9%) and sodium carbonate (also 1·9%). Wattle bark and extract accounted for 1·7%, cotton 1·2% and pineapples (tinned) 1·0%. The other significant items were wool (0·9%), oil seeds, oil nuts and oil kernel (0·7%), scrap metal (0·7%), beans, peas and lentils (0·6%), butter and ghee (0·5%), cashew nuts (0·1%). Other smaller commodities (mainly minerals) accounted for the remainder.

The high place gained by petroleum products follows the opening of the Changamwe Oil Refinery in Mombasa. This industry is based on crude oil imported from the Middle East. We may also note that for a long time copper and alloys accounted for nearly 1% of exports. Unmilled maize has been affected by the vagaries of our climate and from 1964 to 1966 there was nothing available for export, although in 1958 the crop accounted for 6·4% of exports.

West Germany has been the main buyer of Kenya's coffee, purchasing over £K22 million between 1964 and 1967. Over the same period the USA bought coffee worth £K7·8 million and Britain bought to the value of £K1·1 million. Other important buyers are Canada, Sweden and the Netherlands. The bulk of the tea exports is bought by Britain, with the USA, Canada and the Netherlands also featuring. Britain is also the main buyer of meat, wood, oil seeds, pineapples and hides and skins. West Germany dominates the sisal and coffee market. Since 1964 Japan and India have been the main buyers of sodium carbonate, and India also purchases the bulk of the wattle bark.

In all, Britain is the principal buyer of Kenya's exports. In 1967 she bought goods worth £K13·1 million, while West Germany spent £K4·9 million, USA £K3·6 million, Canada £K2 million, Japan £K2·1 million and Zambia £K1·7 million.

In terms of geographical areas and power blocks, the pattern is summarised in Table 15.3.

Table 15.4 *Value of Kenya's imports by geographical areas* (in £K'000) [1]

Area	1960	1961	1962	1963	1964	1965	1966	1967
Western Europe	40 248	36 716	37 125	38 784	41 340	44 084	63 342	62 221
United Kingdom	24 187	24 062	23 308	22 665	23 551	25 164	37 752	34 989
EEC [2]	13 247	9 999	11 449	12 887	14 297	15 261	21 255	23 404
EFTA [3]	2 493	2 374	2 156	2 706	3 007	3 147	3 603	3 751
Eastern Europe	250	234	347	646	1 750	1 870	4 347	2 084
The Americas	4 668	5 035	6 766	4 756	5 154	9 369	12 026	8 525
Africa	5 523	6 255	3 867	3 630	1 993	2 002	1 734	1 711
Middle East	6 889	5 771	6 363	6 692	8 877	9 915	11 309	11 537
Far East and Australia	9 690	10 965	11 258	14 201	13 629	17 574	14 077	14 992

[1] Source: *Statistical Abstracts*, Republic of Kenya, 1968, p. 59.
[2] European Economic Community: West Germany, France, Netherlands, Italy, Belgium and Luxemburg.
[3] European Free Trade Area: United Kingdom, Sweden, Norway, Denmark, Austria, Portugal and Switzerland.

Imports

A country imports the things she requires but does not produce. Thus Kenya's most important imports are machinery and transport equipment (worth £K20–50 million annually), mineral fuels, lubricants and related materials (£K8–12 million annually), food and live animals (£K4–12 million annually), animal and vegetable oils, crude materials (including rubber and synthetic fibres), and chemicals (including medicines, fertilisers, paints and perfume). It is interesting to note in Table 15.3 that government imports increased more than six times between 1963 and 1966 (£K3·4 million to £K19·9 million). A legitimate reason for this is the necessary adjustments which followed Independence, but it does seem to show insufficient concern for cutting down on imports.

Britain is, quite naturally, the principal supplier for most of Kenya's imports. Between 1958 and 1967 Kenya bought goods worth between £K24 million and £K38 million annually from Britain. This also means that Kenya's most unfavourable trade balance is with Britain. The rest of the source areas for the bulk of our imports are summarised in Table 15.4 above:

East African Trade

We have seen that Kenya exports goods worth nearly £K29 million annually to Tanzania and Uganda. This common market, originally developed by the colonial administration before any of the states attained independence, was given a new scope and impetus by the Treaty of East African Co-operation of 1 December 1967. The treaty aims 'to strengthen and regulate the industrial, commercial and other relations of the partner states to the end that there shall be accelerated, harmonious and balanced development and sustained expansion of economic activities, the benefits whereof shall be equitably shared'. It aims at banning all quantitative restrictions on trade but introduces a protective measure of transfer taxes (infra-East African import duties) to ensure that profits are equitably shared.

Indications are that this common market will continue to expand for the good of the East African people.

Trade with Uganda

The imports are mainly food including beverages and tobacco (£K4 237 000 in 1967), manufactured goods (especially cotton piece goods and metal manufactures worth £K4 205 000 in 1967), and basic materials and fuels worth £K1 718 000 in the same year. Under basic materials were such items as electric energy and cotton seed oil. The main items that came under food were sugar (worth over £K1·2 million), and tobacco for the manufacture of cigarettes in Kenya.

On the exports side, manufactured goods (chemicals, soaps, clothing, metal manufactures, etc.) accounted for nearly £K8 million in 1967, while food, beverages and tobacco (of which meat, fruit and vegetables and tobacco were prominent) added another £K3 million. Petroleum products are the most important single item, accounting for £K2·5 million in 1967.

Trade with Tanzania

The most important single items in the import list in the food, beverage and tobacco category include fruits and vegetables, unmanufactured tobacco, cereals and meat. Under basic materials and fuel, cotton, seed oil and oilseeds are important, while blankets, aluminium, metal manufactures, chemicals and footwear are also important.

The main foods exported to Tanzania (mainland) are unmilled wheat, fruit and vegetables, tea, beverages, tobacco, butter and ghee. In the manufactured goods list, chemicals, soaps, paper, cement, metal manufactures, and footwear are the most important. The export of petroleum products has now virtually ceased as

Tanzania now relies on her own products from the refinery in Dar es Salaam.

Some Conclusions

The above survey has shown that Kenya must try to reduce her trade deficit. Imports must be cut down and this can easily be done without any serious adverse effects by stepping up the 'Buy Kenyan' campaign. Also, and despite what may here be termed 'apparent problems', Kenya, as a non-aligned nation committed to 'African Socialism and its applications to planning', should aim at buying in the cheapest markets. Similarly, certain super luxury import items could be deliberately restricted. In this context recent trends in the restrictions on the amount of capital which individuals can take out of the country at any given time are sound. The whole economy should be examined with this in mind. For example, in 1968 half of the motor vehicles in East Africa were registered in Kenya. The Mombasa oil refinery and Nairobi tyre manufacturing factory are therefore very important savers of imports. The logical conclusion must now be to begin thinking of a motor vehicle assembly plant in the republic.

Internal trade can still be expanded considerably. The widely differing ecological regions must surely mean that each province can benefit greatly from what others have to offer and can produce more cheaply. Sugar cane yields in Nyanza and Western Provinces, for example, are much higher with much less expenditure than in Coast Province. In short, Kenya's natural diversity must be made a source of strength by making the nation self-supporting in many more items than is the case at present.

References

GOVT OF KENYA *Development Plan 1970–4*, Govt Printer, Nairobi, 1969.

EAST AFRICAN COMMUNITY *Economic and Statistical Review* (any number of this quarterly publication is a very valuable source of information).

GOVT OF KENYA *Statistical Abstracts*, Govt Printer, Nairobi, annual.

Part 3

Chapter 16
Conclusion and Future Outlook

Conclusion

The physical and human geography of Kenya is a vast field of study, which cannot be covered adequately in a volume such as this. It is hoped that the salient features of Kenya's physical and human geography are given, and that a more thorough scrutiny of the entire field by the present and future generations of geographers can furnish more detail.

In order to carry out detailed rural development, the present provincial organisation does not seem to be the most logical possible and is, indeed, inconvenient in certain instances. For example, to administer a province such as the new Rift Valley from its headquarters located at Nakuru is not an easy task, because the province extends from the Sudanese border in the north to the foot of Mount Kilimanjaro, on the Tanzanian border, in the extreme south. The province also covers a vast area relative to the others such as Central, Western, Nairobi and Nyanza Provinces. A more rational proportioning of the provinces would be more easily manageable from the viewpoint of certain features and phases of development.

To facilitate the economic development of the dry northern parts of Kenya, perhaps the most suitable location for the provincial headquarters for the five districts of Mandera, Marsabit, Wajir, Isiolo and Garissa could be either Wajir or Marsabit. The selected headquarters should be the base for all researches leading to the best utilisation of the arid environment. The main research centre, being so located and re-inforced by several other smaller research stations suitably located over the entire area, could sooner or later be developed into an important institute recognised internationally. It would therefore also be comparable with several other important Kenya research centres such as: a) those at the coast (for instance, that at Mtwapa); b) those in the highlands (such as the National Agricultural Laboratories in Nairobi; the Jacaranda Research Station in the Ruiru-Thika area; the Njoro Plant Breeding Research Station; the Kitale National Agricultural Research Station); and several other smaller research stations in the remaining parts of western Kenya. Most of the above established research stations, especially

those in the highlands, have yielded important international results, apart from providing excellent services locally in the agricultural field, thus fulfilling the national purposes for which they were established.

Kenya provides an area of considerable geological interest, and may well be in the future the centre of detailed work on Tertiary volcanics, tectonics and, especially, for further researches on the Great African Rift Valley. Progress in these fields can only come with further development and expansion of the Mines and Geological Department and the Department of Geology at the University of Nairobi. Interest in geological training must be deliberately fostered because this is a vital area of knowledge in our attempt to solve the many mineralogical, hydrological and a host of other problems concerning development that at present face Kenya.

The location of Kenya on either side of the equator, the richly varied configuration and the modified climatic conditions are all of considerable significance in the economic development of Kenya. There is need for a closer study of local climates in relation to agricultural development. This approach popularly termed agricultural climatology is today one of the great success stories in Kenya, as is noted in the case of the local Katumani hybrid maize, which is well-adapted to the marginal agricultural areas of Kenya. As a result, it has achieved excellent results in increasing yields and practically eliminating the old fear of maize failure.

A proper appreciation of Kenya's organic resources must be based on the results of the investigations into the soil, plant and animal geography of the country, and hence the ecological regions of Kenya. This is bound to yield far richer dividends than have so far been realised, and whilst much effort has been directed by the government to this field the greater part of the problem of developing the resources has yet to be systematically tackled by the relevant ministries of the government and by university research workers.

Kenya's population is growing relatively rapidly, and means must be found whereby it can be distributed more evenly. One way of tackling the problem is to encourage rural development projects so that the 'pull' on the rural population by the towns is arrested. Apart from employment opportunities in the agricultural sector, which is mainly concerned with primary production (often easily saturated), the rural population must be convinced to stay put by the introduction of a number of processing and fabricating industries supported by the associated service industries. Other incentives such as more schools, better medical facilities and similar amenities should be introduced along with the development projects mentioned above. The foregoing comments suggest a planned decentralisation of both the industries and services, and all those other facilities allied to them, to suitable rural areas.

There is no doubt that in agriculture, there is still considerable scope for peasant farming in cotton, tea, coconut, sugar cane, cashew nuts, bananas, cassava and maize, etc. Failure to succeed in such activities appears to be related to lack of proper organisation. Take, for instance, the case of the bananas produced in Kisii District of South Nyanza. These could be sent to the Nairobi market economically if the transport network was improved and utilised by an efficient co-operative society yet to be formed by the growers.

There has been great expansion in the settlement scheme cultivation of rice and sugar cane. Whilst the expansion of rice cultivation depends to a large extent on the availability of irrigation water, the rapidly spreading peasant sugar cane cultivation in Nyanza seems to have much scope, provided the central administrative or managing organisation is considerably improved. Perhaps the best solution to the sugarcane outgrowers' problems (namely, large quantities of over mature cane remaining uncut for processing,[1] limited factory capacity in relation to available cane and unscheduled closures of the factory owing to faulty plant parts) would be a more effective government administrative and financial assistance reinforced by the formation of truly active co-operative societies, each for a major settlement scheme. The societies would assist the small sugar cane outgrowers in such things as planting, weeding, cutting and transporting the cane to the processing factories without the delay as at present. Another feasible approach to the sugar cane outgrowers problems is the creation of a statutory sugar board to assist the growers.

Comprehensive development of both Kenya's forest and fishery resources has yet to be achieved. In the field of mineral exploitation, there is a need for Kenyan geologists specially trained to prospect, assess and exploit mineral resources. It is felt that the Department of Geology at the University in Nairobi should play a much more important role in conjunction with the Mines and Geological Department in terms of training the necessary professional personnel. Given such local personnel, not only for purposes of mineral exploitation but also those trained by the relevant departments in fields such as forestry and fisheries, it should be possible to accelerate the development in these three fields.

[1] Because of lack of reliable labour, poor supervision and limited costly transportation arrangements.

The study of Kenya's manufacturing and service industries has examined the location and structure of the country's 39 individual industries both in their composite groups (such as the agricultural food processing industries, the agricultural non-food manufacturing industries, the non-agricultural manufacturing industries and the service industries), and, to a lesser extent, as individual items. The principal conclusions drawn about industrial location are that:

a Kenya has a discontinuous industrial belt stretching from the Uganda border in the north-west to the Indian Ocean shores in the south-east;

b industrial concentration is higher in a limited number of areas within the above belt, especially in and around the main urban areas;

c the three district industrial units of Nairobi, Thika and Mombasa are, by far, the most favoured industrially. (However, amongst the 41 district industrial units into which Kenya falls, more than 75% of the manufacturing and service industrial workers are concentrated in only ten of the district industrial units);

d most of the industries are orientated either towards the markets or towards the raw materials.

The main conclusions relating to the industrial structure are that:

a only a mere 1% of Kenya's population is employed in the manufacturing and service establishments;

b the majority of the industries process and/or fabricate agricultural products;

c the factories employing 100 or more workers constitute less than 15% of the 2 747 factories employing five or more workers and yet provide employment for more than 64% of the 95 692 manufacturing and service industrial workers then employed;

d the 2 780 factories (each with less than five operatives) surveyed in 1964 proved unimportant both in terms of relative employment and value added by manufacturing (however this category of factories is, perhaps, the most likely foundation for future large African-owned industrial enterprises);

e industrial diversification in the agricultural manufacturing industries is better than in both the non-agricultural manufacturing industries and the service industries.

The great weakness in Kenya's industrial development lies in its relatively intense centralisation, especially in the Nairobi and Mombasa areas, which in 1964 accounted for almost 50% of the national manufacturing and service industrial operatives and about 60% of the national value added by manufacturing for 1961, and more than this in 1964. In order to develop the rural areas faster than can be done through reliance on primary agricultural production decentralisation of the manufacturing and service industries to the more suitable rural areas is overdue. This is, however, closely bound up with the factors of location, particularly the principal factors such as fuller infrastructural development, cheaper capital (preferably local), various types of skills (including managerial skill), most of which are still lacking in Kenya. Availability of raw materials is also an important factor here, but the most influential probably are transport costs and the various aspects of personal considerations.

Important backbone features of the economy such as insurance, commercial and financial facilities are at present over-centralised, particularly in the larger urban areas such as Nairobi, Mombasa, Nakuru, Kisumu and Thika. Thus the rest of the country is poorly provided for. Because the above facilities form a vital part of our economy there is a need for decentralising and expanding them according to a broadly based development plan.

In the field of tourism Kenya seems to have scope for unlimited development. However, it is useful to observe that the tourist trade handles a 'delicate complex commodity'. Its nature is such, therefore, that it could be ruined irretrievably by several adverse factors amongst which are political instability and irrational game and park development and management. So far efforts already put into the development of tourism by the relevant ministries of the government deserve the highest praise. However, what remains to be assessed is the proportion of the financial benefits the trade offers to Kenya, as compared with what is lost to the country through foreign financial manipulations. It is also important to accelerate further our rate of establishing tourist facilities, and finally, we should avoid any kind of negative exploitation of the tourist industry such as excessive prices and all other adverse allied practices noted in some other countries. If such practices are allowed to creep into Kenya's tourist industry we will only have ourselves to blame for the consequences.

Future Outlook

Kenya's Economy during 1968

Predictions of the future can best be appreciated if seen in the context of Kenya's economic position during 1968.

In agriculture, except for sisal and coffee, the level of production of the main crops rose notably in 1968. The reasons for this were the increasing use of improved seeds and fertilizers and good weather conditions. Marketed crops netted nearly £K71·0 million during the year, an increase of about 5·4% as compared with £K67·0 million for 1967. However, the rising volume of farmers' loan debt arrears is a most disturbing feature. As in 1967, the 1968 coffee crop was again badly affected by coffee berry disease, thus reducing the output by 17% from that of 1967 to 39 600 tons (40 233·6 tonnes) for 1968. This compares most unfavourably with the 1966 coffee output of 56 900 tons (57 810·4 tonnes). However, the 1968 coffee prices were 10% higher, and the industry therefore received partial compensation. By far the most significant contribution to the expansion in the agricultural income was made by the cereals, the gross farm

revenue of which increased by about 36% over that of 1967. Maize deliveries reached a record of 350 800 tons (356 412·8 tonnes), about 20% higher than the 1967 output, whilst 225 355 tons (288 960·7 tonnes) of wheat were delivered which again was 20% higher than 1967. Because maize supplies were far in excess of domestic requirements, the 1968 maize export totalled 250 000 tons (254 000 tonnes) valued at £K4·8 million. Similarly, the wheat supplies were in excess of the East African requirements, although the bulk of the surplus was stored owing to low export prices. During 1968 tea production[1] showed a large increase but beef output dropped slightly and totalled only 29 961 tons (30 440·4 tonnes) as compared with 30 463 tons (30 950·4 tonnes) for 1967. Whilst pig deliveries declined in 1968, recorded milk sales increased by about 4%. Sugar production considerably contributed to the farmers' increased incomes, the cane output for 1968 being about 30% above the 1967 figure. The decline in the sisal industry which has for some time been apparent continued in 1968. Pyrethrum production rose slightly (despite the competitive effects of synthetic insecticides) reflecting the increased smallholder production to a level above the quantity each smallholder is licensed to produce.

In the industrial sector the index of manufacturing production in 1968 was 7·2% above the 1967 figure. The rise in output was based mainly on the domestic market, although there was also an increase in exports, reflecting the reduction of quantitative restrictions in East Africa. In some industries, however, the expansion in production was associated with notable increase in stocks which, by the end of 1968, had reached relatively high levels. Output in the textile industry increased by 32% largely because of an increase in the production of cheaper varieties of cloth. The recent rapid increase in production capacity of the textile mills is already creating the problem of over-production as is indicated by a significant increase in stocks for 1968. Output from the Changamwe oil refinery in Mombasa fell slightly during 1968 to 4·96 million gallons (22·55 million litres) as compared with 5·04 million gallons (22·93 million litres) for 1967. Processed sugar output was one third greater than the 1967 figure. However, the sugar industry needs better management to ensure that cane is sent to the factory before over-maturing, and also to keep the factory working to capacity. Owing to a downturn in exports, cigarette production dropped in 1968, although beer production increased. Despite the large increase in maize production, maize meal processing declined. Both wattle extract and pyrethrum extract production (the two principal agricultural commodities in the chemical industry) increased. The completion of the first stage of the Seven Forks Tana River hydro-electricity project at Kindaruma significantly increased Kenya's installed electric power capacity, and the amount of power locally generated rose considerably.

[1] Valued at over £K10 million as compared with about £K8 million for the 1967 production.

In the building and construction industry, the output only increased by 5·3%, indicating a much slower expansion pace as compared with the faster annual expansion rates of recent years. However the value of private building works completed in 1968 in the main towns increased by 16%. In the public sector, works completed during 1968 were valued at £K10·4 million.

In the field of international trade, the total value of Kenya's trade increased by 5% in 1968. This was a poor result overall because the declining trend in 1967 meant that the 1968 level was less than 1% above the 1966 figure. The £K127·1 million worth of imports represented a 6% increase over the 1967 figure, while exports and re-exports worth £K89·3 million were almost 4% higher than 1967. Thus the overall trade deficit (on a customs and excise basis) rose by £K3·5 million to total £K37·8 million, a deficit of £K52 million with overseas countries being partly offset by the traditional surplus with East African countries, which was £K14 million in 1968. The rise in imports occurred despite a fall in goods received jointly from Uganda and Tanzania. Kenya's exports to the other East African countries in 1968 differed little in total from that of 1967, and the slight increase in exports during 1968 was accounted for solely by the non-East African trade. About 31·5% of total overseas imports into Kenya was from the United Kingdom. Imports from the European Economic Community countries differed little from those of 1967 (West Germany was the main source of the EEC imports into Kenya) and amounted to about 20% of total imports. Japanese goods imported into Kenya increased by about 37% while shipments of mineral oil from Iran increased only modestly. Outside Kenya's East African market, the United Kingdom was our leading overseas market accounting for about 25% of our total foreign trade. This figure represented a 7·4% rise in the value of Kenya's exports to the United Kingdom in 1968 as compared with 1967. After an appreciable fall in Kenya's exports to the EEC countries, there was a 20% increase in 1968. Although Kenya's exports to the USA rose in 1968, they failed to reach the 1966 level. An encouraging development in 1968 was the continued growth in Kenyan exports to Zambia.

Coffee continued to be the principal commodity sold abroad, although the value of tea exports is rapidly rising. Because of coffee berry disease, coffee exports were 25% below the 1967 figure. Although this was partially offset by a rise of 10·4% in coffee prices, the total value of coffee exports fell by more than 18%. Tea exports, on the other hand, expanded by nearly 50%, so that despite an 8·7% fall in tea prices, total exports, by value, rose by about 36%. Thus in 1968, coffee accounted for 22·2% of total overseas exports, whilst tea accounted for 17·4%. The respective figures for 1967 were: coffee, 29·4% and tea, 13·9%. Following the bumper maize crop, the value of maize exports was 2·4 times the 1967 figure, making maize the fourth most important commodity after petroleum products. Overseas meat and meat products sales and the sales of pyrethrum showed relatively small increases, but the value of sisal exports dropped.

Looking at Kenya's economic progress as a whole during 1968, it could be stated that the country's economy expanded at a higher rate than the average for recent years. Despite a decreased coffee output, 1968 was a good agricultural year, and there was encouraging progress in the manufacturing and service sectors. However, capital investment was only a little higher than in 1967. Although the trade deficit widened slightly, the balance of payments position was good, and foreign exchange reserves rose. This was due to favourable trends on the invisible and capital accounts. Tourism, in particular, continued to prosper. The banking system was characterised during 1968 by a distinct improvement in the liquidity position of the commercial banks. This was reflected in the eradication of net indebtedness to overseas banks and a rise in deposits at the Central Bank. Provisional estimates of private capital movements suggest a net inflow of £K10·5 million. This figure includes re-investment of undistributed profits of foreign enterprises, but indications are that in 1968, for the first time in recent years, new money was being brought into Kenya by the private sector over and above that provided by the profits earned in the country. Both the private sector and the government made increasing use of capital imports. In the period 1964–8 economic growth in real terms averaged 6·3%, which is the rate projected in the 1964–70 Development Plan. Favourable weather conditions during 1968 led to a satisfactory expansion in agricultural output, both in the cash crop and non-cash crop sectors. The manufacturing sector had a most encouraging year with output rising at a faster rate than at any time since 1964. Activity in the building and construction industries did not expand as fast in 1968 as was the case in recent years, but it was nonetheless at a high level. The various service industries also continued to prosper. The expansion of the transport and communications industries, though somewhat sluggish, nevertheless kept up a reasonable rate of progress, thus reinforcing tourism which once again illustrated its potential for expansion. The wholesale and retail traders showed an increasing turnover due largely to the increased agricultural output, and rising domestic consumption. Capital formation during 1968, at current prices, amounted to £K91 million and was therefore 4·2% above the comparable figure for 1967, although this increase was largely accounted for by prices. This performance was satisfactory in view of the high level of investment in 1967 when the total capital outlay expanded by more than one-third. Moreover, some of the building and construction work which was started during 1968 by the private sector was not included in the capital formation estimates for the year. Expenditure on self-help community schemes in 1968 was more than £K2·5 million. The cost of living during 1968 was relatively stable, although there was a slight rise for both the middle and lower income groups.

The Economy during 1969

According to the 1968 *Economic Survey*, the growth of the economy in 1969 was expected to be lower than that for 1968. At constant (1964) prices, the 1969 growth was only 5·6%. Over the five years (1964–9), however, Kenya's economy advanced at a cumulative annual rate of growth of 6·3% in real terms. Thus, the real rate of growth has been equal to the target set out in the Development Plan for the period 1964–1970, which has now been superseded by the new 1970–4 Development Plan.

In the agricultural sector, overall marketed agricultural production remained quite high, despite dry weather conditions in certain areas which thereby affected food production. During 1969 coffee production rose to 52 616 tons (53 690 tonnes), about 35·6% above the 1968 output. Tea fields increased by 17·5% to 35 344 tons (36 065 tonnes) over the 1968 figure. However, the prices of both tea and coffee were relatively lower than those for 1968, thus the farmers' incomes dropped despite higher production.

1969 showed great improvement, and the quantitative index of manufacturing for the year shows that production increased by 11·0%, while sales rose by 10·7% in value. Food processing which is the largest industrial group in terms of output, had a 20·3% rise despite failure of the long rains. The increase is attributed to the rapid growth of sugar production and grain milling. Beverages and tobacco had a steady rise, while metal products manufacture also increased. However, certain industries, such as textiles, lagged behind others in performance. On the other hand, textile manufacture is now amongst some of Kenya's largest industrial enterprises. Moreover, it is included along with those industries for which a high growth rate is projected in the new 1970–4 Development Plan. The quantitative index for the paper and printing industry, based on imported raw materials, increased much more in 1969, by about 34% over that of the previous year, and sales also rose by about 9%. The negotiations for the long awaited Broderick Falls (Webuye) pulp and paper mill are practically completed and the project, estimated to cost £K13 million, is expected to make Kenya self-sufficient in certain types of paper, when it is opened. In the rubber industry, the major development is that of the £K5·5 million Firestone project, about whose establishment the necessary negotiations were completed in 1969. The factory started production in 1971, beginning with 150 000 tyres and hoping to raise its production to 200 000 tyres per year after three years. The output of the chemical products industry dropped by more than 11% below that of 1968, because of the fall in production of both pyrethrum and wattle bark extracts. However, paint production showed a 23% rise, while that of soap was up by 21%. In the petroleum products industry, the 1969 rise was over 11·0% in the throughput at the Mombasa refinery, and total export of petroleum products rose by about 19% in 1969. The 11·9% rise in the non-metallic mineral products in 1969 was mainly due to the rapid expansion of the cement production, especially at the Bamburi factory at the coast. The metal products industry expanded by 12·3% in 1969, and new steel re-rolling mills have been established at Miritini and Kikuyu. In the building and construction sector, there was an 18% increase in 1969 as compared with the 10% increase during 1968. Since 1964, the average growth rate in this industry has been 13%, and during the 1970–4 Development Plan period, the new average growth rate expected of the industry is 9%. This industry has great significance in the general development of the economy.

Progress under the 1966–70 Development Plan period was fairly satisfactory, and an extra expenditure of £K8 million over the planned total expenditure (for the period) of £K92 million thus amounted to about 8·7%. However, the benefits already being derived and those to be derived from the plan include: improved roads to aid the other sectors of the economy, especially the sugar industry; the large sums of money spent on social services which should result in improved living conditions for many Kenyans; the expenditure on education which should, in the long run, have infrastructural beneficial effects on the economy, especially when the educational facilities are equitably distributed.

Plans involving an outlay of more than £K30 million put before the Kenya government for the development of air traffic in the Nairobi area are signs of a promising future for the economy. Moreover, the completion of the first stage of the Seven Forks Power Project in 1968 has facilitated further development in the area during 1969, and the power line to the coast from Nairobi has now been completed.

Progress in the irrigation projects also continued in 1969, with nearly 10 900 acres (4 400 hectares) of land under irrigation and supporting nearly 3 000 families. In 1969, the gross value of produce from all the schemes (Mwea Tebere, Tana River, Perkerra, Ahero, etc.) was £K582 000, about 20% increase over the 1968 value.

Capital formation at current prices in 1969 was £K95·5 million, which was £K5 million more than in 1968. At constant (1964) prices, growth in absolute terms was of the same order and 5·4% above that of 1968. Except for transport equipment, there was a growth in all other types of assets, especially in machinery and other equipment. Capital formation in construction and works also rose rapidly, although that in the private sector (at constant prices) increased by about £K4 million. The latter was confined almost to machinery and other equipment.

Total exports during 1969 were £K97·3 million as compared with imports, which stood at £K128·8 million. Imports from overseas reached a record figure of £K100 million, although those from Uganda and Tanzania declined both during 1968 and 1969. Exports overseas and to Uganda and Tanzania increased over the 1968 figures by £K5·5 million and £K2·5 million, respectively. Thus the volume of trade with Tanzania and Uganda rose above the 1968 figure. The increase in exports

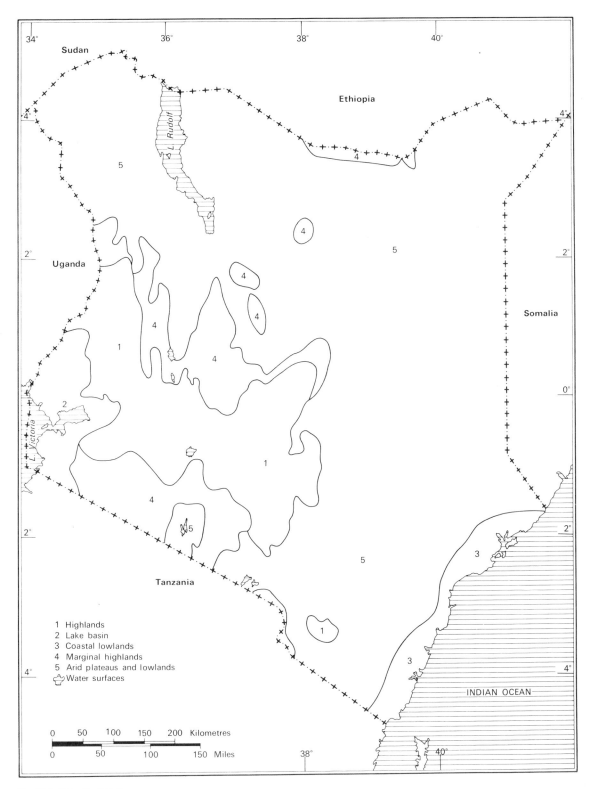

Fig. 16.1 Natural regions

1 Highlands
2 Lake basin
3 Coastal lowlands
4 Marginal highlands
5 Arid plateaus and lowlands
Water surfaces

reduced the overall deficit on merchandise trade in 1969 by £K6·3 million. However, the 1969 balance of trade for Kenya was rather unfavourable and the deficit remained fairly large.

The Future

The long term economic development of Kenya, reinforced by a strong manufacturing core, should be based both on the natural regions (and their potentialities), and the five principal industrial development zones (introduced in Chapter 13). The five major natural regions of Kenya should be evaluated in terms of both their agricultural potentiality and exploitable mineral wealth. Other important resources such as forests, fisheries and all other types of wildlife should be carefully assessed for purposes of properly balanced development.

The five major natural regions of Kenya are indicated in Fig. 16.1. The present state of development in these regions, especially in agriculture, can be gauged from Chapter 9. Further contributions relating to industrial development, etc. are also to be found in the relevant chapters in this book. However, these aspects tell us far less about the long term needs. These could be satisfied better by taking advantage of:

a the organic and inorganic potentialities of the five natural regions (the present and potential organic resources of the regions are treated in detail elsewhere.[1]);

b the spatial relationship between the natural regions and the suggested industrial development zones (Figs. 12.2 and 16.1).

The treatment of the present and potential organic resources referred to above partly takes into account the salient patterns of the commercial and subsistence crops discussed by Brown,[2] and proceeds to indicate the location of the crops in Kenya. The location table, reinforced by the said appendix, also shows the distribution of the domestic animals. Each of the five broad belts of differing land potential (indicated in the map showing broad classification of Kenya's agricultural land) is zoned so that the better parts can be differentiated from those which are worse.

What is important in the future is that the natural regions should be developed to their maximum capacity by basing the development on the relevant organic and inorganic potentiality. The choice of natural regions as the best starting point for our economic development is advantageous, because a natural region is a spatial unit throughout which the conditions of relief, climate, natural and cultivated vegetation, and consequently human activities, are *almost* uniform. The stress is on the word *almost*, because natural regions are, in fact, good examples of 'unity in diversity'. Natural regions are synthetic, in that each region is made up of a number of contrasting though related parts. The latter essentially result in a unity in diversity. In Kenya there are the following natural regions (Fig. 16.1):

a the highlands,
b the lake basin (of Nyanza and Western Provinces),
c the coastal lowlands,
d the marginal highlands, and
e the arid plateau and lowlands.

The two most favourable of the regions are the highlands and the lake basin natural units. The third in rank is the coastal lowlands region, which is followed closely by the marginal highlands region. Parts of the latter are considerably well favoured, although the greater portion of the region is too dry for normal development. The worst-endowed region is the arid plateau and lowlands, which occupies a vast part of Kenya.

The relationship between the development zones (Fig. 12.2) and the natural regions (Fig. 16.1), viewed in the light of the patterns of organic and inorganic resources, is vital, especially in the field of rural development. Along with the above relationship go the necessary plans relating to the present pattern of population density. It should be observed that about 80% of the high potential land in Kenya has always been in the former African land units, and only 20% in the formerly alienated land. Parts of the African section have for a long period been handicapped by population pressure and lack of modern farming technology. Before the entire section could be developed so as to attain its maximum output, the population pattern in the section should be re-organised. It is suggested that in all parts of Kenya where land potential is high, areas with dispersed population patterns must be given closer attention because such dispersed population patterns are, in general, incompatible with the best use of high potential land.

Although limited portions of the central zone (Figs. 12.2 and 16.1) extend into the lake basin and coastal lowlands regions, the bulk of the central zone is located in the highlands region. The latter is therefore both the industrial and general economic core of Kenya. The zone has several weaknesses, however. It suffers from over-centralised industries, poor diversification and uncoordinated economic planning. The other development zones such as the two fringe zones, the problem zone and the negative zone are all, in a graded fashion, less favoured as compared to the central zone as discussed in Chapter 13 and elsewhere.[1]

In planning for the future much more emphasis should be placed on rural development, and to give such development the urgency it deserves perhaps the Minister of Local Government should be put in charge and redesignated the Minister for Rural Development. While urban development should not be ignored, decentralisation of industries to the district head-

[1] See: R. B. Ogendo, *Industrial Geography of Kenya*, East African Publishing House, Nairobi, 1972. Especially Appendix 2, including the 'Agrico-industrial raw materials and location table', in close association with map 75. Also see maps: 65–67, 69, 72 and 74.

[2] L. H. Brown, *A National Cash Crops Policy for Kenya*, Ministry of Agriculture, Nairobi, 1963.

[1] R. B. Ogendo, *Industrial Geography of Kenya*, East African Publishing House, Nairobi, 1972.

quarters, and suitable rural areas should be given more weight. There should be a deliberate policy of optimum size for the district headquarters. Moreover, the present tendencies towards centralisation, especially in Nairobi and its environs, should be strongly discouraged and replaced by a policy of all-round development in the suitable areas of Kenya, which have the potentialities but which are neglected at present.

References

BROWN, L. H. *A National Cash Crops Policy for Kenya*, Min. of Agric., Govt Printer, Nairobi, 1963.

OGENDO, R. B. *Industrial Geography of Kenya*, East African Publishing House, Nairobi, 1972.

Index

Published by Longman Kenya Ltd., P.O. Box 45925, Shell and BP House
(2nd floor), Harambee Avenue, Nairobi and Printed by Kenya Litho Ltd.,
P.O. Box 40775, Changamwe Road, Nairobi.